Making Content Comprehensible for Multilingual Learners: The SIOP® Model

sixth edition

JANA ECHEVARRÍA

Professor Emerita, California State University, Long Beach

MARYELLEN VOGT

Professor Emerita, California State University, Long Beach

DEBORAH J. SHORT

Founder and Director, Academic Language Research & Training

KATIE TOPPEL

English Language Development Specialist, Oregon

Content Development: Jeff Johnston **Product Management:** Drew Bennett
Content Management: Bridget Daly **Product Marketing:** Krista Clark
Content Production: Yagnesh Jani **Rights and Permissions:** Jenell Forschler

Please contact https://support.pearson.com/getsupport/s/contactsupport with any queries on this content.

Cover Image by Shutterstock/mangpor2004

Chapter Opener Photo Credits: Chapter 1: Kali9 /E+/Getty images; Chapter 8: FG Trade/E+/Getty image; Chapter 10: Tracy Fowler/MBI/Alamy Stock Photo.

SIOP® is a registered trademark of Savvas Learning Company LLC in the US and/or other countries.

Library of Congress Cataloging-in-Publication Data
Names: Echevarría, Jana, 1956- author. | Vogt, MaryEllen, author. | Short, Deborah, author. | Toppel, Katie, author.
Title: Making content comprehensible for multilingual learners : the SIOP® model / Jana Echevarría, MaryEllen Vogt, Deborah J. Short, Katie Toppel.
Other titles: Making content comprehensible for English learners
Description: Sixth edition. | Hoboken, NJ : Pearson, 2024. | Includes bibliographical references and index.
Identifiers: LCCN 2022044094 | ISBN 9780137878857 (paperback)
Subjects: LCSH: Revised edition of: Making content comprehensible for English learners. Fifth edition. 2017. | English language—Study and teaching (Elementary)—Foreign speakers. | Language arts—Correlation with content subjects.
Classification: LCC PE1128.A2 E248 2022 | DDC 372.652/1044—dc23/eng/20221027
LC record available at https://lccn.loc.gov/2022044094

1 2022

ISBN 10:   0-13-787885-0
ISBN 13: 978-0-13-787885-7

Pearson's Commitment to Diversity, Equity, and Inclusion

Pearson is dedicated to creating bias-free content that reflects the diversity, depth, and breadth of all learners' lived experiences.

We embrace the many dimensions of diversity, including but not limited to race, ethnicity, gender, sex, sexual orientation, socioeconomic status, ability, age, and religious or political beliefs.

Education is a powerful force for equity and change in our world. It has the potential to deliver opportunities that improve lives and enable economic mobility. As we work with authors to create content for every product and service, we acknowledge our responsibility to demonstrate inclusivity and incorporate diverse scholarship so that everyone can achieve their potential through learning. As the world's leading learning company, we have a duty to help drive change and live up to our purpose to help more people create a better life for themselves and to create a better world.

Our ambition is to purposefully contribute to a world where:

- Everyone has an equitable and lifelong opportunity to succeed through learning.
- Our educational content accurately reflects the histories and lived experiences of the learners we serve.

- Our educational products and services are inclusive and represent the rich diversity of learners.
- Our educational content prompts deeper discussions with students and motivates them to expand their own learning (and worldview).

Accessibility

We are also committed to providing products that are fully accessible to all learners. As per Pearson's guidelines for accessible educational Web media, we test and retest the capabilities of our products against the highest standards for every release, following the WCAG guidelines in developing new products for copyright year 2022 and beyond.

 You can learn more about Pearson's commitment to accessibility at
https://www.pearson.com/us/accessibility.html

Contact Us

While we work hard to present unbiased, fully accessible content, we want to hear from you about any concerns or needs with this Pearson product so that we can investigate and address them.

 Please contact us with concerns about any potential bias at
https://www.pearson.com/report-bias.html

 For accessibility-related issues, such as using assistive technology with Pearson products, alternative text requests, or accessibility documentation, email the Pearson Disability Support team at **disability.support@pearson.com**

 Pearson

About the Authors

JANA ECHEVARRÍA, Ph.D., is Professor Emerita at California State University, Long Beach, where she received her university's Outstanding Professor award for excellence in scholarship, teaching, and service. Prior to receiving her UCLA doctorate, she was a teacher in bilingual, ESL, and special education programs. Dr. Echevarria has published widely on effective instruction for multilingual learners, including those with learning disabilities. She has presented her research throughout the United States and internationally, including at Oxford University (England), Wits University (South Africa), Harvard University (U.S.), Stanford University (U.S.), University of Barcelona (Spain), and South East Europe University (Macedonia), where she was a Fulbright Specialist. She also was a resident instructor at Feng Chia University (Taiwan). Dr. Echevarria is a member of the California Reading Hall of Fame and serves as an expert on English learners for the U.S. Department of Justice, Civil Rights Division.

MARYELLEN VOGT, Ed.D., is Professor Emerita of Education at California State University, Long Beach. She is currently director and reading specialist for Literacy Intervention & Instruction, a nonprofit program for students with reading delays. Dr. Vogt received her doctorate from the University of California, Berkeley, and is author/co-author of numerous articles, chapters, and books for teachers and administrators. Her research interests include literacy intervention, teacher change and development, and disciplinary literacy for multilingual learners. Dr. Vogt has provided professional development in all 50 states and in several other countries, including Germany, where she served as a Visiting Scholar at the University of Cologne. She received her university's Distinguished Faculty Teaching Award, served as President of the International Literacy Association, and has been inducted into the Reading Hall of Fame, an international organization of literacy scholars and researchers.

DEBORAH J. SHORT, Ph.D., founded and directs Academic Language Research & Training, a consulting company, and provides professional development on academic literacy, content-based English as a new language, and sheltered content instruction worldwide. She has directed research and evaluation studies on multilingual learners and educational program designs for the Carnegie Corporation of New York, the Rockefeller Foundation, the U.S. Departments of Education, U.S. Department of Justice, the Southern Poverty Law Center, and others. Publications include *SIOP Model* books for Pearson, *The 6 Principles* books for TESOL, ESL textbooks like *Reach Higher, Inside,* and *Edge* for National Geographic Learning, and professional journal articles. She taught ESL and EFL in New York, California, Virginia, and the DR Congo. She served as president of the TESOL International Association (2020–21) and has presented research in the United States, Canada, New Zealand, South America, Europe, China, and the Middle East.

KATIE TOPPEL, Ed.D., is an English Language Development Specialist at the elementary level, serving multilingual learners through collaboration, co-teaching, and small-group instruction. Dr. Toppel began her career as a preschool teacher in a Bilingual Migrant Head Start classroom. Her instructional background includes experience teaching kindergarten and first grade in addition to serving as a K–12 Support Services Teacher at an international school in Germany. Dr. Toppel is a co-author of the book *DIY PD: A Guide to Self-Directed Learning for Educators of Multilingual Learners.* Her other publications include journal articles, online articles, and book chapters focused on culturally responsive teaching, co-planning, and co-teaching as well as contributions to *99 Ideas and Activities for Teaching English Learners with the SIOP Model* (2nd ed.). She is also the co-founder of #MLLChat_BkClub on Twitter, which is a virtual book club aimed at improving instructional practices for multilingual learners. Dr. Toppel presents and shares her work both nationally and internationally at educational conferences.

Preface: The SIOP® Story

The SIOP Model (formerly known as the Sheltered Instruction Observation Protocol) has been used in schools for over 25 years, and it continues to be a successful model of instruction for teaching multilingual learners and other students. Teachers and administrators throughout the world have implemented SIOP in their schools and districts, not only because SIOP has been empirically validated as an effective instructional model, but also because they know that teaching academic content and academic language concurrently, systematically, and consistently works. The SIOP Model is an instructional framework for helping students reach academic standards while they learn and improve their use of academic English.

Our work on the SIOP Model started in the early 1990s when there was a growing population of multilingual learners in the United States, but no coherent model for teaching this student population. We began by identifying key characteristics of sheltered instruction and effective teaching strategies through literature review and classroom research. A preliminary observation protocol was drafted and field-tested with sheltered instruction teachers. A research project through the Center for Research on Education, Diversity, & Excellence (CREDE) enabled us to engage in an intensive cyclical refinement process and to use the SIOP Model in a sustained professional development effort with teachers on both the East and West Coasts. Through this process of classroom observation, coaching, discussion, and reflection, the instrument was finalized as the Sheltered Instruction Observation Protocol, or as it has come to be known, SIOP (pronounced sī-ŏp). SIOP offers teachers a model for lesson planning and implementation that provides multilingual learners with access to grade-level content based on academic standards. By providing this access, we help prepare students for life after high school in colleges or careers.

Although several approaches to teaching multilingual learners have emerged over the years, at present, SIOP remains the only research-validated model of sheltered instruction. Studies on the efficacy of SIOP have appeared in more than 50 peer-reviewed professional journals. In fact, because of its applicability across content areas, the national Center for Research on the Educational Achievement and Teaching of English Language Learners (CREATE) used the SIOP Model as a framework for comprehensive school-wide intervention in its research aimed at improving the achievement of multilingual learners in middle school. The SIOP Model is now being implemented at all levels of education from pre-K to community colleges and universities. It is used in sheltered content classes (also called integrated ELD in some states), dual language programs, content-based English language development classes, special education instruction, and general education classrooms.

Since the first edition of this book was published, we have continued to develop and refine the SIOP Model, but we have not changed the eight components and 30 features. These components and features have withstood the test of time. In our work with thousands of teachers and administrators throughout the country, our own understanding of effective sheltered instruction and the needs of multilingual learners has grown substantially. We believe, and research on SIOP confirms, that when teachers consistently and systematically implement the SIOP Model's 30 features in lessons for multilingual learners and English speakers alike, the result is high-quality, effective instruction and improvement of student achievement.

We hope that you will use this book as a guide for lesson planning and teaching. SIOP teachers tell us that it is a resource they turn to again and again as they plan and carry out effective lessons, so we encourage you to highlight sections, mark pages with sticky notes, and fill margins with application ideas. As you read, you will find lesson plans, teaching techniques, and many effective activities for working with multilingual learners and other students. Our research confirms that the SIOP Model makes a positive difference academically for all students, so what works well for multilingual learners will work equally well for others in your classroom.

As the authors of this book, we have approached our teaching, writing, and research from different yet complementary fields. Jana Echevarría's research and publications have focused on literacy, language, and in the education of multilingual learners, including multilingual learners with special education needs. MaryEllen Vogt's research and publications focus primarily on improving reading instruction, including comprehension in the content areas, content literacy for multilingual learners, and teacher change and development. Deborah Short is a researcher and former sheltered instruction teacher with expertise in second language development, academic literacy, methods for integrating language and content instruction, materials development, and teacher change. We are delighted to welcome a new author to our team. Katie Toppel's background is in early childhood education, and she currently works as an English language development specialist. She brings a fresh perspective and adds a teacher's point of view to each chapter.

The strength of our collaboration is that we approach the issue of educating multilingual learners with multiple frames of reference. In writing this sixth edition of *Making Content Comprehensible for Multilingual Learners: The SIOP® Model*, we each provided a slightly different lens through which to view and discuss instructional situations. But our varied experiences have led us to the same conclusion: Educators need a resource for planning and implementing high-quality lessons for multilingual learners and other students—lessons that will prepare students eventually for college and careers—and SIOP is fulfilling this need.

■ What's New in This Edition

Enhanced Focus on Multilingual Learners

This sixth edition reflects an advance in perspective for teaching multilingual learners. Multilingual learners bring cultural, linguistic, and experiential assets to the classroom and educators have realized that those assets should be acknowledged and built upon instructionally. SIOP authors have consistently adhered to an asset orientation, but you will find it more prominently presented in this edition, including the change of the book's title (from English Learners to Multilingual Learners) and more explicit attention in chapters as to how teachers can use translanguaging practices and build upon students' home languages and other assets. Further, Feature 19 has been slightly reworded to make it clear that using the home language in class strategically can help students acquire English and deepen their content knowledge.

Enhanced Focus on Technology

Rather than having a separate section on technology as in the past, we have integrated technology throughout the chapters to reflect the competence teachers have developed in embedding technology in their lessons. We have also added more ideas for using technology for remote learning, which remains a reality for some teachers.

New Focus on Multi-Tiered System of Supports for Multilingual Students (MTSS)

In our work with SIOP, we have heard many educators ask questions about multilingual learners who have reading or learning problems and are struggling academically because of them. Few books about teaching multilingual learners address the topic of using data-driven supports to improve students' academic performance. Chapter 10 provides a process for effective MTSS with multilingual learners for educators to follow in their school's MTSS process. The chapter also includes three case studies of struggling multilingual learners and demonstrates how students move through the process.

Enhanced Focus on Implementing the SIOP Model Collaboratively

An important addition to this book, new Chapter 11, "Collaborative Practices for Implementing the SIOP Model," discusses collaborative learning and how educators can get started using SIOP as a common framework. The chapter then moves to a discussion of how to use SIOP in a co-teaching environment. There is a detailed explanation of the co-teaching process that demonstrates how the process can be implemented effectively. Included are profiles of a general education teacher and ELD specialist whose collaboration is used to illustrate the co-teaching process, along with a complete SIOP lesson plan. A detailed *Week at a Glance* planning graphic shows teachers what a co-planned week might look like. Many ELD specialists and general education teachers will find the content of this chapter to be worthwhile.

New Focus on Applying the SIOP Model

Each chapter provides opportunities to apply what you have learned about the SIOP Model through *Application Exercises*. These exercises enable you to watch excerpts from SIOP lessons, and, using the SIOP protocol, rate the degree to which the chapter's SIOP features are present in the lesson you observed. Then readers are asked to provide a rationale for their ratings of each of the SIOP features. There are also reflection questions about the content of each chapter, and how the content relates to the lesson depicted on the respective video excerpts. The Application Exercises are intended for university classes and professional learning workshops and trainings. The SIOP videos that accompany the Application Exercises are found in chapter appendices, located at the end of each chapter in the Pearson eTextbook. The Application Exercises are found in the Learning Management System-Compatible Assessment Bank, which can be downloaded from the Instructor Resources section on Pearson.com.

Key Content Updates for Each Chapter:

Chapter 1 Introducing the SIOP® Model
- Revised chapter objectives
- Updated demographics and research throughout

- Updated discussion of multilingual learners' assets, characteristics, and academic performance
- Up-to-date discussion of academic language and literacy
- New features: Perspectives of SIOP educators and classroom artifacts
- New videos in the Pearson eTextbook to illustrate chapter discussion
- Revised discussion questions

Chapter 2 Lesson Preparation

- Revised chapter objectives
- Updated research throughout
- Enhanced sections discussing content and language objectives and how to write them
- New figures related to Lesson Preparation
- New section on SIOP Lesson planning
- New teaching scenarios and sample lesson plan: Solving Local Problems (Fourth Grade)
- New features: Perspectives of SIOP educators and classroom artifacts
- New videos in the Pearson eTextbook to illustrate chapter discussion
- Revised discussion questions

Chapter 3 Building Background

- Revised chapter objectives
- Updated research throughout including information from the science of reading literature
- Revised substantive discussion of three categories of academic vocabulary
- New feature: Examples of think-alouds that model teaching to specific SIOP features
- New features: Perspectives of SIOP educators and classroom artifacts
- New videos in the Pearson eTextbook to illustrate chapter discussion
- Revised discussion questions

Chapter 4 Comprehensible Input

- Revised chapter objectives
- Updated research throughout
- New teaching scenarios: Economics: Natural Resources and Products (Third Grade)
- New features: Perspectives of SIOP educators' and classroom artifacts
- New videos in the Pearson eTextbook to illustrate chapter discussion
- Revised discussion questions

Chapter 5 Strategies

- Revised chapter objectives
- Updated research throughout including information from the science of reading literature

- Updated description of strategic processing
- New table classifying examples of learning strategies (cognitive, metacognitive, language learning, and socio-affective)
- New table: Strategic Sentence Starters
- New features: Perspectives of SIOP educators and classroom artifacts
- New videos in the Pearson eTextbook to illustrate chapter discussion
- Revised discussion questions

Chapter 6 Interaction

- Revised chapter objectives
- Updated research throughout including information from the science of reading literature
- Revised discussion of the features
- Revised teaching scenarios
- New features: Perspectives of SIOP educators and classroom artifacts
- New videos in the Pearson eTextbook to illustrate chapter discussion
- Revised discussion questions

Chapter 7 Practice & Application

- Revised chapter objectives
- Updated research throughout
- New discussion of language use during practice and application activities
- New features: Perspectives of SIOP educators and classroom artifacts
- New videos in the Pearson eTextbook to illustrate chapter discussion
- Revised teaching scenarios and sample lesson plan: Solar System - Earth, Sun, and Moon
- Revised discussion questions

Chapter 8 Lesson Delivery

- Revised chapter objectives
- Updated research throughout
- Additional ideas for differentiation
- New teaching scenarios: Solving Local Problems (Fourth Grade)
- New features: Perspectives of SIOP educators and classroom artifacts
- New videos in the Pearson eTextbook to illustrate chapter discussion
- Revised discussion questions

Chapter 9 Review & Assessment

- Revised chapter objectives
- Updated research throughout
- Expanded discussion on issues related to the formal and informal assessment of multilingual learners

- New features: Perspectives of SIOP educators and classroom artifacts
- New table: Examples of Formative and Summative Assessments
- New videos in the Pearson eTextbook to illustrate chapter discussion
- Revised discussion questions

Chapter 10 Multi-Tiered System of Supports for Multilingual Students

- Revised chapter objectives
- Updated research throughout
- Revised comprehensive section on multilingual learners and special education
- New graphic: Step-by-step MTSS process for multilingual learners
- New feature: Perspectives of SIOP educators
- New videos in the Pearson eTextbook to illustrate chapter discussion
- Revised discussion questions
- Three case studies of multilingual learners in an MTSS process

Chapter 11 Collaborative Practices for Implementing the SIOP Model

- New chapter objectives
- New ideas for collaborating to learn and implement SIOP
- New discussion of alignment between SIOP and the Collaborative Instructional Cycle
- New discussion of using SIOP to support collaboration and co-teaching
- New vignettes featuring co-planning, co-teaching, co-assessment, and co-reflection practices
- New sample co-teaching lesson plan and Week at a Glance graphic
- New features: Perspectives of SIOP educators and classroom artifacts
- New videos in the Pearson eTextbook to illustrate chapter discussion
- New discussion questions

Appendices

- Appendix A: SIOP protocol (with updated wording for Feature #19)
- New Appendix B: Effective Use of the SIOP Protocol
- Appendix C: SIOP Lesson Plan Templates
- Revised Appendix D: Frequently Asked Questions
- Updated Appendix E: Research on the SIOP Model
- Updated Appendix F: SIOP Professional Development Resources
    - Updated list of resources for further information, including books, journal articles, book chapters, and downloadable research briefs https://siopblog .wordpress.com/
    - Website with information about SIOP professional development, http://siop .savvas.com
    - Website for accessing SIOP Blogs https://siopblog.wordpress.com/ and www .JanaEchevarria.com

■ Pedagogical Highlights in the Book

- **Content and Language Objectives.** One of the hallmarks of the SIOP Model is the inclusion of both content and language objectives for each lesson. Many teachers have found writing these objectives to be challenging, even as they acknowledge their importance both for their own planning and for their students' understanding of the lesson's content goals and language focus. Therefore, you will find expanded sections in Chapter 2 (Lesson Preparation) that provide specific guidance for writing content objectives and language objectives, along with recommendations for how to effectively present them orally and in writing to students.

- **Discussion of the Eight Components and 30 Features of the SIOP.** The beginning of each chapter (2–9) discusses one SIOP component and its various features. For example, the discussion of lesson planning is found in the first half of Chapter 2. As you read about each feature in this section, think about how it would "look" in an actual classroom setting and how teachers might use this information to prepare effective sheltered lessons.

- **Application to Your Classroom.** In this section in Chapters 2–9, you will find a variety of ideas and activities for implementing the eight SIOP components. Most of the ideas are appropriate for students in grades K–12, unless identified otherwise. Some activities may be familiar because you use them in your own classroom. We hope you'll be motivated to try the others because they represent best practice—those ideas and activities that are included have been found to be especially effective for multilingual learners and learners still developing academic literacy skills.

- **Differentiating for Multilevel Classes.** In this section found in Chapters 2–9, we show ways to differentiate SIOP instruction for various levels of language proficiency and academic skills.

- **Teaching Scenarios.** The second half of each chapter about SIOP's components includes teaching scenarios. In these vignettes, teachers, who are teaching the same grade level and content, attempt to include the focal SIOP features, but with varying degrees of success. At the end of each teaching scenario, you will have the opportunity to use that component section of the SIOP to rate the effectiveness of the lesson in implementing the respective SIOP features. For example, as you read the teaching scenarios in Chapter 2, think about how well the three teachers included the features of the Lesson Preparation component in their planning and introduction of the lesson to the class. Note that the illustrated lessons throughout the book range from elementary to high school and they cover a variety of content areas and student language proficiency levels.

- **Discussion of the Three Teaching Scenarios.** Following the description of the three teachers' lessons, you will be able to see how we have rated the lessons for their inclusion of the SIOP features of effective sheltered instruction. We provide detailed explanations for the ratings and encourage you to discuss these with others to develop a degree of inter-rater reliability. You may explain your rating of each teacher's lesson in writing and print a copy for use during discussions in teacher preparation courses, in professional development sessions, or in learning groups at your school site.

- **Final Points.** Each chapter has easy-to-read bulleted information that summarizes the chapter's key points.

- **Discussion Questions.** Based upon input from educators who have used this book, we have revised some of the discussion questions found at the end of each chapter to better reflect actual classroom practice with SIOP. We hope these questions will promote thinking about your own practice, conversations during professional development, and opportunities for portfolio reflection for preservice and inservice courses.

- **Completion of a Lesson Plan.** One language objective in each of Chapters 2–9 asks readers to include features of the specific SIOP component in a SIOP lesson plan. For example, in Chapter 4, a language objective is: *As part of a lesson plan, write several techniques to make academic language accessible for multilingual learners.* By the end of the book, your completed lesson plan will reflect each of SIOP's components and features.

- **The SIOP Protocol.** In Appendix A, you will find both the full version of the SIOP protocol and a two-page abbreviated protocol. The eight components and 30 features of the SIOP Model are identical in both instruments and they are included as options for your personal use. Note that use of students' home language has always been part of SIOP's feature #19, but we decided to clarify its wording. It now acknowledges the important use of translanguaging and reads: *Feature 19: Ample Opportunity for Students to Clarify and Discuss Key Concepts in L1 with Peer, Aide, Teacher, or L1 Text.*

- **Using the SIOP Protocol.** Appendix B offers a discussion of scoring and interpreting the SIOP protocol, explaining how the instrument can be used to measure fidelity to SIOP and to guide teachers in strategically planning lessons for one or more targeted SIOP components.

- **SIOP Lesson Plan Templates.** We have been asked frequently for assistance with lesson planning for SIOP. In this edition, we have included four different formats for lesson plans (see Appendix C); we hope you will find one that is useful for you. In Chapters 2, 5, 7, and 11 you will also find complete plans. These lesson plans are written with different formats, grade levels, and subject areas.

- **Frequently Asked Questions.** In our work with teachers, many of the same questions arise. Answers to these questions are included to guide you as you implement SIOP or help others do so. (See Appendix D.)

- **SIOP Research.** In Appendix E, you will find an overview of the findings from the original SIOP research as well as an updated discussion of the findings of national and international research studies on the SIOP. While not all published SIOP research can be included, it is worth noting that to date there are more than 50 studies supporting the efficacy of the SIOP Model. If you are involved in a research study in your school, district, state, or university and have findings that contribute to the research literature on SIOP, we would greatly appreciate hearing about them.

- **SIOP Professional Development Resources.** In Appendix F, you will find a comprehensive list of resources and books about the SIOP Model. We have written these books in response to teachers' and administrators' requests for additional resources for implementing SIOP. You will find books for administrators and SIOP coordinators, teachers and language specialists, and several books for teachers at all different school levels, from pre-K through high school. The Appendix also includes information about SIOP professional development opportunities: siop.savvas.com as well as useful websites. We hope all these resources are helpful to you as you embark on your SIOP journey!

- **Artifacts.** Each chapter includes examples of student work, lesson ideas, or teacher-made resources. Guiding questions or statements provide the reader with an opportunity to think and make decisions much like a SIOP teacher would.

- **Pearson eTextbook, Learning Management System (LMS)-Compatible Assessment Bank, and Other Instructor Resources**

  - **Pearson eTextbook:** The Pearson eTextbook is a simple-to-use, mobile-optimized, personalized reading experience. It allows you to easily highlight, take notes, and review key vocabulary all in one place–even when offline. Seamlessly integrated videos will engage you and give you access to the help you need, when you need it. To gain access or to sign in to your Pearson eTextbook, visit: https://www.pearson.com/pearson-etext.

  - **Video Examples:** Each chapter in the text includes *Videos* that illustrate principles or concepts aligned pedagogically with the chapter.

  - **LMS-Compatible Assessment Bank:** With this new edition, Application Exercises are included in LMS-compatible banks for the following learning management systems: Blackboard, Canvas, D2L, and Moodle. These packaged files allow maximum flexibility to instructors and trainers when it comes to importing, assigning, and grading.

  - **Application Exercises:** Application Exercises (AEs), new to the sixth edition of this book, are activities and assessment questions for use in college and university teacher education classes, and for school district use for professional learning. As a companion to the text, they offer a way for readers to self-assess, and for instructors and in-district professional developers to teach and assess knowledge and understandings of the SIOP Model. The AEs focus on the SIOP Model components, and they are included for chapters 2 – 9 (Lesson Preparation through Review & Assessment). We also have questions for Chapter 1 (Introducing the SIOP Model) for in-class discussion and/ or assessment. The SIOP videos for the Application Exercises are found in each chapter of the Pearson eTextbook, following the Discussion Questions. These exercises can be downloaded from the Instructor Resources section on Pearson.com.

NOTE: The AEs and accompanying videos are NOT intended, nor is permission granted, for use as professional development by for-profit or not-for-profit companies or individuals outside of school districts, colleges, or universities without written approval from Pearson Rights & Permissions.

▉ Acknowledgments

Many educators throughout the United States and in other countries have contributed to this book through their work as SIOP teachers, bilingual specialists, curriculum coordinators, school and district administrators, university professors, and professional learning experts. We thank them for their insights and critical analyses of the SIOP Model and protocol.

We also thank the many teachers and administrators in whose schools we have conducted research on the SIOP Model, both past and present. Their willingness to let us observe and discuss their teaching of multilingual learners has enhanced our understandings and validated our work. The contributions of these fine educators to the ongoing development of SIOP are many, and we are grateful for their continued interest and encouragement. Our colleagues and fellow researchers on these projects deserve our gratitude as well.

Special thanks go to Allyson Newton, Senior SIOP Product Manager, for Savvas Learning Company, for her deep knowledge about and unwavering support for multilingual learners and the SIOP Model. Further, we would like to thank the individuals who provided quotes and video clips for this book which added important voices to the content: Helene Becker, Tim Blackburn, Maggie Brewer, Mary Casto, John Davis, Tania Drexler-Gutierrez, Francheska Figueora, Molly Haag, Carlota Holder, Tan K. Huynh, Karlin La Porta, Nicole Teyechea McNeil, Angie Medina, Irina McGrath, Kirstin Miller, Deb Painter, Cara Richards-Tutor, Andrea Rients, Kelsins Santos, Ana Segulin, Scott Wade, and Marilyn Amy Washam. We'd also like to express our gratitude to Susan Hurt, who conducted a literature review for us on new SIOP research and dissertation studies.

We are grateful for the students, parents, teachers, and administrators in the Shakopee (MN) Public Schools who opened their schools and classrooms so we could video-record their SIOP lessons which are used in the new Application Exercises and eTextbook Videos. The teachers and district SIOP trainers who are featured include: Gust Abdalla, Trish Boltman, Charmin Erickson, Rachel Klick, Monica Miller, Andrea Rients, Myrlene Schenck, Emily Schmitz, and Jennifer Tabios. We also acknowledge the support, enthusiasm, and contributions of Jeffery Johnston at Pearson, for his assistance with this sixth edition and in particular, the creation of the new Application Exercises.

We appreciate the contributions of those who have participated in the annual SIOP National Conference and at other SIOP professional learning events (see savvas.com/SIOP). At each of these, we gain new understandings about our work from those who engage in professional learning about the SIOP Model.

We found the comments and suggestions from the following reviewers to be very helpful: Lottie Baker, George Washington University; Loren Jones, University of Maryland; Shim Lew, University of West Florida; Monica Vuksanovich, University of North Texas; and Amani Zaier, Texas Tech University. Thank you for taking the time to provide feedback.

The original SIOP work was supported under the Education Research and Development Program, PR/Award No. R306A 60001, the Center for Research on Education, Diversity & Excellence (CREDE), as administered by the former Office of Educational Research and Improvement, now the Institute of Education Sciences (IES), National Institute on the Education of At-Risk Students (NIEARS), and U.S. Department of Education (ED). The contents, findings, and opinions expressed here are those of the authors and do not necessarily represent the positions or policies of IES, NIEARS, or ED. Additional SIOP research was supported by the Carnegie Corporation of New York, the Rockefeller Foundation, and the U.S. Department of Education, Institute of Education Sciences, under the CREATE research center.

Finally, we express appreciation to our families, whose ongoing support has enabled us to pursue our professional interests.

je   mev   djs   kt

Contents

8 Lesson Delivery   214

9 Review & Assessment   235

10 Multi-Tiered System of Supports for Multilingual Students   262

11 Collaborative Practices for Implementing the SIOP Model   279

Introducing the SIOP® Model

CONTENT OBJECTIVES

This chapter will help you to . . .

- List characteristics of multilingual learners that may influence their success in school.
- Distinguish between content-based language instruction and sheltered instruction.
- Explain the research supporting the SIOP Model.

LANGUAGE OBJECTIVES

This chapter will help you to . . .

- Describe the assets your multilingual learners bring to your classroom.
- Develop a lexicon related to the SIOP Model.
- Compare your typical instruction with SIOP instruction.

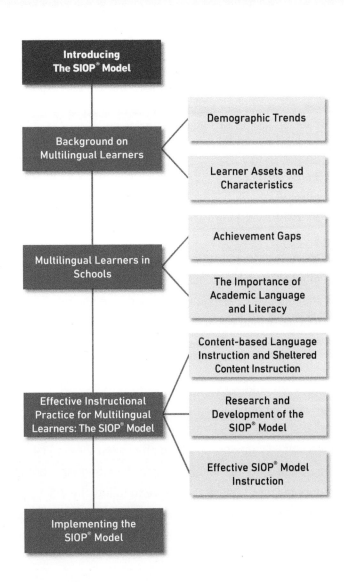

1

Dolores worried about her biology class, her first period class for the new school year. Last year she struggled in science and math. Her teachers would lecture and expect her to take notes, but they talked very quickly. The students were to read the chapters in the textbooks at night and answer questions or do math problems. It was hard for her to understand the information in the books because she didn't know many of the words, and in class she relied on her table mates for assistance. She never volunteered to speak if the teachers asked a question. If one called on her, she usually didn't know how to respond in English even when she had an idea of the answer, and the teacher would quickly call on someone else.

So, she walked into Biology with trepidation. She saw two friends already in the room at a lab table and sat with them. She looked around and saw vocabulary charts on the wall. There were words with pictures and sentences using each word. There were also charts of phrases that started sentences like "A key similarity/difference is __," "It is harder/easier __," and "In comparison/ In contrast, __." The whiteboard had some writing. "CO: We will explore the camouflage adaptation in an experiment. LO: We will use comparisons to describe the results." At the lab table she saw two sheets of paper—one white, one black sheet—and two envelopes. Looking inside, she saw white dots in one and black dots in the other.

The biology teacher, Ms. Ruiz, introduced herself and explained the lesson. She pointed to the sentences on the board: "Today we will do a lab so you can learn about animal adaptations like camouflage, and then we will write about our results using some comparative phrases." She gestured to the chart with sentence starters as she reminded the class about ways to state comparisons. She asked students to turn to a partner and define *camouflage* and *adaptation*, or give examples, if they knew of any. Dolores was pleased. She knew those words in Spanish. Where she grew up in Mexico, she had seen green leaf frogs and vine snakes. They blended in with the leaves and trees. She told her friend Alicia about them. When Ms. Ruiz asked students to share, she nervously raised her hand and described them. When she stumbled over a word in English, Ms. Ruiz encouraged her to say it in Spanish.

Ms. Ruiz next pointed to a vocabulary chart and discussed the words. She had the students pronounce them and then copy them in their notebooks. After that, she started a National Geographic video clip and explained it showed some camouflage adaptations among animals. They watched the brief clip twice, with closed captions, and then she asked them to compare two of the animals they saw. She encouraged students to use comparative language, both the phrases on the chart and others that students knew. Dolores was able to follow the discussion.

Next, Ms. Ruiz introduced the experiment and displayed directions on the interactive whiteboard. She passed out tweezers, a worksheet, and an index card to each student. She told the students to gently pour the white dots on the black paper. They would have one minute to pick up as many dots as possible. They would count them and record the number collected on the worksheet. Then they would move the dots to the white paper and do the same. After that, they would work with the black dots, first on white paper, then black. Using a document camera, she modeled how to spread out the dots, pick them up, and record the information.

When they finished the experiment, Ms. Ruiz asked the lab partners to discuss what they discovered and connect the camouflage results to things they see in real life. She then asked the students to share out their conclusions. She reviewed the objectives for the day and said, "Post one thing that you learned on the class tablet before you leave." Dolores was surprised when the bell rang. The time went by so fast. She felt like she understood all that they had done. ∎

Dolores had different learning experiences from one year to the next. The previous year, her science teacher used a more traditional approach. He lectured primarily and had the students work frequently in textbooks. He provided little language development or scaffolding for his multilingual learners—indeed, little scaffolding for any of his students. Dolores was quiet in class because she didn't know how to articulate her ideas in English. She had difficulty comprehending the textbook. She didn't learn much academic English in either science or math class.

This year, in contrast, held the promise of a more positive learning environment. Ms. Ruiz, the biology teacher, made the lessons easy to understand. She had pictures with words on the walls and showed video clips. She explained words and how to form different types of sentences. She let them do experiments and talk about them with their lab partners. Dolores gained the confidence to speak up in class. She could share things she knew from her life in Mexico. She could use her native language as a resource. Most importantly, she felt like she was learning English while learning science.

Dolores is fortunate to have a Biology teacher who uses the SIOP Model. Her thoughtful lesson planning enables all the students in class to learn the science content. Dolores and the other multilingual students benefit in particular because they are able to learn the material through English, their new language. Ms. Ruiz provides supports and engages them in activities that give them access to the grade-level curriculum. We have written this book to help more teachers learn the techniques that Ms. Ruiz uses, so that many more multilingual learners will have a chance to develop academic literacy in English and be successful in school.

■ Background on Multilingual Learners

English is the most popular new language to learn around the world. Some people learn English for their job or studies; others because they want to travel or communicate with speakers of English. In the United States, English is the medium of instruction in most elementary and secondary classrooms, so students with a home language other than English need to learn it to be successful in school.

In this book we refer to students who are not yet proficient in English language and literacy as *multilingual learners*. This term is similar to various names for these students that have been used by the federal government and state and local education agencies, such as *English language learner*, *English learner*, and *emergent bilingual*. With this term, we choose to emphasize the language assets these learners have rather than the language they are in the process of acquiring.

Multilingual learners typically receive language support services in their schools and may be at any level of English proficiency. Upon enrollment, they are identified for services via a home language survey and a subsequent English language proficiency assessment. They are usually assigned a proficiency level (e.g., beginning or entering) and placed in a bilingual, dual language, or English-medium program depending on the school or district options. Like the learners, these programs have different names. Most multilingual learners will receive a class period or two of designated English language development as well as instruction in the subject areas delivered through their home language or sheltered instruction. They exit language support programs when they meet the criteria, which usually includes at a minimum passing the state English language proficiency assessment.

Figure 1.1 lists common terms and acronyms for multilingual learners and their educational programs. Your district may use some of them, and you will also find these terms in research studies and federal and state educational policies. Note however, that definitions for some of these terms are fluid and may vary somewhat in your state. For further discussion about the use of categories, see Gunderson, 2021.

Demographic Trends

Dolores is one of many multilingual learners in our schools. In fact, she represents the fastest growing group of K–12 students (U.S. Dept. of Education, Office of English Language Acquisition, 2021a). Recent data report that in Fall 2019, 10.4% of the students in U.S. K–12 schools were multilingual learners, equaling more than 5.1 million students out of a total enrollment of 49.2 million. It is noteworthy that multilingual learners in Grades K–2 constitute 15% or more of the total student enrollment in each grade. In terms of elementary and secondary proportions, 60.3% of the multilingual learners were reported in grades K–5 and 39.5% in grades 6–12 (U.S. Department of Education, National Center for Education Statistics, 2021).

The five states that enroll the largest numbers of elementary and secondary multilingual learners are California, Texas, Florida, New York, and Illinois. Those with the fewest number of multilingual learners in school are Vermont, Wyoming, West Virginia, North Dakota, and New Hampshire. Fourteen states enroll multilingual learners in greater percentages than the national average (ranging from 19.6% to 10.6%) when compared to total student enrollment: Texas, California, New Mexico, Nevada, Illinois, the District of Columbia, Rhode Island, Alaska, Washington, Delaware, Maryland, and Massachusetts (U.S. Department of Education, National Center for Education Statistics, 2021).

Although close to 400 different languages are spoken in the homes of our elementary and secondary students, a very large percentage of multilingual learners (75.7%) have Spanish as a home language. The other top languages, albeit at much

FIGURE 1.1	Common Terms Associated with Multilingual Learners and Their Educational Programs

Student-related

Dual language learner (DLL)
Emergent bilingual (EB)
English language learner (ELL)
English learner (EL)
English learner student with a learning disability (ELSWD) [also dually identified student]
English only (EO) [monolingual English speaker]
English speakers of other languages (ESOL)
Ever EL—Someone who was an identified English learner at some time in school
Former English (language) learner (FEL/FELL)
Fully English proficient/Fluent English proficient (FEP)
Limited English proficient (LEP)
Long-term English (language) learner (LTEL/LTELL)
Multilingual learner (ML/MLL)
Never EL—Someone who was never identified as an English learner
Newcomer—Someone who is newly arrived to the United States and new to English [definitions/criteria vary]
nonEL—Non-English learner (may be someone who was an English learner but has reached proficiency; may be someone who was never an English learner)
Students with (limited or) interrupted formal education (SIFE/SLIFE)

Program-related

Bilingual education (BE)
Content-based ESL (CBESL)
Content-based language instruction (CBLI)
Dual language (DL)
English as a new language (ENL)
English as a second language (ESL)
English as an additional language (EAL)
English language development (ELD)
English language proficiency (ELP)
English to speakers of other languages (ESOL)
Home language survey (HLS)
First language (L1) [also home language, primary language, native language]
Languages other than English (LOTE)
Multi-tiered systems of support (MTSS)
Response to Intervention (RTI)
Second language (L2)
Sheltered instruction (SI)
Specially designed academic instruction in English (SDAIE)
Structured English immersion/Sheltered English immersion (SEI)
Transitional bilingual instruction (TBI)
Two-way immersion (TWI)

smaller scale, are Arabic (2.6%), a variety of Chinese (2.0%), and Vietnamese (1.5%). The other languages are spoken by fewer than 1% of the multilingual learner population (U.S. Department of Education, National Center for Education Statistics, 2021).[1]

---

[1] It may be noted that 2.1% of the multilingual learners were reported as having English as their home language. This might include students who were adopted from another country but live in a household that speaks English and students in households where multiple languages are spoken.

It is also important to recognize that the number of multilingual learners reported in the data refers to the students who have been identified as eligible for language support services in their school districts; these students were evaluated by a home language survey and an English language proficiency assessment tool. The number does not include the multilingual learners who have exited the language support programs but are still struggling with some aspects of *academic* English, the language used to read, write, listen, and speak in subject area classes to perform academic tasks and demonstrate knowledge of the subject standards. The increases in multilingual learner enrollment will continue over the next several decades, so all educators need to be prepared to address these students' language and academic needs.

Learner Assets and Characteristics

In order to develop the best educational programs for multilingual learners, we need to know our students and understand their diverse backgrounds. Our learners bring a wide variety of educational and cultural experiences to the classroom as well as considerable linguistic assets and other funds of knowledge (Gonzalez, Moll, & Amanti, 2005; Paterson, 2021; TESOL, 2018). They differ in a number of ways as well, from home language and country of origin to former educational experiences to age of arrival in the United States and socioeconomic status. These characteristics have implications for instruction, assessment, and program design. When we know our students' backgrounds and abilities, we can incorporate effective techniques and materials in our instructional practices.

> We need to know our kids well as individuals, and as interactive members of our classroom community, in order to balance all of their needs and create a flexible learning environment that helps to move everyone forward.
>
> Kirstin Miller, High School Math Teacher, Kentucky

Multilingual Learner Assets.   Let's begin by considering our multilingual learners' strengths. Their assets are related to language and cultural practices in the home, schooling in other countries, and individual abilities and qualities. Teachers therefore need to be aware of the language and literacy skills their students have and use outside of school. When we leverage these assets in the classroom, we promote student agency and access in service of educational equity. We encourage students to draw on their meta skills (e.g., metalinguistics and metacognition) and full repertoire of knowledge, no matter the language context in which it has been learned.

We know, for example, that children make guesses and predictions at home. These then act as precursors to academic language development in school, where the students learn to call these notions *estimates, hypotheses*, or *theories* depending on the subject area. In some cultures, older children mentor younger siblings in performing chores and other tasks. Teachers can build on these relationship roles to construct collaborative learning environments in the classroom. Multilingual learners may have social-emotional skills, such as resilience and acceptance of ambiguity, that can serve them well as they deal with challenging assignments and unfamiliar academic discourse. See Figure 1.2 for some of the assets that teachers should learn to recognize in their multilingual learners.

Diverse Characteristics.   Next let's turn to other characteristics that make our multilingual learners diverse. We cannot plan programs and pathways through school by assuming these students are all alike, because they are not. They enter our classrooms with a wide range of language proficiencies (both in English and

FIGURE 1.2 | **Multilingual Learner Assets**

Oral language skills in the home language—Many aspects of the home language learned through oral interaction can apply or transfer to learning academic English (August & Shanahan, 2006; Genesee et al., 2006; Guglielmi, 2008). These include phonemic awareness and phonics; grasp of vocabulary cognates; knowledge of prefixes, suffixes, and roots; listening comprehension strategies; and functional language use (e.g., comparing, evaluating, describing).

Reading and writing skills in the home language—Knowing how to read and write in the home language facilitates learning those skills in a new language (August & Shanahan, 2006; Genesee et al., 2006). Consider students who can read and find the main idea in a home language text. Those learners have mastered the cognitive reading strategy already. They may need to learn the words and syntax of English, but not how to find the main idea.

Metalinguistic awareness—Having the big picture of how language works (as a concept) provides a foundation for learning a new language. For example, knowing that words can be nouns and verbs and that a relationship between a noun and a verb gives meaning to an utterance can be applied to the new language even if the order of words in a sentence differs from the home language.

Out-of-school literacy skills—Students use literacy outside of school, sometimes for family purposes (e.g., making a shopping list, reading a utility bill) and sometimes for personal reasons (e.g., using social media, listening to music). These practices help them understand that literacy is used for different purposes and is found in different formats. These skills also allow students to learn new knowledge outside of school that may be applicable to a lesson.

Educational backgrounds—Through schooling in their home country, some children may be at or above grade level relative to the curricula in their U.S. school. These students need to learn English, but have few gaps in their academics.

Language brokering roles—School-age multilingual learners often assume the role of language broker in families where the adults do not speak English well. Students learn to engage with others using English, experiencing different interaction patterns, and being responsive to others' utterances. They learn to turn-take turns in conversation, answer questions, ask for clarification, paraphrase, interpret, and translate, among other functions.

Cultural funds of knowledge—In their homes, children participate in language and cultural practices and activities that can be shared in the classroom. Teachers may learn about these funds of knowledge through home visits, interviews, and projects that students complete. Teachers may select instructional materials and plan authentic classroom tasks around these funds that connect with the curriculum. They may invite parents or members of the community as guest speakers.

Familial supports—Family support and parental engagement have positive impacts on children's schooling success. Teachers can partner with the families to determine ways that families can support at home what is being learned at school. Parents, other family members, and guardians can in turn convey family values, communication patterns, storytelling practices, work goals, and aspirations for their children to the teachers.

Life experiences—Our students do not enter schools as blank slates. Many have had life experiences that are pertinent to the curricula. Some students farmed in their home countries and know about plant growth, animal reproduction, and more. Other students' families had market stalls, and they learned about supply and demand, revenue, and debt. Some have lived in different climatic zones and biomes or have traveled across countries and continents. These learners have much to offer the instructional process and can help build background on certain subject-area topics for others in the class.

Social and emotional skills—Many multilingual learners have or are developing social and emotional skills and competencies. Their varied experiences and backgrounds may have led to their development of skills such as persistence, planning and organization, perspective taking, team work, analysis and decision making, emotional awareness, and more. These skills can be building blocks for academic development, especially when teachers foster affirming and supportive learning environments.

Individual talents and abilities—All students have unique qualities. Some may be athletic and learn teamwork and perseverance during sports. Some may have musical gifts and can translate symbols into sounds. Some have part-time jobs where they learn responsibility, problem solving, and resourcefulness. Others draw, dance, write poems, make videos, cook, construct, garden, and more. These abilities and interests can be highlighted in lessons for making input comprehensible and for making output relevant.

in their home languages) and much divergence in their subject matter knowledge. We find diversity in their educational backgrounds, literacy levels in the home language, expectations of schooling, socioeconomic status, age of arrival, personal experiences while coming to and living in the United States, parents' education levels and proficiency in English, and much more. Of course, our learners have individual personalities and talents as well. Some multilingual learners are newcomers (i.e., new arrivals to the United States), some have lived in the United States for several years, and many were born in the United States. Foreign-born multilingual learners may be immigrants, refugees, asylees, unaccompanied minors, permanent residents, or naturalized citizens.

The following discussion offers a broad overview of some of the multilingual learners who enter our schools:

- A number of our foreign-born multilingual learners had strong academic backgrounds before coming to the United States. Some are at or above equivalent grade levels in certain subjects—math and science, for example. They are literate in their native language and may have started studying a second or even a third language. Much of what these learners need is English language development so that as they become more proficient in English, they can transfer the knowledge they learned in their native country's schools to the courses they are taking in the United States. A few subjects not previously studied, such as U.S. history, may require special attention. These students have a strong likelihood of achieving educational success if they receive appropriate English language and content instruction in their U.S. schools.

- Other foreign-born students had very limited formal schooling or an interrupted education—perhaps due to war in their native countries, life in a refugee camp, the need to work, or the remote, rural location of their homes. These students have little or no literacy in their native language, and they may not have had such schooling experiences as sitting at desks all day, changing classrooms for different subjects, or taking high-stakes tests. They have significant gaps in their educational backgrounds, lack knowledge in specific subject areas, and need time to become accustomed to school routines and expectations. These multilingual learners with limited formal schooling and below-grade-level literacy are most at risk for educational failure.

- In the past decade, the number of foreign-born, unaccompanied minors has increased. These students, who are younger than 18 years old, come to the United States without a parent. Many experience hardships and trauma during the journey. Some are able to connect with relatives living in the United States and others are housed with a court-appointed guardian. Many have weak educational backgrounds and face challenges once in U.S. schools.

- There are also many multilingual learners who have grown up in the United States but who speak a language other than English at home. In fact, these students comprise the majority of multilingual learners in both elementary and secondary school programs. Some students in this group are literate in their home language, such as Mandarin, Arabic, or Spanish, and will add English to their knowledge base in school.

Among the types of multilingual students described above, we also have some students with other characteristics that have implications for educational services.

- Students who are newly arrived to the United States may be referred to as *newcomer students*. They may be placed in a specialized newcomer program if they have very low levels of English language proficiency and/or are below grade level in their academics, especially if they enroll in middle or high school, as they have less time to catch up before graduation. Students with limited or interrupted formal education are a subset of newcomer students. (Custodio & O'Loughlin, 2017; Short & Boyson, 2012)

- Multilingual learners who do not exit their language support program after five or more years in U.S. schools are referred to as *long-term English learners* (U.S. Department of Education, 2016). They typically have oral proficiency in English but lack English reading and/or writing skills. They struggle academically (Kieffer & Parker, 2016; Menken, Kleyn & Chae, 2012; Rodriguez, Carrasquillo, Garcia & Howitt, 2020) and often are unable to pass state English language proficiency tests and/or other measures that are required for them to be reclassified as fully English proficient (Saunders & Marcelletti, 2013). Targeted interventions may be planned for these students, especially if they have completed all the available levels/years of service in the language support programs.

- Forty percent of school-aged migratory children (also known as *migrants*) are multilingual learners (U.S. Department of Education, Office of English Language Acquisition, 2021d). They move from school to school within the same academic year as their family travels for work. This situation jeopardizes their learning with absences and potentially incompatible curricula and assessments across districts or states.

- A small number of immigrant students have temporary protected status, a designation by the federal government that may be granted to foreign-born individuals who are unable to return to their country primarily due to safety concerns, such as an ongoing war or the aftermath of a major natural disaster. They, too, may have experienced hardships and trauma.

Some students are dually identified, meaning they should receive services from two educational categories. For example, besides being multilingual learners, some children have learning disabilities or are gifted and talented.

- Multilingual learners tend to be over- or underrepresented in special education because their school districts struggle to determine if a student's difficulty is due to a learning disability, a lack of schooling, a delay in developing second language proficiency, or another reason (National Center for Learning Disabilities, 2020). It is not recommended that a school wait longer than one year to begin the referral process for special education consideration; interventions can begin sooner, however. When students are appropriately identified, federal regulations require that they receive instructional hours for English language development as well as for identified special education needs (U.S. Department of Justice, Civil Rights Division, & U.S. Department of Education, Office of Civil Rights, 2015).

- Some multilingual learners and former multilingual learners who score poorly on reading assessments may need additional services to improve their reading achievement, such as Tier 2 or Tier 3 in a Multi-tiered System of Support (MTSS) (or Response to Intervention [RTI]) program. We believe that the SIOP Model we present in this book is the best option for Tier 1 instruction and may help avoid Tier 2 and 3 placements (see Chapter 10).

- Some students have abilities that fit the criteria for gifted and talented services, but their participation in these programs is much lower than that of students who have English proficiency. Schools may struggle to identify them, particularly if they have low or no proficiency in English and speak a language other than Spanish. Some schools may have barriers to participation such as certain course prerequisites, English proficiency, reclassification status, and false assumptions that teachers of these courses can't provide scaffolds to give students access to the subject material. As a result, multilingual learners are underrepresented in gifted and talented programs and in advanced coursework, such as higher-level mathematics and Advanced Placement and International Baccalaureate courses (Kiefer & Thompson, 2018; U.S. Department of Education, Office of English Language Acquisition, 2021c). The U.S. Department of Education, however, directs school districts to make sure their admission policies and practices do not limit multilingual learners' participation in these programs and courses (U.S. Department of Education, Office of English Language Acquisition, 2017).

The diverse characteristics described above represent some of the background factors that should be considered when planning programs and instruction so multilingual learners can succeed in school. Figure 1.3 shows these characteristics and additional important points that influence multilingual learners' educational attainment and should be kept in mind.

FIGURE 1.3	Diverse Characteristics of Multilingual Learners

Status Related to Country of Origin

- U.S. born
- Naturalized U.S. citizen
- Permanent resident
- Immigrant
- Refugee
- Asylee
- Unaccompanied minor
- Temporary protected status

Knowledge of the English Language

- Exposure to English (social and academic)
- Familiarity with Roman alphabet and Arabic numbers
- Familiarity with English sounds (phonemes)
- Proficiency in oral English (speaking and listening)
- Proficiency in written English (reading and writing)
- English being learned as a third or fourth language

(continued)

FIGURE 1.3 Diverse Characteristics of Multilingual Learners *(continued)*

Knowledge of the Home Language

- Proficiency in home language oral skills (speaking and listening)
- Proficiency in home language written skills (reading and writing)
- Metalinguistic awareness
- Cross-linguistic transfer

Educational Background

- On grade-level schooling in home country
- On grade-level schooling in U.S. schools (in home language or English)
- Partial/interrupted schooling in home language
- No schooling in home language
- Entrance age in U.S. schools
- Partial/interrupted schooling in English
- No schooling in English
- Receiving language support services for five years or less
- Receiving language support services for more than five years
- Expectations for schooling
- Degree of absenteeism

Social, Cultural, Emotional, and Economic Factors

- Age of arrival in the United States
- Poverty level
- Free or reduced lunch status
- Mobility
- Living situation (e.g., homelessness, crowded conditions)
- Exposure to trauma, violence, abuse, and other serious stressors
- Refugee or asylee status
- Undocumented status
- Parents' educational background
- Parents' level of English proficiency
- Cultural norms for communication
- Access to technology (e.g., equipment, Internet, bandwidth)
- Access to health/mental health services

Other Educational Categories

- Special education status
- Tier 2 or Tier 3 intervention (MTSS or RTI)
- Gifted and talented status
- Migrant status
- Exited/Former/Reclassified/Monitored multilingual learner—Years 1 and 2 after exit
- Exited/Former/Reclassified multilingual learner—Years 3 and 4 after exit

Multilingual Learners in Schools

Our multilingual learners enter U.S. schools where academically rigorous, standards-based instruction and assessment is the norm. The federal government holds schools accountable for the success of all students, and each state has standards for mathematics, reading/language arts, English language development, and science, at a minimum. All states are required to administer high-stakes tests based on these standards and report results annually. A positive change over the past two decades is that schools and districts are expected to teach grade-level academic content to multilingual learners right from the start, either in English or in their home language, in addition to English language development classes.

As a result of changes in education policy since 2001, the education of multilingual learners is a regular part of school improvement conversations, with attention given to providing better educational opportunities for the learners and monitoring their language proficiency growth and academic progress. Schools now regularly analyze assessment data to determine the progress of their efforts and to adjust programs, instruction, and resources as indicated. Some federal and state funding is available to help practicing teachers strengthen their instruction so students develop academic literacy skills and can access core content. Schools can tap these funds to provide sustained professional development opportunities, including job-embedded coaching. Some states have also allocated additional resources for multilingual learner programs, such as grants for specialized services for newcomers and students with interrupted educational backgrounds (Short & Boyson, 2012).

Unfortunately, although national standards for teacher education colleges and universities state that prospective teachers need to understand how to work with diverse students, including multilingual learners, and that they should keep students' culture and language differences in mind when planning lessons (see http://caepnet. org/standards/introduction), the standards do not detail specific coursework that should be taught. English language development teachers, bilingual teachers, and dual language teachers are well trained to teach in and about English, but courses on second language acquisition, ELD techniques for integrating language and content, and cross-cultural communication are rarely required for others studying to be teachers in U.S. schools (National Academies of Sciences, Engineering, and Medicine, 2017). Consequently, many general education teachers are underprepared to serve multilingual learners when they exit their preservice institutions (National Council on Teacher Quality, 2015). The burden for preparing these general education teachers to meet the educational needs of multilingual learners therefore falls on schools and districts and must be accomplished through inservice professional development.

Achievement Gaps

Despite more attention being given to multilingual learners and the programs serving them, the challenging academic standards and assessments have not resulted in closing the achievement gap between multilingual learners and students proficient in English. For the past 20 years, the achievement gap between these student groups on national tests has changed very little, a difference of more than 20 points in mathematics and more than 30 points in reading and in science. Consider the following statistics:

- The average scale score gap between English learners[2] and non-English learners on the fourth-grade National Assessment for Educational Progress (NAEP) exam for reading ranged from 35 points in 2003 to 33 points in

---

[2] The U.S. Department of Education, which oversees NAEP, uses "English learners" for the students we refer to as "multilingual learners" in this book.

2019, with minor variation during the intervening years. A similar gap existed in the eighth-grade reading exam, albeit with slight widening, from 43 points in 2003 to 45 points.

- The average scale score gap between English learners and non-English learners on the fourth-grade NAEP mathematics exam remained almost the same, 23 points in 2003 to 24 points in 2019. The gap widened somewhat in the eighth-grade mathematics exam, from 38 points in 1996 to 42 points in 2019.

- Similarly, the average scale score gap between English learners and non-English learners on the NAEP science exam was relatively the same, from 32 points in 2005 to 33 points in 2019. The gap also widened somewhat in the eighth-grade science exam, from 42 points in 1996 to 46 points in 2019.

A closer look at the most recent data available at the time of this writing can be found in Table 1.1. In this table showing the performance of English learners and non-English learners in 2019 on the fourth-grade and eighth-grade NAEP reading, mathematics, and science exams, you can see that the achievement of all students is quite low. In none of the three subjects did even half of the non-English learners

TABLE 1.1   **Performance of English Learners and Non-English Learners on NAEP Exams in 2019**

Reading/Language Arts

4th Grade	Average Scale Score	Below Basic	Basic	At or above Proficient	Advanced
non ELLs	224	29%	32%	29%	10%
ELLs	191	65%	25%	8%	1%
8th Grade					
non ELLs	266	24%	40%	31%	4%
ELLs	221	72%	24%	4%	0%*

Mathematics

4th Grade	Average Scale Score	Below Basic	Basic	Proficient	Advanced
non ELLs	243	16%	39%	35%	10%
ELLs	220	41%	43%	15%	1%
8th Grade					
non ELLs	285	28%	36%	25%	11%
ELLs	243	72%	22%	4%	1%

Science

4th Grade	Average Scale Score	Below Basic	Basic	Proficient	Advanced
non ELLs	155	23%	38%	38%	1%
ELLs	122	59%	33%	8%	0%*
8th Grade					
non ELLs	157	29%	34%	35%	2%
ELLs	111	81%	16%	3%	0%*

Sources: National Student Group Scores and Score Gaps reports for Reading/Language Arts, Mathematics, and Science on website, https://www.nationsreportcard.gov

reach the proficient level. For English learners, the results are more troubling. For five of the six exams reported, 90% to 97% of the students who are still acquiring English failed to reach the proficient level.

- National assessments are not the only area of achievement where multilingual learners do more poorly than students who are proficient in English.

- Multilingual learners are more likely to drop out of high school than all students. In 2019, 5.1% of all students were status dropouts[3] but the rate was 17.5% for students identified as speaking a language other than English at home and speaking English less than very well (U.S. Department of Education, National Center for Education Statistics, 2021).

- Although the 4-year cohort high school graduation rates for all students improved from 2010–11 to 2017–18, multilingual learners still graduated at a lower rate (68%) than all students (85%), a group which includes multilingual learners. The gap between the two groups has narrowed somewhat during this time (U.S. Department of Education, Office of English Language Acquisition, 2020).

- In 2017–18, multilingual learners were overrepresented in the number of students who were retained (i.e., not promoted) in grades K–12 (U.S. Department of Education, Office of English Language Acquisition, 2021b).

Why do these achievement gaps continue to exist for multilingual learners as a group, despite decades of educational reform?

- One factor is the assessments themselves. Multilingual learners take subject-area tests in English (except in a few states) before they are proficient in the language. Compounding the situation is that these assessments have been designed and normed on native English speakers. These tests are not valid or reliable for multilingual learners (Abedi & Linquanti, 2012), so it is not surprising they do not attain the testing achievement targets set for native English speakers.

- Another factor is the quality of instruction. We discussed earlier the underpreparation of many general education teachers. Many have had to learn on the job how to effectively instruct multilingual learners. In 2017–18, 64% of all teachers reported having at least one multilingual learner in class. However, only 10% had a major, minor, or certification in ESL and only 44.8% of them took any undergraduate or graduate course on teaching these learners before their first year of teaching (U.S. Department of Education, National Center for Education Statistics, 2021). Related to this are the low expectations that teachers, administrators, and counselors may hold for multilingual learners, which can lead to placement in low-level academic courses and a mistaken belief that challenging assignments and higher-order thinking tasks should be avoided due to the students' limited proficiency in English (Sugarman, 2019).

- Localized policies for admission to gifted and talented programs and advanced coursework, such as requiring English proficiency, reclassification status, certain prerequisite courses, and lack of identification assessments in languages other

---

[3] Status dropout refers to students who are not enrolled in high school and do not have a high school credential (e.g., a regular diploma or GED).

than English, limit multilingual learners' access to challenging curricula. Similarly, policies pushing for a 4-year high school graduation rate may cause students with limited or interrupted educational backgrounds to drop out because they do not believe they have time to learn English and pass all the required courses for a diploma (Rodriguez, Carrasquillo, Garcia, & Howitt, 2020).

Pearson eTextbook

Video Example 1.1

Watch this video to hear Dr. Jim Cummins discuss learning a new language and explain BICS and CALP. Where are your students on the continuum between social language and academic language?

https://www.youtube.com/watch?v=OLw6XRyoPrE

- Another important reason is perhaps the simplest. Acquiring a new language takes time. Moreover, as students move up in proficiency level and in grade level, they have more language and content to learn. We know that conversational fluency (also known as *social language* or *basic interpersonal communicative skills* [BICS]) develops inside and outside of the classroom and can be attained in one to three years (Thomas & Collier, 2002). However, the language that is critical for educational success—academic language (or cognitive/academic language proficiency [CALP]) (Cummins, 2000)—is more complex and develops more slowly and systematically in academic settings. Multilingual learners typically need four years of instruction or more to reach grade-level proficiency in academic English (Greenberg Motamedi, 2015; Kieffer & Parker, 2016).

In contrast to the disappointing findings when current multilingual learners are compared to all students, there is some hopeful news. When school districts and states disaggregate data and analyze the achievement of their former multilingual students—those who have reached proficiency in English and exited their language support programs—some positive achievement outcomes have come to light. The biennial report to Congress on Title III programs (U.S. Department of Education, Office of English Language Acquisition, 2021a) examined the performance of former multilingual learners on statewide assessments of mathematics, reading/language arts, and science tests. Although these tests and achievement levels vary by state, and not all states submitted data, a review of the percentage of students who participated and reached the proficient or above proficient level shows how well former multilingual learners did compared to current multilingual learners and all students who took the exams.

In Table 1.2, we can see that former multilingual learners outperformed all students, as well as current English learners, in mathematics and reading/language arts in the 2017–18 school year.[4] They did not, however, outperform all students in science.

TABLE 1.2 **Students Who Scored At or Above Proficient on Statewide Assessments for School Year 2017–2018**

	Mathematics	Reading/language arts	Science
All students	45.2%	50.5%	55%
English learners	25.4%	23.8%	21%
Former English learners	46.3%	52.6%	44%

Source: U.S. Department of Education, Office of English Language Acquisition, 2021a

---

[4] 2017–2018 was the most recent school year for which data analyses were available at the time of this writing.

We also see that when policies and programs are established with second language acquisition research and evidence-based practices in mind, multilingual learners perform well. For example, studies have shown that students instructed through two languages outperformed those who studied only in English on academic and English language proficiency measures, including the state tests (Steele, et al., 2017; Umansky & Reardon, 2014; Valentino & Reardon, 2015). A study of New York City's graduation rates revealed former multilingual learners outperformed students as a whole (New York City Department of Education, 2022). These findings remind us that for the vast majority of our students, acquiring English as a new language is a temporary endeavor; once they have achieved English proficiency, the cognitive benefits of bilingualism can lead to their academic success.

The Importance of Academic Language and Literacy

One key area where we know that multilingual learners need support is in developing academic language and literacy skills in English. These skills serve as the foundation for school success because we learn primarily through language and use language to express our understanding. Age-appropriate knowledge of the English language is a prerequisite in the attainment of content standards because as the grade levels rise, language use becomes more complex and more content area-specific. The skills students need to be college and career ready are more extensive than knowledge of vocabulary words and paragraph formation. They include analytical reading and writing, effective communication and interaction, critical thinking, and creativity. The emphasis on teaching academic language is reflected in national and state standards and assessments for English language proficiency. (See, for example, standards from California, ELPA21, New York, Texas, and WIDA).

We argue that academic language is a second language for *all* students. Even native English speaking students do not enter kindergarten or first-grade classrooms using embedded clauses and long, modified noun phrases in their conversations, nor do they analyze text for an author's use of imagery or write problem–solution essays about local issues. They learn these ways of using language for specific purposes over time in school. And school is where children and young adults mostly use academic language.

In *Developing Academic Language with the SIOP® Model* (Short & Echevarría, 2016, p. 2), we explain that academic language is different from everyday conversation:

> [W]hile there is no singular definition, there is consensus that academic language includes the application of reading, writing, listening, and speaking skills to knowledge of vocabulary, language structures, language functions, genres, discourse patterns, and strategic competencies that students need to be successful in school with spoken and written academic text. There is also agreement that academic language demands and linguistic elements vary, at least partially, by subject area.

Although academic language is used in school settings by all students, this type of language use is particularly challenging for multilingual learners who are beginning to acquire English at the same time that school tasks require a high level of

English usage. Multilingual learners do double the work: they must develop literacy skills for each content area *in* their second language as they simultaneously learn, comprehend, and apply content area concepts *through* their second language (Short & Fitzsimmons, 2007).

Using English, multilingual students, for example, must be able to

- read and understand the expository prose in textbooks and reference materials,
- write persuasively,
- argue points of view,
- take notes from teacher lectures or Internet sites, and
- articulate their thinking processes—make hypotheses and predictions, express analyses, draw conclusions, and so forth.

In content classes, multilingual learners must integrate their emerging knowledge of the English language with the content information they are studying in order to complete the academic tasks. They must also learn *how* to do these tasks—generate the format of an outline, negotiate roles in cooperative learning groups, interpret charts and maps, and much more. These three knowledge bases—knowledge of English, knowledge of the content topic, and knowledge of how the tasks are to be accomplished—constitute the major components of academic literacy (Short & Echevarría, 2016). Teachers and curriculum developers should pay attention to this full range of academic language.

■ Effective Instructional Practice for Multilingual Learners: The SIOP® Model

When we first started working on the SIOP research in the mid 1990s, we had a vision for the education of multilingual learners. We wanted them to receive grade-level content curricula through specialized instruction that would use techniques to make the content comprehensible and that would also promote their English language development. We wanted them to be placed in content classes from the start of their schooling, not wait 2–3 years and only receive ESL and electives during that period, as was the standard practice in the early 1990s. We had a vision that all teachers would teach both language and content to the multilingual learners. Thus, all teachers would hold high expectations for the learners and be responsible for their success in school.

For this to happen, the general education teachers needed to learn and apply what were then common ESL techniques and also develop an understanding of how academic language is used in their subject areas and then learn how to teach aspects of that language to the students. We referred to this practice as *sheltered content instruction*. In addition, the ESL teachers had to shift how they taught English to make it more content-based and relevant to the language demands of the other classes that students took. So language teachers were asked to integrate content topics and teach related vocabulary, incorporate reading and writing tasks that would reflect the genres found in core subject areas, and promote academic conversations.

Of course, those who taught newcomer students at the lowest proficiency levels also had to cover social and school communicative language as well.

Educational reforms over the past two decades have led schools and districts to focus on developing academic language and literacy skills in students who struggle academically, including multilingual learners. Schools have sought to improve the educational programs, instructional practices, and the curricula and materials being offered to these students. Opportunities for ongoing professional development are moving teachers in the right direction. There is still work to be done along with consistent application of legal requirements and best practices[5], but progress is being made. There is, for instance, general agreement that it is best to teach academic language to multilingual learners with some targeted focus on the lexical, semantic, and discourse levels of the language as they are applied in school settings (Saunders & Goldenberg, 2010; WIDA, 2020). A growing number of researchers have found that letting students use everyday vernacular and/or their home language before learning the academic and technical language helps them assimilate the content better (García, Ibarra Johnson, & Seltzer, 2017; Gibbons, 2015; Paterson, 2021).

Content-based Language Instruction and Sheltered Content Instruction

Now, more than 25 years after we started researching SIOP, content-based language instruction (also known as *Content-based ESL* and *Designated ELD*) and sheltered instruction (also known as *Integrated ELD* in CA and *Sheltered/Structured English Immersion*) are acknowledged methods for developing academic English and providing multilingual learners access to core content coursework in grades K–12 (U.S. Department of Education, Office of English Language Acquisition, 2021a). Ideally, these two approaches work in tandem: one focuses on academic (and where needed, social) language development while addressing content topics; the other focuses on making content standards and topics accessible while teaching the academic language of the particular subject area.

As you see in Figure 1.4, in the content-based language classes, the curricula are tied to the state standards for English language proficiency, the students are all multilingual learners, and the teacher is certified in ELD/ESL or bilingual education. In sheltered content instruction classes, the curricula are tied to the state subject area standards, and the students may be all multilingual learners or mixed with native English speakers and former multilingual learners. The teachers have elementary or secondary content certification and may have an endorsement or certification in ELD/ESL or bilingual education.

In content-based language instruction, material from multiple subject areas is often presented through thematic or interdisciplinary units. For example, one theme might be "The Marketplace," and lessons could include objectives drawn from economics, science, geography, history, and mathematics. Students might create maps showing how goods move from farms and manufacturing plants to city markets;

---

[5] Federal guidance accentuates the need for effective programming and attention to academic language and literacy development. See, for example, U.S. Department of Education, Office of English Language Acquisition, 2017; and U.S. Department of Justice, Civil Rights Division, & U.S. Department of Education, Office of Civil Rights, 2015.

FIGURE 1.4 Courses That Integrate Content and Language Instruction

Type of Class	Content-based language instruction, also known as content-based ESL/ELD, or Designated ELD	Sheltered content instruction, also known as Integrated ELD, SDAIE, or structured/sheltered English immersion (SEI)
Language Goals	Academic English proficiency (When used in a dual language program, proficiency in English and the target language is the goal.)	Academic English proficiency (When used in a dual language program, proficiency in English and the target language is the goal.)
Academic Content Goals	May emphasize English language arts in some states; introduces content topics from the other core areas (math, science, social studies) too; may help fill in gaps in educational backgrounds	Typically focuses on the curriculum and standards from a content area (e.g., sheltered Algebra); the language is modified and scaffolding techniques are used so the grade-level concepts can be addressed
Standards	English language proficiency and/or English language arts standards	Content standards (any or all subjects)
Language of Instruction	English, some native language for translanguaging	English, some native language for translanguaging
Student Characteristics	Variety of language/cultural backgrounds	Variety of language/cultural backgrounds
	All English proficiency levels, although some districts target the newcomer through intermediate levels	All English proficiency levels. Some programs mix native English speakers and multilingual learners and former multilingual learners in certain courses, particularly as multilingual learners reach intermediate and advanced proficiency levels
Grades Served	All grades (until students exit language support program)	All grades (until students no longer need language support, usually decided on a case-by-case basis by content area)
Teachers	ESL/ELD/Designated ELD teachers; typically ELD- or bilingual-certified or endorsed, sometimes English language arts certified with specialized training	Content-certified teachers - some with ELD or bilingual certification or endorsement, some are content-certified with specialized training
Role of the SIOP Model	For lesson planning and delivery	For lesson planning and delivery
Additional Information	The number of hours of instruction per week may be reduced as proficiency levels rise.	These courses are often the bridge to general education content courses while students are developing academic English skills. May be used in any class where students need to develop academic literacy.

design a brochure or make a video ad to sell a good or service; use online reference materials to learn about the supply and demand of certain goods; or develop a business plan for a good or service they would like to sell. They might study comparative and persuasive language to advertise their good or service. Multilingual learners may contribute valuable insights to this topic because some have lived in places where their parents or neighbors moved goods to market. Some may have experienced the effects of adverse weather on the production of foodstuffs or the effects of poor infrastructure on the transportation of goods.

In general, content-based language teachers seek to develop the students' English language proficiency by incorporating information from the subject areas that students are likely to study or from courses they may have missed if they are new immigrants. Whatever subject matter is included, for effective content-based language instruction to occur, teachers need to provide practice in academic skills and tasks common to regular, grade-level classes.

In sheltered content classes, teachers deliver grade-level objectives for the different subject areas to multilingual learners through modified instruction that makes the information comprehensible to the students while promoting their academic English development. The goal is to teach content to students learning English through a developmental language approach.

Effective sheltered instruction is *not* simply a set of additional or replacement instructional techniques that teachers implement in their classrooms. Instead, it draws from and complements methods advocated for second language and mainstream classrooms. For example, some techniques include cooperative learning, connections to student experiences, culturally responsive activities, targeted vocabulary development, slower speech and fewer idiomatic expressions for less proficient students, use of visuals and demonstrations, and use of online resources.

In the 1990s, there was a great deal of variability in the design of sheltered instruction courses and the delivery of sheltered lessons, even among trained teachers and within the same schools. There was no model for teachers to follow and few systematic and sustained forms of professional development. That situation, along with the underachievement of multilingual learners, was the impetus for our research: to develop a valid, reliable, and effective model of sheltered instruction that would improve the academic performance of these students.

Research and Development of the SIOP® Model

We therefore developed the SIOP Model, with the participation of many schools and teachers, as an approach to integrate content and language instruction for multilingual students. Teachers would employ techniques that make the content concepts accessible and also develop the students' skills in the new language. Details of the SIOP Model research studies can be found in Appendix E of this book and we present a brief overview here.

The first version of the Sheltered Instruction Observation Protocol (the original name for SIOP) was drafted in the early 1990s. We used it exclusively as a research and supervisory tool to determine if observed teachers incorporated key sheltered techniques consistently in their lessons. This early draft, like subsequent ones, integrated findings and recommendations from the research literature with our professional experiences and those of our collaborating teachers on effective classroom-based practices.

Pearson eTextbook

Video Example 1.2

Watch this video to hear a brief overview of the SIOP Model's framework and research findings. What aspects of SIOP are new to your instruction?
https://www.youtube.com/watch?v=3lEQciprSuc

The protocol evolved into a lesson planning and delivery approach, known as the SIOP Model (Echevarría, Vogt, & Short, 2000), through a seven-year research study, "The Effects of Sheltered Instruction on the Achievement of Limited English Proficient Students," sponsored by the Center for Research on Education, Diversity & Excellence (CREDE) and funded by the U.S. Department of Education. The study began in 1996 and involved collaborating middle school teachers who worked with the researchers to refine the features of the original protocol.

Over four years, we piloted the model and assessed student learning. In 2000, we finalized SIOP with 30 features of instruction organized in eight components—Lesson Preparation, Building Background, Comprehensible Input, Strategies, Interaction, Practice & Application, Lesson Delivery, and Review & Assessment (Echevarria, Vogt & Short, 2000). The CREDE research showed that multilingual learners whose teachers were trained in implementing the SIOP Model performed statistically significantly better on an academic writing assessment than a comparison group of multilingual learners whose teachers had no exposure to the model (Echevarría, Short, & Powers, 2006). A subsequent study confirmed the SIOP (protocol) to be a valid and reliable measure of sheltered instruction (Guarino et al., 2001).

SIOP is the term for the empirically validated model of sheltered instruction designed to make grade-level academic content understandable for multilingual learners while at the same time developing their academic English language proficiency. It was formerly spelled out as the Sheltered Instruction Observation Protocol. SIOP refers to the observation instrument for rating the fidelity of lessons to the model (see Appendix A) and to the instructional model for lesson planning and delivery that we explain in detail in the following chapters. It is also used as an adjective (e.g., SIOP teachers, SIOP lessons, and SIOP classrooms), and as a verb (e.g., to *siopize* a lesson plan).

We continued to test and refine the SIOP Model. From 1999 to 2002, we field tested the SIOP professional development program, which includes professional development institutes, videotapes of exemplary SIOP teachers, facilitator's guides, and other materials. (See Appendix F.) From 2004–07, we replicated and scaled up the SIOP research in a quasi-experimental study in two districts at the middle and high school levels. Multilingual learners with SIOP-trained teachers made statistically significant gains in their average mean scores for oral language, writing, and total proficiency on the state assessment of English language proficiency, compared to the comparison group of English proficient learners (Short, Fidelman, & Louguit, 2012).

From 2005–12, we participated in the Center for Research on the Educational Achievement and Teaching of English Language Learners (CREATE), looking at the SIOP Model first in middle school science classrooms (Himmel, Short, Richards, & Echevarría, 2009) and later as the professional development framework for a school-wide intervention (Echevarría & Short, 2011). In this set of studies, we used an experimental-control design; and multilingual learners, former multilingual learners, and native English speakers were part of the student population. The results showed that students with teachers who implemented the SIOP Model with greater fidelity performed better on criterion-referenced assessments than those whose teachers did not implement SIOP to a high degree (Echevarría, Richards–Tutor, Chinn, & Ratleff, 2011). So, the level of implementation mattered. Further, students in SIOP curriculum groups outperformed control students on criterion-referenced vocabulary, science, and social studies measures (Echevarría, Richards-Tutor, Canges, & Francis, 2011; Short & Himmel, 2013). These findings indicate that English-speaking students are not disadvantaged when they are in SIOP classes with multilingual learners and that they also benefit from SIOP practices.

FIGURE 1.5 **Overview of the SIOP®'s Eight Components**

- The features under *Lesson Preparation* initiate the lesson planning process, so teachers include content and language objectives, use supplementary materials, and create meaningful activities.
- *Building Background* focuses on making connections with students' background experiences and prior learning, and developing their academic vocabulary.
- *Comprehensible Input* considers how teachers should adjust their speech, model academic tasks, and use multimodal techniques to enhance comprehension.
- The *Strategies* component emphasizes teaching learning strategies to students, scaffolding instruction, and promoting higher-order thinking skills.
- *Interaction* prompts teachers to encourage students to elaborate their speech and to group students appropriately for language and content development.
- *Practice & Application* provides activities to practice and extend language and content learning.
- *Lesson Delivery* ensures that teachers present a lesson that meets the planned objectives and promotes student engagement.
- *Review & Assessment* reminds teachers to review the key language and content concepts, assess student learning, and provide specific academic feedback to students on their output.

A number of school districts have also conducted program evaluations on their implementation of the model. Several can be reviewed in *Implementing the SIOP® Model Through Effective Professional Development and Coaching* (Echevarría, Short, & Vogt, 2008). In addition, many other researchers have studied SIOP Model professional development programs and student achievement in the United States and other countries. (For a sampling, see Batt, 2010; Coppersmith, Slapac, & Song, 2019; Daniel & Pray, 2017; Ebedy, 2019; Koura & Zahan, 2017; Li et al., 2016; McIntyre et al., 2010; Piazza et al., 2020; and Song, 2016a).

Figure 1.5 provides brief descriptions of each component. You will read about each component and its features in subsequent chapters of this book. We are gratified that the original model has stood the test of time; no features have been added or removed. The model has been shown to be effective in numerous districts and schools across the United States and in other countries as well.

Effective SIOP® Model Instruction

In this book, *Making Content Comprehensible for Multilingual Learners: The SIOP® Model*, we introduce you to the research-based model for sheltered instruction and content-based language instruction. We provide teaching ideas for each of the model's eight components, suggest ways to differentiate instruction in multi-level classrooms, and demonstrate through lesson scenarios how the model can be implemented across grades and subject areas. The model will guide you to the best practices for multilingual learners. It has been used successfully in both language and content classrooms, and in programs that use primarily English and those that use English and another language. With this approach, you will help your multilingual learners attain the skills and knowledge associated with success in school and beyond.

In effective SIOP lessons, language and content objectives are systematically woven into the curriculum of one particular subject area, such as kindergarten math, fourth-grade language arts, or high school biology, or in one ELP level, such as beginner, intermediate, or advanced. Teachers develop the students' academic language proficiency consistently and regularly as part of the lessons and units they plan and deliver.

ARTIFACT 1.1   Content and Language Objectives

Posting and reviewing content and language objectives for each lesson is a hallmark of the SIOP Model. Here are objectives from classrooms in Portland, Oregon.

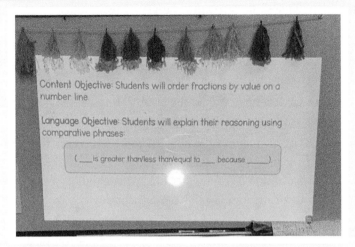

Content Objective: Students will order fractions by value on a number line.

Language Objective: Students will explain their reasoning using comparative phrases:

(___ is greater than/less than/equal to ___ because _____)

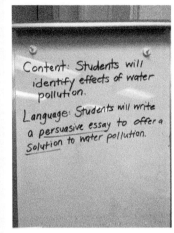

Content: Students will identify effects of water pollution.

Language: Students will write a persuasive essay to offer a solution to water pollution.

> When teachers implement the SIOP Model, multilingual learners in both language and general education classes are more engaged and participate more fully. The SIOP Model gives them the tools to engage in rigorous academic content that would otherwise be out of their linguistic reach.
>
> Helene Becker, retired District EL Director, Connecticut

In subsequent chapters, you will explore the components and features of the SIOP Model in detail and have the opportunity to try out numerous techniques for SIOP lessons. You will see that the SIOP Model shares many features recommended for high-quality instruction for all students, such as collaborative discussion groups, strategies for reading comprehension, writers' workshop, and differentiated instruction. However, the SIOP Model adds key features for the academic success of these learners, such as the inclusion of language objectives in every content lesson, the development of background knowledge, the acquisition of content-related vocabulary, and the emphasis on academic literacy practice. The final two chapters demonstrate how SIOP is effective with struggling students and serves as the basis for co-teaching.

Here we briefly describe some of the instructional practices that effective SIOP teachers use. You can compare your typical instruction with them, and you might find that you are already on the path to becoming a skillful SIOP teacher!

- Classroom teachers provide rigorous, grade-level instruction aligned with state content standards through specialized techniques, although some targeted curricula may be designed for children who have significant gaps in their educational backgrounds or very low literacy skills.
- Classroom teachers identify how academic language is used in the different subjects and give students explicit instruction and practice with it.
- Language teachers advance students' English language skills with curricula addressing language proficiency standards, but also by incorporating the types of texts, vocabulary, and tasks used in core subjects to prepare the students for success in the regular, English-medium classroom.
- SIOP teachers incorporate technology for remote learning and in-class lessons. Students have access to various apps and Internet tools for many purposes, ranging from online simulations and virtual field trips, to speaking practice through audio recordings, to self-paced research, and writing and editing tools.

Accomplished SIOP teachers determine students' baseline understandings in their subject area and move them forward, both in their content knowledge and in their language skills through a variety of techniques.

- SIOP teachers make specific connections between the content being taught and students' experiences and prior knowledge, and they focus on expanding their vocabulary base.

- SIOP teachers modulate the level of English they use and carefully select the texts and other materials used by students.

- SIOP teachers make the content comprehensible through techniques such as the use of visual aids, multimedia and online resources and text features, modeling, demonstrations, graphic organizers, vocabulary previews, cooperative learning, peer tutoring, and home language support.

- Besides increasing students' factual knowledge, SIOP teachers highlight and model procedural knowledge (e.g., how to accomplish an academic task) along with study skills and learning strategies (e.g., note-taking and self-monitoring comprehension when reading).

In effective SIOP lessons, students have agency. They interact with each other and the teacher and engage with the texts and tasks, which leads to elaborated discourse and critical thinking.

- SIOP teachers promote language learning through social interaction and contextualized communication, guiding students to construct meaning and understand complex concepts from texts and classroom discourse (Vygotsky, 1978).

- Multilingual learners are explicitly taught functional language skills, such as how to negotiate meaning, confirm information, describe, compare, and persuade. SIOP teachers help them articulate their content knowledge both orally and in writing, often with sentence starters and language frame scaffolds.

- SIOP teachers introduce students to the classroom discourse community and demonstrate skills such as taking turns in a conversation and interrupting politely to ask for clarification.

- SIOP teachers encourage students to use their full linguistic repertoires, such as their home language, and other assets to learn, discuss, and apply their knowledge.

Not all teaching is about the techniques in a lesson. SIOP teachers also consider their students' affective needs, cultural backgrounds, and learning preferences. They strive to create a nonthreatening environment where students feel comfortable taking risks with language.

- SIOP teachers engage in culturally responsive teaching and build on the students' potentially different ways of learning, interacting, and using language.

- They socialize multilingual learners to the implicit classroom culture, including appropriate behaviors and communication patterns.

- SIOP teachers connect with the families of multilingual learners. They partner on ways to support the students at home and at school. For example, they may

> " SIOP helps students understand how language works so they can take ownership of their learning whether they are using L1 or L2 to access the content. When students begin to understand how language objectives show them, in a more tangible way, how language development increases through content knowledge, ownership becomes evident. "
>
> Dr. Francheska Figueroa, Postdoctoral Research Scholar, Arizona

seek to determine the funds of knowledge in the children's households and orient parents and guardians to the expectations of schooling in the United States.

SIOP teachers offer multiple pathways for multilingual learners to demonstrate their understanding of the content too, getting a more accurate picture of their knowledge and skills than is possible through one standardized test. Otherwise, some students may be perceived as lacking mastery of content when actually they are following the normal pace of the second language acquisition process.

- SIOP teachers plan pictorial, hands-on, or performance-based assessments for individual students; group tasks or projects; oral reports; written assignments; and portfolios, along with more traditional measures such as tests and quizzes to check student comprehension and language growth.
- Teachers use rubrics to measure student performance on a scale leading to mastery, and they share those rubrics with students in advance.

It is important to recognize that the SIOP Model does not require teachers to discard their favorite techniques or to add copious new elements to a lesson. Rather, this model of sheltered instruction brings together *what* to teach by providing a framework for *how* to teach it. It acts as an umbrella, allowing teachers the flexibility to choose techniques they know work well with their particular group of students (see Figure 1.6). It reminds teachers to pay attention to the language development needs of their students and to select and organize techniques that facilitate the integration of district- or state-level standards for English language proficiency and for specific content areas.

FIGURE 1.6   **The SIOP® Model Framework for Organizing Best Practices**

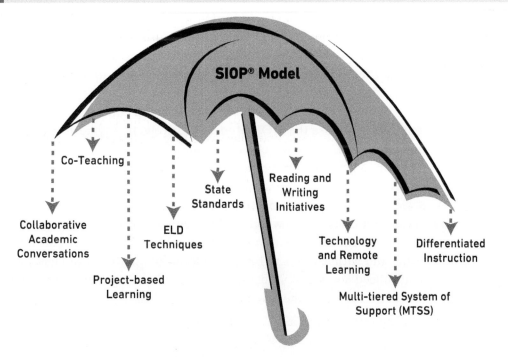

■ Implementing the SIOP® Model

Pearson eTextbook

Video Example 1.3

Watch Dr. Jana Echevarria describe how SIOP implementation advances equity for multilingual learners. How would SIOP fit into your school or program? Discuss how it can promote equity if well-implemented.

https://www.youtube.com/watch?v=DzFVJk5zOxI&t=236s

The goal of this book is to prepare teachers to teach content and academic language and literacy skills effectively to multilingual learners. The SIOP Model may be used as part of a program for preservice and inservice professional development, and used as a coaching tool, a planner for sheltered content and content-based language lessons, and a training resource for university faculty. Research shows that professional development approaches that improve teaching include the following: sustained, intensive development with modeling, coaching, reflection, and problem solving; collaborative endeavors for educators to share knowledge and give feedback; experiential opportunities that engage teachers in actual teaching, assessment, and observation; and development grounded in research but also drawing from teacher experience and inquiry, connected to the teachers' classes, students, and subjects taught (Darling-Hammond, Hyler, & Gardner, 2017; Short, 2013).

In our research studies, we found that SIOP implementation does not happen quickly. Teachers may take one to two years before they implement the model consistently to a high degree, and coaching helps get them to that level (Short, Fidelman, & Louguit, 2012). McIntyre and colleagues (2010) suggest that teachers' proficiency in implementing the model may depend on their background teaching experiences and the design of their professional development.

Effective implementation of the SIOP Model is one key to improving the academic success of multilingual learners. Preservice teachers need to learn the model to develop a strong foundation in best practice for integrating language and content in classes with multilingual learners. Practicing teachers need the model to strengthen their lesson planning and delivery and to provide students with consistent instruction that meets language and content standards. Site-based supervisors and administrators use the model to train and coach teachers and systematize classroom observations. Teacher education faculty present the SIOP Model in their methods courses and use it in student teacher supervision.

Any program in which students are learning content through a nonnative language could use the SIOP Model effectively. It may be an ELD program (with pull-out or self-contained classes), a late-exit bilingual program, a dual language program, a newcomer program, a sheltered program, or even a foreign language immersion program. The model has been designed for flexibility and tested in a wide range of classroom situations: with children who have strong academic backgrounds and those who have had limited formal schooling; with students who are recent arrivals and those who have been in U.S. schools for several years; and with learners at beginning levels of English proficiency and those at advanced levels. For students studying in language support programs, SIOP instruction provides the bridge to the general education program.

■ Final Points

As you reflect on this chapter and the impact of the SIOP Model on multilingual learners' content and academic language learning, consider the following main points:

- Students who are learning English as a new language are the fastest-growing segment of the school-age population in the United States, and almost all candidates in teacher education programs will have linguistically and culturally diverse students in their classes during their teaching careers. However, many of these future teachers—as well as most practicing teachers—are underprepared to instruct these learners.

- When teachers use the SIOP Model, they build creative and supportive classroom environments that help students succeed. There is a high level of engagement, and student assets are valued and incorporated into lessons. Teachers use the SIOP Model to give multilingual learners access to the core curriculum, meet state standards, and prepare for college and careers.

- The SIOP Model has a strong, empirical research base. It has been tested across multiple subject areas and grade levels. The research evidence shows that the SIOP Model can improve the academic literacy of multilingual learners.

- The SIOP Model does not mandate cookie-cutter instruction; instead, it provides a framework for well-prepared and well-delivered lessons in any subject area. As SIOP teachers design their lessons, they have flexibility. Nonetheless, critical instructional features must be attended to in order for teachers to respond appropriately to the unique academic and language development needs of multilingual learners.

- The model is operationalized in the SIOP protocol, which can be used to rate lessons and measure the level of SIOP implementation.

- Our research shows that both language and content teachers can implement the SIOP Model fully to good effect. The model is best suited for content-based language and sheltered content classes that are part of a program of studies for multilingual learners. It is effective in general education classes, too. Altogether, these classes offer a promising pathway to help students progress through the grades and eventually graduate from high school.

■ Discussion Questions

1. In reflecting on the content and language objectives at the beginning of the chapter, are you able to:
   a. List characteristics of multilingual learners that may influence their success in school?
   b. Distinguish between content-based language instruction and sheltered instruction?
   c. Explain the research supporting the SIOP Model?

    d. Describe the assets your multilingual learners bring to your classroom?

    e. Develop a lexicon related to the SIOP Model?

    f. Compare your typical instruction with SIOP instruction?

2. Consider one class of multilingual learners. Identify the individual and sociocultural factors that might influence the educational success of these students. In what ways might instruction using the SIOP Model help them?

3. Are the multilingual learners in your school successful when they exit English language support programs and are placed in regular classrooms? Explain how you know and what contributes to their success or lack of success.

4. Many sheltered content teachers fail to take advantage of the language learning opportunities for students in their classes. Why do you think this is so? Offer two concrete suggestions for these teachers to enhance their students' academic language development.

5. The SIOP Model has been implemented by teachers since 2000. Why do you think it is still relevant today?

6. Look at one of your own lesson plans. Which characteristics of the SIOP Model do you already incorporate? Consider the components and features of the model as found in Appendix A.

Lesson Preparation

CONTENT OBJECTIVES

This chapter will help you to . . .

- Identify content objectives for multilingual learners that align to state, local, or national standards.
- Incorporate supplementary materials suitable for multilingual learners into a lesson plan.
- Apply knowledge of students' educational background and skills to adapt content to their language proficiency and cognitive levels.

LANGUAGE OBJECTIVES

This chapter will help you to . . .

- Generate language targets for multilingual learners that align to standards and address how language is used in academic settings.
- Discuss advantages of including both language and content objectives in a lesson and sharing the objectives with students.
- Explain the importance of meaningful academic activities for multilingual learners.
- As part of a lesson plan, write content and language objectives linked to standards and the lesson topic.

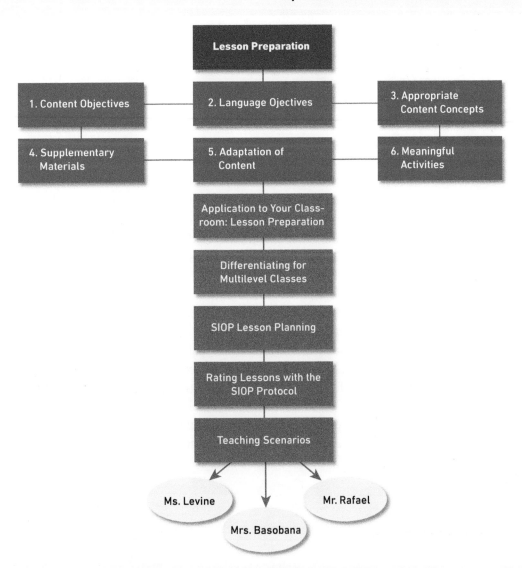

In this chapter, and in subsequent chapters, we explain each SIOP Model component and its features. Each chapter begins with an explanation of the component, offers classroom activities, and then describes how three teachers approach the same lesson. The lesson scenarios throughout the book are about varied topics and represent different grade levels.

This chapter introduces the first component of the SIOP Model, Lesson Preparation. We present background information and the rationale for each of the six features in this component and list some ideas for applying the features and differentiating instruction in multilevel classes. The chapter concludes with teaching scenarios that illustrate how three Grade 4 teachers, who each have classes with students learning English as a new language, implement this component in their lessons. As you read the scenarios, we encourage you to check your understanding of the SIOP features explained in the chapter by rating the scenario lessons according to best practice. Reflect on how effectively each lesson meets the needs of multilingual learners in relation to each feature. Look for evidence in the text. At the conclusion of the teaching scenarios, we discuss our assessment of the teachers' efforts to provide SIOP instruction, and we invite you to compare your appraisal to ours. ■

■ Background

Lesson planning is critical to both student and teacher success. For maximum learning to occur, planning must produce lessons that target specific learning goals, enable students to make connections between their own knowledge and experiences and the new information being taught, give students practice using and applying the new information, and assess student learning to determine whether to move on or reteach the material. With careful planning, we make learning meaningful and relevant by including appropriate motivating materials and activities that foster real-life application of concepts studied.

We have learned that if multilingual students' exposure to content concepts is limited by vocabulary-controlled materials or watered-down curricula, the amount of information they learn over time is considerably less than that of their peers who use grade-level texts and curricula. The result is that the learning gap between native English speakers and multilingual learners widens instead of closes, and eventually it becomes nearly impossible for multilingual learners to catch up

(Carnoy & Garcia, 2017; Gándara & Rumberger, 2008). However, multilingual learners who have learned English and exited ELD programs have, over time, narrowed the performance gap on national math and reading exams (Kieffer & Thompson, 2018). Therefore, it is imperative that we plan lessons that promote the acquisition of academic English and include age-appropriate content and materials. Our lessons, however, must provide appropriate scaffolds so our students can meet the rigor of state standards over time and be prepared for college and careers.

This component, Lesson Preparation, is very important to the SIOP Model and provides the basis for successful lessons. If properly prepared, a lesson will include most of the SIOP features in advance. It is then up to you, the teacher, and your class to accomplish the learning goals and tasks as the lesson unfolds. Another component, Lesson Delivery, helps you monitor the implementation of the lesson. As we explained in Chapter 1, we know from 20+ years of research that SIOP lessons enhance student language development and content knowledge. So, to guide your SIOP lesson planning, let's explore each feature in the SIOP component of Lesson Preparation.

You will begin with the end in mind by setting your goals for student learning through content and language objectives. These objectives should evolve from the lesson topic and be part of the instructional plan. After you write content and language objectives, post them, and discuss them with the students at the start of class, you must, at some point in the lesson, provide explicit instruction on these objectives. We know from research that explicit instruction speeds up language development (TESOL, 2018). Your multilingual learners then need practice opportunities aligned to the objectives, and, at the close of the lesson, they should be assessed on their progress toward meeting those objectives. The lesson cycle is complete when you reflect on your instruction and student progress to inform the planning of your next lesson.

> " Sheltered instruction (SIOP) has shifted my practice from delivering content to facilitating experiences where students process the content by using language.
>
> Tan Huynh, Secondary School Social Studies Teacher, Thailand "

 SIOP®   **SIOP® FEATURE 1:**

Content Objectives Clearly Defined, Displayed, and Reviewed with Students

Content objectives identify what students should know and be able to do as a result of instruction on a subject area topic. They usually derive from state standards. Teachers can often write them based on learning targets found in curricular frameworks of the subject areas. In effective SIOP lessons, content objectives are clear and measurable. They must guide the teaching and learning process, and they should be shared with students at or near the beginning of a lesson.

Here are some sample content objectives from different subject areas:

- Students will be able to solve multiplication problems.
- Students will use map skills to plot the route of a product or good from harvesting or manufacturing to market.
- Students will collect and organize data during a science experiment.
- Students will be able to cite evidence to show how a character advanced a story plot.

Additional examples are found in each chapter of this book.

Sources of Content Objectives.   Teachers have several sources to help them identify content objectives.

- *State subject area standards.* State standards are the main source of content objectives for teachers. Some districts have local standards or rely on national standards, particularly for subjects that may not have a state standard equivalent (e.g., history, technology).
- *State or district-level curriculum frameworks.* Many states and districts have translated the standards into curriculum frameworks. These break down the standards into unit or lesson topics and these can be useful guides for content objectives.
- *Course textbooks and teacher guides.* Many textbooks and teacher guides identify learning goals for units of study.
- *Colleagues.* Some subjects lack state standards, so teacher collaboration is critical for setting objectives to ensure consistent learning goals. Also, ELD teachers sometimes seek assistance in identifying appropriate content objectives to add to their content-based language lessons. They may feel unprepared for in-depth instruction on a content topic, they may not know the key concepts that should be taught, and they may not know what types of activities usually support the topic. In many schools, ELD teachers serve students from several grade levels at the same time. For these reasons, we strongly advocate that content and language teachers collaborate closely as they prepare lessons to help their students meet content and language goals. (Chapter 11 discusses teacher collaboration.)

Identifying and Writing Content Objectives.   SIOP teachers plan objectives that support content standards and learning outcomes, but if the objectives are not denoted in the curriculum materials, teachers must deconstruct the standards to determine what the intention for student learning is, such as knowledge of a concept, a skill to master, a reasoning process to learn and apply, or a subject-specific product to produce. Then, within a given unit of study, teachers identify the sequence of learning objectives that lead up to meeting or making progress toward the full standard and build lessons around these objectives (Chappuis, Commodore, & Stiggins, 2017; Tobiason, Chang, Heritage, Jones, & Herman, 2014). When they write the content objective statements for each lesson, they must consider the proficiency levels of the multilingual students to ensure that they use language the students will understand.

When writing content objectives for your lessons, keep the following guidelines in mind to support your multilingual learners:

- Write lesson-level objectives (something that can be taught and learned in one or two days). State standards are frequently complex and not written in a manner that is accessible to multilingual learners or students in primary grades. Often standards are too generic or broad—such as "The student will collect and analyze data, determine the equation of the curve of best fit in order to make predictions, and solve practical problems, using mathematical models of linear and quadratic functions." (Virginia Dept. of Education, 2016)—to be useful as a single lesson's learning goal.

- If you are an ELD teacher, write content objectives related to the lessons that multilingual learners receive in subject-area classes to support their academic language needs. You might draw from one content area, focus on one subject per quarter, or concentrate on academic tasks of those subjects (e.g., extracting information from text to create a timeline, writing a descriptive essay, explaining steps in an experiment).

- State the objectives in terms of student learning, not as an agenda item or an activity. See Figure 2.1 for several ways that teachers in our research studies have stated their objectives. You will note that all focus on the student.

- Use active verbs so objectives are observable and measurable.

- Use student-friendly language that suits the age and proficiency levels in the class. For example, some kindergarten and first-grade teachers post key words for the objectives rather than complete sentences or add illustrations to the objective statements.

- Limit the number of content objectives to only one or two per lesson to reduce the complexity of the learning task and to ensure that instruction can meet the objectives.

- Share objectives with your students, orally and in writing, for every lesson. In this way, students know what they are supposed to learn each day and they can share the responsibility for learning.

- Provide explicit instruction and practice opportunities related to each objective in your lesson.

- Review the objectives at the end of the lesson to determine if your multilingual learners have mastered them. Use that informal assessment when deciding whether to move to the next topic or spend some time reteaching.

Pearson eTextbook

Video Example 2.1

Watch Monica Miller introduce her content and language objectives for her math lesson. How does she help her second graders understand the goals for the day?

Presenting Objectives to Students. We know from our research studies and professional development experiences that teachers need to get into the routine of presenting objectives to learners each day. Rest assured, the effort is worth it! Teachers consistently report the value of displaying and clearly stating content objectives for all students. As one teacher said, "I just wanted to say that defining the objectives each day definitely brings more focus to my planning and thinking, and it helps bring order to my classroom procedures." Another teacher remarked, "It's our GPS for the lesson." Students can take some ownership for their learning when they know the goal of the lesson.

FIGURE 2.1	How to Start an Objective

Students will be able to (SWBAT) _____

Students will (SW) _____

We will _____

Today I will _____

I can _____

Our job is to _____

_____

Some content teachers have asked how to present objectives for inquiry lessons, worried that the objective might "give away" the discovery moment. We have two suggestions. One is to write the objective in a more general way. For example, "Students will investigate what factors influence plant growth" is better with an inquiry lesson than "Students will investigate the effect of water on plant growth." The other is to present the objectives after students have completed an introductory activity or experiment at the start of the lesson to set up the inquiry frame of mind.

Some teachers also ask how to present objectives to newcomers with little English proficiency or students with interrupted educational backgrounds. In that case, you may have to build background first. You can write a content objective like "Identify parts of a plant and their functions." When you explain it, elaborate and use instructional supports: *"Today you will learn about parts of a plant* (showing a picture or real plant). *You will be able to identify the parts* (point to the different parts) *and tell what the parts do* (e.g., *Leaves make food for the plant.*)." *Plant, part,* and *function* would be vocabulary terms to teach in the lesson.

The bottom line for multilingual learners is that content objectives need to be written in terms of what students will learn or do; they should be stated simply, orally and in writing, use active verbs, be tied to specific grade-level content standards, and shared with the students every day.

SIOP® **SIOP® FEATURE 2:**

Language Objectives Clearly Defined, Displayed, and Reviewed with Students

Pearson eTextbook

Video Example 2.2

Watch Professor Cynthia Lundgren explain why teachers need to include language objectives in their lessons and how objectives help students meet standards. What role does language play in your content area?

https://www.youtube.com/watch?v=del47uaZMJs

Language objectives are what students need to learn about English in order to

- learn, express, practice, and apply new information,
- demonstrate knowledge, and
- perform academic tasks.

Language objectives direct the academic language learning in a given lesson. They typically derive from state English language proficiency or English language arts standards. For any lesson, multiple language objectives are possible depending on the academic language needs of the multilingual students: objectives related to vocabulary, reading and writing skills, oral language practice, and more. Teachers select from the possibilities for each lesson to determine the one or two that would best help students understand and work with the new material and advance their language proficiency. Across lessons in a unit, however, SIOP teachers reliably present a variety of language objectives.

Here are some sample language objectives:

- Students will be able to write a conclusion to a science report.
- Students will use key vocabulary when summarizing a text.
- Students will be able to rehearse a speech with a partner.
- Students will explain a solution to a math problem orally.

Additional examples are found in each chapter of this book.

ARTIFACT 2.1   Bilingual Summer School Class Objectives

Content and language objectives and student work from Ms. Osorio's bilingual/ESL summer school Kindergarten classroom in Tyler ISD, Tyler, Texas.

Ana Segulin permission

The guidelines we discussed earlier for content objectives apply to planning language objectives too:

- Language objectives should be written clearly and simply with active verbs, and students should be informed of them in each lesson, both orally and in writing.
- The objectives should be limited in number for a given lesson and reviewed at the end.
- They should be drawn from the state English language proficiency standards and English language arts standards.
- The objectives should represent an element of academic language that students need to learn or master.
- Teachers should provide explicit instruction on the objectives, create opportunities for students to practice, and assess their progress toward meeting them.

Effective SIOP teachers must incorporate language objectives, in addition to content ones, into their lesson plans to support multilingual learners' academic language development. In fact, academic language is a second language for all learners, so both types of objectives are equally essential in SIOP lessons. Teachers with newcomer students may have to build social and classroom-related language skills too.

Although incorporating language objectives in all content lessons is a hallmark of the SIOP Model, we recognize that some classroom and content area teachers are not used to thinking about the language demands of the subjects they teach, apart from language arts specialists. Yet every teacher uses language as a tool to communicate knowledge to students, to have students complete assignments, and to determine whether students are learning.

If you are a classroom or content area teacher, it is not sufficient to only have deep knowledge of topics in your subject area. Rather, to be effective, you also need to know how language is used in the subject area in order to convey information (whether orally or in text) and to apply that information (through class reading, writing, and discussion activities). In addition, you need to know your students' English proficiency levels so the language objectives can be targeted to what students need to learn about the academic language of history, science, mathematics, or other subjects, yet not be at a level too high for their current understanding. Every SIOP teacher, therefore, is a teacher of language and content.

Because it may be a new way of thinking for you, here are key points from research on second language acquisition to keep in mind when developing lessons:

- *Remember that acquiring a second language is a years-long process.* Just as a baby takes years to learn its first language, our students learning English as a new language need time to become familiar with English sounds and words, sentence formations, discourse styles, and more. They need to practice using the language and to try out new formulations to construct meaning on their own, even if they make mistakes along the way. When students master a new language it means they can use their language knowledge and skills fluently, accurately, automatically, and creatively; this process can take thousands of hours to achieve. (See Gass, Behney, & Plonsky, 2020; NASEM, 2017; and TESOL, 2018 for more information.)

- *Plan language objectives to reflect a progression of learning about an aspect of language, from process-oriented to production-oriented.* In your lessons, give your multilingual learners a chance to explore and then practice before demonstrating mastery of an objective. The following objectives from a SIOP language arts class show the progression of objectives that might be taught over several days:

Students will be able to

Day 1. Recognize figurative language and its function in text. (Process)

Day 2. Discuss the types of figurative language such as similes and metaphors. (Process)

Day 3. Write examples for types of figurative language. (Production)

Day 4. Write a character description that incorporates figurative language. (Production)

For the first lesson (Day 1), students learn to recognize figurative language in text, focusing on descriptive terms and key words *like* and *as*, and discuss the purpose of figurative language. After that (Day 2), they might explore types (e.g., similes and metaphors) and discuss reasons why authors use figurative language. On Day 3 they generate their own examples in decontextualized sentences. They then write for an authentic purpose, like a book or movie review, drafting a paragraph that describes a character using figurative language on Day 4.

- *Teach all four language skills from the start.* Multilingual learners tend to develop receptive skills (listening and reading) faster than productive skills (speaking and writing), but all the skills should be worked on in an integrated manner. Students don't have to learn to speak, for instance, before they learn to read and write. Furthermore, the skills reinforce one another to develop academic English. Reading a story can be a model for writing a text or a way to deepen the meaning of vocabulary. Planned speaking practice with language frames (e.g., Our data showed . . . , The purpose of _____ was . . .) can aid in reading comprehension when a similar phrase is encountered. (See August & Shanahan, 2006; TESOL, 2018; and Zwiers & Soto, 2017 for more information.)

- *Focus on function* and *form to move students to advanced proficiency levels of academic English.* ELD and English language arts teachers play important roles in developing students' academic language skills, but teachers should not let students coast in class during the other subjects. If your multilingual learners are ready to produce more sophisticated language (e.g., during an oral presentation, in science lab report), challenge them to do so. Skillful teachers take advantage of oral interaction, for instance, to move their learners from informal, everyday explanations of a content topic (e.g., a scientific process) to a more academic register of the formal written and spoken code. When SIOP teachers plan language objectives around specialized grammar and lexical forms related to their subject area, they set their students up for success because multilingual learners will encounter more rigorous text and be expected to use more complex language as they progress in their proficiency levels. (See Balconi & Spitzman, 2021; Gibbons, 2015; and Turkan, de Oliveira, Lee, & Phelps, 2014 for more information.)

Pearson eTextbook

Video Example 2.3

Watch this video to see different approaches for incorporating translanguaging practices in your SIOP classroom. Reflect on ways you can tap your students' home language assets to help them succeed in class. https://www.youtube.com/watch?v=KSYKXIOL6-k

- *Translanguaging can support language development and content learning.* Translanguaging is a process by which an individual makes a strategic choice to use one language or another at a particular moment in oral or written discourse for a communicative purpose. Bilingual individuals periodically employ translanguaging in a dynamic way when they interact with others. They might, for example, choose a word from one language instead of another because of its nuanced meaning, or ask an important question in the language they are most proficient in to ensure clarity. In the classroom, students who are using English to convey information may switch to another language to fill in a gap in their vocabulary knowledge. Being able to translanguage is a resource that multilingual learners can call on to participate in class, gain knowledge, or work on lesson tasks. It gives the students agency and offers flexibility.

Research on translanguaging has revealed that multilingual learners have one complex linguistic system that can include two or more "named" languages, like English and Spanish. The borders between these languages are porous, and certain knowledge, skills, and strategies such as phonological awareness, knowledge of print, listening and reading comprehension skills, and narrative skills can be shared across the languages or can transfer from one to another. Effective SIOP teachers encourage students to use all their linguistic resources as they participate in class, make sense of new information, and apply knowledge, knowing that the ultimate outcome is proficiency in academic English. (See Ebe, Soto, Freeman, & Freeman, 2021; García, Ibarra, Johnson, & Seltzer, 2017; NASEM, 2017; Paterson, 2021; and Seilstad & Kim, 2020 for more information.)

- *Give feedback on students' language use.* In order to acquire a new language, students need feedback to determine if what they produce in English is comprehensible and if their interpretations of what they read or heard are correct. The tasks you assign and the feedback you give can be modulated by the students' proficiency levels. For example, when asking a question, allow for approximations and multiple-word responses rather than complete sentences from those at early stages of English development, but expect learners with greater proficiency to respond in complete sentences. This practice develops language skills because it requires multilingual learners to move beyond what may be their comfort zone in using English. (See Lyster & Saito, 2010 and Nassaji & Kartchava, 2017 for more information.)

- *Assess the language objectives to determine if students are making progress toward mastery.* It is important to find out if students met the language goals in your lesson. This knowledge can help you decide if students need more practice or feedback, and if you need to reteach or can move forward. One way to do so is by monitoring how students are using English in the lesson tasks and activities. Another way is to use a group-response technique at the end of a lesson (e.g., thumbs-up/thumbs-down to questions posed) or an exit ticket where students write to a prompt that demonstrates their learning. You will find this topic discussed in more detail in Chapter 9.

Sources of Language Objectives.   As you plan, you may want to explore different sources of language objectives.

- *State English language proficiency (ELP) standards and curricular frameworks.* By using these resources, your objectives will be aligned to the language goals your state has set for multilingual learners.

- *WIDA Can-Do descriptors.* The WIDA consortium has compiled a list of "Can Do" descriptors that can help teachers identify the kind of language tasks students should be able to perform according to five differing levels of English proficiency and different grade-level clusters. (To view them, search for "Can Do Descriptors" at www.wida.wisc.edu.)

- *State English language arts standards and curricular frameworks.* It is important that multilingual learners achieve the language arts standards, so you can draw ideas from these documents for objectives. Note that some states also have other content area standards that include a strand focused on communication and can provide ideas as well.

- *Colleagues.* One critically important source for successful content and language integration is your colleagues.

  - If you are a content or grade-level classroom teacher, pair up with an ELD or bilingual teacher. Tap that teacher's expertise for potential language objectives and knowledge of the multilingual learners' academic language needs.

  - If you are an ELD or reading teacher, you have a plethora of language objectives at your disposal. Partner with one or more content teachers to identify content objectives and lesson tasks that the multilingual learners need assistance with and align those content goals to your language objectives. You may want to focus on thematic units to cover a variety of content topics or focus on one subject area per quarter. (See Chapter 11 for an example of teacher collaboration.)

- *Course textbooks, teacher guides, and other instructional materials.* Review instructional materials to be used in class to determine if there are language skills and academic vocabulary that the multilingual learners need to develop in order to comprehend the information or perform the assignments. Also check out the teacher guides because publishers have recognized the need for more attention to academic language and have incorporated some explicit suggestions that can lead to language objectives.

Identifying and Writing Language Objectives.   As you begin to craft language objectives, the possibilities abound because our multilingual students have so much to learn about academic English. In some lessons, language objectives may focus on developing students' vocabulary, introducing new words and concepts, or teaching word structure to help multilingual learners discern the meaning of new words. Other lessons may lend themselves to practice with reading comprehension skills or the writing process. Some objectives will highlight functional language use, such as how to request information, justify opinions, negotiate meaning, provide detailed explanations, and so forth. Higher-order thinking skills, such as articulating predictions or hypotheses, stating conclusions, summarizing information, and analyzing an author's purpose are potential language objectives, too. Sometimes specific grammar points can be taught as well; for example, learning about different verb tenses that indicate sequence or continuity in the past when studying historical periods.

Our goal is to help you select and write language objectives that address the type of academic language your multilingual learners need in order to understand the content and perform the activities in the lesson. But it is important to make clear that activities are not language objectives, although they may provide language practice. For example, "Students will complete a Venn diagram" is not a language objective. A Venn diagram is a tool that can help a student demonstrate meeting an objective such as "Students will read a text to find and record similarities and differences between two animals." If they complete the graphic organizer after reading, the teacher can see whether they can read for a purpose and find details. The Venn diagram might in fact be used later as a resource to support another language objective such as "Students will use comparative language to discuss similarities and differences with a partner," but while it has captured information and is used to talk about that information, it is not the learning objective.

Remember: Writing an agenda or list of activities on the board is *not* the same as writing the content and language objectives!

Categories of Language Objectives.   In each lesson you want to target an aspect of language to teach your learners. That target is the core of your language objective. We suggest you draw from the following four categories to identify language targets and generate language objectives.

- **Academic Vocabulary.** You may focus an objective on the key words needed to discuss, read, or write about the topic of the lesson (e.g., names of important people, places, and events; technical terms; scientific and mathematical processes; social studies or health concepts). In doing so, you may select vocabulary from three subcategories, which are described in more detail in Chapter 3.
  - *Content vocabulary:* These key words and technical terms are subject specific. They are often highlighted in textbooks. Students need them to understand lesson concepts, but many are low-frequency words (i.e., not regularly used outside of the classroom).
  - *General academic vocabulary:* These words include cross-curricular academic terms (e.g., *circumstances, impact, observe*), transition words and logical connectors (e.g., *however, because, next*), and language function words (e.g., *compare, persuade*). This category includes medium- and high-frequency words that are used in academic and social conversations.
  - *Word parts:* This category refers to roots, prefixes, suffixes, and base words. Attention to the structure of words can help expand a student's vocabulary knowledge considerably. For example, if multilingual learners know that *re* is the prefix meaning "to repeat," they can begin to guess the meaning of words like *reread, rewrite,* and *recycle.* This is also an area where home language knowledge can facilitate word learning, especially for students from Latin-based language backgrounds.
- **Language Skills and Functions.** Your language objectives might focus on one of the skills or subskills of the four language domains—reading, writing, listening, and speaking, or on a language function (e.g., retell, persuade) that indicates the purpose for which students use language in the lesson.
  - Multilingual learners need some direct instruction in the four language skills, along with opportunities to practice. The skill selected needs to link to the topic of the lesson. For example, in a language arts class, students may need to *read and find key details* in the text to cite as evidence in an essay. In history, they may need to *listen to a recording* of a debate in order to determine two positions on a controversial issue. In science, they may have to *record their observations* during an experiment.
  - Lessons also call for students to use language for a specific purpose—to *describe, compare,* or *predict,* for example. Multilingual learners need instruction and models here as well, particularly in ways to articulate their descriptions, comparisons, predictions, and the like.

- **Language Structures or Grammar.** Students also benefit when you write objectives that reflect the common language structures in the written or spoken discourse of your subjects. For example, your students might be struggling with a text that includes the passive voice or if-then sentences. If so, you may teach students how to interpret these sentences. If you are an ELD teacher, this category offers the opportunity to teach grammatical forms that will really advance your students' language proficiency.

- **Language Learning Strategies.** By planning objectives to teach language learning strategies, you can set students up with resources to learn on their own. Examples include

  - corrective strategies (e.g., reread confusing text),

  - self-monitoring strategies (e.g., make and confirm predictions),

  - prereading strategies (e.g., preview headings, relate to personal experience),

  - language practice strategies (e.g., repeat or rehearse phrases, imitate a native speaker), and

  - cognate strategies (e.g., teach students with Latin-based or Greek-based native languages to consider cognates when they see new academic terms).

More discussion on strategies is found in Chapter 5.

Selecting Potential Language Objectives. One of the difficulties teachers face is narrowing down the wide range of possible language objectives. Multilingual learners need lots of academic language development, so how should a teacher select one or two language targets for a lesson? We suggest that you think about the four categories of language as you analyze how language will be used in your lesson or unit of study. You may find it helpful to reflect on the 4Ts:

- Texts—what language students need to know to comprehend reading passages and written instructions,

- Talk—what language students need to know to understand your speech and to participate in class discussions,

- Tasks—what language students need to know to complete activities and assignments, and

- Tests—what language students need to know to comprehend test questions or prompts and demonstrate their knowledge.

As you consider the language that will be needed for a lesson or unit, you can organize your ideas in a language targets chart, as seen in Figure 2.2. Jot down your ideas according to the categories and use it as a brainstorming tool.[1]

The next step is to think about your multilingual students. What do they know and what can they do with language already? Where might your students need assistance with the potential language targets you listed in the chart? How can you

---

[1] See *Developing Academic Language with the SIOP® Model* (Short & Echevarría, 2016) for detailed information on selecting and writing language objectives for SIOP lessons and for activities to help you apply the guidelines to your own classes.

FIGURE 2.2 **Language Targets Chart**

Language Targets Chart

Academic Vocabulary	Language Skills / Functions
Language Structures / Grammar	Language Learning Strategies

Source: *Developing Academic Language with the SIOP® Model* (Short & Echevarría, 2016), Chapter 3. Used with permission.

advance their academic English with this lesson? Figure 2.3 illustrates questions to ask yourself as you plan your lessons or units.

If you are planning one lesson, select one or two objectives from your Language Targets Chart that are most useful to the students and relevant to the topic. If you are planning a unit, sequence the objectives across the days so you tap the range of categories and build language proficiency.

Writing Language Objectives. For some of you, writing language objectives will be a new process. We want to acknowledge that there is no single way to write these

FIGURE 2.3 **Questions to Ask When Selecting Objectives**

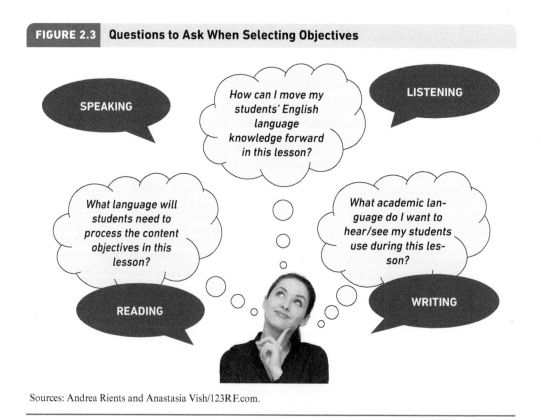

Sources: Andrea Rients and Anastasia Vish/123RF.com.

objectives, but remember they need to reflect an aspect of academic English that students need to learn or improve.

To help you with the process, we offer the following language frames as scaffolds (Short & Echevarría, 2016). To complete them, follow the suggestions we made earlier: Think about which category of academic language your students need to learn and where in the lesson (e.g., the text or task) the language will be needed or practiced. Use this analysis to determine a language target. Then include the language target with a language function in a statement like one of the following:

A: **Students will <u>(language function: active verb)</u> using/with <u>(*language target*)</u>.**

B: **Students will [use] <u>(*language target*)</u> to <u>(language function: active verb)</u>.**

C: **Students will <u>(*language target as active verb*)</u> [with/to___].**

You will notice that there is some flexibility with the frames according to the target and function selected. Here are some examples of these objectives from the frames above. The language target is italicized:

A: Students will explain a science experiment using *if-then statements*.

B: Students will *use cognates* to determine word meaning.

C: Students will *read to find the main idea*.

As you write your objectives—content and language, you may want to keep the verbs in Figure 2.4 in mind. You'll see that they are all active verbs. In SIOP lessons, you should avoid using verbs like *learn*, *know*, and *understand* because the processes are not observable. Although the verbs in the chart are not exclusive to one category or another, they are more commonly used with the category presented. Over time, add to this list to further distinguish between the content and language goals of your lesson.

In Figure 2.5, we show how language objectives might be written for these four categories. One column shows language objectives for a first-grade social studies class. The next column shows language objectives for a third-grade math lesson on geometric shapes. The third column shows language objectives for a middle school

FIGURE 2.4 **Sample Verbs for Writing Content and Language Objectives**

Verbs for Content Objectives	Verbs for Language Objectives
Identify	Listen for
Solve	Retell
Investigate	Define
Distinguish	Find the main idea
Hypothesize	Compare
Create	Summarize
Select	Rehearse
Draw conclusions about	Persuade
Determine	Write
Find	Draft
Calculate	Defend a position on
Observe	Describe

FIGURE 2.5 Sample Language Objectives by Category with Instructional Practices

Type of Language Objective	Grade 1 Social Studies Example	Grade 3 Math Example	Middle School Language Arts Example	High School Chemistry Example
Academic Vocabulary	We will use key words (e.g., *park, library, school, apartment building, house*) and prepositions (e.g., *next to, beside, across*) to describe locations in the neighborhood.	Students will be able to define the terms *square, rectangle, rhombus, trapezoid,* and *parallelogram* orally and in writing.	Students will be able to state the figurative and literal meanings of expressions of hyperbole.	Students will be able to define the terms *chemical reaction, chemical change,* and *physical change* orally and in writing.
What it means instructionally	Teacher teaches students key terms and prepositions and models how to use them to describe the locations of different buildings in the neighborhood.	Teacher teaches (or reminds) students how to define a term: state attributes, give an example, draw a picture, or use it in a sentence.	Using examples (e.g., "my feet are killing me"), the teacher explains what hyperbole is and the difference between figurative and literal language. Students evaluate sample statements as hyperbolic or not and explain why.	Teacher teaches (or reminds) students how to define a term: state attributes, draw an illustration, use in a sentence, give an analogy, provide an antonym, or identify group membership and distinguishing characteristics.
Language Skills and Functions	We will compare features of neighborhood locations using comparative phrases.	Students will be able to listen to teacher descriptions in order to draw different types of parallelograms.	Students will be able to express an opinion orally in a formal and an informal manner.	Students will be able to formulate questions and generate hypotheses before conducting an experiment.
What it means instructionally	Teacher teaches comparative language frames, such as "Both ___ and ___ have." and "___ and "___ are alike/different because ___."	Teacher teaches a listening comprehension skill—paying attention to key words—and asks students to draw the shapes or construct them on a geoboard.	Teacher demonstrates an oral book review as she might tell it to a friend and as she might tell it to a teacher. She calls attention to word choice, intonation, and rhetorical style. She asks students to prepare a similar report on a book, song, or movie.	Teacher teaches (or reminds) students of the way to form these language functions: formulate a question and then state a hypothesis, perhaps with sentence starters like "Will the ___?" and "We predict that ___."

Language Structures or Grammar →	We will use singular and plural nouns with past tense irregular verbs.	Students will be able to use comparative phrases, such as *greater than, larger than, smaller than, less than,* and *equal to* orally and in writing when comparing geometric figures and angles.	Students will be able to use conjunctions and dependent clauses to join ideas in compound and complex sentences.	Students will be able to use adverbs of time in their lab report to describe their observations.
What it means instructionally →	Teacher introduces (or reviews) the difference between singular and plural nouns (using neighborhood examples) and models sentences with past tense irregular verb forms (e.g., *I went to two stores on Ash Street*).	Teacher introduces (or reviews) these comparative phrases and also shows the corresponding mathematical symbols (i.e., $>$, $<$, and $=$).	Teacher introduces (or reviews) conjunctions and dependent clauses and how their use can create a variety of sentences with two or more related ideas. Students practice writing such sentences.	Teacher teaches (or reviews) adverbs of time (e.g., *first, next, later, after three minutes, for several hours*) and shows models of usage in a lab report.
Language Learning Strategies →	We will listen for key words to mark a journey on a map and monitor our result.	Students will be able to visualize and relate the geometric shapes to their lives.	Students will be able to rehearse an oral presentation with a peer.	Students will be able to monitor subject-verb agreement in written lab reports.
What it means instructionally →	Teacher models a jigsaw activity where one student gives directions orally and a partner records the route on a map. The pairs check for accuracy.	Teacher explains how to visualize and make a personal connection and how to articulate the mental image, using a think-aloud.	Teacher teaches class how to listen and give feedback to an oral presentation based on certain criteria (e.g., word choice, intonation) and provides class time for rehearsing.	Teacher discusses subject-verb agreement and points out examples in a model lab report. Teacher then shows students how to check a sentence for subject-verb agreement, particularly for noun phrases (e.g., *potassium and sodium combine to form salt*).

language arts class, and the final column shows language objectives for a high school chemistry class. These objectives are illustrative and would not all be addressed in one lesson; instead, they could be used over a series of lessons. The chart also explains how SIOP teachers would address the objectives in the lessons, in the rows labeled "What it means instructionally." As you write your plans, remember, there must be some instruction and practice related to the language objective.

As you get started writing your own objectives, remember that it is important to include a variety of language objectives over the course of each week. Many teachers feel comfortable teaching vocabulary as their language objective. This is a good first step, but it is not the complete picture of the language development our multilingual learners need to be successful in school and beyond. So draw from all four categories as you plan a series of lessons or a unit of study.

Some teachers who have students with mixed levels of English proficiency in class have asked if they need to write language objectives for each proficiency level. The answer is no. Instead, write an objective that all students should attain based on the content concepts in the lesson, but adjust the intended outcome or performance task to match the students' ability levels. For example, consider the example above "Students will read to find the main idea." You can differentiate the text students read based on proficiency level and/or adjust the activity by which students demonstrate that they know the main idea. Some multilingual learners may master the objective by the end of the lesson; others will be at some point on a path toward mastery.

Connecting Content and Language Objectives.   As you write content and language objectives for your lessons, you may find that they are closely linked at times, but not always. Because you are continually adjusting the language objectives to your students' academic language learning needs, this is understandable. In the following upper elementary math lesson, there is a close alignment.

- Students will solve word problems using a two-step process.
- Students will write a word problem requiring a two-step process for a classmate to solve.

The first statement is the content objective. It focuses on a mathematical procedure students must learn. The second is the language objective. Students use their math writing skills to apply their knowledge of the procedure.

At other times, the language objective might extend the content knowledge, as in this European History lesson:

- Students will explain the causes of the economic recovery of Europe after World War II.
- Students will write and present a podcast summarizing Europe's economic growth over the five years following the end of WWII.

In this lesson, students use the text and other sources to determine how the economy in Europe improved over time, finding events that occurred or steps that governments took. The teacher may have to explain the Marshall Plan and other initiatives. The teacher may then have to guide students in creating a podcast: how to organize the ideas, write a script, and rehearse. Besides helping students articulate their information orally, the teacher may also encourage them to focus on some paralinguistic aspects of the presentation, such as intonation and vocal speed.

For language arts and reading teachers, distinguishing language and content objectives can be tricky. Certain curriculum concepts like *plot* and *setting* are clearly candidates for content objectives because they are specific to the language arts subject, but other possibilities like "produce writing that conveys a clear point of view" could be either a language or a content objective. It could even be a language objective in a history class.

Despite possible overlap, we advise language arts and reading teachers to consistently identify both a content and a language objective for each lesson, even if the decision seems arbitrary because one might be placed in either category. Or, you may decide that reading and writing-related objectives will be content objectives and speaking, listening, and vocabulary targets will be language objectives. Because we are aiming for whole-school implementation of the SIOP Model, having students recognize and expect both types of objectives in all their classes is a valuable goal.

When multilingual learners practice objectives that are explicit learning targets, they advance their knowledge base. Objectives, in sum, are the learning targets related to the content and language knowledge students must acquire, and they are necessary for students to be able to accomplish the activities and master the curriculum.

Checking Your Objectives. The final task after you have written your content and language objectives is to evaluate them. This checklist can help you do so:

_____ The objectives are aligned to state or district standards.

_____ The objectives are observable.

_____ The objectives are written and will be stated simply in language that multilingual learners can understand.

_____ The objectives are written in terms of student learning.

_____ The content objective is related to the key concept of the lesson.

_____ The language objective promotes student academic language growth (i.e., it is not something most students already do well).

_____ The language objective has an instructional connection to the lesson topic or activities.

_____ The objectives are measurable. I have a plan for assessing student progress on meeting both types of objectives during the lesson.

> " Lesson Preparation benefits students so that I do not waste instructional time due to lack of preparedness. When I have my GPS in place, my content and language objectives, we know where we are going and how we are getting there!
>
> Dr. Francheska Figueroa, Postdoctoral Research Scholar, Arizona "

SIOP® **SIOP® FEATURE 3:**

Content Concepts Appropriate for Age and Educational Background Level of Students

SIOP teachers must carefully consider the content concepts they wish to teach, and use district curriculum guidelines and grade-level content standards as guides. In SIOP classrooms, this entails ensuring that although materials may be adapted to meet the needs of multilingual learners, the content is not diminished. When planning lessons around content concepts, consider the following:

- your multilingual students' first language literacy,
- their English language proficiency,
- their schooling backgrounds and academic preparation for grade-level work,
- their background knowledge of the topic,
- the cultural and age appropriateness of instructional materials, and
- the difficulty level of any text or other material to be read.

Our goal as SIOP teachers is to provide the grade-level curriculum to our multilingual learners. By employing the type of techniques we propose in the SIOP Model, teachers skillfully make that content comprehensible to them. Sometimes you may adapt the materials being read or the materials used to accomplish a task. If so, keep the following considerations in mind.

- In general, it is inappropriate to use the curriculum materials and books from much earlier grades. Students also deserve books with age-appropriate illustrations. If necessary when using grade-level or near grade-level material, provide the scaffolding that multilingual learners need to understand the content concepts and complex text used in the lesson.

- In some cases, students with major gaps in their educational backgrounds may be placed in newcomer programs or specialized classes. You should still use the SIOP Model, but can pull objectives and content concepts from earlier grades in order to provide the foundational knowledge the students need to perform grade-level work successfully and catch up to their classmates (Custodio & O'Loughlin, 2017; Samway, Pease-Alvarez & Alvarez, 2020; Short & Boyson, 2012). We recommend that schools develop specialized courses to accelerate the learning of multilingual learners with limited formal schooling. (See, for example, the courses developed in New York under the Bridges to Academic Success project [https://bridges-sifeproject.com]).

- Be mindful of concepts multilingual learners have already acquired through their life experiences or prior schooling. An illustration, demonstration, or video clip can help students recall a concept and then the SIOP teacher can help them learn new English words to describe the concept and add to their understanding of it.

- To help multilingual learners make connections to the content topics, reflect on the amount of background knowledge needed to learn and apply the concepts, and plan ways to build or activate students' prior knowledge related to them. For example, middle school students typically learn about the U.S. Civil War, yet some newly arrived high school multilingual learners may not have studied this topic. Rather than diminish the content, use what prior knowledge students do have, perhaps about conflicts in their home countries, and then explicitly build background from there as a foundation for the lesson.

- Another way to build background for a small group of learners is through a minilesson that precedes the regular whole-class lesson (Vogt & Echevarria, 2022). This minilesson provides a "jump-start" by reviewing key background concepts and introducing vocabulary. It develops context and gives access to students who may lack appropriate background knowledge or experience with the grade-level content concepts. In some dual language programs, this practice is part of Preview/Review and is conducted in the home language or non-instructional language of the students (Ebe, Soto, Freeman, & Freeman, 2021). Chapter 3 details several ways to accomplish this background building, such as leading a picture walk through the reading material, watching a video clip online, and having learners participate in experiential activities.

- In schools where an ELD teacher and a classroom teacher work collaboratively with the same group of students, the ELD teacher can offer lessons that build background and vocabulary before the multilingual learners study the topic in their regular class. See Chapter 11 for a fuller discussion of teacher collaboration for co-planning and co-teaching.

SIOP® **SIOP® FEATURE 4:**

Supplementary Materials Used to a High Degree, Making the Lesson Clear and Meaningful

Pearson eTextbook
Video Example 2.4
Watch this eighth grade history lesson and notice how the teacher incorporates supplementary materials. How do these items help students understand the content? What else does the teacher do to support her multilingual learners?

When SIOP teachers contextualize information, they help multilingual learners understand the core curriculum and complete more cognitively demanding tasks. Effective SIOP instruction accomplishes this in part through the use of supplementary materials. These materials can especially assist students who do not have grade-level academic backgrounds and/or who have language and learning difficulties, because lectures and activities centered on a text are often difficult for them. Supplementary materials enhance meaning and clarify confusing concepts, making lessons more relevant.

A variety of supplementary materials also support different learning styles and multiple intelligences because information and concepts are presented in a multifaceted manner. Multilingual learners can see, hear, feel, perform, create, and participate in order to make connections and construct relevant meanings. The use of technology (e.g., interactive whiteboards, pre-loaded apps on tablets) and multimedia can enhance student understanding and engagement with the content topics and related language practice opportunities.

Supplementary materials can help create a culturally responsive classroom as well (Shin, Savic & Machida, 2021; Snyder & Staehr Fenner, 2021). They can provide a real-life context and enable students to bridge prior experiences from their own backgrounds with new learning. They also honor the diversity of backgrounds, experiences, and cultures that our students bring to the classroom. Further, they provide the occasion for a multilingual learner to be the expert in class, emphasizing an asset-based approach to teaching and learning.

Examples of supplementary materials and resources that can be used to create context and support content concepts include the following:

- **Pictures and Visuals:** Visual supports can build background knowledge and help students explore a wide variety of content and vocabulary concepts. Photographs, illustrations, graphs, charts, timelines, and maps are available that depict nearly any object, process, action, or setting. Sources of images include websites, magazines, commercial photos, books, and hand drawings. Many teachers have electronic document viewers and interactive whiteboards that they use to display book pages, photos, and other artifacts to the class. Students who have difficulty processing a large amount of auditory information particularly benefit when instruction is supported with visual clues.

- **Multimedia:** Multimedia materials such as video clips, podcasts, and Internet resources can enhance teaching and learning. Media in the students' native language can also be valuable sources of information, with audio links as well as written text. It is important to preview websites for appropriateness and readability, especially when using them with students at beginning and intermediate language levels or with young learners.

- **Related Literature:** A wide variety of fiction and nonfiction texts can be included to support instruction, including material written or recorded in the students' home languages or tied to their cultural experiences. Some thematic book sets (e.g., *Civil Rights Leaders Around the World*) cover unique but related topics and are written at different reading levels (e.g., one below-level book, two on-level books, one above-level book). Other book sets may have several versions of the same book available, each written at a different reading level. Some websites such as www.newsela.com offer articles aligned to grade-level curriculum standards that are written for different reading levels, too. These resources are useful for classes that have students with multiple proficiency levels in English.

- **Class Libraries:** Many teachers create class libraries with trade books and leveled readers on key topics. Some teachers ask librarians to find books on related topics as well.[2] Student-written books may be included, too. Children can read these materials as supplements to the textbook. They offer a motivating way to look at a topic in more depth. Class libraries can promote more independent reading among students, which is valuable for vocabulary development and reading comprehension practice.

- **Manipulatives:** These can include anything from counter chips for math to microscopes for science to interactive maps for geography. Manipulating objects physically can reduce the language load of an activity; beginning-level students in particular can still participate and demonstrate their understanding. Technology tools allow students to move items around a computer screen, too. Be sure to demonstrate how to use materials so that students can accomplish lesson tasks (e.g., measuring liquid in a beaker, using fraction bars).

- **Realia:** These are real-life objects that enable multilingual learners to make connections to their own lives. Examples include play money (coins and bills) for a unit on money; realia such as photos, recordings, and artifacts for a social studies unit; or nutrition labels on food products for a health unit.

- **Chapter Summaries:** Some textbook publishers provide one-page summaries of each chapter, which present the key ideas. The summaries are often available in Spanish and sometimes in other languages as well. They can be used to preview the topic or to review it afterward.

---

[2] See Short, Cloud, Morris, and Motta (2012) to learn about a project organizing library books by lesson topic and English proficiency level and creating bookmarks for book sets.

Adaptation of Content to All Levels of Student Proficiency

In many schools, teachers are required to use textbooks that are too difficult for some of their multilingual learners to read, yet the students cannot be expected to learn all content information by listening to lectures either. We must therefore find ways to make the text and other resource materials accessible for all students. We do not advocate "watering down" text because content concepts are frequently lost when the text is adapted in this way; rather, we adapt our instruction and materials so that the content concepts are left intact.

- **Native language supports.** If some of your multilingual learners are literate in their native language, use texts written in that language to supplement a textbook or clarify key concepts. For students who are not literate in their native language but have oral skills, native language broadcasts, podcasts, and audio books may be additional sources of information. For some multilingual learners, multiple exposures to the audio version of a text may result in a more thorough understanding.

  Our goal is to help students understand text and information presented orally in English, and our job is to teach the vocabulary, sentence structure, connections between sentences and paragraphs, and other necessary information to the multilingual learners so they can increase their independence. If we can give them the gist of what they will be learning beforehand through their native language, we can then build on that new knowledge, and, with careful lesson planning, advance their English language skills and strengthen their content knowledge.

- **Text summaries.** Summarize the text to focus on the key points of information to help students focus on key historical events, steps for solving a math problem, or a story plot, for example. The new text might be written as an outline, a list of bulleted points, or a graphic organizer like a flow chart. You can use it as a prereading instructional strategy, as an aid during reading, and as a postreading method for organizing newly learned information.

- **Text elaboration.** There are several ways to elaborate a text: (1) provide a companion glossary that defines vocabulary and explains key concepts; (2) prepare a study guide with questions to consider as students read sections of a text or other annotations to the text; (3) rewrite portions of the text, being sure to maintain critical content information, but perhaps simplifying the sentence structure, starting all paragraphs with the topic sentences, embedding definitions of difficult words, and/or adding more visuals or background information.

So far, we have discussed adapting the text used to deliver content information. Other types of adaptations in class may involve the worksheets and other instructional supports that students use to complete a task. Some students might benefit from having a word bank available while they are writing a summary or paragraph about a topic while others will not need that support. If the students are to take notes in a T-chart format (e.g., main ideas in left column and key details in right), some students might use a blank chart and others might have a version that is partially completed. You can also adapt the task. Students may conduct research using native language materials (in print or online), for example, and share the information with classmates in English. In other words, by differentiating the materials or the task, you can adapt the content to student proficiency levels. But note, as proficiency advances, less to no adaptation is needed.

On the SIOP rating form, a lesson may receive an N/A for feature #5 if the content does not need adaptation for student comprehension.

SIOP® SIOP® **FEATURE 6:**

Meaningful Activities That Integrate Lesson Concepts with Language Practice Opportunities for Reading, Writing, Listening, and/or Speaking

Pearson eTextbook
Video Example 2.5
Watch Jennifer Tabios and Andrea Rients collaboratively plan a World History lesson with meaningful activities that will support their students' academic writing. What can you add to your lessons to promote language practice?

To the extent possible, lesson activities should be planned to promote language development in all skills while multilingual learners are mastering content objectives. We want to provide oral and written language practice that is relevant to the lesson concepts, but remember: Activities that generate language practice are not language objectives. Language objectives require explicit instruction, for example, about a language skill or structure needed to accomplish the activities.

Multilingual learners are more successful when they are able to make connections between what they know and what they are learning by relating classroom experiences to their own lives. These meaningful experiences are often described as "authentic," because they represent a reality for students. That is, classroom experiences mirror what actually occurs in the learner's world. Authentic, meaningful experiences are especially important for multilingual learners because they are learning to attach labels and terms to things already familiar to them. Their learning becomes situated rather than abstract when they are provided with the opportunity to actually experience what they are being taught.

In some classrooms, however, multilingual learners have been assigned activities that are not meaningful and are unrelated to the content and activities pursued by their English proficient classmates. It is essential that content standards that apply to students with English proficiency also apply to multilingual learners, and that the planned activities reflect and support these standards.

Consider a middle school science class where students are studying animal adaptations. While the rest of the class learns about adaptations that help animals survive or thrive in their environments, the teacher has the beginning-level learners color and cut out pictures of birds from the Galapagos Islands. This activity is neither authentic nor relevant for these students. In this instance, the teacher has obviously not provided meaningful activities that support the grade-level science content standards. (A SIOP teacher however would have many ways to engage multilingual learners in this lesson—the use of videos to demonstrate adaptations like color camouflage and physical characteristics, preteaching vocabulary and comparative sentence patterns, partnering students for discussion, and experiential tasks like using different utensils to pick up food items [e.g., nuts, seeds, beans], to name but a few.)

The activities planned in the lessons may be for guided practice or application. When SIOP teachers add student choice opportunities, such as for projects, they can incorporate and sustain students' cultures and backgrounds. When studying geometric shapes, for example, multilingual students might examine artwork, architecture, or fabric prints from their countries and report on common shapes or designs. When studying forms of national governments, students might compare the U.S. form of representative democracy to the government of a country of their own choosing.

As you continue to read this chapter and the remaining ones, you will find a host of teaching ideas for meaningful activities that integrate the concepts with language practice. The resources listed in Appendix F provide many more as well.

Application to Your Classroom: Lesson Preparation

- **Presenting Objectives to the Class.** Effective SIOP teachers do more than just go through the motions by writing the objectives on the board and reading them quickly to the class. Involve your students in thinking about the objectives and the upcoming lesson in the first few minutes. Here are some ways to make the presentation of objectives more productive.

  - Ask students to pick out important words from the objective and highlight them—for example, the verbs and nouns.

  - Ask students to paraphrase the objectives with a partner, each taking a turn, using the frame: "We will ___."

  - Present the objective and then do a Timed-Pair-Share, asking students to predict some of the things they think they will be doing for the lesson that day.

  - Begin the lesson with a 3–5 minute activity or demonstration and then ask students to infer what the objectives might be.

- **Number 1, 2, 3 for Self-Assessment of Objectives.** In this activity, students are asked to diagnose their knowledge about a topic and then take some responsibility for learning new information during the lesson. At the beginning of the lesson, display the objectives and ask students to rate themselves on how well they understand each one. You may read each aloud and have students show with their fingers which of the following ratings fit:

  1. I understand this concept.

  2. It looks familiar, or I have studied something like this before.

  3. I don't know this.

At the end of the lesson, return to the objectives and ask students to rate again, "How well did you meet the objective today?"

1. I can teach the concept to someone else.

2. I understand most of it, but not everything.

3. I don't understand completely. I need more time/practice/examples.

- **Jigsaw Text Reading** (Aronson et al., 1977). This technique works well with multilingual learners when there is a difficult-to-read or very lengthy text.

   1. Form cooperative learning "home" groups and then have one or two members from each group come together to form a new group of "experts."

   2. Assign each new "expert" group a different section of the text to read. This group can take turns reading the text aloud, have partners read to each other, or have group members read the text silently.

   3. Following the reading, each "expert" group reviews and discusses what was read, determining the essential information and key vocabulary. You may prepare a worksheet for them to record key information and guide their comprehension.

   4. Check carefully with each "expert" group to make sure all members understand the material they have read.

   5. After you are confident that the "experts" know their assigned information, have them return to their "home" groups and teach fellow group members what they learned. You may have another worksheet for the group to complete.

   This process scaffolds the learning of multilingual learners because in both groups they are working with others to understand the text. Some classmates may have more background information on the topic. Text can be read with other students, reducing the demands of tackling lengthy sections alone. Depending on English proficiency, multilingual learners may join an "expert" group individually or with a partner. It works best when you form the "expert" groups rather than letting students choose their own group members.

- **Graphic Organizers.** Graphic organizers include story maps, text structure charts, Venn diagrams, timelines, word webs, thinking maps, and flow charts. These schematic diagrams are ubiquitous in today's classrooms, but that does not reduce their value. When preparing a lesson, teachers should think about possible graphic organizers that can provide conceptual clarity for information that is difficult to grasp. Graphic organizers help students identify key content concepts and make relationships among them (McLaughlin & Allen, 2009). They also provide multilingual learners with visual clues they can use to supplement written or spoken words that may be hard to understand.

   ◆ When used *before reading*, graphic organizers can build background for complex or dense text. The type of organizer (e.g., Venn diagram, flow chart, tree map) can preview the text structure, too. For example, a Venn diagram forecasts a comparison-contrast text and a flow chart suggests a cause-effect text.

- When used *concurrently with reading*, they focus students' attention and act as a guide to the information. They help students make connections (e.g., a 2-column chart can elicit comparisons), take notes, and understand the text structure (e.g., a timeline informs students the text will be organized chronologically).

- When used *after reading*, graphic organizers can be employed to record key content information, personal responses, or connections to other texts or topics. They can also be used as prewriting tools for various tasks that might be developed from state writing standards, such as when students have to "draw evidence from literary or information texts to support" written analysis or reflection.

- **Videos.** Gone are the days when we would pop a videotape in a VCR player, but using videos to teach students is still worthwhile. Videos are often motivating for multilingual learners and the images convey knowledge without the potential comprehension struggle of written text. Technology now allows us to bring video clips into the classroom through interactive whiteboards, computers, and smartphones. Some teachers play videos with the sound off the first time to help students focus on the gist of the message or assign watching a video clip for homework before beginning a new unit. Video clips related to grade-level curricula can be found at sites like www.discoveryeducation.com, www.pbs.com, and www.nationalgeographic.com. Other sites, like www.brainpop.com and https://ed.ted.com offer a wide range of material for students in grades K–12, video clips along with lesson ideas, quizzes, and/or other features.

■ Differentiating for Multilevel Classes

The Lesson Preparation component offers teachers multiple opportunities to meet the needs of students with different abilities or language proficiency levels in their classrooms. Although it takes time to prepare a lesson for different groups of students, the investment pays off when all of your students learn the material and you do not have to reteach.

- The first step is knowing your students: their literacy skills both in English and in their native language, their schooling backgrounds (including the number of years they have completed in school), their learning styles, and their multiple intelligences. With this knowledge you can have realistic expectations about what they can accomplish and plan activities accordingly. The WIDA Can-Do descriptors can help you set these expectations.

- The second step is to consider where in your lesson students will need some differentiated instruction.

  - Is it when you introduce new content? If so, should you use different texts or a different presentation style? Should you modulate your speech? Preteach vocabulary?

  - Is it when the learners must perform a task to practice or apply the new information or language target? If so, you may have to consider how you will group the students. Or you may assign different tasks to different groups (based on language proficiency or learning style, for example). You may prepare different handouts or other materials.

◆ Is it when you are checking for comprehension? Then you might plan leveled questions so you can address students in ways that they will be able to comprehend the question and have a chance to respond. Or you may prorate the assignment students complete (e.g., a one-page report for some, a three-page report for others).

A few specific examples of differentiated activities follow.

● **Differentiated Sentence Starters** (Short, Vogt, & Echevarría, 2011a, pp. 30–31). This technique converts teacher-developed leveled questions into sentence starters that the students might use orally or in writing.

1. Begin with the essential question of a lesson.
   For example: How do animals change as they grow?

2. Write questions at a variety of levels of difficulty.
   For example: (a) What does a caterpillar change into as it grows up?
   (b) Do all animals look different when they grow up? Explain.
   (c) Why do animals change as they grow?

3. Convert the questions into sentence starters.
   For example: (a) When a caterpillar grows up, it . . . .
   (b) Yes, all animals look different because . . . . [or] No, not all animals look different. For example, ...
   (c) Animals change as they grow for several reasons. For one, ...

4. Post the questions and have the students respond, either by self-selecting a sentence starter or by being assigned one.

● **Leveled Study Guides.** Study guides to accompany assigned text or a unit's topics can be specifically written for diverse students' needs and their stages of language and literacy development. All students are expected to master the key concepts in the text or unit; however, some need support for comprehension while others can delve more deeply into the material on their own.

◆ For students who can easily read the text material, write a study guide so they can extend and enrich their knowledge of the topic, and be sure to include challenging questions or tasks.

◆ For those who need a little support, write a study guide with definitions and "hints" for unlocking the meaning to lead them through the text. Include a few challenging questions and tasks.

◆ For some multilingual learners and struggling readers, create a study guide with brief summaries of the text or topic along with more manageable questions and tasks.

   Of course, the option to try a more challenging guide should be open to all students.

● **Scaffolded Outlines.** Teacher-prepared outlines equip students with a form they can use for note-taking while reading dense portions of text, watching a video, or

FIGURE 2.6 **Scaffolded Outlines**

Beginning Level

The Circulatory System

   I. Major Organs
      A. Heart
         1. Pumps blood throughout the body
         2. _____
      B. Blood vessels
         1. _____
         2. _____
  II. Major Vessels
      A. Artery
         1. Takes blood away from heart
         2. _____
      B. Vein
         1. Brings blood back to the heart
         2. _____
      C. Capillaries
         1. Connects arteries and veins
         2. _____
 III. Types of Blood Cells
      A. Red blood cells
         1. _____
      B. _____
         1. Fights disease
      C. Platelets
         1. _____

Intermediate–Advanced Level

The Circulatory System

   I. Major Organs
      A. Heart
         1. _____
         2. _____
      B. _____
         1. _____
         2. _____
  II. Major Vessels
      A. Artery
         1. _____
         2. _____
      B. Vein
         1. _____
         2. _____
      C. _____
         1. _____
         2. _____
 III. Types of Blood Cells
      A. Red blood cells
         1. _____
      B. _____
         1. Fights disease
      C. _____
         1. _____

listening to a speech, thus providing scaffolded support. These are especially helpful for students at beginning and intermediate language levels if some of the major concepts, or even some details, are already filled in. The students can then add other information to the outline as they read, watch, or listen. For some students, a completed outline becomes a useful tool for review. Figure 2.6 shows an example of two versions of a scaffolded outline for a science reading on the circulatory system.

■ SIOP Lesson Planning

"How do I start implementing SIOP lessons?" is a frequent question from teachers new to the SIOP Model. We suggest that

- elementary school teachers begin with one subject area, and
- secondary school teachers begin with one course.

It is better to begin on a small scale so you do not have to write multiple SIOP lessons each day while you are learning the model. In some cases, teachers learn the SIOP Model over time, component by component in a cumulative manner, and they

Pearson eTextbook

Video Example 2.6

Watch this video to see Lindsey Dunifon, a high school history teacher, describe how she approaches SIOP lesson planning and the impact that SIOP implementation has on her students. Which of her comments resonate with you at this point in your SIOP experience?

build their lesson planning skills in the same way. That, in fact, is how we designed this book. One discussion question in each chapter will direct you to develop a SIOP lesson, adding more features and refining it as you learn about the model.

It's helpful to recognize that it takes time to get good at SIOP lesson planning! As you begin SIOP implementation, we strongly encourage you to write out lesson plans in detail and keep the short form of the SIOP protocol (Appendix A) handy as a checklist to ensure all of the features are incorporated. You may want to try one or more of the lesson plan templates in Appendix C or the templates in Chapter 7 of *Implementing the SIOP® Model Through Effective Professional Development and Coaching* (Echevarría, Short, & Vogt, 2008). These templates have been used successfully in a variety of classrooms and across grade levels. Once you have internalized the model, you may write less detailed lesson plans, and you will probably find that writing SIOP lessons across subject areas or courses is easier.

When planning, teachers often ask how they can meet all 30 features in a given class period. We explain that one SIOP lesson may be completed in a single day or it may require 2–3 days, depending on the topic covered and tasks assigned. Over the course of several days, all 30 features should be met, however.

Besides writing lessons from scratch, another option is to *SIOPize* a lesson you have already written. Using the checklist, see which features are already present and then enhance your lesson with the missing features. You may need to add explicit instruction for a language objective or more activities for oral interaction, for instance.

■ Rating Lessons With The SIOP® Protocol

As we mentioned at the start of this chapter, we want to give you the opportunity to check your understanding of the SIOP features and learn to use the SIOP protocol. So, with each component we present scenarios of three teachers who teach the same concepts at the same grade level. After we describe each teacher's lesson, we will ask you to rate the SIOP features for this component on a scale of 4–0, with 4 meaning the feature was well implemented in the lesson and 0 meaning it was not present. You will probably notice that some ratings for the features will seem quite obvious (usually those that merit 0, 1, or 4 on the scale), while others will be more challenging to discern. You can then compare your assessment of the features' implementation with ours in the Discussion section that follows.

Your goal is to have a clear understanding of each feature and how it "looks" during a SIOP lesson. These scenarios are a way to begin that process. It is very helpful to discuss with other teachers, teacher candidates, coaches, supervisors, or professors how you determined your ratings on the various SIOP features for the lessons depicted in this book. Ask yourself: What evidence can you find in the scenarios to justify your scores? Does your judgment match the information shared in this chapter about each feature?

In a number of schools, SIOP teacher groups meet to read the scenarios and discuss the ratings. To deepen their understanding of how the features should be implemented, they also watch video clips of teachers delivering instruction and rate those lessons, too. These collaborative discussions help promote transfer of the growing knowledge about SIOP to lesson planning.

Please note that although we organized this book so that you can rate the lessons as you read, in real life you may not want to give ratings to each feature, especially as you and colleagues are learning to implement the model. You could record comments and note if a feature is present or absent, and then use the protocol to offer targeted feedback. You will also notice that 5 of the 30 features have an N/A option (see Appendix A). After years of research, we determined that those 5 (e.g., Adaptation of Content, in Lesson Preparation) might not be needed in every SIOP lesson. Adaptation of Content, for example, may not be necessary in a class with multilingual learners who are at advanced proficiency levels.

■ The Lesson

The lesson described below is intended to teach fourth-grade children about analyzing a social science problem from a local perspective.

Solving Local Problems (Fourth Grade)

The classrooms depicted in the teaching scenarios in this chapter are in a suburban elementary school. Multilingual learners represent approximately 30% of the student population, and the children speak a variety of languages. In the fourth-grade classrooms of teachers Levine, Basobana, and Rafael, the majority of the multilingual learners are at the intermediate stage of English fluency. Native English speakers and multilingual students who have exited the English language development program are present along with those who are still in the language program.

At their curriculum planning meeting, the teachers decided on their next unit. It would be devoted to solving a problem in their local community, an introduction to the social science analysis standard, "Explain individual and cooperative approaches people have taken, or could take in the future, to address local, regional, and global problems, as well as predict possible results of those actions." It would also give students more application with another social science standard "Construct explanations using reasoning, correct sequence, examples, and details with relevant information and data." The teachers chose the theme, "Making a Difference," and agreed on a Big Question to guide the lessons and the culminating project: "What is a problem at school or in our community? How could changing it make a difference?" For the unit assessment, the teachers would have students prepare a project about solutions and outcomes to a local issue. The school district does not have an adopted social studies textbook, so the teachers would develop lessons for 6–7 days and find materials on their own.

■ Teaching Scenarios

The scenarios take us into the classrooms of Ms. Levine, Mrs. Basobana, and Mr. Rafael and describe their planning process and the first two days of the unit. In Chapter 8 we will revisit these classrooms and consider whether the delivery of the lessons was effective or not.

Ms. Levine

Ms. Levine, an experienced SIOP teacher, likes to create a unit-at-a-glance chart before she writes her lesson plans. She thinks about the assessment and what students need to learn to accomplish it. That reasoning helps her write the content and language objectives. Then she slots in the main lesson tasks, adds notes about language elements and student groupings—especially ideas she gets from Ms. Aronson, the ELD teacher who knows her students—and lists the materials they will use.

For Making a Difference, Ms. Levine wanted to focus on youth activists who solved problems in their communities. She anticipated that their stories would be motivating for her students and would demonstrate that young people can have agency. Given this, she worked back from the assessment. Her students appreciate having choice in assignments—their own agency—so she thought they could select how they'd like to present the local problem, possible solutions, and outcomes. Deciding to frame it as a Call to Action, she thought the student groups might want to make a poster or infographic, record a PowerPoint presentation, or produce a video clip for a PSA (public service announcement) or news broadcast. In order to set her students up for success, she would have to teach vocabulary terms and support them in the reasoning process and in expressing problems, solutions, and outcomes.

They would also need some modeling. How does one solve a problem in the community? She began looking for resources on kid activists. She found many sites online and also asked the school librarian for recommendations. She decided to begin with the story of Bellen Woodard, a third-grader who created packs of crayons representing 12 different skin colors. One article was available in Spanish and English. She also found a videoclip where Bellen was interviewed. She could use this story to model the process. The class could summarize the problem and solution with the SWBST (Somebody Wanted But So Then) graphic organizer they used occasionally in language arts. Then in cooperative groups, they could read other stories about youth activists and share out. She would use reciprocal teaching in the groups because the students were familiar with the process (Palincsar & Brown, 1984; Oczkus, 2018) and she could assign the roles—predictor, clarifier, questioner, and summarizer—strategically to accommodate the students' reading and English language skills. In this way, they will be exposed to multiple approaches for solving a local problem.

As Ms. Levine jotted these ideas down in her unit-at-a-glance chart, she had a clearer picture of how the unit would evolve and what the students needed to learn. She then drafted content and language objectives. (See Figure 2.7.) But as she thought about the activities, she realized that some of her multilingual learners need more support, so she would have to adapt some tasks. She would work in a small group with the students at beginning levels of English during the reciprocal teaching activity and also guide them with the SWBST organizer. For the project she would let them choose their groups based on interest, but assign another student in the group as a language buddy to help.

Before the unit began, Ms. Levine wrote her lesson plans, developed her graphic organizers, and gathered the instructional resources. She bookmarked key websites

FIGURE 2.7 **Ms. Levine's Unit-at-a-Glance Chart**

	Day 1	Day 2	Day 3	Day 4	Days 5–6
Unit Theme	Making a Difference				
Big Question	What is a problem at school or in our community? How could changing it make a difference?				
Objectives	CO: SW identify problems and their causes, solutions, and outcomes in texts. LO: SW read a text and write a summary of the problem, solution, and outcome.		CO: SW research a community problem and propose solution and action steps. LO: SW use cause-and-effect language to explain a problem and possible solution. SW make predictions of outcomes.		CO: SW design their Call for Action project. LO: SW give an oral presentation about their project using modal verbs (must, should, could, might).
Activities	Bellen Woodard reading SWBST summary	Youth Activists Reciprocal teaching SWBST summary	Research community problems Generate possible solutions and predict outcomes	List action steps to solve a community problem	Call to Action project: choices: poster, infographic, PSA, video, PowerPoint
Supplementary Materials	Bellen Woodard article, video SWBST graphic organizers	Youth activist stories (Kevin Patel, Marley Dias, Greta Thunberg, Malala Yousafzai)— different reading levels	Bookmarked websites Problem-solution-outcome chart	Sample PSA Do Something.org Problem-solution-outcome chart	Tablets, headphones with mics Poster board, markers
Language and Grouping notes	activist, effect suffixes (-ion, -ist, -ive) whole class	outcome, evaluate cooperative groups (assign roles for recip. teach.) T-led group for beginning readers	____ is a problem because . . . Due to ____, . . . If ____ happens, then . . . We predict that ____	cooperative groups	We must/have to ____ People should ____ It might help if ____ cooperative groups

and posted links in the online class platform. She wrote the content and language objectives for the first two days on her whiteboard:

CO: SW identify problems and their causes, solutions, and outcomes in texts.

LO: SW read a text and write a summary of the problem, solution, and outcome.

She also posted the Big Question for the unit on the bulletin board: What is a problem at school or in our community? How could changing it make a difference?

Figure 2.8 shows the lesson plan for the first two days of the unit. During these days, Ms. Levine explained the unit would be about solving local problems and connected the process to work students do in math. She defined key terms act/action/activist, effect/effective, and outcome and looked at the word parts to show how the suffixes changed the meaning of the words. She asked students to record the words with an representative picture or sentence (in English or their native language) in their notebooks.

FIGURE 2.8 **Ms. Levine's SIOP® Lesson Plan for Grade 4 Social Studies**

Date: Mar 21 - 22   Grade/Class/Subject: *Gr 4 Social Studies*
Unit/Theme: *Making a Difference*   Standards: *Social Studies Analysis 4.24, 4.21*
Content Objective: *SW identify problems and their causes, solutions, and outcomes in texts.*
Language Objective: *SW read a text and write a summary of the problem, solution, and outcome.*

Key Vocabulary	Supplementary Materials
cause, effect, problem, solution, action (review terms)	*Bellen Woodard story*
outcome, activist, result, consequence, effective (new terms)	*Print and online stories of 4 youth activists, photos of them*
	Somebody Wanted But templates (2 versions)

SIOP ® Features

Lesson Preparation
✓ Adaptation of Content: templates, stories at diff. levels
✓ Links to Background
✓ Links to Past Learning
✓ Strategies incorporated: *Brainstorm, Predict, Evaluate*

Scaffolding
✓ Modeling
✓ Guided practice
✓ Independent practice
✓ Comprehensible input

Grouping Options
✓ Whole class
✓ Small groups
✓ Partners
___ Independent

Integration of Processes
✓ Reading
✓ Writing
✓ Speaking
✓ Listening

Application
___ Manipulatives/movement
✓ Meaningful
✓ Linked to objectives
✓ Promotes engagement

Assessment
___ Individual
✓ Group
✓ Written
___ Oral

Lesson Sequence

Day 1
1. Present content and language objectives. Connect "problem-solution" to math.
2. Brainstorm: What's a problem you see at school or in your community? How could changing it make a difference?
3. Preteach new vocab and review other terms. Point out word relationships in act/action/activist; effect/effective
4. Introduce Bellen Woodard story with a brief summary and text walk. Show graphic organizer template Somebody, Wanted, But, So, Then. Ask students to recall when they used it in language arts and for what purpose (summarizing).
5. Read Bellen story aloud, periodically ask comprehension Qs (think-pair-share), orally explain other vocabulary as needed.
6. Model completing the graphic organizer with student input. Model turning the information from the organizer into sentence or two.
7. Wrap-up: How did Bellen's crayon sets make a difference? (partner share)

Day 2
1. Review objectives. Have students make "Oh Yesterday , we/I . . ." statements to tell what they learned or did the day before.
2. Present task: read story using reciprocal teaching and complete gr. org. Show photos. Group students by reading levels (4-5 per group). Assign texts about youth activists by level and distribute organizers (2 versions for differentiation: SWBST, SWBBST). Work with group of beginning readers.
3. Groups read, discuss, and complete their organizers. Then write one or more sentences using the organizer to describe the problem and solution they read about.
4. Have reporter from each group show and explain the completed organizer (use document camera). For each, ask students, Was that a good solution? Can you think of another one? (think-pair-share)
5. Wrap-up. Four corners: Students move to the corner of the room representing the problem and solution they think was most effective. Review objectives. (1, 2, 3)

Reflections:
Students enjoyed the discussions. Had to cut some discussions of other solutions short when the groups were presenting due to time! Most were able to write their sentences based on the organizer.

Ms. Levine referred to the Big Question and asked students to brainstorm some responses with a partner. She offered an example: *One problem I see is when school ends, sometimes students have to wait for buses outside in the rain. If we solve it, they won't get so wet.* When the pairs reported out, she recorded their ideas on chart paper. She explained the unit project plan briefly and introduced Bellen Woodard as a young activist who identified a problem and took action to solve it. Next she previewed the story about Bellen with a text walk, and then she read it aloud, pausing occasionally to ask comprehension questions.

Ms. Levine explained they would read the story again to identify the problem, its cause, Bellen's solution, and the outcome. They would summarize it with the SWBST organizer that she projected from her computer to the whiteboard. After the second read-through, she elicited ideas from the students to complete the organizer and then as a class they crafted the summary. (See Figure 2.9). To wrap up, she asked students to tell a partner how Bellen's crayon sets made a difference. For homework, she assigned watching a video interview of Bellen that was bookmarked on the class web page.

As the second day began, Ms. Levine had a few students do the "Oh Yesterday" technique[3] to recap the prior day and then reviewed the objectives. Next, she showed them photos of the four young activists that they would read about. She explained they would divide into reciprocal teaching groups to read one of the four stories and complete a Somebody Who summary. They would then share out what they learned, which could give them a range of ideas for their own projects later in the week. She arranged the students into cooperative groups, assigned their reciprocal teaching roles, and passed out the corresponding text and organizer to each group. She planned to work directly with a small group of her three multilingual students who were at beginning levels of English. The two reading groups with stronger readers had an organizer that added a Because section (Somebody Wanted Because But So Then).

When the groups finished, a reporter from each group displayed the organizer using the document camera and explained the problem, solution, and outcome. Ms. Levine invited students to ask questions. After each report, she asked pairs to discuss if they thought it was a good solution and if they could think of another one.

FIGURE 2.9	Graphic Organizer Completed by Ms. Levine's Class
Somebody	Bellen Woodard, third grade
Wanted	crayons for different skin colors
But	most crayon boxes had only a peach color for skin
So	she ordered crayons for diverse colors and made her own packs
Then	she donated the packs to local schools

Bellen Woodard was in third grade and wanted crayons for different skin colors, but most crayon boxes had only a peach color for skin. So, she ordered crayons with diverse colors and made her own crayon packs. Then she donated the packs to local schools.

---

[3] Three students took turns completing this sentence, "Oh Yesterday, we studied/learned/practiced . . . ," to connect to the previous lesson.

FIGURE 2.10 Lesson Preparation Component of the SIOP® Model: Ms. Levine's Lesson

4	3	2	1	0	
1. **Content objectives** clearly defined, displayed, and reviewed with students		**Content objectives** for students implied		No clearly defined **content objectives** for students	
4	3	2	1	0	
2. **Language objectives** clearly defined, displayed, and reviewed with students		**Language objectives** for students implied		No clearly defined **language objectives** for students	
4	3	2	1	0	
3. **Content concepts** appropriate for age and educational background level of students		**Content concepts** somewhat appropriate for age and educational background level of students		**Content concepts** inappropriate for age and educational background level of students	
4	3	2	1	0	
4. **Supplementary materials** used to a high degree, making the lesson clear and meaningful (e.g., computer programs, graphs, models, visuals)		Some use of **supplementary materials**		No use of **supplementary materials**	
4	3	2	1	0	N/A
5. **Adaptation of content** (e.g., text, assignment) to all levels of student proficiency		Some **adaptation of content** to all levels of student proficiency		No significant **adaptation of content** to all levels of student proficiency	
4	3	2	1	0	
6. **Meaningful activities** that integrate lesson concepts (e.g., interviews, letter writing, simulations, models) with language practice opportunities for reading, writing, listening, and/or speaking		**Meaningful activities** that integrate lesson concepts but provide few language practice opportunities for reading, writing, listening, and/or speaking		No **meaningful activities** that integrate lesson concepts with language practice	

To wrap up, Ms. Levine posted the four activist photos in each corner of the room and then asked the students to move to the corner representing the problem and solution they thought was most effective. They had two minutes to discuss why and then she asked one person from each corner to report out. They reviewed objectives as the time ended, rating their understanding as 1 (I got it), 2 (I'm making progress), or 3 (I need more practice).

Check your understanding: On the SIOP form in Figure 2.10, rate Ms. Levine's lesson on each of the Lesson Preparation features.

Mrs. Basobana

Mrs. Basobana was excited about this unit. A newshound personally, she likes bringing current events into the classroom. She believes the class has rich discussions and she doesn't like to overprepare. She'd rather design the lessons based on student interests and ideas that come up organically, but did decide on a general plan for each day:

Day 1: SW review the local newspaper for issues in the community and discuss with class.

Day 2: SW generate a list of community and school problems.

Day 3: SW generate possible solutions to a class-selected problem.

Day 4: SW research the solutions and evaluate.

Day 5: SW write a newspaper article for the future, by which time they will have solved their problem to report on their actions and outcomes.

Day 6: SW edit newspaper articles.

For Day 1 she brought in copies of the local newspaper from the past three days and also loaded the website on the class tablets. Since students were already sitting in desk groups, she asked each group to look through one of the papers and find an issue that was a local problem. As the students began the task, many requested help with the articles, asking questions ranging from "Is a robbery a local problem?" to "What does litigation mean?" to "The paper says it will rain tomorrow and that's a problem for our soccer game." Several students complained they couldn't understand the articles.

After ten minutes of this work yielded little progress for many students, she called for the class's attention and asked for a volunteer to report a problem. One student identified an article about the building of a new highway that was going to be close to people's homes. Mrs. Basobana agreed, found the article in her copy, and read the article aloud. Then she asked the class to talk about what they heard, writing some questions on the board:

1. What is the problem?

2. Why is it a problem?

3. What is the solution?

4. Is it a good solution?

During the ensuing discussion, only four students volunteered to respond. Mrs. Basobana had some exchanges with them and as needed, rephrased their ideas to correct or clarify. She invited others to add their thoughts and even called some students by name, but few more participated. She spent a few minutes explaining *eminent domain* and *infrastructure funding* and then asked the class to vote by raising their hands if they thought the solution in the article was a good one.

On the second day, Mrs. Basobana explained the project for the end of the unit. The students would write a newspaper article for the future in which they would identify a problem, describe some possible solutions, select one, pretend that it happened, and tell the result. As a class they would decide on the problem, solution, and outcome, but each group would write its own article, or if someone wanted to write independently that would be okay, too.

To start them off, she asked students to state some problems at the school or in the community. She created a list on the whiteboard. Suggestions included lunch in the cafeteria, trash on the streets, homework, the heater in the music room, people sleeping on the ground, and climate change. Not all students offered an idea but they all paid attention. After the list was finished, she asked students to rank their top three choices of a problem to solve on a slip of paper and give it to her. She then asked one student to tally the votes on the list posted on the board while she read the slips aloud. During the six minutes needed to collect and count the votes and decipher handwriting, two students started to argue at their seats, engaging the interest of those around them until Mrs. Basobana had the instigators move their desks apart. The winning problem was people sleeping on the ground. She told the students this problem is often referred to as homelessness and shared some of the reasons that people become homeless.

With 5 minutes left in class, Mrs. Basobana suggested students sketch their ideas for solving the problem and said they would work on solutions the next day.

Check your understanding: On the SIOP form in Figure 2.11, rate Mrs. Basobana's lesson on each of the Lesson Preparation features.

FIGURE 2.11 **Lesson Preparation Component of the SIOP® Model: Mrs. Basobana's Lesson**

4	3	2	1	0	
1. **Content objectives** clearly defined, displayed, and reviewed with students		**Content objectives** for students implied		No clearly defined **content objectives** for students	
2. **Language objectives** clearly defined, displayed, and reviewed with students		**Language objectives** for students implied		No clearly defined **language objectives** for students	
3. **Content concepts** appropriate for age and educational background level of students		**Content concepts** somewhat appropriate for age and educational background level of students		**Content concepts** inappropriate for age and educational background level of students	
4. **Supplementary materials** used to a high degree, making the lesson clear and meaningful (e.g., computer programs, graphs, models, visuals)		Some use of **supplementary materials**		No use of **supplementary materials**	
5. **Adaptation of content** (e.g., text, assignment) to all levels of student proficiency		Some **adaptation of content** to all levels of student proficiency		No significant **adaptation of content** to all levels of student proficiency	N/A
6. **Meaningful activities** that integrate lesson concepts (e.g., interviews, letter writing, simulations, models) with language practice opportunities for reading, writing, listening, and/or speaking		**Meaningful activities** that integrate lesson concepts but provide few language practice opportunities for reading, writing, listening, and/or speaking		No **meaningful activities** that integrate lesson concepts with language practice	

Mr. Rafael

Mr. Rafael was new to SIOP, but engaged in learning about it. He chose to approach the unit from the historical perspective of civil rights. He thought he could capture the students' interest with a video of a civil rights activist. Because it was March, Women's History Month, he chose to showcase Harriet Tubman. He reviewed many videos online to find one about her life that was appropriate for his fourth-graders and he checked that the clip would have closed caption options, believing the words on the screen would help his multilingual learners. He found a short biography of her for elementary students and loaded the weblink to his class's learning management system. He identified key terms in the text he wanted to preteach—*activist*, *civil rights*, *slavery*, *protest*, *results*, and *outcome*—and prepared a worksheet the students could complete that included a word bank for students to use if needed.

He decided it would be fun for the class to write a short play about a problem in their community and perform it like reader's theater as their project. He knew the importance of practicing reading, writing, listening, and speaking and felt he could assign roles to students based on their language levels. The class had read a scene from a play in language arts in the fall, so they were familiar with the genre. His plan for the unit was to introduce the local problem–solution concept on the first day, select a topic for the play and begin writing on day two, continue writing on days three and four, and maybe five, and then rehearse and perform on day six. He would record the performance.

As he considered the two social science standards that he had to address, he realized that one could be the content objective for the unit and the other could be the language objective. He rewrote them slightly in this way:

Content: SW explain individual approaches people have taken, or could take in the future, to address local or national problems, and predict results of those actions.

Language: SW write about problems and solutions using reasoning, correct sequence, examples, and details with relevant information in a play.

When class began on the first day, Mr. Rafael had trouble loading the video clip on the computer and displaying it on the whiteboard. When it was finally streaming, seven minutes had passed, so to save time, he skipped sharing the objectives with the students and decided to highlight some key vocabulary as he quickly talked about Harriet Tubman. He explained their unit was about problems and solutions. He asked who had heard of Harriet Tubman and several students raised their hands. He acknowledged they knew of her work with the Underground Railroad, but now they would look at her actions in terms of problems and solutions. As he introduced the video clip, he introduced the key vocabulary orally by mentioning that she was an activist and worked on civil rights to end slavery and promote women's right to vote.

Mr. Rafael passed out the worksheet with basic questions about problems Harriet Tubman confronted and ways she solved them. He encouraged students to pay attention to the video and turned on the closed captions in English. After they watched the 6-minute clip, he instructed students to try to answer the questions, encouraging them to work with a partner, if desired. After five minutes, he explained that like good historians they would look at another source for information and had students bring up the article about Tubman on their tablets. He called on one student after another to read paragraph by paragraph aloud. As needed, he explained unknown words and helped with pronunciation. When they finished, he had the students continue with the worksheet. After he noticed most students were done, he went over the answers with the whole class. To wrap up the lesson, he asked the students to share with a partner one way Harriet Tubman made a difference.

The next day, Mr. Rafael explained his idea for the project and showed the students the content and language objectives for the unit. He next displayed the Big Question: "What is a problem at school or in our community? How could changing

---

FIGURE 2.12   Lesson Preparation Component of the SIOP® Model: Mr. Rafael's Lesson

4	3	2	1	0	
1. **Content objectives** clearly defined, displayed, and reviewed with students		**Content objectives** for students implied		No clearly defined **content objectives** for students	
4	3	2	1	0	
2. **Language objectives** clearly defined, displayed, and reviewed with students		**Language objectives** for students implied		No clearly defined **language objectives** for students	
4	3	2	1	0	
3. **Content concepts** appropriate for age and educational background level of students		**Content concepts** somewhat appropriate for age and educational background level of students		**Content concepts** inappropriate for age and educational background level of students	
4	3	2	1	0	
4. **Supplementary materials** used to a high degree, making the lesson clear and meaningful (e.g., computer programs, graphs, models, visuals)		Some use of **supplementary materials**		No use of **supplementary materials**	
4	3	2	1	0	N/A
5. **Adaptation of content** (e.g., text, assignment) to all levels of student proficiency		Some **adaptation of content** to all levels of student proficiency		No significant **adaptation of content** to all levels of student proficiency	
4	3	2	1	0	
6. **Meaningful activities** that integrate lesson concepts (e.g., interviews, letter writing, simulations, models) with language practice opportunities for reading, writing, listening, and/or speaking		**Meaningful activities** that integrate lesson concepts but provide few language practice opportunities for reading, writing, listening, and/or speaking		**No meaningful activities** that integrate lesson concepts with language practice	

it make a difference?" and restated some responses students made the day before about Harriet Tubman. He then asked the student pairs to discuss the question and generate a list of school and community problems which he recorded on chart paper. When they reached ten items, he stopped the discussion and asked students to vote. No item got a majority. He spent a few minutes talking about voting by majority versus plurality and also asked students to think which idea might make a good play. Then he crossed off all but the three items with the most tallies and had the class vote again. The winner was "trash in the river."

Mr. Rafael shared his plan for the play to have three acts: one to tell the problem, one to identify solutions, and the third to resolve the problem and show the outcome. Each act would be written by a different group of students. He assigned students to the groups, making sure to divvy up his multilingual learners among them. The students had many questions: who would be the actors, what are the characters' names, is it a story or real life, and so on. Mr. Rafael pointed out these were good questions that they had to answer before they started writing and led a class discussion to design the outline of the story they would tell. Not all the students participated in the discussion but those who did had many different ideas. He tried to capture them on the board and redirected the discussion multiple times to focus on the problem-solution-outcome frame, but no decision was reached when the class had to go to lunch. Mr. Rafael asked the students to chat with each other at lunch and think about it overnight. They could share ideas with their family too. Tomorrow they would decide.

Check your understanding: On the SIOP form in Figure 2.12, rate Mr. Rafael's lesson on each of the Lesson Preparation features.

■ Discussion of Lessons

Review your rating form and think about the reasons you scored the lessons as you did. Look for evidence in each scenario. Read on to see our analyses.

1. *Content Objectives Clearly Defined, Displayed, and Reviewed with Students*
   Ms. Levine: 4
   Mrs. Basobana: 0
   Mr. Rafael: 1

- **Ms. Levine** planned her unit content objectives in advance and sequenced them so students would have enough knowledge to be successful on the unit project. She wrote the content objectives on the whiteboard and she clearly, explicitly, and simply stated them in a manner that was comprehensible to her students on both days. She also connected the objectives to the unit's Big Questions. She used the text about Bellen and the graphic organizer to help her students meet the objective. Her lesson received a "4."

- **Mrs. Basobana** wrote the activities for the week but did not present them to the students as objectives, nor did she share an overview of the unit. The activities relied on her active involvement. Without any modeling or scaffolding, the students struggled to read the newspaper articles to identify local problems.

She tried to generate a class discussion about a problem but few students participated. Without providing objectives and setting the stage for the unit, her multilingual learners and others had difficulty understanding the purpose of the activities they were asked to do. The sketching activity at the end of the second day was disconnected from the newspaper task. Her lesson was rated "0" for this feature, but could have been improved by writing and presenting the objectives to the students, providing instruction, modeling the newspaper task, and making sure the activities aligned to the learning goal.

- **Mr. Rafael** wrote only one content objective for the unit and it was a restatement of the state standard. This was much too broad for this unit and impossible to accomplish in one lesson. Further, he failed to share it with the students on the first day, opting to jump into the first activity without setting a learning goal for the class. His multilingual learners would not know what was expected of them, and if they were unfamiliar with the biography of Harriet Tubman, they were at a disadvantage. Although he did read the objective aloud at the start of the second day, he did not connect what they did the day before with the objective. If he had unpacked the standard into manageable learning chunks for each lesson and introduced them to students each day, the students would have had a better chance of success. His lesson received a "1."

2. *Language Objectives Clearly Defined, Displayed, and Reviewed with Students*
Ms. Levine: 4

Mrs. Basobana: 0

Mr. Rafael: 1

- **Ms. Levine** wrote the language objectives on the whiteboard and reviewed them with the students. She planned opportunities for students to meet the objectives by teaching key vocabulary, introducing the story with a text walk, modeling the graphic organizer, and grouping the students appropriately with differentiated materials. By the end of the two days, the students were able to meet the gist of the objective: read a problem-solution text and write a summary. Those students at beginning levels of English were also able to succeed because she worked directly with them. At the end of the lesson, she orally reviewed the language objectives for the students. Her lesson was rated a "4."

- **Mrs. Basobana** did not include any language objectives in her lesson plan, although it had many opportunities for language learning, such as reading a newspaper article to find the answers to the discussion questions, or having students use persuasive language to argue for or against the choice of a problem. She did not discuss the meanings of the key terms nor did she encourage her students to participate in the discussion. Mrs. Basobana mostly conveyed information orally, and she did all the writing. The lesson would have been more effective if she planned a language objective and provided some instruction and an activity to support it. Her lesson received a "0."

- **Mr. Rafael** had a language objective, but to save time, he did not present it to the students until the second day. As with the content objectives, this decision meant the students did not know what they were going to learn during the first lesson. Further, the language objective was also a restatement of a state standard, not suitable for an individual lesson. The first day could have focused on listening skills to identify problems and solutions in Harriet Tubman's life and the second day could have focused on one or more elements of the play, including plot, character, and setting. His lesson was rated a "1."

3. *Content Concepts Appropriate for Age and Educational Background Level of Students*

   Ms. Levine: 4

   Mrs. Basobana: 4

   Mr. Rafael: 4

   In the scenarios each of the fourth-grade teachers, **Ms. Levine, Mrs. Basobana,** and **Mr. Rafael,** planned a unit to address a local problem, potential solutions, and possible outcomes. The content concepts were appropriate because they are congruent with the fourth-grade state standards for the social studies curriculum. Each lesson was rated a "4."

4. *Supplementary Materials Used to a High Degree, Making the Lesson Clear and Meaningful*

   Ms. Levine: 4

   Mrs. Basobana: 0

   Mr. Rafael: 2

   - **Ms. Levine** used a number of supplementary materials to make the content more accessible to the learners: the article about Bellen Woodard, texts about other youth activists at different reading levels; a differentiated graphic organizer, photos, bookmarked websites, and a video clip about Bellen. Her lesson received a "4" on this feature.

   - **Mrs. Basobana** had print and online news articles for the students but failed to ensure that the texts were accessible and meaningful to the fourth-graders. She did not show any visuals to support student learning. Her lesson received a "0."

   - **Mr. Rafael** reviewed several videos about Harriet Tubman and selected one suitable for his fourth-graders along with a biography written for young learners. The video enabled his multilingual learners and other students to connect visually with Harriet's problems and solutions, but he did not preteach any vocabulary that might have helped his multilingual learners understand the audio or the biography text. He did prepare a worksheet to check student comprehension with a word bank for additional support, but he did not include any other supplementary materials (e.g., some pages from a script) that might have helped him explain the unit project—the class play—better to his learners. His lesson was rated "2."

5. *Adaptation of Content to All Levels of Student Proficiency*

   Ms. Levine: 4

   Mrs. Basobana: 0

   Mr. Rafael: 1

- **Ms. Levine** adapted the grade-level content for her multilingual learners in a number of ways. She worked directly with the students at beginning levels of English during the reciprocal teaching activity and prepared a variation of the organizer (SWBBST) for some groups. By arranging reciprocal teaching groups with students of mixed reading abilities and assigning roles according to student skill levels, she supported the multilingual learners who were not yet strong readers. For the project, once the groups were formed, she planned to assign a language buddy to each student at the beginning level of English. Her lesson was rated a "4."

- **Mrs. Basobana** did not adapt the content for her multilingual learners. She relied on local newspapers and oral discussion to convey information. Without scaffolding for the task or defining key vocabulary, her multilingual learners had difficulty participating and likely did not learn much about the key concepts just by listening and reading independently. Her lesson planning did not include any way to adapt the content or text. Her lesson rated a "0."

- **Mr. Rafael** did not adapt the content very much in his lesson. Although he displayed the closed captioning on the video about Harriet Tubman as one adaptation, he did not preteach any vocabulary that might have helped his multilingual learners understand the audio. Nor did he plan ways to support his multilingual learners at beginning and intermediate levels of English to read the fourth-grade level biography and complete the worksheet other than encouraging them to "work with a partner." If he had created different versions of the text, perhaps through Newsela or Rewordify, and taught key terms more explicitly, the opportunities for the students to comprehend the key information would have improved. On the second day, he arranged groups so multilingual learners were distributed with others who might assist as needed, but he did not adapt the task. His lesson received a "1."

6. *Meaningful Activities That Integrate Lesson Concepts with Language Practice Opportunities for Reading, Writing, Listening, and/or Speaking*

Ms. Levine: 4

Mrs. Basobana: 0

Mr. Rafael: 2

- **Ms. Levine** included many meaningful activities in the lesson. The class then worked on a vocabulary categorization activity. Her lesson received a "4."

- Without objectives, language supports, and activities aligned to the learning goals, **Mrs. Basobana's** lesson was not very meaningful for her class. Her plan for students to read newspapers and find local problems was not well-thought-out. The students had too many articles to look through, the articles were written at reading levels above most students' abilities, no vocabulary was taught, and few students participated in the class discussion. She got sidetracked at one point and discussed topics not particularly relevant to the lesson at hand (infrastructure and eminent domain). The voting on paper, tallying, and re-voting wasted time and did not prompt any language practice, although she could have asked students to present pros and cons for the options, using persuasive language. The sketching activity at the end of the day was busywork. Students did it independently and it was never reviewed by Mrs. Basobana or discussed. The class project in principle could be meaningful and lead to language practice in later lessons, but she did not teach students how to write a news article, did not provide models, and set up an unlikely premise that they would report on something that they imagine would happen in the future by looking back on the outcome from a further future perspective. Mrs. Basobana's lesson received a "0."

- **Mr. Rafael** planned some meaningful activities on the first day of the lesson. He used two sources of information for students to consider problems Harriet Tubman faced and solutions she explored, modeling the disciplinary literacy of history *and* tapping three learning modes (listening, viewing, and reading); however, the students would have benefitted from more language support. The worksheet offered some writing practice and was intended to capture basic facts but could have included more challenging questions that asked students to evaluate Harriet's choices, for instance. On the second day, Mr. Rafael's lesson was less meaningful. The voting for a class problem was teacher-directed and generated little productive discussion practice; and the introduction of the class project was problematic. He gave the students no choice in their groups, he assumed the students remembered what a play was and what elements it contained, and he failed to plan for a class-generated plot, setting, and characters. To his credit, when he realized students needed more guidance, he altered his lesson to try to generate an outline for the play and identification of characters. His lesson was rated a "2."

■ Final Points

As you reflect on this chapter and the benefits of lesson planning with clear content and language objectives in mind, consider the following main points:

- Lesson Preparation is a critical foundation for delivering a high-quality SIOP lesson. Thoughtful planning leads to effective teaching—but a great plan does not always guarantee a great lesson for multilingual learners. Teachers must plan lessons that are aligned to the grade-level curriculum and based on content standards and learning outcomes, but they must also be culturally responsive to student needs and acutely aware of how well students are learning during a lesson in case adjustments to the plan are needed.

- All SIOP lessons need attention to language with at least one objective devoted to furthering the multilingual learners' academic English development. This should be a learning objective—an achievement target, not an activity—and teachers must teach to it during the lesson.

- If students lack background knowledge and experience with content concepts, effective sheltered teachers provide it through explicit instruction, and they enhance student learning with appropriate supplementary materials. They provide scaffolded support by adapting dense and difficult text.

- SIOP teachers situate lessons in meaningful, real-life activities and experiences that involve the students in reading, writing, and discussing important concepts and ideas.
- The principles of effective sheltered instruction and content-based language instruction should be reflected in teachers' lesson plans. As we explore the other features of the SIOP Model and see how teachers apply other important principles in their classrooms, remember that the first step in the instructional process is comprehensive lesson design.
- In sum, teachers must learn to identify and then teach the academic language of their subject explicitly in their lessons and use a variety of techniques to build background, convey new information to multilingual learners in accessible ways, plan for meaningful tasks that practice and apply the content and language knowledge, and then review what has been learned.

■ Discussion Questions

1. In reflecting on the learning outcomes in the content and language objectives at the beginning of the chapter, are you able to:
   a. Identify content objectives for multilingual learners that are aligned to state, local, or national standards?
   b. Incorporate supplementary materials suitable for multilingual learners into a lesson plan?
   c. Apply knowledge of students' educational background and skills to adapt content to their language proficiency and cognitive levels?
   d. Generate language targets for multilingual learners that align to standards and address how language is used in academic settings?
   e. Discuss advantages of including both language and content objectives in a lesson and sharing the objectives with students?
   f. Explain the importance of meaningful academic activities for multilingual learners?
   g. As part of a lesson plan, write content and language objectives linked to standards and the lesson topic?

2. What are some advantages to writing both content objectives and language objectives for students to hear and see? How might written objectives affect teacher and student performance in the classroom?

3. Think of a lesson you have recently taught or one you might teach. What would be an appropriate content objective and language objective for that lesson?

4. In many schools, one ELD teacher supports multilingual learners from several classrooms, sometimes across different grade levels. How can the ELD and grade-level or subject-area teachers collaborate to share the responsibility for teaching both language and content objectives to these students? Try this: Co-plan a mini-unit in which some lessons will be taught by the ELD teacher and others by the grade-level classroom teacher or the secondary subject-area teacher. (More information on co-planning is found in Chapter 11.)

5. Many teachers rely on mini-lectures or textbook chapters for teaching key concepts. Think of a curricular area (e.g., science, language arts, math, social studies) and discuss some meaningful activities that could be used to teach a concept in that area. What makes each of these activities "meaningful," and how would they provide language practice?

6. Begin writing a SIOP lesson. Identify the topic and your content and language objectives. Find or create supplementary materials and adapt content as needed. Determine at least one meaningful activity the children can engage in during the lesson. Decide how many class periods will be needed to complete the lesson. When you finish, share your initial lesson plan with a colleague and solicit feedback. Revise your lesson.

■ Pearson eTextbook Application Videos

The purpose of the Pearson eTextbook Application Videos is to provide you with an opportunity to observe and reflect on SIOP teaching and learning practices. There are multilingual students in each of the classrooms with varying levels of English proficiency. The teachers you will observe are at different levels of SIOP implementation, from second-year SIOPers to veterans. As you observe the lessons they have created, focus on the students and the lesson objectives, keeping in mind that becoming a high-implementing SIOP teacher takes time, practice, and support to refine teaching practices. We are grateful to each of these SIOP educators for welcoming us into their classrooms, and for their dedication to SIOP, their multilingual learners, and other students.

Pearson eTextbook Application

Video Example 2.1

Co-Teachers' Interview: Planning the Grade 2 SIOP Math Lesson

Two teachers discuss the SIOP lesson plan template

Pearson eTextbook Application

Video Example 2.2

Co-Teachers Teach Grade 2 SIOP Math Lesson on Place Value

Pearson eTextbook Application

Video Example 2.3

Co-Teachers' Post-Lesson Reflections: Grade 2 SIOP Math Lesson on Place Value

Building Background

CONTENT OBJECTIVES

This chapter will help you to . . .

- Identify techniques for connecting students' prior knowledge, personal experiences, and past learning to a lesson's content concepts.
- Identify ways to develop background knowledge for students who have a mismatch between what they know and have experienced, and the content concepts found in a lesson.

LANGUAGE OBJECTIVES

This chapter will help you to . . .

- Select vocabulary for a SIOP lesson from three categories of words: Key content and technical words; general academic words; and word parts—roots and affixes.
- For your SIOP lesson plan, write several prompts for activating students' prior knowledge about the lesson's content concepts.

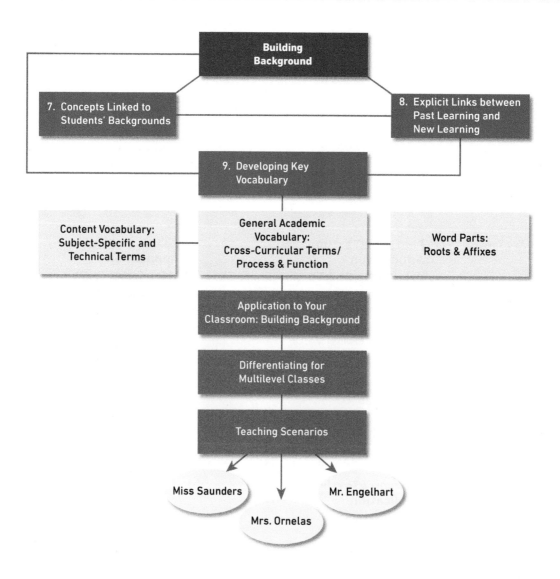

Reflect on two instances when you attended workshops for professional development.

- During one workshop, you were highly motivated, totally engaged, and you came away from the training renewed and eager to implement in your classroom what you had learned. What aspects of this professional learning activity clicked for you?
- Now, recall a workshop during which you were unmotivated by the speaker, disengaged, disconnected, and bored by what the facilitator was talking about. You had little interest in trying out anything that was discussed during the session. Why was this professional development workshop such an unsatisfying experience?

There might be several reasons for the differences in your reactions, including your motivation for attending the workshop, the effectiveness of the facilitator, the time of day, your physical comfort, and so forth. But consider another possibility: There was a mismatch between what you know and have experienced with your own students, and the concepts and information that were being presented. Because of your background knowledge and personal experiences, you didn't understand what was being presented; or you didn't care about what was being presented because of the mismatch; and/or you couldn't connect with what was being taught, so you turned off and became disengaged. Now, ponder what these two workshops would have been like if the facilitator had been speaking in a language that you did not understand fully. ■

■ Background

Multilingual learners, particularly recent immigrants, are frequently disadvantaged because their schooling experiences—whether little schooling, ineffective schooling, or excellent schooling—may be considerably different from U.S. educational contexts. For example, the K–12 curriculum varies from country to country, and depending on circumstances, some students may have experienced interrupted schooling, especially if they have been refugees or lived in remote areas. Further, multilingual learners, including both immigrants and students born in the United States, may lack the academic language and key vocabulary necessary to understand grade-level content information. However, not all multilingual learners lack background experiences and academic language. Some may have rich experiential backgrounds and sufficient academic language in their native tongue, but they do not know the equivalent English terms and thus are unable to connect with the concepts being taught.

Pearson eTextbook

Video Example 3.1

In this video, Dr. MaryEllen Vogt explains the Building Background component of the SIOP Model. And, yes, you'll see the use of transparencies (remember those?), but the concepts Dr. Vogt is discussing have stood the test of time. After watching the video, what questions do you have about the Building Background component? Jot them down and see if you find answers to them as you read this chapter.

https://www.youtube.com/watch?v=ytXeEFCTMbg

Effective teaching takes students, including multilingual learners, from where they are and leads them to higher levels of understanding. Effective SIOP teachers present information in a way that students can understand, bearing in mind their language development needs and possible gaps in their educational experiences. In SIOP lessons, new information is explicitly linked to students' backgrounds and experiences, and instructional scaffolding provides multilingual learners and other students with access to grade-level content concepts. This chapter focuses on Building Background, which is closely tied to Lesson Preparation and the teacher's assessment of students' knowledge of and experience with the topic at hand.

You will find three teachers' lessons in the Teaching Scenarios section. As you read about each of the Building Background features and then the Scenarios, reflect on the multilingual students you are teaching, have taught, or have observed. Which, if any, may have had a mismatch between their background knowledge and experiences and the content they were being taught? Which, if any, struggled with academic vocabulary?

SIOP®

SIOP® FEATURE 7:

Concepts Explicitly Linked to Students' Background Experiences

"
The Building Background component in SIOP helps teachers make connections to multilingual learners' cultural and linguistic experiences while accessing the content. At the same time, teachers are modeling a tenet of culturally responsive teaching as they adapt to the diversity of classrooms today.

Francheska Figueora, Ph.D
Postdoctoral Research Scholar, Arizona
"

It is a widely accepted notion among experts that a learner's "schemata"—knowledge of the world—provides a basis for understanding, learning, and remembering facts and ideas found in texts. Individuals with knowledge of a topic have better recall and are better able to elaborate on aspects of that topic than those who have limited knowledge of the subject (Kaefer, 2020). Background knowledge is essential for developing reading comprehension, and it predicts comprehension skill development throughout a student's schooling (Barnes, Ahmed, Barth, & Francis, 2015). Therefore, students benefit when teachers assess, develop, and use their background knowledge to create lessons that provide a path to reading and academic success, as has been described over the decades by the Science of Reading research studies (see Glossary) (Duke, Ward, & Pearson, 2021).

TESOL, an international professional organization for teachers of multilingual learners (www.tesol.org), has published the *6 Principles for the Exemplary Teaching of English Learners*, which provides a foundation for excellence in English language teaching (TESOL, 2018). The first principle is directly related to SIOP feature #7: Know Your Learners. The better we know each of our students, the more likely we are to provide appropriate instruction that taps into their prior knowledge and builds upon what they already know.

One of the most important things teachers of multilingual learners can do is to learn the pronunciation of all students' names within the first few days of a new school year, by teaching all students to learn to say each other's names. Esther Park, a talented and highly effective teacher of multilingual learners, suggests beginning this process with the oral reading of the book, *Teach Us Your Name*, by Huda Essa (2016). On the cover of the book, in the title, the word, *Tell* is crossed out, and the word *Teach* is inserted, gently emphasizing the importance of each child's name. On her website, www.mrspark.org/free, Esther shares her process, called Teach Us Your Name, by beginning with her own name, modeling its origin and pronunciation. You are free to download the other steps in this important and meaningful lesson from her website.

Culturally responsive teaching suggests that teachers also tap into and value students' backgrounds, experiences, languages, and cultures. Luis Moll (1994) contributed seminal research about the impact of students' backgrounds and experiences, with a focus on Hispanic students and students of color. Many of the children and youth he studied were schooled in middle-class, mostly White classrooms that were not necessarily designed to allow non-White and/or non-middle-class students to showcase what Moll refers to as their "funds of knowledge." He describes these *funds* as sources of knowledge and experience that are grounded in the students' homes and communities. These experiences are rich and they frequently include practical opportunities for practice, often provided by multi-generational family members.

However, instead of being viewed as assets, too often multilingual learners' backgrounds "are perceived as coming from homes with limited intellectual capital and possessing limited intellectual capability" (Tracy & Morrow, 2017, p. 164). Moll refers to this as a *deficit perspective*, and he argues in his writing that teachers must know their students well, all aspects of them, in order to recognize and use instructionally the assets that students bring to the classroom.

With asset-driven teaching, teachers use what students know and have experienced as conduits for language, literacy, and content learning. Examples include providing sentence frames (see Chapter 4) and Talk Moves (see Chapter 6), in English and in the home language, so multilingual learners have a chance to participate fully in a lesson.[1] Effective literacy and content instruction for multilingual learners includes focused attention on helping students forge connections with texts, topics, and classroom activities that build on their background knowledge, experiences, and past learning. Teachers make connections to students' home languages and cultures by linking them to the content concepts and key vocabulary they are teaching (Duke, Ward, & Pearson, 2021; Neuman, Kaefer, & Pinkham, 2014).

In addition, SIOP teachers develop multilingual learners' background knowledge by:

- Recognizing that students from culturally diverse backgrounds may struggle with comprehending a text or concept presented in class because their schemata do not match those of the culture for which the text was written. In the United States, most school reading materials, such as content area texts, rely on assumptions about students' prior knowledge, especially related to curriculum. Therefore, when introducing a new concept, SIOP teachers often use visuals (pictures, photos, and artifacts) to provide context and a reference point for multilingual learners. Students can share in their home languages the name for what a picture represents, and native English-speaking students can practice saying the words in their classmates' languages, thus validating one of the greatest assets of multilingual learners, their native languages. Then, the English word can be introduced and explained.

---

[1] There are several translation sites online, such as Google Translate and Word Translate. If possible, check with a speaker of the language to verify accuracy of the translation.

- Acknowledging that many multilingual learners emigrate from other countries and bring an array of experiences that are quite different from those of the majority. Multilingual learners' cultures may have an impact on their reading comprehension development, even for those who were born in the United States. Again, culturally responsive teaching is especially important. Consider this example: As a teacher reads, *"The barking dog ran toward the boy on the bike,"* do all students get a sense of fear or danger? Anderson (1994), a pioneer in schema theory research, questioned whether we can assume that students from every culture will have the same experience with, or emotional reaction to a story or article, or whether we should expect the same outcomes from them. For an example of cultural mismatch of schemata that occurred in a middle school's self-contained special education class with a small group of multilingual learners, see Figure 3.1.

FIGURE 3.1 **An Example of a Mismatched Schema**

A teacher was participating in a research study using instructional conversations, an approach that explicitly links students' background to text (Echevarría, 1995). He read a passage from a grade-level novel about a young man, Mike, who was reading a magazine (his favorite subscription) while riding a public bus home. He left the magazine on the bus and as he exited, he spoke a quick Italian greeting to some passengers whom he had overheard speaking Italian. The story explains that Mike had learned a few phrases from his brother-in-law who is Italian. After Mike got off the bus, he noticed the bus make its next stop with quite a commotion. He turned to see the Italians running toward him, angrily! After taking a circuitous route home, he got to his second-floor apartment, breathing a sigh of relief. He had no idea why the Italians were so angry with him, but he was relieved that he had lost them. A half-hour later he heard a noise outside, looked out the window, and saw the Italians coming into his building.

At this point, the teacher paused and asked the students how the Italians could possibly have found where Mike lived when the story made it clear that he had lost them. She expected that the students would remember that Mike had left the magazine, with his address label on it, on the bus. However, one student volunteered that the Italians found Mike by asking his brother-in-law. The teacher admitted that she found the answer to be "out in left field" and would ordinarily have tactfully asked someone else for the answer. But the nature of instructional conversations is to discuss ideas, drawing out students' thoughts and linking them to the text. So, the teacher asked the student to elaborate. He explained that in their community, which was 99% Latino with a small population of Samoans, if he needed to know where a certain Samoan person lived, he'd simply ask someone from the Samoan neighborhood.

The teacher admitted that she had learned an important lesson: The students' schemata were different from hers, yet just as valid. Moreover, she had nearly dismissed the student's excellent contribution because she was looking for a specific answer that matched her schemata, but none of the students in her group had any idea about magazine subscriptions and address labels. In that student's experience, if one wanted a magazine, one merely walked to the store and bought it.

This example clearly demonstrates that the student and teacher had very different ideas and assumptions about the characters and events in the story and a different "magazine" schema. Some of the differences might be attributed to cultural variation and a difference in home environments.

Teachers of multilingual learners need to be aware that what may appear to be poor comprehension and weak memory skills may in fact be students' lack of experience or background knowledge associated with or assumed by a message or a text. Further, what might look like a lack of prior knowledge may be a lack of accessibility in previous lessons that were taught. Background material may have been "covered," but it was not learned meaningfully. Through the SIOP Model, we urge teachers to activate students' background knowledge explicitly and provide links from their experiences to the key concepts. The interactive emphasis of the SIOP Model (see Chapter 6 for specific features) enables teachers to elicit students' prior knowledge and discuss ideas, issues, concepts, or vocabulary that are familiar and unfamiliar, to develop requisite background information.

An Important Distinction: Activating Prior Knowledge and Building Background

As you begin to write SIOP lessons with techniques to develop students' background knowledge, reflect on the following questions:

- What is meant by activating prior knowledge?
- What is meant by building background?
- How do they differ instructionally?

In the past, we have used the terms *activating prior knowledge* and *building background* somewhat synonymously. Yet, we now know there are some instructional differences that need to be considered when teaching multilingual learners. All students have prior knowledge gained from schooling and life experiences, and teachers can informally assess through a variety of activities what students know and can do, as well as determine any mismatches in schemata. Some familiar activities for activating students' prior knowledge include brainstorming, structured discussion, quick-writes, and research-validated activities, such as KWL: What do we know? What do we want to know? What have we learned? (Ogle, 1986).

Some other examples of prompts for activating prior knowledge at the beginning of a SIOP lesson include:

- *Try to picture . . . (topic) . . . . in your mind. What does it look like? Describe your mental picture with a partner. Are your pictures alike or different?*
- *In the last lesson, you learned about . . . (concept) . . . . What are three important things you remember about this topic? Share what you remember with your partner/small group.*
- *How many of you have seen a . . . . or have seen a picture of it? Describe what you saw to your partner/small group.*
- *Yesterday in social studies (or another subject), your content objective was . . . . Explain to your partner what you did to meet that objective. Your language objective was . . . . Explain to a new partner what you did to meet that objective.*

You will find additional prompts for activating students' prior knowledge in Mrs. Ornelas's lesson in the Teaching Scenarios section of this chapter.

Using prompts to elicit students' prior knowledge about a topic represents an important assessment opportunity. If you find that some multilingual learners have little or no prior knowledge about a content topic, brainstorming about it may not be helpful because the brainstormed terms, names, and places may be unfamiliar to

Pearson eTextbook

Video Example 3.2

In this video, you will watch a teacher activate middle school, multilingual students' background knowledge about bats. Note how she begins with a riddle, and then she moves back and forth between teacher-led and student-led discussion. How does she encourage students to identify not only what they know about bats, but also how they came to know the information?
https://www.youtube.com/watch?v=4Bnd-uzD1oE&ab_channel=TylerISDBilingual%2FESL

these students. For example, if students are from countries where there have been revolutions, they may know something about them, but not about the American Revolution. According to Kaefer (2020, p. S175), "activities meant to activate background knowledge are not always helpful. When students have incorrect background knowledge, activating it may actually inhibit comprehension, even if the prereading activities attempt to correct that misinformation." Therefore, it is prudent to circulate among students while they are participating in activities to activate prior knowledge, listening to their conversations to clarify misconceptions or misunderstandings. Doing so may fill in gaps in knowledge and help students connect what they do know with what is being taught. And when teachers' explanations are made more concrete with supplementary materials (e.g., photos, models, illustrations, etc.), students are more likely to make the appropriate connections. Essential questions, found in many textbooks and required in some districts, can be developed from a lesson's content and language objectives. They can assist students in thinking about and making connections to a lesson's topic, using their background knowledge, and experiences.

SIOP® | **SIOP® FEATURE 8:**

Links Explicitly Made between Past Learning and New Concepts

In addition to activating prior knowledge and building background for students, it is also important for teachers to make explicit connections between new content concepts and vocabulary, and those concepts and vocabulary that were taught in one or more previous lessons. Decades of research clearly shows that for learning to occur, new information must be integrated with knowledge students have previously acquired (Duke & Cartwright, 2021; Kaefer, 2020; Rumelhart, 1980). In other words, a SIOP teacher builds a bridge between previous lesson concepts and vocabulary, and the concepts and vocabulary in the current lesson.

Examples of ways to explicitly link students' past learning and new learning follow:

- Compare yesterday's objectives to today's content and language lesson objectives.
    - *Here are our objectives from yesterday* (read them aloud). *What did you learn while working on them? Tell a partner. Here are our content and language objectives for today's lesson. What do you think you'll be learning today that you didn't know yesterday? Share with your group.*
- Explicitly review the previous lesson's key concepts and vocabulary:
    - *Let's review the graphic organizer we used yesterday to help us compare and contrast acids and bases. With your partner, share two or more ways they are different, and two ways they are the same. You may look at your notes and graphic organizer if you need some help remembering. Be ready to share with the class.*

- Refer to a previous lesson's PowerPoint slides, a text that was read, or other visuals that are related to the topic. By preserving and explicitly referring to photos, word banks, illustrations, charts, maps, and graphic organizers, teachers have tools for helping students make critical connections between previous learning and new learning.

  ◆ *Here are the pictures we talked about yesterday. In your group (or with a partner), explain to each other how the pictures are related to the topic of . . . . Here are two pictures we will be talking about today. Using today's objectives and these pictures, predict what content and language concepts you think you will learn in today's lesson.*

- Incorporate Exit Tickets (Vogt, Echevarria, & Washam, 2015, p. 188) and/or Self-Assessment Rubrics (Vogt & Echevarria, 2022, p. 235) as opening and closing routines for lessons.

  ◆ Exit tickets can be sticky notes on which students record their responses to posted Outcome Sentences (see Chapter 9). An example of an Outcome Sentence is: *Something I still don't understand is _____.*

  ◆ The Self-Assessment Rubric provides an opportunity for students to review and assess the degree to which they have met or are making progress in meeting each of the content and language objectives. Young children can respond with 😊 (*I understand*), ? (*I still have a question*), and ☹ (*I don't understand*). Older students can respond by indicating the number on a rubric (3, 2, 1) that corresponds with their level of understanding (3 = I fully understand; 1 = I do not understand).

Explicit links to past learning are particularly important for multilingual learners who receive a great deal of input through the new language. An explicit, if brief, review of the content and academic vocabulary from prior lessons focuses on the key information that students should remember. This review is not intended to be remedial; instead, it is an important part of a SIOP lesson that is beneficial for all students.

SIOP® **SIOP® FEATURE 9:**

Key Vocabulary Emphasized (e.g., introduced, written, repeated, and highlighted for students to see)

Vocabulary development, critical for multilingual learners, is strongly related to academic achievement (August & Shanahan, 2006). Furthermore, for over 80 years we have known of the powerful relationship between vocabulary knowledge and reading comprehension (Duke, Ward, & Pearson, 2021; Stahl & Nagy, 2006). As an integral aspect of a learner's background knowledge, vocabulary plays a major role in language, literacy, and content teaching. Systematic and comprehensive vocabulary instruction, therefore, is particularly necessary for multilingual learners. Rigorous state standards require that students be able to read texts of increasing complexity that include sophisticated academic vocabulary across a variety of content areas. State content and literacy assessments rely on wide-ranging vocabulary knowledge, so multilingual learners' academic vocabulary instruction must be accelerated to meet rigorous content standards.

Vocabulary experts recommend a combination of plentiful and wide-ranging language experiences that include learning individual words, reading a wide variety of texts, employing word-learning strategies, and developing word consciousness, which is loosely defined as an appreciation of and interest in words. All are needed in a comprehensive vocabulary program for multilingual learners (Vogt, 2020). What follows are some interesting and important facts about vocabulary learning for native English speakers and multilingual learners:

- It has been estimated that students need to learn approximately 3000 new words per year, if they are to complete high school with sufficient vocabulary knowledge (Hiebert, Goodwin, & Cervetti, 2017).

- Older students need to know about 2000 high-frequency words to understand about 85% of most texts (Blachowicz & Fisher, 2000, p. 514). However, there is a paradox: Less-frequent words that students need to know are attained mostly through reading, but many multilingual learners do not know enough words to be able to read well (Carr, Shearer, & Vogt, 2019).

- Over the years, literacy researchers have found that students need multiple exposures to new words and terms. The number of encounters necessary for vocabulary to enter long-term memory ranges from 8–10 to 35 or more, depending on who is making the recommendation. The numbers differ because of the variability of students in any given study, so rather than aiming for a particular number, be sure to provide multiple exposures and opportunities for students to read, write, and orally use the key vocabulary you are teaching. Exposures to instructional words via multimedia-enhanced texts have been found to lessen the gap in vocabulary knowledge between multilingual learners and non-multilingual learners (Silverman & Hines, 2009).

- Not surprisingly, multilingual learners and struggling readers need even more exposures to newly learned vocabulary. Again, depending on the students, they may need as many as 20 or more encounters, if we take retention beyond the immediate posttest as the criteria for learning (Waring & Nation, 2004). The more exposures, the more likely it is that the words will be learned and long-term retention will be greater. In all, students must learn tens of thousands of words, so they need multiple and meaningful language and vocabulary practice opportunities with a variety of instructional approaches, and ongoing encouragement.

Teachers frequently ask how many words they should be teaching during a lesson or unit. Some studies suggest that a limited number of words should be taught per lesson or per week, and those words should be key words in the text the students will read. Others recommend teaching multilingual learners the meanings of basic words, such as those that native English speakers already know. Beck, McKeown, and Kucan (2002), have developed a three-tier scheme for teaching vocabulary words that is widely used in U.S. schools. Within the tiers, teachers identify basic or common words (Tier 1); words that are used across the curriculum and multiple meaning words (Tier 2); and content specific vocabulary (Tier 3). Identifying vocabulary for instruction within the three tiers helps teachers select words important to a topic, thus limiting words to a manageable number.

What is clear is that students must know many more words than teachers can possibly teach. Therefore, in SIOP lessons, teachers purposefully select words that are critical for understanding texts and content concepts, and then provide a variety of ways for students to learn, remember, and use those words. When planning vocabulary lessons, a SIOP teacher returns to the lesson objectives and considers the following questions about which and how many words to teach:

- What words or terms do students need to know to meet the content objectives of this lesson?
  - *The topic of this lesson is westward expansion. In the chapter, the following words are in italics: "transcontinental, expansion, relocation, reservation, treaty, and disease." I will concentrate on "transcontinental" and "expansion" for the first lesson because we will be using these terms throughout the unit. I will teach "reservation, relocation, treaty, and disease" tomorrow, while reviewing the three words taught today. All of these are content words necessary for understanding the next few lessons.*

- What words or terms do students need to know to meet the language objectives of this lesson?
  - *In the chapter, the author provides information in a sequential manner. I need to make sure that all students know the word "sequence," so that is part of the language objective. I also need to informally assess the degree to which students recognize the academic words that are in the chapter, including "originally, after a while, subsequently, meanwhile, another." There are other sequence words that are included ("first, then, afterwards, finally"), but most of the students know these. I'll double-check to ensure my students with lower English proficiency can identify these words.*

If teachers have too many words to teach in a lesson, students, especially multilingual learners, will become lost because of so many definitions. Therefore, fewer words at a deeper level are better than a lot of words that are lightly touched upon.

Academic Vocabulary

The words and terms about westward expansion, discussed in the previous two examples, are *academic vocabulary*. A subset of academic language, as described in Chapter 1, academic vocabulary involves the use of more sophisticated sentence structures and forms of expression than are found in everyday conversation. Academic vocabulary includes words and phrases that are used widely in the academic disciplines. Deep knowledge of the academic vocabulary of the content subjects taught in schools is necessary for students' overall academic success. In SIOP lessons, academic vocabulary is an important category for developing language objectives, and it involves more than just defining words. Generating new words (e.g., with word families and base words/roots/affixes), using vocabulary strategies, and working on

Pearson eTextbook

Video Example 3.3

In this video, Dr. Deborah Short discusses "Shades of Meaning," a vocabulary activity that investigates synonyms in terms that vary in intensity or depth. It can be used with nouns, verbs, adjectives, and adverbs.

https://www.bing.com/videos/search?q=Deborah+short+Shades+of+Meaning&&view=detail&mid=246BADDAE82B00CE7A89246BADDAE82B00CE7A89&&FORM=VRDGAR&ru=%2Fvideos%2Fsearch%3Fq%3DDeborah%2Bshort%2BShades%2Bof%2BMeaning%26go%3DSearch%26qs%3Dds%26form%3DQBVR

word choice in writing tasks are also examples of language development that can serve as sources of language objectives.

For better understanding of the varied types of academic vocabulary that teachers need to focus on, especially for multilingual learners, we have classified them into three groups. Each should be considered during the planning of SIOP lessons when deciding vocabulary to teach and when writing language objectives.

1. **Content Vocabulary—Subject-Specific and Technical Terms:** These are the key words and terms associated with a particular topic being taught (e.g., the words provided in the example of westward expansion; or a language arts lesson on parts of speech: *nouns, verbs, adjectives, adverbs*). These words and phrases are found primarily in the informational and expository texts that students read, and frequently they are highlighted or bolded in the students' textbooks. More important than listing words for students to learn is conveying the importance of knowing particular words related to a given topic.

2. **General Academic Vocabulary—Cross-Curricular Terms/Process & Function:** These are words and phrases students must learn because they are used in all academic disciplines, such as *sequence* in the preceding example. Often, these words are not explicitly taught; yet they are the ones that frequently trip up multilingual learners and struggling readers. This category also includes words with multiple meanings. These words may have both a social language and an academic language use, such as *a dining room table* and *table with information*. Or the word's meanings may differ according to academic subject, such as the distinction among legislative *power*, electrical *power*, and logarithmic *power*.

   a. Cross-curricular terms: Most of the general academic vocabulary terms can be used across the curriculum. They describe relationships (*friendship, conflict, encounter*) and actions (*describe, argue, measure*). They help illustrate information (*chart, model, structure, symbol*), and are used to speculate (*predict, infer*) and conclude (*effect, result, conclusion, drawback*). They are expressions we usually only see in academic texts (*In addition to . . . , Moreover . . . , Subsequently . . .*), and terms we might use in casual conversation, as well as in academic discussions (*situation, circumstances, source, evidence, modify*).

   b. Language processes and functions: Another subset of the general academic terms indicates what we want to do with language—the kind of information we convey or receive, and the tasks we engage in that require language to accomplish. Some multilingual learners may know the terms in their home languages, but they may not know the English equivalents. Examples of some of these language process and function words and phrases that are common in classroom discourse are *discuss, skim, scan, question, argue, describe, compare, explain, list, debate, classify, support your answer, provide examples, summarize, outline, give an opinion*, and so forth. Additional examples are words and phrases that indicate transitions and connections between thoughts, such as *therefore, in conclusion, whereas, moreover*, and *furthermore*, and words that indicate sequence such as *first, then, next, finally*, and *at last*. This category also includes the verbs that students encounter in state tests and during other assessments, such as *determine, identify, select, critique, define, match, estimate*, and *contrast*.

Pearson eTextbook

Video Example 3.4

As you watch this video and listen to Amy Washam discussing signal words, think of cross-curricular terms that you regularly use in your teaching. Do they need to be taught and practiced by students? Probably so. Add to the word lists that Amy Washam describes and create your own for your classroom.

https://www.bing.com/videos/search?q=YouTube+Building+Background+SIOP&docid=608037725812321137&mid=9D26093B88AD295E35E49D26093B88AD295E35E4&view=detail&FORM=VIRE

3. **Word Parts: Roots and Affixes:** These include word parts that enable students to learn new vocabulary, primarily based upon English morphology. By grade 6, students have acquired thousands of words that include roots and affixes. There is no way that multilingual learners can realistically learn all these words through instruction and memorization. Therefore, all teachers must help students understand that many English words are formed with roots, to which are attached prefixes and suffixes (affixes).

For example, if a science teacher is teaching photosynthesis, they can help students learn the meaning of *photosynthesis* by introducing the meaning of the root, *photo-* (light). By comparing the words *photosynthesis, photocopy, photograph, photography, photoelectron, photo-finish*, and *photogenic*, students can see how these English words are related by both structure (prefix + root + suffix) and meaning. The root *photo* means "light," thus providing a clue to a word's meaning if it has this root. "In fact, in English and other languages with Latin and Greek roots, words that are related by structure are also frequently related by meaning" (Bear, Invernizzi, Templeton, & Johnston, 2019).

■ Application to Your Classroom: Building Background

Effective activities that activate prior knowledge, build students' background knowledge, and develop academic vocabulary include the following:

- **Use What You Know.** With partners or small groups, a SIOP teacher asks students to solve a problem related to a content topic, using prior knowledge and experiences. For example, in a middle school lesson on water conservation, the teacher tasked the students with proposing multiple ways to desalinate ocean water, prior to researching the problem on the Internet or in a text. All students, including multilingual learners, were able to contribute because the meanings of words related to conservation of water and desalinization had been taught, supported with visuals, modeled, and reviewed. In addition, home language (L1) support was provided with key terms and phrases in the students' L1. Classroom posters included English and other languages for the technical vocabulary. (Always check translations for accuracy when using Internet translation tools with multilingual students.)

- **Pair-Share-Chart** (Vogt, Echevarría, & Washam, 2015). This activity begins with a structured partner-share about a familiar topic, as determined by the SIOP teacher. After 2–3 minutes, students share their conversations with the whole class. As students share what they know or think they know about the topic, the teacher records their thoughts on chart paper. Using the information that is charted, the teacher introduces a new concept and helps students make connections between what they already know and the new topic. The charted information is saved and added to during the lesson or unit, and the teacher continues to help forge connections with new information.

- **Pretest with a Partner** (Vogt & Echevarria, 2022, p. 48). This activity is helpful for students in grades 2–12 and is appropriate for any subject area. The purpose of Pretest with a Partner is to allow students the opportunity at the beginning of a lesson or unit to preview the concepts and vocabulary that will be assessed at the conclusion of that lesson or unit. One pretest and a pencil are distributed to each pair of students. The pretest, created by the SIOP teachers, should be similar or identical to the posttest that will be administered later. The partners pass the pretest and pencil back and forth to one another. They read a question aloud, discuss possible answers, come to consensus, and write an answer on the pretest. This activity provides an opportunity for students to activate prior knowledge and share background information, while the teacher circulates to assess what students know, noting gaps and misinformation.

- **Word Sorts** (Bear et al., 2019; Helman, Bear, Templeton, & Invernizzi, 2012). During a word sort, students categorize previously introduced words or phrases into groups predetermined by the teacher. Words or phrases can be typed on a sheet of paper (46-point type on the computer works well), many sorts are available through the *Words their Way* books (citations above), or they can be downloaded from several websites by doing a search for "words for word sorts." The teacher or students cut the paper into word strips and then sort the words according to meaning or similarities in structure. For example, in a SIOP history classroom, a variety of words related to the American Revolution are listed in mixed order on a sheet of paper. After the teacher has orally read the words and students have chorally read them, the students sort them according to structure (endings: *-tion, -sion, -tation*) (see Artifact 3.1). This activity can be differentiated by having some students also determine the verb forms for words (e.g., *revolt*, *tax*, *participate*, *solve*, *frustrate*, *represent*). Then they can compare those words to the other words that are nouns (e.g., *nation, passion, mission, vision, plantation*).

  Other examples of word sorts involve words and phrases related to the content concepts being taught (see Artifact 3.2). Adding the "oddball" column in word sorts encourages students to think about both examples and non-examples during the classification activity.

- **Contextualizing Key Vocabulary.** SIOP teachers peruse the material to be learned and select several key terms that are critical to understanding the lesson's most important concepts. The teacher introduces the terms at the outset of the lesson, systematically defining them, showing a picture for each, as appropriate, and showing how the term is used within the context of a sentence. For additional scaffolding, embed definitions within a sentence, such as:

  - *Sara, an athletic teen <u>who is healthy, strong, and active</u>, won the race.*

  - *The migratory birds, <u>those that fly in a group from one place to another in autumn</u>, have stayed near our lake for several days before flying on.*

  - *Amphibians, such as <u>frogs and salamanders that have smooth, scale-less skin that must stay wet</u>, are most active at night when there is less evaporation of water.*

ARTIFACT 3.1 Word Sorts (American Revolution—Example 1)

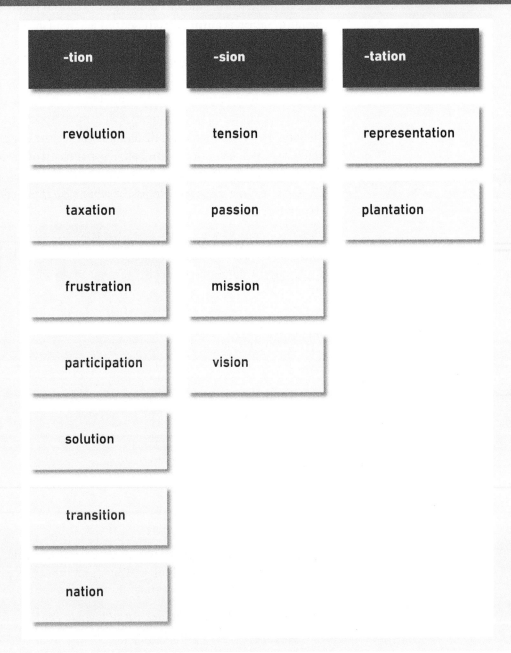

-tion	-sion	-tation
revolution	tension	representation
taxation	passion	plantation
frustration	mission	
participation	vision	
solution		
transition		
nation		

- **Vocabulary Self-Collection Strategy (VSS)** (Ruddell, 2007). Following the reading of a content text, students self-select several words that are essential to understanding key concepts. Words may be selected by individuals, partners, or small groups, and they are eventually shared with and discussed by the entire class. The VSS words may be entered into a word study notebook, and students may be asked to demonstrate their knowledge of these words through written or oral activities. Or teachers may wish to use Google Apps for Education (GAFE), a free suite of apps that include *Docs, Sheets*, and *Forms*, which provide an easy way to create surveys and collect information from students. *Forms* can be used with VSS to expedite the process for students when collecting their VSS words.

The teacher creates a form for the text being read and shares it on the class website. For homework, students enter the words and terms they selected (VSS), and the information is automatically sent to a spreadsheet, where it is sorted into columns corresponding to those on the teacher's survey form. Research on VSS indicates that when students are shown how to identify key content vocabulary, they become adept at selecting and learning words they need to know, and, given opportunities to practice VSS, comprehension of the text improves (Shearer, Ruddell, & Vogt, 2001). This approach is most appropriate for multilingual students with high-intermediate and advanced English proficiency, for native English speakers, and for those in the upper elementary and secondary grades.

ARTIFACT 3.2   Word Sorts: American Revolution—Example 2

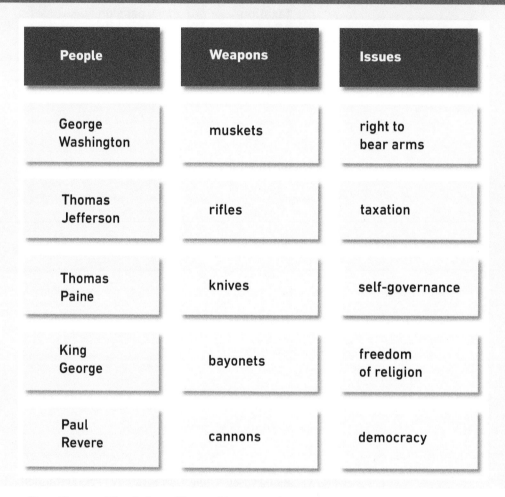

People	Weapons	Issues
George Washington	muskets	right to bear arms
Thomas Jefferson	rifles	taxation
Thomas Paine	knives	self-governance
King George	bayonets	freedom of religion
Paul Revere	cannons	democracy

- **Four Corners Vocabulary Charts** (Vogt & Echevarría, 2008). These charts provide more context and "clues" than typical word walls because they include an illustration, definition, and sentence for each vocabulary word (see Artifact 3.3). For academic words that are challenging or impossible to illustrate (e.g., *discuss* or *summarize*), simply take a photo of your students during a discussion or when summarizing, and insert the photo on the chart as a reminder of the word's meaning. Including multilingual learners' home languages for the key vocabulary word not only helps their comprehension and retention of the word but also validates students' home languages (L1).

Justin Cowart/NASA,
JPL-Caltech, UCLA,
MPS, DLR, IDA

1. **Picture or Illustration**	3. **Sentence with Embedded Definition**
	There are currently five known dwarf planets, including Pluto, which was formerly called a planet until 2006.
2. **Definition**	4. **Word or Term**
A celestial body that orbits the sun and is not a moon; has enough mass to assume a nearly round shape, but is not large enough to disturb other objects from its orbit	English: Dwarf Planet Spanish: planetas enanos Vietnamese: hành tinh lùn Arabic: كواكب قزمة

■ Differentiating for Multilevel Classes

Many of the teaching ideas in the previous section provide ways to differentiate instruction while developing students' background and vocabulary knowledge. The following idea is geared specifically to differentiating instruction according to multi-lingual learners' levels of English proficiency. (If you need to refresh your memory of the stages of language acquisition, please see the Glossary, where they are described.)

- **Differentiated Cue Tips.** Cue Tips (Vogt & Echevarria, 2022, p. 8) are an effective way to provide multilingual learners (and other students) with words related to language functions, such as *comparing/contrasting, determining cause/effect, sequencing events, summarizing, drawing conclusions, making generalizations,* etc. Rothenberg and Fisher (2007) suggest that these words can be differentiated for varied levels of language proficiency (see Figure 3.2). One caution: Remember to

FIGURE 3.2   Examples of Differentiated Cue Tips for Sequencing

Entering and Beginning (Levels 1 and 2)	Developing and Expanding (Levels 3 and 4)	Bridging and Reaching (Levels 5 and 6)
first	while	prior to
second	before	previously
third	now	since
next	after	eventually
later	finally	subsequently
then	in the past	furthermore

adjust differentiated Cue Tips as multilingual learners gain more English proficiency. A goal for all students is for them to learn to use grade-level terminology, including more sophisticated vocabulary.

■ The Lesson

Short Story: *Two Were Left* by Hugh B. Cave (Sixth Grade)

Three teachers in an urban middle school with a large population of multilingual learners are teaching a suspenseful short story. Although it was written in 1942, it remains an exciting, suspenseful, and intriguing story for upper elementary and middle school students. Each of the teachers' self-contained classes includes multilingual learners with a variety of levels of English proficiency. The classes are heterogeneously mixed with native English speakers and multilingual learners, and all students are reading at a variety of reading levels. This story is part of a larger literature unit focusing on stories and poetry, with the theme of "Decisions and Their Consequences."

The short story, *Two Were Left*, begins with a description of a boy named Noni and his devoted husky, Nimuk, stranded on a floating ice island in the sea. It is not evident from the text exactly how they got there, but it is implied that the boy and dog had been with village hunters, and the ice they were on had broken away from the others. Noni and Nimuk had been there for an undetermined time, and both were exhausted, hungry, and increasingly wary of each other. Noni's leg had been hurt at a previous time, and he was wearing a simple brace made of a harness and iron strips. The boy decided to make a weapon in case the starving Nimuk decided to attack him. In Noni's village, it was not uncommon to use dogs for food in times of hunger. The story continues as Noni works on making a knife, and boy and dog become increasingly weak. The suspense builds as Noni considers the consequences of attacking his dog. Eventually, he decides he can't possibly kill his beloved dog, and he flings the crude knife away from them. It lands point first in the ice some distance away. Nimuk growls in a frightening way, but eventually licks Noni's face and falls, exhausted, by his owner. Sadly, boy and dog cuddle together, unable to save themselves any longer. Not much later, an airplane pilot sees two figures on the ice island and swoops in for a closer look. He settles his plane on the ice and saves an unconscious Noni and his dog, Nimuk. What had caught the pilot's attention was the reflection of a quivering knife stuck in the ice.

The following standards guided the development of the three lessons.

Key Ideas and Details

1. Read closely to determine what the text says and make logical inferences about its meaning, cite specific evidence from the text, in writing or when speaking, to support conclusions.

2. Analyze the development of central ideas or themes in a text; summarize the main ideas and supporting details.

3. Analyze how and why individuals, events, and ideas develop and interact over the course of a text.

Note: The story, *Two Were Left*, can be found on the Internet by searching the title and author.

■ Teaching Scenarios

The teachers have prepared their own lesson plans for teaching the short story, *Two Were Left* by Hugh B. Cave. Their individual instructional approaches and SIOP ratings follow.

Miss Saunders

Miss Saunders began her lesson by reviewing with her students the lesson's content objectives (connecting the day's story to the theme of "Decisions and Consequences") and language objectives (reading a story; locating and defining vocabulary words) that were written on chart paper. Next, she asked the table groups to turn over the four photos that were face down on their tables. Each was a photo of Alaska: One was of a glacier, another was of the tundra, the third was of the sea with large, broken pieces of ice floating in it, and the fourth was of an Inuit village. Miss Saunders asked her students to do a Think-Pair-Share and consider what they observed in the photos, what they had questions about, and what they thought life must be like for the people living in the village. She then described her experiences on a vacation to Alaska and showed some of her photos.

Miss Saunders next introduced several vocabulary words that were taken from the story. She mentioned that understanding these words would help students better understand the story. She wrote the following on the board: *Noni, Nimuk, ice island, momentarily, intentions, suspiciously, unconscious.* She explained the first two words were the characters' names in the story. Miss Saunders then distributed copies of the two-page story and asked students to find the remaining vocabulary words in the story. Once they found the words, students were asked to highlight them, and, with a partner, try to define the words using contextual clues. Then, the students, in pairs, were expected to match their informal definitions with those found in the dictionary and make corrections, as needed.

When everyone was finished with the vocabulary assignment, Miss Saunders and the class went over the vocabulary words' definitions. She then asked the students to read the story silently. The evening's homework assignment was to create a "storyboard" of *Two Were Left*. Miss Saunders reminded the class of what the word *sequence* means and noted that events in a story generally follow in an order or sequence. She said, "You remember when we talked about this, right?" Her students nodded affirmatively. She then asked the students what the first event was in *Two Were Left*. A student responded that Noni and Nimuk were on a piece of ice that broke off from a larger piece. "That's right, Louis!" She then distributed a large piece of white construction paper to each student with the instructions to fold it into eighths and draw the first event in the first box in the upper left-hand corner. After a few moments, Miss Saunders asked the class to take the construction paper home and to continue making the storyboard sequence by drawing pictures that depicted seven other important events in the story. She quickly went over the day's objectives, with mixed feelings about her students' progress toward meeting them, and the bell rang shortly thereafter.

Check your understanding: On the SIOP form in Figure 3.3, rate Miss Saunders's lesson for each of the Building Background features.

FIGURE 3.3	Building Background Component of the SIOP® Model: Miss Saunders's Lesson

4	3	2	1	0	N/A
7. **Concepts explicitly linked** to students' background experiences		**Concepts loosely linked** to students' background experiences		**Concepts not explicitly linked** to students' background experiences	

4	3	2	1	0
8. **Links explicitly made** between past learning and new concepts		**Few links made** between past learning and new concepts		**No links made** between past learning and new concepts

4	3	2	1	0
9. **Key vocabulary emphasized** (e.g., introduced, written, repeated, and highlighted for students to see)		**Key vocabulary** introduced, but not emphasized		**Key vocabulary** not introduced or emphasized

Mrs. Ornelas

Mrs. Ornelas began the story, *Two Were Left*, by asking her students to close their eyes for a moment and put their heads down on their desks. She then turned down the lights and turned on a recording of heavy winds blowing. Then, she said in a slow and careful cadence: "Imagine for a moment . . . you are in the Arctic, farther north than Alaska, where the winds blow almost continuously. You live here with your family in a small village. During the winter, it snows every day until there are so many feet of snow piled high that all walking paths are solid ice. The only time there is any natural light is around lunch time and it's only a glimmer; then it becomes black as night once again. In the summer, the sun never sets so you need to put heavy cloth or tarps on window openings so you can sleep. This is your home, and you share it with your parents and best friend, your dog. You are happy that you have family, good friends, and enough food. However, one day, everything changes. You and your dog become separated from the other hunters in your village, and you end up alone on a chunk of ice, floating with only your dog. Think about what you might do in this situation to save yourself."

Mrs. Ornelas then turned off the recording and raised the lights. She turned on the document reader so the students could see the brief paragraph that she had just read to them. She read aloud the directions that followed the paragraph: "With your group members, jot down the ways that your lives are different from this boy's life. Think of as many different things as you can. Now, how are your lives like this boy's life?" Mrs. Ornelas asked each student to draw a Venn diagram graphic organizer (this was familiar to them) on a piece of paper, and as they talked among themselves, they filled out the organizer. The class then briefly reported out what they had discussed.

Mrs. Ornelas then read aloud and explained the lesson's content objectives (comparing and contrasting their lives with the main character's life; predicting events in the story) and language objectives (finding examples of foreshadowing in the story; reading the story while confirming or disconfirming predictions).

Following the objectives, Mrs. Ornelas displayed on the smartboard a map of the Arctic area, so all students had an idea of the setting for the story they were going to read. Mrs. Ornelas pointed to Alaska and northern Canada, and asked students if they had ever read, seen, or heard anything (other than what she had just read) about this part of the world. One girl said, "I remember when we were studying climate change in Science and we looked at photos of melting glaciers. That's what I thought of when you started telling us your story." Mrs. Ornelas displayed on the whiteboard several large photos of glaciers and said, "You mean these pictures, Esmeralda? You're right. The setting for today's story is very much like what we talked about in science, so think about these photos as you begin reading about the setting in today's story."

Mrs. Ornelas next displayed on the smartboard the following academic vocabulary words: *predicting* and *foreshadowing* because these words are critical to understanding the story deeply. She reviewed the meaning of *predicting* because this was a familiar process while reading stories. She then introduced *foreshadowing* by pointing to the word on the board and asking what *fore* made them think of. Someone said "Before?" Another said, "Doesn't it have something to do with golf?" She wrote on the board *foreground* and *forethought*, and asked students to try to figure out the words' meanings, with *fore* meaning "before or in front of;" then she asked them to have a partner conversation about whether the three words might be related because of the prefix *fore*. Mrs. Ornelas walked around the room listening while her students grappled with their task. She then asked the students to share with their partner what *shadowing* might mean. Nearly everyone knew what a shadow was, but they were struggling with the term *foreshadowing*. Mrs. Ornelas asked the students if, when she was reading the brief vignette at the beginning of class, they had formed any ideas of what today's story might be about. Many students' hands flew into the air. After taking a few responses, Mrs. Ornelas told the class, "I used foreshadowing to help you think about the story we're going to read before we actually read it. You're now already making some predictions based on the hints I provided, right? What are they?"

After taking some responses, Mrs. Ornelas told the students that in the story, *Two Were Left*, the author would also give some hints about what was going to happen later in the story. She said, "These hints are called *foreshadowing*. Throughout our reading, we will make predictions and as we continue, we will either confirm or disconfirm our predictions, sometimes based on the foreshadowing the author provides." Mrs. Ornelas reminded students that they had worked with confirming and disconfirming predictions before in other stories, and she reminded them about how to use the strategy. She also told them that the author's use of foreshadowing would help them predict what would happen in the story. She encouraged them to see if they could find examples of *foreshadowing* and to underline them while they read the story together. Mrs. Ornelas then distributed copies of *Two Were Left* and the class engaged in a familiar group reading activity called the Directed Reading-Thinking Activity (DR-TA) (see Chapter 5 for more details).

Mrs. Ornelas began by asking the students to cover with another piece of paper everything but the title, *Two Were Left*. She then asked, "With a title like *Two Were Left*, what do you think this story is going to be about?" The students laughed and said, "About a boy and a dog!" Mrs. Ornelas directed the students to uncover and read the next brief paragraph that provided more information. She then said, "Okay . . . now you have new information. What do you think is going to happen next? Why do you think so?" And off they went, uncovering more and more of the story while reading, predicting, discussing, confirming, and disconfirming their ideas, until Noni and Nimuk were finally rescued. Most students could find some foreshadowing, starting with the title, and some even identified the quivering knife that eventually signaled the pilot. The story concluded with a brief discussion of the unit's theme (Decisions and Consequences) and Noni's decision to throw away the knife. After reviewing the content and language objectives, students and teacher alike agreed that their objectives had been met.

The next day, for a follow-up vocabulary activity, the students in pairs or triads selected their favorite part of *Two Were Left* and typed it into a word cloud box on their tablets. The most frequent words from the story were emphasized on the word clouds. Later, the students discussed how important these words were to the story and they compared their word clouds (see Artifact 3.4).

Check your understanding: On the SIOP form in Figure 3.4 on the following page, rate Mrs. Ornelas's lesson for each of the Building Background features.

Mr. Engelhart

Mr. Engelhart began his lesson by telling his students the objectives: *You will learn some new words from the story we are going to read and complete a story plot graphic organizer.* He then distributed a worksheet that had vocabulary word definitions

ARTIFACT 3.4 **Word Cloud from *Two Were Left***

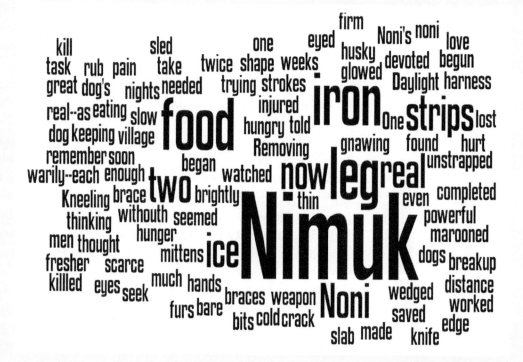

FIGURE 3.4 **Building Background Component of the SIOP® Model: Mrs. Ornelas's Lesson**

4	3	2	1	0	N/A
7. **Concepts explicitly linked** to students' background experiences		**Concepts loosely linked** to students' background experiences		**Concepts not explicitly linked** to students' background experiences	

4	3	2	1	0
8. **Links explicitly made** between past learning and new concepts		**Few links made** between past learning and new concepts		**No links made** between past learning and new concepts

4	3	2	1	0
9. **Key vocabulary emphasized** (e.g., introduced, written, repeated, and highlighted for students to see)		**Key vocabulary** introduced, but not emphasized		**Key vocabulary** not introduced or emphasized

and sentences from the day's story, *Two Were Left*. He gave each student eight index cards so that they could copy the information from the worksheet, one vocabulary word per card so that students would have eight flash cards for practice. The words on the worksheet included the following: *marooned, warily, labored, inventions, thrust, aroused, feebly, quivering*.

The following are examples of four of the vocabulary words, definitions, and sentences that the students copied onto their index cards from the words on the worksheet.

Marooned: to place or leave alone without hope of escape; "And, now, the two, completely alone, *marooned* on the ice, eyed each other warily."

Warily: careful and watchful for danger; "And, now, the two, completely alone, marooned on the ice, eyed each other *warily*."

Labored: to move with great effort; "He could see hunger and suffering in the dog's *labored* breathing and awkward movements."

Intentions: a planned way of acting; "Closer Nimuk came, aware of Noni's *intentions*."

After the students had copied the words, definitions, and sentences onto their eight vocabulary cards, Mr. Engelhart distributed copies of the *Two Were Left* story. He then asked for volunteers to take turns reading the story aloud. He directed students to underline the sentences where the eight vocabulary words were found. When the story was completed, Mr. Engelhart asked students how they liked the story, and all said it was good. A discussion followed on what the students liked about the story, and why. A graphic organizer for the story's plot was assigned as homework. He collected the vocabulary cards for checking and concluded the lesson, satisfied that his goals had been met.

Check your understanding: On the SIOP form in Figure 3.5, rate Mr. Engelhart's lesson for each of the Building Background features.

FIGURE 3.5	Building Background Component of the SIOP® Model: Mr. Engelhart's Lesson

4	3	2	1	0	N/A
7. **Concepts explicitly linked** to students' background experiences		**Concepts loosely linked** to students' background experiences		**Concepts not explicitly linked** to students' background experiences	

4	3	2	1	0
8. **Links explicitly made** between past learning and new concepts		**Few links made** between past learning and new concepts		**No links made** between past learning and new concepts

4	3	2	1	0
9. **Key vocabulary emphasized** (e.g., introduced, written, repeated, and highlighted for students to see)		**Key vocabulary** introduced, but not emphasized		**Key vocabulary** not introduced or emphasized

■ Discussion of Lessons

Look back at your rating form and think about the reasons you scored the lessons as you did. What evidence is in the scenarios? Read on to see our analyses.

7. *Concepts Explicitly Linked to Students' Background Experiences*

Miss Saunders: 3

Mrs. Ornelas: 4

Mr. Engelhart: 0

- **Miss Saunders's** lesson received a "3" for this feature. She chose to develop students' background knowledge for the story, *Two Were Left*, by showing them photographs of Alaska that were similar to the setting of the story. The Think-Pair-Share activity was a good one to choose so that students could share their impressions of the photos with each other and the class. While Miss Saunders's vacation photos and stories were interesting, they didn't directly relate to the setting of the story the students were going to read. To earn a "4" rating, Miss Saunders might have shown a video clip from the Internet and, depending on the location of their school, asked students to contrast their living conditions (such as southern California or Florida) to the story's setting. This may have been more meaningful. Also, since the main characters are a boy and a dog, bringing students' feelings about their pets (or others' pets they know) could have prepared them for the emotional aspect of this story.

- **Mrs. Ornelas's** lesson received a "4" for this feature. She spent about 15 minutes activating her students' prior knowledge and building their background about the setting of the story, *Two Were Left*. Because the setting and the situation were so very different from the students' experiences, the time was well spent. It's not just the actual setting that is so different (the Arctic area), but it's also the culture of the people in the story, where dogs aren't pets, but rather commodities that can mean the difference between life and death. (For this story, it might be interesting to mention to students that keeping dogs as pets might also be a cultural difference for other people, including some cultures where dogs are food, and in others, where neither dogs nor cats are pets.) In the lesson, the students' predictions and ability to grapple with a challenging literary device like foreshadowing were enhanced by the visualization exercise (with students' eyes closed and the wind blowing) and the comparison/contrast of their lives to Noni's via the Venn diagram. Also, the DR-TA is a powerful activity that enables teachers to really understand where students' predictions and ideas are coming from while they're reading. Students use their background experiences and knowledge throughout a DR-TA to make and then confirm/disconfirm their predictions while developing comprehension of the story. Note that confirming predictions requires citing text evidence.

- **Mr. Engelhart's** lesson received a "0" for this lesson. He didn't attempt to activate students' background knowledge or build background information related to the story's content concepts or vocabulary. He did state his goals, but these were not written as content and language objectives because the verb *learn* isn't measurable or observable, and "completing a graphic organizer" doesn't indicate the cognitive work the students will be engaged in. When objectives are well written, they provide information that begins to activate students' prior knowledge and build background knowledge.

8. *Links Explicitly Made between Past Learning and New Concepts*

Miss Saunders: 1

Mrs. Ornelas: 3

Mr. Engelhart: 0

- **Miss Saunders's** lesson received a "1" for this feature. She made only one reference to the students' past learning, and it was toward the end of the lesson. When she asked her students if they recalled when they talked about story sequence, the students gamely replied with a unison nod. Because understanding story sequence was critically important for the homework assignment, explicitly reviewing (and if necessary, re-teaching) the steps taught previously (e.g., introduction, rising action, falling action, climax, conclusion; or beginning, event 1, event 2, . . . conclusion) was very important. Multilingual learners would have benefitted from working together with the teacher and/or a small group to identify the story sequence prior to creating the storyboard. There will also most likely be confusion when doing the homework if the number of boxes (8) doesn't match the number of story events they identify at home.

- **Mrs. Ornelas's** lesson received a "3" for this feature. She was prepared to make an explicit link between the students' previous learning about the Arctic area and the story they were going to read in this lesson. She had the photos from the Science lesson ready to display on the interactive whiteboard so students could make the connections. For this feature to have been a "4," Mrs. Ornelas would have needed to be more explicit in reminding students of how readers make predictions, and more importantly, how they could confirm and disconfirm predictions while reading. This was especially important because Mrs. Ornelas was connecting making predictions to the author's use of foreshadowing in the story. This might have been confusing to some multilingual learners and struggling readers who still needed more practice in understanding predicting as a metacognitive strategy as a metacognitive strategy (see Chapter 5 for more information about metacognitive strategies).

- **Mr. Engelhart's** lesson received a "0" for this feature because it included nothing to connect past learning to today's lesson in terms of content concepts, vocabulary, or language. Although students may have completed vocabulary cards previously, there was no attempt to connect former vocabulary to today's new words.

9. *Key Vocabulary Emphasized*

Miss Saunders: 2

Mrs. Ornelas: 4

Mr. Engelhart: 1

- **Miss Saunders's** lesson received a "2" for this feature. She selected some interesting and perhaps tricky words from the story for her students to work with. However, the time that was spent on finding informal and formal definitions of these words was not necessarily going to enable the multilingual learners (and other students) to better understand this story. That is, they were not critical to the story's outcome, especially character names, which are easily learned. It would have been more relevant to this story and the objectives (sequencing the events in the story) if she had spent the time reviewing the academic vocabulary related to sequencing, perhaps with signal words the students could have used on their storyboards (*first, next, then, finally, in the end*, and so forth). She then could have identified and talked about some of the more interesting and challenging words in the story, working with the students to use the context clues for the informal definitions.

- **Mrs. Ornelas's** lesson received a "4" for this feature. She chose to teach explicitly two academic vocabulary words that she felt were essential to fully comprehending the story. One is an important literary term related to author's craft (*foreshadowing*), and the other is a critical strategy for reading (*predicting*). Notice how she introduced these concepts with the visualizing activity. She then divided the word *foreshadowing* into two parts (*fore* + *shadowing*) before writing *foreground* and *forethought* on the board, leading students to generalize the meanings of the three words. There are many other interesting words in this story, and on the following day, the students worked with them when creating their word cloud designs. Because the word clouds emphasized the most frequent words in the passages the students chose, they could readily compare them with the interesting, but less frequently used words.

- **Mr. Engelhart's** lesson received a "1" for this feature. He provided his students with a list of vocabulary words, definitions, and sentences from the story they read, but the students' assignment to copy them onto the flash cards didn't have a clear purpose and it's unlikely the words carried much meaning for them. Making connections to the words would have been difficult to do since several were somewhat unique to this story, and thus challenging for grade 6 students. One exposure to these words would not ensure retention of either the words or their meanings. Mr. Engelhart's students may have enjoyed listening to and reading the story, but his lesson missed many opportunities to develop his students' content and language knowledge.

Final Points

As you reflect on this chapter and the impact of connecting students' background knowledge and learning experiences to the content being taught, and the importance of explicitly teaching academic vocabulary, consider the following main points:

- Explicitly linking a lesson's key content and language concepts to students' background knowledge and experiences enables them to forge connections between what they know and what they are learning.
- In addition, explicitly connecting past content and language learning to a new lesson's content and language concepts assists students in understanding that their previous learning connects to the lesson they will have today.
- Multilingual learners may have a difficult time with the academic vocabulary of various disciplines. Three types of academic vocabulary discussed in this chapter are: (1) content vocabulary: subject specific and technical terms; (2) general academic: cross-curricular terms/process & function; and (3) word parts: roots and affixes.
- Teaching ideas, such as using visuals to provide concrete meanings, Four Corners Vocabulary charts, differentiated signal words, and word clouds, engage students in interactive practice with words that promote academic vocabulary development for multilingual learners.

Discussion Questions

1. In reflecting on the content and language objectives at the beginning of the chapter, are you able to:
   a. Identify techniques for connecting students' prior knowledge, personal experiences, and past learning to a lesson's content concepts?
   b. Identify ways to develop background knowledge for students who have a mismatch between what they know and have experienced, and the content concepts found in a lesson?
   c. Select academic vocabulary for a SIOP lesson using words from these three groups: content vocabulary, general academic vocabulary, word parts: roots and affixes?
   d. As part of a lesson plan, write several prompts for activating students' prior knowledge about the lesson's content concepts?

2. In culturally responsive SIOP classrooms, teachers validate their students' backgrounds, experiences, cultures, and native languages. Reflect on what you have just read in this chapter and in Chapter 1 that demonstrates this type of sensitivity and respect for native English speaking and multilingual students. Which SIOP features that you have learned about to this point focus on teaching to students' assets? Be specific.

3. Think about a joke or cartoon that you didn't understand, such as from a late-show monologue or a political cartoon. Why was it confusing or not amusing? What information would you have needed for it to make sense? What are the implications for teaching content to all students, including multilingual learners?

4. Add to the SIOP lesson plan you have started. Think about how you will activate students' prior knowledge and build background. What explicit connections to past learning can you make? What are your key academic vocabulary words, and how will you teach them? Choose some techniques or activities for the lesson.

■ Pearson eTextbook Application Videos

The purpose of the Pearson eTextbook Application Videos is to provide you with an opportunity to observe and reflect on SIOP teaching and learning practices. There are multilingual students in each of the classrooms with varying levels of English proficiency. The teachers you will observe are at different levels of SIOP implementation, from second-year SIOPers to veterans. As you observe the lessons they have created, focus on the students and the lesson objectives, keeping in mind that becoming a high-implementing SIOP teacher takes time, practice, and support to refine teaching practices. We are grateful to each of these SIOP educators for welcoming us into their classrooms, and for their dedication to SIOP, their multilingual learners, and other students.

Pearson eTextbook Application
Video Example 3.1
SIOP Lesson: Grades 10–12;
Nutritional Choices for
Healthy Eating

Comprehensible Input

CONTENT OBJECTIVES

This chapter will help you to . . .

- Identify three techniques for presenting content information that enhance comprehension for multilingual learners.
- Name elements necessary for providing clear directions for completing academic tasks.

LANGUAGE OBJECTIVES

This chapter will help you to . . .

- Discuss modifications to teacher speech that can increase student comprehension.
- As part of a lesson plan, write several techniques to make academic language accessible for multilingual learners.

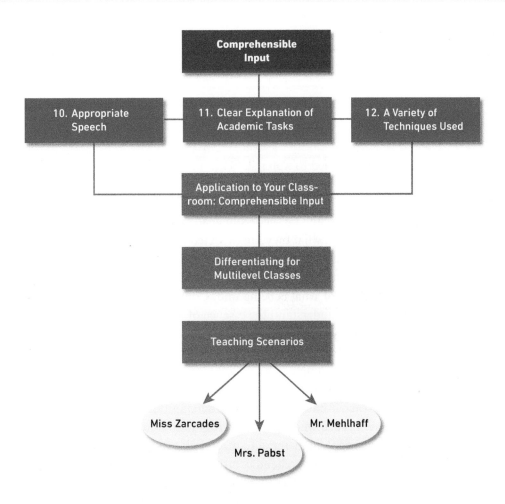

As you look through SIOP's features, you will see that they reflect what we know about effective instruction for all students—English speakers and multilingual learners alike. However, some SIOP features are essential for making instruction meaningful for multilingual learners (August & Shanahan, 2006, 2010). The features of the Comprehensible Input component make SIOP instruction different from "just good teaching." Making a message understandable for students is referred to as *comprehensible input* (Krashen, 1985). A culturally responsive SIOP teacher considers the unique linguistic needs of multilingual learners and modifies teaching accordingly. Regardless of classroom setting—whether a designated English language development/ESL lesson, a lesson in a dual language program, or a content area lesson—using comprehensible input techniques is necessary for making subject matter accessible and also for developing second language proficiency. ■

■ Background

> "Teaching students in a Dual Immersion program makes the use of comprehensible input non-negotiable. Many of our students come in with little to no experience in the target language. Ensuring comprehensible input techniques are used during our lessons is the key that allows students to unlock the content."
>
> —Angie Medina, Dual Immersion Literacy Teacher, California

Have you ever tried to water ski without a boat? Impossible, right? No matter how badly you want to ski, it can't happen without a boat. A teacher using the features of Comprehensible Input functions as the boat because multilingual learners, no matter how motivated, can't be successful academically if they don't understand what the teacher is saying, what they are expected to do, or how to accomplish academic tasks. Humans don't "pick up" language solely from exposure. For example, many of us have been around speakers of Spanish, Vietnamese, or Farsi, but we understand little, if anything of what is being said. Comprehensible input techniques are necessary for students to understand the essence of what is being said or presented. A SIOP teacher makes verbal communication more understandable by consciously using supports that are matched to students' levels of English proficiency.

Mandarin Chinese has a concise way of expressing the sentiments of many multilingual learners. *Ting bu dong* literally means *I hear but I don't understand.* Students hear the teacher but don't always understand the message. Specialized teaching techniques are needed when working with multilingual learners who are expected to master rigorous content material to meet high academic standards in a language they do not yet speak or comprehend completely. Acquiring a new language takes time and is facilitated by many "clues"—by speech that is geared to individual proficiency levels and by techniques that are used consistently in daily teaching routines.

Comprehensible input entails much more than simply showing pictures as visual clues during a lesson. While visuals are important, SIOP teachers make a conscious effort to make the lesson accessible through a wider range of supports. Communication is made more understandable through speech that is appropriate to students' proficiency levels. Teachers enunciate and speak more slowly, but in a natural way, for students who are beginning English speakers. More repetition may be needed for beginners and, as students gain more proficiency in English, teachers adjust their speech levels to match the students' needs. Teachers will increase students' understanding by using appropriate speech coupled with a variety of techniques that will make the content clear.

These techniques are particularly important as students aim to meet the high academic standards in each grade level. Across grade levels, students are expected to comprehend information presented orally and to express their understanding in a variety of ways, such as recounting key ideas and details, and paraphrasing or summarizing the information presented. The way information is presented orally will have a significant impact on the degree to which multilingual learners will be able to achieve these expectations.

In this chapter, we will discuss a number of ways to make teacher talk comprehensible to students so that lessons are understandable for them. In the scenarios that follow later in the chapter, you will see examples of third-grade teachers who use comprehensible input techniques with varying degrees of effectiveness when teaching an economics lesson.

SIOP® **SIOP® FEATURE 10:**

Speech Appropriate for Students' Proficiency Levels

For this feature, speech refers to (1) rate and enunciation and (2) complexity of language. The first aspect addresses *how* the teacher speaks and the second aspect refers to *what* is said, such as level of vocabulary used, complexity of sentence structure, and use of idioms.

Students who are at the beginning levels of language proficiency benefit from teachers who slow down their rate of speech, use pauses, and enunciate clearly while speaking. Sometimes it is easy to rush through information or instructions because of the time pressure of teaching by the clock or because you want the pace to move along so that students don't lose interest. For multilingual learners, a brisk speaking pace is difficult to follow, especially if care isn't taken to enunciate clearly. When each syllable of each word isn't pronounced properly but naturally, words get slurred together. Students have difficulty understanding, especially if there is other noise around the room. As students become more comfortable with the language and acquire higher levels of proficiency, a slower rate isn't as necessary. In fact, for advanced and transitional students, teachers should use a rate of speech that is normal for a regular classroom. Effective SIOP teachers adjust their rate of speech and enunciation to their students' levels of English proficiency.

Pearson eTextbook

Video Example 4.3

Watch this video of a third grade social studies lesson. Notice how teacher Deb Painter enunciates in a natural but effective way for multilingual students. Think about other techniques she uses and select one you might use with your students.

Likewise, students will respond according to their proficiency level. The following example illustrates the variation in responses that may be expected when students at six different levels of English proficiency are asked to describe the setting in a story. The levels reflect the WIDA performance definitions (https://wida.wisc.edu/sites/default/files/resource/WIDA-ELD-Standards-Framework-2020.pdf).

- Entering: "Cold day."
- Emerging: "Day is cold and there snow."
- Developing: "The day is cold and there is lots of snow."
- Expanding: "The day is very cold and heavy snow is falling."
- Bridging: "It is a cold, winter day and it is snowing more heavily than usual."
- Reaching: "The unusually heavy snow on the day the story takes place causes a number of problems for the characters."

While still providing multilingual learners with exposure to grade-level language, SIOP teachers carefully monitor the vocabulary and sentence structure they use in order to match the students' proficiency levels, especially with students at beginning levels of English proficiency. Teachers simplify sentence structures by using subject–verb–object format with beginning students and reduce or eliminate embedded clauses and passive voice. For example, in a social studies lesson, the teacher may use the following complex sentence structure that is difficult to understand:

> "English colonists brought free enterprise, the idea of owning and controlling their own businesses, from England but because England's leaders wanted the colonies' financial support, laws were passed to limit the free enterprise system in the colonies."

It might be better stated as,

> "English colonists brought the idea of owning and controlling their own businesses from England. This idea is called free enterprise. England's leaders wanted the colonies' financial support, so the laws were passed to limit the free enterprise system in the colonies."

Reducing the complexity of language is effective for beginners but should be used judiciously. Oversimplification of spoken or written language eliminates exposure to a variety of sentence constructions and language forms (Crossley et al., 2012), especially the complex text called for in most state standards.

Finally, using idioms may create confusion for multilingual learners, especially beginners who are trying to make sense of a new language, since these common sayings do not have exact translations. Some common idioms include "below the belt" for unfair; "put one's foot down" meaning to be firm; "see eye to eye" for agreeing; "get the hang of" meaning to become familiar with; and "get a person's back up" indicating to make someone annoyed.

Multilingual learners are better served when teachers use language that is straightforward, clear, and accompanied by a visual representation that contributes to comprehensible input and helps students to understand the lesson's content. It is

"

Comprehensible Input benefits students by inviting all students to access grade-level learning while they continue to build on their social and academic language skills.

Dr. Nicole Teyachea McNeil, Senior Learning Specialist, Arizona

"

difficult for students to learn if a teacher's delivery of information is too fast, too complex, or inarticulate.

SIOP®

SIOP® FEATURE 11:

Clear Explanation of Academic Tasks

Pearson eTextbook
Video Example 4.4
Listen to Professional Learning Coordinator Andrea Rients explain the importance of comprehensible input in teaching. Consider videotaping your own lesson as Andrea did. The information gained is invaluable!

Multilingual learners at all levels (and native English speakers) perform better in academic situations when the teacher gives clear instructions for assignments and activities. In their discussion of working memory, which is central to learning, Bailey and Pransky (2014) point out that when students are confused about the lesson's topic or the activity's purpose, they either disengage or frantically try to make connections with what they already know. In this process, they are wasting valuable working memory processing space. So, when the teacher isn't clear, there is more at stake than just taking up time repeating unclear instructions.

Effective teachers present instructions in a step-by-step manner, preferably using modeling or demonstrating the task for students. Ideally, a finished product such as a business letter, a research report, or a graphic organizer is shown to students so that they know what the task entails. Oral directions should always be accompanied by written ones so multilingual learners can refer back to them at a later point in time as they complete the assignment or task. Students with auditory processing difficulties also require clear, straightforward instructions written for them to see.

According to case study data collected from multilingual learners in sheltered instruction classes (Echevarría, 1998), middle school students were asked what their teachers do that makes learning easier or more difficult. The following are student comments from the study that you would likely hear from students today:

- "She doesn't explain it too good. I don't understand the words she's saying because I don't even know what they mean."
- "She talks too fast. I don't understand the directions."
- "He talks too fast. Not patient."
- "It helps when he comes close to my desk and explains stuff in the order that I have to do it."

These students' comments illustrate the importance of providing a clear explanation of teachers' expectations for lessons, including delineating the steps of academic tasks. This point cannot be overstated. In our observations of classes, many "behavior problems" are often the result of students not being sure about what they are supposed to do. A cursory oral explanation of an assignment can leave many students unsure about how to get started. The teacher, frustrated with all the chatter, scolds students, urging them to get to work. However, students do not know *how* to get to work and often do not know how to articulate that fact to the teacher. Bottom line: Making expectations clear to students contributes to an effective and efficient classroom.

As you can see in Artifact 4.1, the teacher provided clear, comprehensible instructions for how to complete the activity. First, the graphic helps students

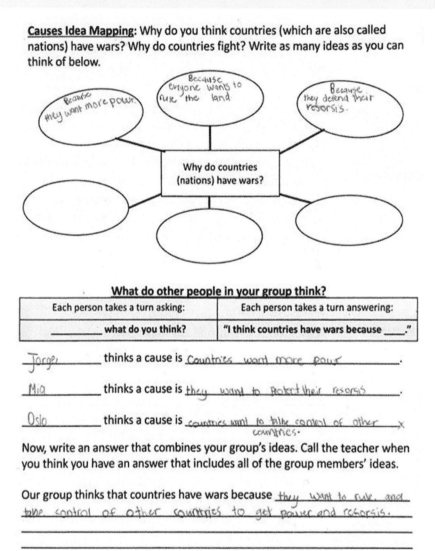

Causes Idea Mapping: Why do you think countries (which are also called nations) have wars? Why do countries fight? Write as many ideas as you can think of below.

[Idea map with central box "Why do countries (nations) have wars?" connected to ovals containing handwritten text: "Because they want more power", "Because everyone wants to rule the land", "Because they defend their resorsis." and three empty ovals.]

What do other people in your group think?

Each person takes a turn asking:	Each person takes a turn answering:
_____ what do you think?	"I think countries have wars because ____."

Jorge thinks a cause is _Countries want more powr_ .

Mia thinks a cause is _they want to Protect their resorsis_ .

Oslo thinks a cause is _countries want to take control of other_ x
countries.

Now, write an answer that combines your group's ideas. Call the teacher when you think you have an answer that includes all of the group members' ideas.

Our group thinks that countries have wars because _they want to rule, and_
take control of other countries to get power and resorsis.
_____
_____
_____

understand that they need to write several ideas. Next, the sentence frame facilitates discussion as each student took a turn answering. Finally, students combined their ideas into a single answer with the sentence starter that was provided. These clear instructions, including visuals and sentence frames, enable multilingual learners to participate in activities with grade-level material.

The same is true for inquiry lessons, but with some modifications. Teachers sometimes misinterpret having a clear explanation of the lesson's expectations as being incompatible with an inquiry approach when in fact all lessons, inquiry or not, have expected outcomes for students that require some explanation. While explaining each part of the lesson may give away the inquiry process, usually teacher directions at the beginning of the lesson are brief and are limited to introducing materials and describing the task. Recall the last student quote above that "It helps when he . . . explains stuff in the order that I have to do it." Inquiry lessons need to provide enough language support so that multilingual learners aren't disadvantaged. Students usually work in cooperative groups, which provides an opportunity for students less proficient in English to be helped by their peers. However, multilingual learners likely will become frustrated if they don't understand what their peers are talking about or exploring. Some initial explanation and review of vocabulary is necessary, as well as teacher supervision of groups during different phases of the inquiry lesson, so that clarification can be provided, as needed.

Typically, SIOP teachers go over every aspect of the lesson, showing visuals with each step, if needed. For example, in a reading class, the teacher wants students to complete a graphic organizer with information about the characters, setting, problem, resolution of the problem, and theme of a piece of literature the class has been reading. Using this information, students will write a summary. Figure 4.1 contrasts clear directions and step-by-step instruction with unclear directions and unguided instruction. Which column more closely applies to the way you present directions to your students?

The teacher described in the left column uses a written agenda so that if students don't understand, weren't paying attention, or simply forgot, they have the

---

FIGURE 4.1   **Clear Explanation Contrasted with Unclear Explanation**

Clear Explanation

The teacher writes on the board:
1. Review your notes from yesterday.
2. Use your notes to answer the five questions on the board.
3. Write your answers on your whiteboard.
4. Complete the graphic organizer.

After giving students a few minutes to review their notes and discuss with a partner (more fluent speaker paired with less-proficient; additional information is added as needed), the teacher gives them a set amount of time to answer the first of five questions. She gives them a 30-second signal and then asks the class to "show me" their whiteboards where they have written their answers. She can see from a glance at their boards who got it right and who needs assistance or clarification. This process continues until all five questions are answered. The teacher shows a copy of a graphic organizer on the document reader and completes the first part with the class. Then students take the information from the five questions and use it to complete the graphic organizer. Students are allowed to work with a partner on completing the graphic organizer, while the teacher circulates and observes to make sure that both partners have mastered the content. She asks questions and prompts to ensure understanding.

Unclear Explanation

The teacher gives an oral review of what was discussed in the story the previous day. Then she asks a series of questions about the characters, the story's problem, and how the problem in the story was resolved. Several students raised their hands to answer the questions. The teacher talks about the theme and the importance of recognizing a story's theme.

Then the teacher hands out a graphic organizer and tells the students that they have the remainder of the period to complete it using the story and the information they have talked about.

written steps to guide them and keep them on task. Depending on the age and proficiency levels of the group, the teacher may need to model one or more of the steps. By the time students complete the graphic organizer, they have received feedback on the accuracy of the information they will use and have seen a model of a partially completed graphic organizer. Likewise, using information in the graphic organizer to write a summary is modeled for them. This type of teaching facilitates writing of an accurate, complete summary.

In contrast, the teacher in the right column gives information and instructions orally, and only a handful of students participate in the whole-class, teacher-dominated Q&A. When it is time to complete the graphic organizer, most likely many students are unsure about where to begin or what information is pertinent. A critical academic task, writing a summary, is left to be done as homework. Undoubtedly, few students will be able to complete the assignment because the teacher gave the students no model, guidelines, or practice before asking them to do the work independently.

As a check of how clear your task explanations are, you might write out the directions you would give your students for completing an academic task and ask a colleague to follow them. Better yet, record yourself giving directions and watch/listen to see how comprehensible the explanation was. It can be eye opening!

In the area of writing, students need to be shown very specifically—and have opportunities to practice what has been clearly explained—the essential elements of good writing. Showing students what constitutes good writing, explaining it clearly, and providing opportunities to practice will result in improved writing (Boswell, 2015; Graham, 2019; Linares, 2018). For intermediate and advanced students, focused lessons on "voice" or "word choice" may be appropriate, while beginning students benefit from models of complete sentences using adjectives or forming a question.

Pearson eTextbook

Video Example 4.5

Watch this video as Dr. Jana Echevarria describes an interactive writing technique. Note how modeling and other comprehensible input techniques are essential. Consider using interactive writing with your students.

https://www.youtube.com/watch?v=O2y8YoVeMVI

SIOP®

SIOP® FEATURE 12:

A Variety of Techniques Used to Make Content Concepts Clear

Effective SIOP teachers make content concepts clear and understandable for multilingual learners using a variety of techniques. We have observed some teachers who teach the same way for multilingual learners as they do for native English speakers, but rely on pictures to illustrate words for multilingual learners. While visual supports are effective and necessary, multilingual learners benefit from a wider range of supports to make the material understandable. The actual techniques a teacher uses should match the task. For example, when explicitly teaching academic vocabulary words in depth, the teacher might use examples and non-examples, video clips, and other concrete representations of the words (Baker et al., 2014; TESOL, 2018; Zucker, et al., 2021). High-quality SIOP lessons offer students a variety of ways for making the content accessible to them. Some techniques include:

- Use gestures, body language, visuals, and objects to accompany speech. For example, in a lesson on informational text the teacher points to a poster that illustrates text features and says, "There are a number of features used in informational text that help the reader. One is (holds up 1 finger) headings (points to the heading). Headings tell us what the text will be about. What is the heading for this text? (Class reads together.) Another feature is captions (points to the caption below an illustration). Captions give information about a photo or illustration. There are also bold words (points to bold words). These words are important for understanding the text." In this case, the teacher used gestures and visuals to make the oral explanation more understandable for students. SIOP teachers also include visuals, as seen in Artifact 4.2, Vocabulary Dice Game, on worksheets to make the oral explanation clear. The teacher describes the steps of the game, pointing to each step on the game board worksheet. Since the steps and icons are part of the game board, they are visible for student reference and eliminate confusion.

- Model a process, task, or assignment. As an example, when a teacher discusses the process of water changing to ice she doesn't only rely on an explanation of the process. She uses several techniques to augment the information presented verbally. First, she shows or draws a model of the process as it is being described. When students are later instructed to record conditions under which the change

ARTIFACT 4.2   **Vocabulary Dice Game**

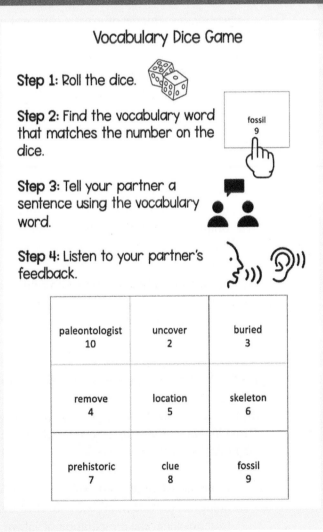

in ice from a solid to a liquid is accelerated or slowed, the teacher shows an observation sheet that is divided into three columns on a document reader, interactive whiteboard, or chart paper. The teacher shows several pictures (e.g., lamp, sun, and refrigerator) that depict various conditions such as heat and cold. She demonstrates the first condition, heat, with a picture of the sun and models how students will describe the condition in the first column (e.g., heats). Then the teacher asks students what effect the sun, or heat, has on ice. The students answer and in the second column the teacher records how the ice changed (e.g., melted), and in the third column indicates if the process was accelerated or slowed by the condition (e.g., accelerated). Providing a model as the students are taken through the task verbally eliminates ambiguity and gives the message in more than one way. Students are then able to complete the rest of the worksheet. Furthermore, in this case, there is a written example students can consult if they have questions later.

The importance of modeling isn't limited to multilingual learners. One time the SIOP authors were asked to film a description of "use-tomorrow" activities for teachers. The request was easy enough to fulfill but we were unsure of what it entailed: a demonstration, a PowerPoint presentation of the activity, an oral description? After a slew of emails, we were sent a short video clip that modeled what was needed. Simple! Once we saw a model of exactly what was expected, the task was easy.

- Preview material for optimal learning. When students' attention is focused on the specific material they will be responsible for learning in the lesson, they are able to prepare themselves for the information that is coming, making it more comprehensible for them. Further, they have an opportunity to access prior knowledge and make the connections that they will need to understand the lesson. Previews can occur through book walks, anticipation guides, brief video clips, and the like.

- Allow students alternative forms for expressing their understanding of information and concepts. Often multilingual learners have learned the lesson's information but have difficulty expressing their understanding in English, either orally or in writing. Hands-on and kinesthetic activities can be used to reinforce the concepts and information presented, with a reduced linguistic demand on these students. In a kindergarten class, children might mime the stages of plant growth: squatting with arms around knees for a seed, extending one arm for a sprout, standing with a foot extended and arm extended for root and seedling, standing with both arms up and feet apart for plant.

■ Application to Your Classroom: Comprehensible Input

In the section that follows, you will find ideas you can apply to your own classroom. Teaching ideas and activities should be planned with a purpose in mind. That said, identify how each of the ideas are connected to SIOP's Features 10–12.

- **Capitalize on technology.** SIOP teachers use the video and audio aspects of technology to provide many ways for their multilingual learners to learn. It's fairly easy to supplement the presentation of information with images, videos (e.g., YouTube and PBS Kids), slides (e.g., PowerPoint, Google Slides, Haiku Deck), and the innumerable websites and apps available to make a lesson's content more understandable for multilingual learners. However, make sure that students aren't overwhelmed by the tools used. When using slides, consider limiting a presentation to fewer than a dozen slides. This limitation causes teachers to be precise in their language use and not risk overwhelming students with too much information. For example, in a lesson on buoyancy, a teacher wanted to make sure students were engaged and had access to the content. The first slide read, *Sink vs. Float: What is buoyancy?* On that initial slide, in addition to the title, the teacher inserted images that clearly represented those concepts. The subsequent slide revealed the objectives of the lesson. Following the objectives were slides with important vocabulary accompanied by related images. For example, for the word *predict*, he added clipart images of a fortuneteller and the weather forecast. The final slides described the tasks the students must complete. The teacher decided to limit the presentation to eight slides so students wouldn't be frustrated by too much information. In addition to the clipart images, the teacher searched YouTube and found several videos showing experiments with buoyancy. He also added an animation showing the equation for density and a problem being solved. This presentation format ensured an accessible amount of information was shown in a comprehensible manner.

- **Use graphic organizers effectively.** New ideas and concepts presented in a new language can be overwhelming for multilingual learners. Graphic organizers take the information, vocabulary, or concept and make it more understandable by showing the key points graphically. SIOP teachers make sure that the graphic organizer they use matches the task and leads to attaining the lesson's objectives. To paraphrase the saying "a picture is worth a thousand words," a graphic organizer can capture and simplify a teacher's many potentially confusing words.

  Some graphic organizers may be simple, such as a problem/solution chart or a web with vocabulary definitions. For older students, graphic organizers may be more elaborate. For example, prior to giving a presentation that requires argumentation or an argumentative writing assignment, a scaffold might be to have students complete the following Argumentation Map, which provides an overview of the argumentation process:

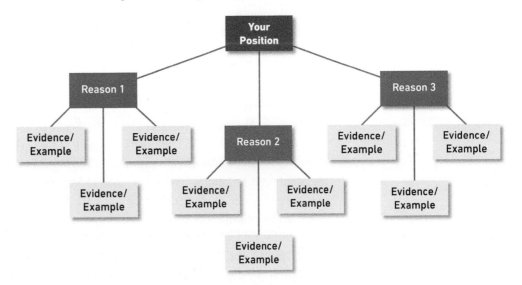

See Vogt and Echevarría (2022) *99 Ideas and Activities for Teaching English Learners with the SIOP® Model* (2e) for many SIOP-appropriate graphic organizers.

- **Provide repetition**. It is well established that repetition strengthens connections in the brain (Jensen & McConchie, 2020) and repetition of vocabulary and language structures helps with language acquisition (Rogers, 2019). Multilingual learners are learning through a new language, and in order for input to be comprehensible, they need multiple exposures to words, concepts, and skills. Frequency of encounters has been found to be important in vocabulary learning (Webb & Nation, 2017); however, excessive practice of a single word or skill can become monotonous and defeat the purpose.

  SIOP teachers provide context when using repetition to teach vocabulary and language structures. For example, the math activity called *Every Student Gets a Chance* (Vogt & Echevarria, 2022) begins with the teacher writing the words and their corresponding numbers for the following: million (1,000,000), thousand (1000), hundred (100), tens (10), and ones (1) on the board. The teacher reads each word, pointing to its number, then asks a volunteer to read each word as the teacher points to the number. Next, a second volunteer reads aloud the same information, and so it continues so that each student who feels comfortable can choose to read the information aloud. Once students are able to recognize and repeat the words used in place value and reading large numbers, write a large number such as 182,672,824. Show students how to identify numbers in sets of three, e.g., 182 (one hundred and eighty-two *million*), 672 (six hundred seventy-two *thousand*), 824 (eight *hundred* twenty-four). The same process is followed by asking for a volunteer to read the number; ask a second volunteer to read the same number, and so on. Finally, break students into small groups and continue practicing in small groups with a variety of large numbers. The teacher circulates to provide support.

  By contextualizing the words and providing practice, the vocabulary terms are more meaningful and the repetition is more likely to result in language retention.

- **Explicitly teach cognates.** SIOP teachers make a habit of looking for and pointing out cognates to their multilingual learners throughout all their lessons. Cognates provide many multilingual students with a unique linguistic resource to use in making sense of words. Cognates are words with "ancestral roots" that are similar in appearance and meaning (G.E. García & Godina, 2017), and they occur in English and other ancestrally related languages, such as Spanish–English, French–English, Italian–English, Romanian–English, German–English, and Greek–English (Garcia, et al., 2020). Some examples of cognates include *colony* (English)/*colonia* (Spanish), *diagram* (English)/*diagrama* (Spanish), and *invention* (English)/*invención* (Spanish) (Vogt and Echevarría, 2022). Multilingual students can be taught to use cognates to improve their spelling, writing, and reading (Garcia, et al., 2020). Cognates are found across content areas and can be used to enhance comprehension. For example, using "calculate the mass/volume ratio" (*calcular* in Spanish) may be easier for some students to understand than "figure out the mass/volume ratio." Explicitly teach cognates to students, point out the cognates you encounter in teaching materials, write cognate pairs for students to see, have students keep a cognate notebook to record when they find a cognate in their independent reading, engage students in activities such as circling all the cognates in a reading passage, and the like.

- **Employ flipped lessons.** A flipped classroom offers potential for multilingual learners since content is learned at home, typically through a device, and allows students to stop, pause, and replay as needed. SIOP teachers use flipped lessons so that their multilingual learners have the opportunity to work at their own pace, reviewing content as many times as is necessary. Students can write down questions at home and bring them to class. In-class time is spent with individual and group work; students often work at their own pace. For example, in a secondary science lesson, students view at home the assigned video presentation on the concept of periodic motion and relate it to the movement of a pendulum. In a Google document, students answer the following questions covered in the video:

1. What is a pendulum?
2. What is simple harmonic motion?
3. Where is velocity the greatest in a swinging pendulum?
4. Where is the restoring force the greatest in a swinging pendulum?
5. What is angular frequency?

When students return to class, they participate in a jigsaw activity with each of five groups discussing one of the questions. Next, each group presents its answer to the class. As each group does their presentation, other students clarify the answer they wrote at home with the information presented. Finally, students complete a worksheet that allows them to apply the information learned.

Pearson eTextbook

Video Example 4.6
Watch this video for additional teaching ideas, and how to adapt them for remote learning. Identify comprehensible input techniques that you might employ.
https://www.youtube.com/watch?v=zMQCUs9EGcM

Differentiating for Multilevel Classes

> When I'm teaching a SIOP lesson, comprehensible input provides students with multiple opportunities to access language while ensuring my output is comprehensible, at times through my actions. Furthermore, I can add cultural relevancy and increase comprehensibility through translanguaging. Students use of L1 provides access to L2.
>
> Dr. Francheska Figueroa, Postdoctoral Research Scholar, AZ

We know that most classes with multilingual learners have students with multiple proficiency levels. Some students have stronger listening skills than writing skills or stronger reading skills than speaking ones. Many multilingual learners adapt to the classroom environment by pretending they understand, when, in fact, they may not. SIOP teachers use frequent checks to gauge how well students comprehend material and to discern how speech may need to be differentiated based on student proficiency.

- **Use home language.** In SIOP classes, all the students' linguistic resources are welcomed into the classroom and are used purposefully. When the teacher and/ or peers use multilingual learners' home language strategically during lessons, it provides the comprehensible input they need to gain conceptual knowledge. Even monolingual educators can take steps to acknowledge multilingual students' *translanguaging* (Garcia, 2020), or the ability of multilingual learners to use all their linguistic and cognitive resources to make sense of the academic content being delivered in a new language. They may switch between English and Spanish (or another language) while speaking, discussing topics, and completing tasks. Translanguaging should be acknowledged as a resource to be used while students are learning and practicing English.

- **Offer choice.** When students explore content information on their own, let them make choices for themselves. Bookmark a variety of websites with a range of text and visual options, and, if possible, include some in the native languages of your students. Work with the school librarian to create a temporary classroom library with books at different reading levels on the topic being studied. Provide a picture glossary for key terms that the students are likely to encounter when exploring the topic.

- **Record step-by-step instructions.** These instructions can be used for completing a task or project, using an electronic tablet application. Multilingual learners, individually or in pairs, listen to the instructions as many times as needed, using the speech speed feature to slow the output to their level of understanding. You may also generate questions for partners to ask each other, such as "Which pages do we read before completing the graphic organizer?" or "Are the words we use in the graphic organizer found in the reading passage or somewhere else?" In this way, students listen to the instructions again with a focus on specific questions whose answers will help them complete the task. Multilingual learners may be unaware that the headings or bolded words in a text are those used to complete a graphic organizer.

- **Address social-emotional needs.** Using the techniques discussed in this chapter to differentiate teaching for levels of proficiency communicates to multilingual learners that they are important and are as equally valued as their English-speaking peers. Remember that you make a huge contribution to your students' attitude toward school. Particularly in the early grades, students' experiences form their impressions about school and learning. At any age, students in a positive environment are more likely to experience enhanced learning, memory, and self-esteem (Jensen & McConchie, 2020).

- **Permit differentiated responses.** Allow students to provide differentiated responses to questions and assignments. For oral responses, provide sentence frames for those students who need them. With written assignments, beginning speakers may require partially completed information (e.g., Cloze procedure), while advanced speakers may only need a word bank, or other support, to complete the assignment. Level of support should be differentiated so that students at each level of proficiency are able to understand expectations and be successful in lessons.

- **Provide audiotape texts.** There are a variety of commercially available resources that provide an audio version of a story or book. Publishers often include access to audio versions of a text. Also, software exists for creating MP3 files by scanning text and reading it aloud. Students can listen to the file on a smartphone or tablet. Having an audio version of the text not only allows for multiple opportunities to hear the text but also enables adjustments for different proficiency levels. When the teacher (or someone else) records the text themself, the same passage may be read more slowly with clear enunciation for beginning speakers, or synonyms may be substituted for difficult words.

■ The Lesson

Economics: Natural Resources and Products (Third Grade)

The following lessons take place in an urban elementary school where multilingual learners make up approximately 30% of the school population. In the classrooms described, a mix of language proficiency levels are represented, ranging from beginning speakers to advanced English speakers. Students have varying levels of literacy in their native languages.

Teachers in this school have a weekly grade-level planning meeting, where they co-plan lessons. During this time, teachers develop content and language objectives and share ideas for the week's lessons, thus ensuring that they follow similar pacing. As you will see, although the objectives are the same, the teachers have their own ways of teaching the lessons.

Third-grade teachers Miss Zarcades, Mr. Mehlhaff, and Mrs. Pabst are all teaching a unit on Economics. The lessons described focus on distinguishing the difference between a natural resource and a product, and address the standard: *Determine the meaning of general academic and domain-specific words and phrases in a text relevant to a grade 3 topic or subject area.* The classes have been studying natural resources, learning about which ones are renewable and nonrenewable, and examining the problems associated with scarce resources.

The current lesson takes place over two days. On the first day, the three teachers introduced the lesson by pointing out that we use products every day and that most come from natural resources. They used the example of paper (product) being made from trees (natural resource) and the classes read a text about the production of paper. Then the students were told that they would be asked to select a product they wanted to research. The vignettes that follow describe Day 2 of the lesson.

The lesson's objectives are:

Content: Students will

- investigate how a product is made and the natural resources used to produce it.
- distinguish between a finished product and a natural resource.

Language: Students will

- write a summary of the production process using key vocabulary.
- orally present their research findings.

■ Teaching Scenarios

Miss Zarcades

As was her practice, Miss Zarcades reviewed the content and language objectives she had posted for students. She asked students to read along with her, pointing to each word as she read aloud so that all students, including multilingual learners, could follow along. She began this second day of the lesson by asking each group to quickly say what product they had researched the previous day from texts and Internet sources. Since she had distributed a worksheet to guide—or scaffold—their information gathering, she reviewed on the document reader a sample completed worksheet about the production of a pencil. She went through each section, being careful to enunciate clearly and repeat the specific academic vocabulary words that were key terms in the lesson, such as *renewable resource*, *product*, and *production*. She paused periodically to make sure that all group members were following along on their own worksheets and checking that they had filled in the section correctly. She told the groups that they had ten minutes to review their worksheets and add any additional information. She set an online timer on her interactive whiteboard. As students worked together, Miss Zarcades circulated around the classroom, assisting groups or individuals who needed support.

Next, she distributed poster board and pointed to the samples displayed on the wall. She instructed groups to use their creativity to draw a similar poster that would reflect the production process outlined on their worksheet. Each member of the group chose one section of the worksheet to illustrate—that is, the product, the natural resource used in the product, the source of the natural resource, and whether it was a renewable or nonrenewable resource. The groups were given fifteen minutes to complete a simple illustration of the process as a visual to accompany their oral presentations. Again, Miss Zarcades set the online timer.

After the posters were completed, the groups gave oral presentations of their projects. Each member of the group told about their part of the poster using complete sentences and academic terms. Miss Zarcades had written sentence frames on the whiteboard for those students who needed language support: "The product we researched was ____." and "Production of ____ uses ____ resources" (renewable or nonrenewable). After the oral presentations were made, Miss Zarcades played a quick game of Stand Up/Sit Down. She named an item and asked students to stand if it was a finished product or sit if it was a natural resource. Throughout the lesson, Miss Zarcades used language structures and vocabulary that she believed the students could understand at their level of proficiency. For beginning learners, she spoke slowly, often contextualizing vocabulary words, and enunciated clearly. Also, she avoided the use of idioms, and when she sensed that students did not understand, she paraphrased to convey the meaning more clearly. At the conclusion of the lesson, she reviewed the content and language objectives with her students.

Check your understanding: On the SIOP form in Figure 4.2, rate Miss Zarcades's lesson on each of the Comprehensible Input features.

Mr. Mehlhaff

Mr. Mehlhaff enjoys his students and is friendly but he has a traditional approach to teaching. He began the lesson by reading the content and language objectives. Then he told students to continue researching the products they had started investigating the day before. He had asked each student to select a product and work independently to gather information. Some students seemed lost about how to extract pertinent information from text and Internet sources. Quite a few sat quietly, while others began talking among themselves. Mr. Mehlhaff sensed that some students were off task, so he stood and repeated the directions orally, speaking rather quickly

FIGURE 4.2	Comprehensible Input Component of the SIOP® Model: Miss Zarcades's Lesson

4	3	2	1	0
10. **Speech appropriate** for students' proficiency levels (e.g., slower rate, enunciation, and simple sentence structure for beginners)		**Speech** sometimes inappropriate for students' proficiency levels		**Speech** inappropriate for students' proficiency levels
4	**3**	**2**	**1**	**0**
11. **Clear explanation** of academic tasks		**Unclear** explanation of academic tasks		**No** explanation of academic tasks
4	**3**	**2**	**1**	**0**
12. **A variety of techniques** used to make content concepts clear (e.g., modeling, visuals, hands-on activities, demonstrations, gestures, body language)		Some techniques used to make content concepts clear		**No techniques** used to make concepts clear

and curtly. He wrote on the board: *Product, Natural Resources Used*, to help guide students in completing the task. He pointed to the words and repeated that they were supposed to be looking for information about their product (pointed to word) and writing down which natural resources (pointed to word) were used. He gave students more time to "get to work."

After a while, Mr. Mehlhaff paired students and told the class that the partners were going to share information about their products with one another. He reminded them that they needed to use academic language, including the specific terms that were the focus of the lesson. He referred them back to the language objective and read it to them, stressing that he wanted to hear students using key academic terms and phrases. He called on two of the top students in class and asked them to come up and demonstrate what partners were supposed to do. The students faced each other, and Mr. Mehlhaff told one, "Ask him the name of his product" and the student asked his partner, who then answered. Next Mr. Mehlhaff prompted, "Now, what about natural resources?" and the student asked his partner which natural resources were used to make the product. After this demonstration, Mr. Mehlhaff told the class that partners were going to follow the same questioning format, asking one another about their products. Students began talking with their partners, asking and answering questions with varying levels of success.

Check your understanding: On the SIOP form in Figure 4.3, rate Mr. Mehlhaff's lesson on each of the Comprehensible Input features.

Mrs. Pabst

Mrs. Pabst asked the class to chorally read the lesson's content and language objectives, which were written on the board. She was sure to read slowly so that all students, including multilingual learners, were able to follow along. She asked

FIGURE 4.3 Comprehensible Input Component of the SIOP® Model: Mr. Mehlhaff's Lesson

4	3	2	1	0
10. **Speech appropriate** for students' proficiency levels (e.g., slower rate, enunciation, and simple sentence structure for beginners)		**Speech** sometimes inappropriate for students' proficiency levels		**Speech** inappropriate for students' proficiency levels
4	3	2	1	0
11. **Clear explanation** of academic tasks		**Unclear** explanation of academic tasks		**No** explanation of academic tasks
4	3	2	1	0
12. **A variety of techniques** used to make content concepts clear (e.g., modeling, visuals, hands-on activities, demonstrations, gestures, body language)		Some techniques used to make content concepts clear		No **techniques** used to make concepts clear

if there were any questions from the previous day's assignment and requested a show of hands of students who knew what their product was. All students raised hands. The previous day Mrs. Pabst had let students pick a partner and then work in pairs to select a product and gather information about its associated natural resources.

Mrs. Pabst told the students that today they would identify where the natural resources in their products came from. She pointed to the large map on the wall. Students were told that they would create a symbol that represented each resource used in their product. As Mrs. Pabst explained this process, she used her normal, somewhat rapid speaking style that she used with her English-speaking students. Then she passed out paper for making two copies of each symbol—one to put on the large world map and the other for the map key, or legend. She pointed out that a *map legend* is a key to the symbols used on a map. "It is like a dictionary so you can understand the meaning of what the map represents." She modeled what the students would complete by showing a symbol for trees (paper products) and placed one on the map where logging takes place and another on the map legend, writing "trees for paper production" next to the symbol. Mrs. Pabst then told students to get started working with their partners to create a symbol and find the location of their product's natural resources. Most pairs could design a symbol, but several struggled locating the sources. After all students had completed this task, Mrs. Pabst had each pair come to the map and tell the name of the product, the natural resource used, and where the natural resource came from. They then put one symbol on the map and the other on the map key. When all students had completed their oral report, Mrs. Pabst reviewed the content and language objectives and asked if they were met.

Check your understanding: On the SIOP form in Figure 4.4, rate Mrs. Pabst's lesson on each of the Comprehensible Input features.

FIGURE 4.4 Comprehensible Input Component of the SIOP® Model: Mrs. Pabst's Lesson

4	3	2	1	0
10. **Speech appropriate** for students' proficiency levels (e.g., slower rate, enunciation, and simple sentence structure for beginners)		**Speech** sometimes inappropriate for students' proficiency levels		**Speech** inappropriate for students' proficiency levels

4	3	2	1	0
11. **Clear explanation** of academic tasks		**Unclear** explanation of academic tasks		**No** explanation of academic tasks

4	3	2	1	0
12. **A variety of techniques** used to make content concepts clear (e.g., modeling, visuals, hands-on activities, demonstrations, gestures, body language)		Some techniques used to make content concepts clear		No **techniques** used to make concepts clear

Discussion of Lessons

Look back at your rating forms and think about the reasons you scored the lessons as you did. What evidence is in the scenarios? Read on to see our analyses.

10. *Speech Appropriate for Students' Proficiency Level (Rate and Complexity)*

Miss Zarcades: 4

Mr. Mehlhaff: 0

Mrs. Pabst: 1

- **Miss Zarcades** was attuned to the benefit of modulating her speech to make herself understood by the students. She slowed her rate of speech and enunciated clearly to accommodate beginning learners, and she adjusted her speech for the other, more proficient speakers of English. She used a natural speaking voice, but paid attention to her rate of speech and enunciation. Further, Miss Zarcades repeated key academic vocabulary terms, which helps all students, but especially multilingual learners. Finally, she adjusted the level of vocabulary and complexity of the sentences when speaking and used sentence frames so that all students could participate at their level of proficiency. For this reason, Miss Zarcades's lesson received a "4" for this feature.

- **Mr. Mehlhaff** seemed unaware that his students would understand more if he adjusted his oral presentation to accommodate the proficiency levels of multilingual learners in his class. He gave few instructions to assist students in completing the task, and those instructions he gave did not take into consideration his rate of speech or complexity of speech, variables that impact multilingual learners' ability to comprehend information in class. Also, making sense of written information independently and creating original sentences are inordinately difficult tasks for multilingual learners. Unwittingly, Mr. Mehlhaff set the students up for failure, and then he was frustrated when they were off task. He spoke quickly and curtly, which did not enhance comprehension. Mr. Mehlhaff's lesson was given a "0" for this feature.

- Generally, **Mrs. Pabst's** rate of speech and enunciation were similar to that used with native English speakers. She didn't consciously adjust her speech (rate or complexity) to the variety of proficiency levels in the class, although she did have students chorally read the objectives slowly so all could follow along. Mrs. Pabst could have paraphrased some of her instructions and questions, using simpler sentence structure, when some students struggled to understand. Because Mrs. Pabst made minimal adjustments while speaking to multilingual learners, her lesson received a "1" for this feature.

11. *Clear Explanation of Academic Tasks*

Miss Zarcades: 4

Mr. Mehlhaff: 2

Mrs. Pabst: 3

Making your expectations crystal clear to students is one of the most important aspects of teaching, even if it's an inquiry lesson. When working with multilingual learners, explicit, step-by-step directions can be critical to a lesson's success. It is difficult for almost any student to remember directions given only orally, and oral directions may be incomprehensible to many multilingual learners. A lesson is sure to get off to a rocky start if students don't understand what they are expected to do. Written procedures provide students with a guide. Although Mrs. Pabst modeled using the map and legend, she didn't write instructions for student reference, nor did she review sources where students could find information, which resulted in a delay in some students getting started. Otherwise, she would have received a "4" for this feature.

- **Miss Zarcades's** lesson received a "4" for this feature because she used a teaching style that supported student success by making her expectations for completing academic tasks clear and understandable. She modeled almost every task students were expected to complete. During the lesson she first checked for understanding by using a "popcorn" approach, quickly asking each group the name of their product. Then she modeled for the class a completed worksheet and gave each student a chance to check their own work from the previous day. If an individual student or group was confused or had done the worksheet incorrectly, it was important for Miss Zarcades to make sure they all understood what to do and were doing it correctly before they spent more time on the task. She then provided time for them to make their own additions or corrections, and was careful to oversee their work. Throughout the lesson, tasks were modeled so that students at all levels of English proficiency knew the expectations and, with the scaffolding she offered, were more likely to be successful in completing the work. She took into account the linguistic differences in her class and differentiated accordingly. The sentence frames let the students know exactly the kinds of complete sentences that were expected during their oral presentations.

Using the online timer for time management, Miss Zarcades provided students with boundaries for the tasks—letting them know how much time she expected them to spend—and helped them learn to manage their time. Overall, she understood the value of being explicit in what she wanted the students to do balanced with developing their own independent learning.

- Although **Mr. Mehlhaff** was a veteran teacher, he did not provide the kind of guidance that all students benefit from and that is critical for multilingual learners. He expected young students to work independently, gathering information from text and Internet sources. Exposing students at all levels of English proficiency to complex text is important, but scaffolding is essential to help students access the information. Many students, and especially multilingual learners, were unsure of the expectations or process for completing the assignment. When students were off task, Mr. Mehlhaff attempted to explain further by rereading the objectives, but that probably did little to make the task clearer. He did assist by having two students model how to work in pairs asking questions about the assignment. This gave students an idea about how to conduct their pair work. Thus, Mr. Mehlhaff's lesson was given a "2" for this feature.

- **Mrs. Pabst** first got students focused on the task by reading the objectives and asking them to remember the product they had chosen the previous day. She told them explicitly what they were going to do first: Identify where the natural resources came from that were used to make the products. This kind of clarity helps multilingual learners to know precisely what is expected. In addition, she modeled part of the task that students were to work on. She showed the symbol she had created to represent paper products and put it on the map, just as they would do when they finished. Even without words, the students, including multilingual learners, could see what the process was: Find out where your natural resource comes from, draw a symbol, and prepare to place it on the map and legend with a brief explanation. The lesson would have received a higher rating had Mrs. Pabst actually modeled or explained how students were to extract information about where the natural resources come from. She said that they would create a symbol to represent the resource, but didn't sufficiently explain how they would go about finding the information that their symbol would represent. A worksheet to guide them, as Miss Zarcades provided, would have scaffolded the task better for students. Mrs. Pabst's lesson received a "3" for this feature.

12. *A Variety of Techniques Used to Make Content Concepts Clear*

Miss Zarcades: 4

Mr. Mehlhaff: 1

Mrs. Pabst: 2

- Throughout the lesson, **Miss Zarcades** used a number of techniques that supported students' learning and helped them be successful in completing the assignment. She provided a worksheet to scaffold students' organization of information and she showed the sample completed worksheet, carefully going through each section. All of the visuals she showed and pointed to increased students' comprehension. By giving students a worksheet and poster board for their illustrations, she made the lesson more engaging and provided more than one way to express the information they had gathered. One can imagine that the atmosphere in Miss Zarcades's class is positive, encouraging, and nonthreatening for multilingual learners. This kind of environment instills confidence in students about their ability to learn and be successful in school. Because of the variety of effective techniques used, Miss Zarcades's lesson received a "4" for this feature.

- **Mr. Mehlhaff** is a kind and friendly teacher, but he did not use many teaching techniques that increased students' comprehension of the lesson. His teaching style was one of teacher lecture and student performance without scaffolding. He expected young learners to work independently, which is difficult for most young students, especially multilingual learners who may not even understand the words in the text. Thus, completing a summary of the natural resources used to produce a product was a nearly impossible task. He modeled how to discuss the information in pairs, but one might expect that few multilingual learners had actually independently gathered sufficient information for the oral exchange. Think about the difference between Miss Zarcades's scaffolded lesson and Mr. Mehlhaff's reliance on independent work. This lesson received a "1" for use of comprehensible input techniques.

- **Mrs. Pabst** used teaching techniques in the lesson, but some of her choices were not useful, especially for multilingual learners. First, she asked if there were any questions. Few multilingual learners typically ask for clarification or assistance in front of the class. Then she provided them with the application activity of creating a symbol to place on the map. However, there was no technique used to check for understanding as to whether the students investigated how a product was made and learned about the natural resources used to produce it (the objective). Although she modeled how to create a symbol and place it on the map, she depended on the map symbol activity to guide students' understanding of the content. Instead, she might have used a technique for checking understanding of the production process, or provided an outline or graphic organizer for students to make sense of the information they were expected to gather. Gestures, modeling, activities that promote manipulation, and the like are important for increasing multilingual learners' understanding of the lesson, but these techniques must lead to meeting the lesson's objectives. For these reasons, Mrs. Pabst's lesson received a "2" for this feature.

    (For more examples of lesson and unit plans in history and social studies for grades K–6, see Short, Vogt, and Echevarría, 2011.)

■ Final Points

As you reflect on this chapter and consider the impact of comprehensible input on learning, consider the following main points:

- Although comprehensible input techniques are critical for multilingual learners, English speakers are not disadvantaged by their use. All students benefit from well-articulated speech, a clear explanation of tasks, and techniques that make information understandable.

- Effective SIOP teachers constantly modulate and adjust their speech to ensure that the content is comprehensible.
- Concepts are taught using a variety of techniques, including modeling, gestures, hands-on activities, and demonstrations, so that students understand and learn the content material.
- Effective SIOP teachers provide explanations of academic tasks in ways that make clear what students are expected to accomplish and that promote student success.

■ Discussion Questions

1. In reflecting on the content and language objectives at the beginning of the chapter, are you able to:

   - Identify three techniques for presenting content information that enhance comprehension for multilingual learners?
   - Name elements necessary for providing clear directions for completing academic tasks?
   - Discuss modifications to teacher speech that can increase student comprehension?
   - As part of a lesson plan, write several techniques to make academic language accessible for multilingual learners?

2. Many times in classrooms, discipline problems can be attributed to students not knowing what they're supposed to be doing. If students don't know what to do, they find something else to do. What are some ways that you can avoid having students become confused about accomplishing academic tasks?

3. If you have traveled in another country, or if you are a multilingual learner, reflect on difficulties you had in understanding others. What are some techniques people used to try to communicate with you? What are some techniques you can use in the classroom?

4. For the lesson on economics, what are some comprehension checks that are quick, nonthreatening, and effective for determining if a student is ready to move on?

5. Using the SIOP lesson you have been developing, add to it so that the Comprehensible Input features in the lesson are enhanced.

■ Pearson eTextbook Application Videos

The purpose of the Pearson eTextbook Application Videos is to provide you with an opportunity to observe and reflect on SIOP teaching and learning practices. There are multilingual students in each of the classrooms with varying levels of English proficiency. The teachers you will observe are at different levels of SIOP implementation, from second-year SIOPers to veterans. As you observe the lessons they have created, focus on the students and the lesson objectives, keeping in mind that becoming a high-implementing SIOP teacher takes time, practice, and support to refine teaching practices. We are grateful to each of these SIOP educators for welcoming us into their classrooms, and for their dedication to SIOP, their multilingual learners, and other students.

Pearson eTextbook Application

Video Example 4.1

SIOP Lesson: Grade 5 Language Arts; Annotating Fiction While Reading

Strategies

CONTENT OBJECTIVES

This chapter will help you to . . .

- Identify and build on students' strategy use during content lessons: cognitive, metacognitive, language learning, and socio-affective.
- Select effective teaching techniques for verbal, procedural, and instructional scaffolding.

LANGUAGE OBJECTIVES

This chapter will help you to . . .

- Write questions and tasks that are differentiated for students' English proficiency levels and are at different levels of cognition.
- Include in a lesson plan, instruction and practice with one or more learning strategies, scaffolding for those who need it, and higher-level questions and tasks.

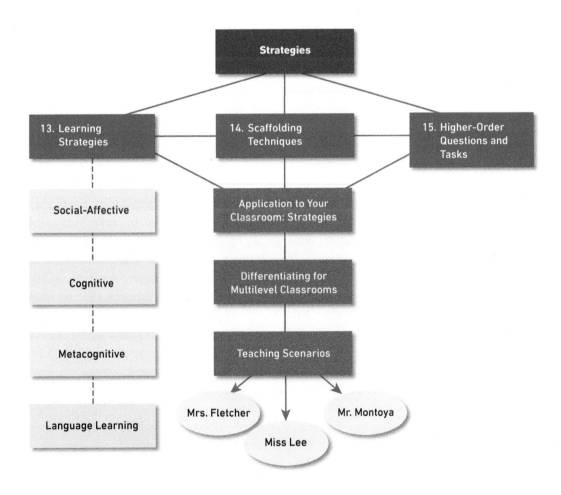

Think about a time when you had to solve a really challenging problem. For example, you are driving in an unfamiliar city, trusting your rental car's GPS to get you safely to your destination. At some point, you realize that you don't recognize landmarks, and you wonder if you're heading in the wrong direction. At this point, you have a decision to make: (1) trust the rental car's GPS; (2) switch to your trusted GPS on your phone; or (3) try to figure out where you are and where you need to go to arrive at your location. If you choose #2, how do you know that your phone's GPS is more trustworthy that the one in the rental car? If you choose #3, how are you going to get to your destination in a timely manner?

In this age of GPS dependence, most likely this has happened to every driver at least once. What did you do to when this happened to you? More than likely, as an experienced driver, you activated a plan for dealing with the dilemma and you relied on a repertoire of strategies you have developed over the years for finding your way from point A to point B, in an unfamiliar environment. As you think about the possible strategies you used, which were taught to you by someone with more experience? Which did you learn by yourself through trial and error? ■

■ Background

A growing body of research suggests that skilled readers and learners are mentally active, engaged, and strategic (August & Shanahan, 2010; Duke, Ward, & Pearson, 2021). Effective learners self-regulate by activating a variety of skills and strategies, such as self-questioning and generating mental images while reading. Active self-regulation involves motivation, engagement, and executive function skills, including cognitive flexibility, working memory, and inhibitory control, such as suppressing distracting information (Duke & Cartwright, 2021). For reading, strategy use is defined as, "deliberate, goal-directed attempts to control and modify the reader's efforts to decode text, understand words, and construct meaning" (Afflerbach, Pearson, & Paris, 2008, p. 368).

Teachers of multilingual learners may have difficulty determining their students' proficiency with learning strategies and self-regulatory skills, especially in the beginning stages of English acquisition. They may confuse students' lower levels of English proficiency with poor or underdeveloped learning strategies.

Therefore, in this chapter, we discuss the importance of teaching and providing practice with a variety of cognitive, metacognitive, and language learning strategies that facilitate knowledge acquisition, and socio-affective strategies that impact engagement and motivation. We also suggest that all students, including multilingual learners, benefit from questions and tasks that involve higher levels of cognition. To accomplish these goals, teachers must carefully scaffold instruction for multilingual learners and other students who need additional support.

Note that in SIOP, we distinguish between *instructional strategies* and *learning strategies*. We use the term *strategies* when discussing how a learner cognitively processes knowledge and language. When referring to instruction, we use terms such as *techniques, activities, methods,* and *approaches.* It is important to understand these differences as you move forward with SIOP.

> "
> The Strategies component provides students access to their funds of knowledge while building linguistic confidence through strategic thinking.
>
> Dr. Francheska Figueroa
> Postdoctoral Research
> Scholar Arizona
> "

You will find three teachers' lessons in the section, Teaching Scenarios. As you read about each of features in the Strategies component, followed by the Scenarios, reflect on the multilingual learners you are currently teaching or have taught previously. Who are the strategic thinkers and problem solvers, who can readily answer questions and tackle tasks that require higher-order thinking? Who are challenged by tasks that require strategic thinking and problem solving? Are you aware of students who use their knowledge of their home language strategically when they are translanguaging? (See the definition of *translanguaging* in the Glossary). What types of scaffolding might be beneficial for the students you have identified? These are the important questions we address in the Strategies component.

SIOP® **SIOP® FEATURE 13:**

Ample Opportunities Provided for Students to Use Learning Strategies

Research studies focused on highly effective readers and learners have shown they use a variety of strategies in an interactive and recursive manner. These individuals use strategies that are flexible and appropriate to the task. As multilingual learners develop English proficiency, it is important that their language, literacy, and content instruction include a focus on learning and practicing a variety of strategies so that they can activate, self-regulate, and transfer these cognitive processes to thinking and learning in English.

Reflect again on the opening scenario in this chapter, in which you were asked to think about a time when you questioned the accuracy of the GPS in your car. What cognitive and metacognitive strategies did you employ to solve the problem of not knowing if you were traveling in the right direction? Think about your answer to this question as you read about the following cognitive, metacognitive, language learning, and socio-affective strategies (See Table 5.1 for a list of the four types of strategies). Strategies that can be taught and that generally transfer to new learning include the following.

- **Cognitive Strategies.** Cognitive strategies are used when learners mentally and/or physically manipulate information, or when they apply a specific technique to a learning task. While some cognitive strategies may need to be taught, others develop naturally, as when we solve a problem and figure things out. Whether taught or learned, cognitive strategies are often remembered for future use and application.

Example: A SIOP teacher models a cognitive strategy during a lesson through a think-aloud that focuses on an important aspect of a text, such as the Essential Question: "*When I see this question in big, bolded words at the beginning of the chapter, I know it is important, because I need be able to answer it after I read.*"

- **Metacognitive Strategies.** Metacognition encompasses both the awareness of one's cognitive processes (thinking about one's thinking = metacognitive knowledge), and the facility to self-regulate these cognitive processes (metacognitive monitoring and control). Educational research includes considerable evidence that substantiates the importance of metacognition in learning and academic achievement (Fleur, Bredeweg, & van den Bos, 2021). The active use of metacognitive strategies implies awareness, reflection, and interaction, and effective learners use these strategies in an integrated, interrelated, and recursive manner. Science of Reading research studies have found that when metacognitive strategies are taught explicitly and practiced frequently, before, during, and after reading, reading comprehension is improved (Duke & Cartwright, 2021; Duke, Ward, & Pearson, 2021; Shanahan, Callison, Carriere, Duke, Pearson, Shatschneider, & Torgesen, 2010).

  Example: SIOP teachers use think-alouds to model metacognitive strategy use, such as: "*When I am reading, I like to stop occasionally, to think about what I just read. If there are three points the author made, I try to remember them and repeat them in my head before going on. I try to summarize or think about the information in the order that I read it. This helps me understand and remember what I am reading.*"

- **Language Learning Strategies.** Language learning strategies are defined as, "Mental strategies that [people] use to make sense of oral and written text, to organize information, to monitor language production, and to apply skills to language tasks" (Short & Echevarria, 2016, p. 21). These mental processes and ways of thinking give multilingual learners resources to learn on their own. As they do with other aspects of learning, effective language learners consciously use a variety of strategies to increase their facility in speaking and comprehending the new language.

  Example: SIOP teachers encourage multilingual learners to use their home language (L1) as described in Chapter 6. *With your partner, explain combustion, using English or your primary language. In your explanation, include our key vocabulary: mass, reactant, chemical reaction.*

  Using translanguaging and code-switching can reduce the affective filter, an invisible, mental screen that can either aid or deter the process of language acquisition (Krashen, 1985). When the affective filter is reduced, the multilingual student feels safer and language acquisition occurs.

- **Socio-Affective Strategies.** O'Malley and Chamot (1994) originated the concept of teaching and reinforcing strategies that were not cognitive in nature, but instead, were more aligned with the social and emotional development of the multilingual learner. These strategies can ease the anxiety and discomfort for language learners who are placed in a classroom with a dominant language group (TESOL, 2018). With the increased focus on students' social-emotional learning (SEL) and the call for student-centered classrooms, socio-affective strategies are important to include in this discussion of strategies that can be taught and reinforced for multilingual learners.

  ◆ *Examples:* SIOP teachers include routines in their lessons, such as how to take turns when talking, how to use sentence frames, how to appropriately agree or disagree with another student during a discussion, how to praise another student for something they said or did, and so forth. These examples are not just intended for young children, because multilingual learners of all ages may have had varied educational experiences in their former schools, if they've had schooling. Modeling socio-affective strategies is important for all students, but especially for multilingual learners.

Furthermore, the social aspects of language learning require practice to build confidence. In a classroom setting, SIOP teachers discuss and model how to participate in instructional conversations (see Chapter 6), including knowing which English words and phrases are appropriate, turn-taking, asking questions, paraphrasing, and so forth. Practice with socio-affective strategies can be beneficial for multilingual learners and native-English speakers, alike.

Take a moment and review the examples of cognitive, metacognitive, language learning, and socio-affective strategies that are important and beneficial for multilingual learners (see Table 5.1). Which of these could you model and teach to your students?

TABLE 5.1 Examples of Cognitive, Metacognitive, Language Learning, and Socio-Affective Strategies

Cognitive Strategies	Metacognitive Strategies	Language Learning Strategies	Socio-Affective Strategies
■ Previewing a text before reading	■ Predicting and inferring	■ Conscientiously applying reading strategies, such as previewing, skimming, scanning, self-questioning, summarizing, and reviewing	■ Seeking out conversational partners
■ Establishing a purpose for learning	■ Generating questions and using the questions to guide comprehension		■ Taking risks with the new language
■ Consciously making connections with past learning	■ Monitoring and clarifying (*Am I understanding? If not, what can I do to help myself?*)	■ Analyzing and using consistent forms and patterns in English, such as: *prefix + root + suffix* (im + port + ed), and *prefix + base word + suffix* (pre + read + ing)	■ Practicing the target language when alone
■ Using mnemonics (hints or systems for remembering information)	■ Evaluating and determining the importance of what is read and/or learned		■ Combatting inhibitions about using the target language by having a positive attitude
■ Highlighting, underlining, or using sticky notes to identify important information	■ Summarizing and synthesizing	■ Making logical guesses based on contextual and syntactic information	■ Asking for clarification, even though it may be difficult to do so

(continued)

| TABLE 5.1 | Examples of Cognitive, Metacognitive, Language Learning, and Socio-Affective Strategies *(continued)* |

Cognitive Strategies	Metacognitive Strategies	Language Learning Strategies	Socio-Affective Strategies
■ Taking notes or outlining ■ Rereading to aid understanding ■ Identifying key vocabulary ■ Identifying, analyzing, and using varied text structures to aid comprehension	■ Making mental images (visualizing) ■ Using mental and sensory images: *What might it smell like? What picture(s) do you see in your mind? How might this feel?*	■ Breaking words into component parts (*un + break + able = unbreakable*) ■ Purposefully grouping and labeling words (*nouns, verbs, adjectives, adverbs, conjunctions, compound words,* etc.) ■ Drawing pictures and/or using gestures to communicate when words do not come to mind ■ Self-monitoring and self-correcting while speaking English (also a metacognitive strategy) ■ Substituting a known word when unable to pronounce an unfamiliar word ■ Guessing and deducing ■ Using verbal and nonverbal cues to know when to pay attention ■ Imitating behaviors of native English-speaking peers to successfully complete tasks ■ Translanguaging: Expressing ideas in more than one language: using one's target and native language as resources to build understanding (see Glossary)	■ Encouraging and rewarding oneself for participating in a group or completing a task ■ Lowering anxiety and reducing stress by reminding oneself of learning goals ■ Asking for help or assistance ■ Learning to clarify and confirm understandings ■ Working with others to achieve a common goal and/or to complete a task together ■ Taking risks by engaging in a discussion ■ Experimenting aloud with the target language, even though errors may be made ■ Recognizing feelings of pride upon meeting a lesson's content and language objectives ■ Motivating oneself by noting when the target language is used correctly; and/or when communicating effectively with another person

Teaching Strategies

What follows are some more tips for effectively teaching strategies:

- Cognitive, metacognitive, language learning, and socio-affective strategies transfer to learning in the new language. For example, once you know how to make predictions while reading in your first language (L1), you can predict with a text in your target language when you have the language proficiency to do so.

Pearson eTextbook

Video Example 5.1

In this excerpted lesson, you will see multilingual learners in a high school classroom grappling with challenging academic words and synonyms. See if you can identify examples of strategies the students are using from Table 5.1. Note that the teacher, Ms. Drexler-Guitierrez, has provided them with partially completed sentences, so they can use the vocabulary in sentences that they read aloud to their peers.

http://mediaplayer.pearsoncmg
.com/_blue-top_640x360_ccv2/
ab/streaming/myeducationlab/
ell/MN/rc/TDG_ELL_HS_
02VocabSynonymsPtA.mp4

You may have multilingual learners who have been well schooled in their home language (L1), and they have developed a variety of strategies that they can use and talk about once they learn the English terms for them. Sentence frames and sentence starters can be very helpful for providing the necessary language bridge for student engagement. (See Table 5.4 in this chapter in the Differentiating for Multilevel Classes section; and Chapter 6 for more information about sentence frames and starters.)

- You also may have multilingual learners in the classroom, including refugees, who have had interrupted formal education (SIFE). The temptation might be to think of these students as "less than"—as being without strategies and skills. However, many of these students have developed a repertoire of survival strategies that they can apply to their learning. Whenever you can, tap into these strategies and assist students in making connections between what they've experienced and learned, and what you are teaching.

- When teaching strategies, it is important that students understand how these strategies work together in an integrated fashion. For example, consider the metacognitive strategies that we use when reading fiction and nonfiction. Here's an example of a think-aloud that could be used with upper grade students to help them understand the interrelatedness of metacognitive strategies:

  - *When reading a short story, we usually make mental predictions about the plot, the characters, the setting, and so forth—sometimes based on the description of the book, other stories we've read by the same author, illustrations, or the first few paragraphs of Chapter 1.*

  - *As we are reading, we ask ourselves questions, such as: "What just happened? Who is this new character and where did he come from? It's beginning to snow heavily, and they can't see where they're driving. Are they going to have an accident? What's going to happen?"*

  - *These questions (in our heads) lead to either confirming (it happened) or disconfirming (it didn't happen) our previously made predictions, based on where the author has taken us in the story. What's fun about reading fiction is that we may think one thing is going to happen, and we're surprised when it doesn't.*

  - *While reading, we should stop, once in a while, to recapitulate, summing up in our heads what we've just read. We then add new predictions and ask new questions for the next paragraph or chapter we're going to read.*

- Introduce and model a variety of strategies and then give students ample practice in using them in an integrated manner (see Mr. Montoya's lesson and lesson plan in this chapter). Encourage students to think of strategies as being housed in a *mental toolbox*, from which they can select one or more depending on the task at hand. It is not good practice to interrupt students' reading of a text by having them stop, label, and write the name of the strategy they're using. There is no research that supports this practice.

- Lipson and Wixson (2013) contend that strategies should not be taught in isolation, one at a time. Rather, teachers need to teach and reinforce strategy use as an integrated process during which readers employ declarative, procedural, and conditional knowledge:

  - *Declarative knowledge*: What is the strategy?
  - *Procedural knowledge:* How do I use this strategy?
  - *Conditional knowledge*: When and why do I use this strategy?

Finally, note that teaching these strategies can serve as the basis of a lesson's content objectives and language objectives. For example, each of the following objectives include strategy practice:

- Content Objectives: You will. . .

  - Preview (skim) a chapter and think of 2–3 questions you have about the earth's ozone layer. *Cognitive strategy: skimming; metacognitive strategy: self-questioning*
  - Jigsaw, with small group members, information about preserving and restoring the Earth's ozone layer. *Socio-affective strategy: actively participating in a small group; language learning strategy: orally sharing information with other group members through the adapted Jigsaw procedure[1].*

- Language Objectives: You will. . .

  - Select three key vocabulary words or terms that you think are important to the topic of climate change. *Cognitive strategy: highlighting or underlining text; metacognitive strategy: evaluating*
  - Write an informal definition, using what you know and have read for each word or term, and share your definitions with a partner. *Language learning strategy: making a logical guess; metacognitive strategy: predicting word meaning; social-affective strategy: explaining information to another person.*

SIOP®   **SIOP® FEATURE 14:**

Scaffolding Techniques Consistently Used, Assisting and Supporting Student Understanding

Scaffolding is a term coined by Jerome Bruner (1983) that is associated with Vygotsky's (1978) theory of the Zone of Proximal Development (ZPD). In essence, the ZPD is the difference between what students can accomplish alone and what they can accomplish with the assistance of a more experienced individual. The assistance that is provided by this individual is called *scaffolding*.

---

[1]Adapted Jigsaw procedure: Partners or small group members read an assigned section of a text, and prepare information on notes or a graphic organizer, to teach to other students in a small group.

> Allowing students to work collaboratively before working independently not only scaffolds the task at hand, but also sends the message that everyone's input is valued and is a key factor in creating positive interdependence.
>
> Ana Segulin, ESL Administrator, Texas

Undoubtedly, you have seen scaffolding on buildings that are under construction. They are intended to provide the workers with access to the building as it is being built. Once the building is completed, the scaffolding is no longer necessary, and it is removed. The scaffolding metaphor is effective for education because when teachers provide scaffolding, they are enabling access to content concepts and academic language, for as long as is necessary. The scaffolding is removed when students no longer need it because they can access the content and academic language on their own.

Pearson and Gallagher (1983) described ZPD and scaffolding as the "gradual release of responsibility" (GRR), as it relates to classroom practices. The intent of the GRR model is to move from reliance on the teacher to student independence in applying key content concepts and vocabulary, but as we all know, a lesson may not move smoothly from one phase to the next.

What has been mostly absent in GRR explanations (*I do, We do, You do*), is the notion that teaching is a recursive, rather than linear process. Therefore, we offer an alternative to the traditional explanation of GRR. In this model (see Figure 5.1),

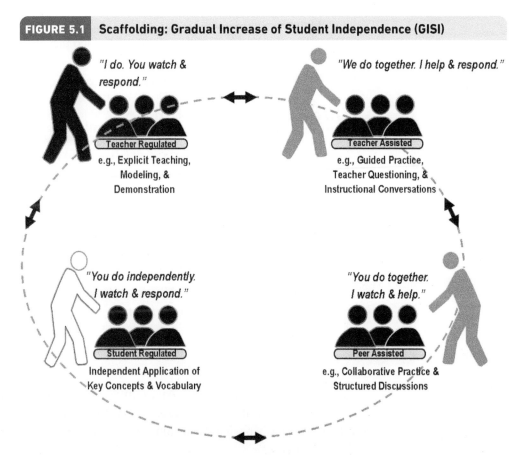

FIGURE 5.1 | **Scaffolding: Gradual Increase of Student Independence (GISI)**

"I do. You watch & respond."

Teacher Regulated

e.g., Explicit Teaching, Modeling, & Demonstration

"We do together. I help & respond."

Teacher Assisted

e.g., Guided Practice, Teacher Questioning, & Instructional Conversations

"You do independently. I watch & respond."

Student Regulated

Independent Application of Key Concepts & Vocabulary

"You do together. I watch & help."

Peer Assisted

e.g., Collaborative Practice & Structured Discussions

Reproduction of this material is restricted to use with Echevarría, J., Vogt, M.E., Short, D., & Toppel (2023). *Making Content Comprehensible for Multilingual Learners. The SIOP Model* (6th Ed.). Boston: Pearson.

the focus is on the student, and on recursive teaching, which is more in keeping with what goes on in a real classroom. A description follows:

- The Gradual Increase of Student Independence (GISI) offers explicit teaching (*I do. You watch and respond.*), and immediate practice with assistance from the teacher (*We do together. I help and respond.*).

- Students who are successful apply their learning with other students with minimal supervision (*You do together. I watch and respond.*).

- For some students, it may be necessary to take a step back and reteach and re-model before moving on to supported practice.

- Of course, the goal for all students is independent application of key concepts and vocabulary (*You do independently. I watch and respond.*).

- This process leads to more differentiated teaching, enabling those who can move forward to do so. But for those who need additional modeling and support, opportunities are provided.

- This model also provides varied starting points for a lesson, depending on lesson objectives and student needs.

Whatever your content standards, it is essential for all students, including multilingual learners, to have appropriate, scaffolded instruction that leads to eventual independence.

Three Types of Scaffolding

Three types of scaffolding can be used effectively with multilingual learners: Verbal, Procedural, and Instructional. A description of each type of scaffolding follows.

1. **Verbal Scaffolding.** SIOP teachers use prompting, questioning, and elaboration to facilitate students' movement to higher levels of language proficiency, comprehension, and thinking. Examples include:

   - Paraphrasing: Restating a student's response in another form or in other words to clarify and model correct English usage aids students' language development and comprehension.

   - Using think-alouds: These models of how effective strategy users think and monitor their understandings usually are provided by the teacher, but they can also involve other students.

   - Embedding definitions: An example: *Aborigines, the people native to Australia, were being forced from their homes.* The phrase, *the people native to Australia,* provides a partial definition of the word *Aborigines* within the context of the sentence.

   - Gesturing; using body language; acting out, modeling, and/or demonstrating

   - Providing correct pronunciation by repeating students' responses: When teachers repeat multilingual learners' correct responses, enunciating carefully and naturally, students have an additional opportunity to hear the content information, pronunciation, and inflection.

- Providing or asking for translation in the students' first language
- Eliciting more language and information from students: Rather than accepting one- or two-word responses, ask students to add on, tell more, or explain their ideas more fully, giving them the chance to advance their language skills. Use prompts, such as:
  - *Tell us more about that.*
  - *Can you add some more information?*
  - *What else do you know about ___?*
  - *That's interesting! I'd like to know more about ___.*
  - *How did you learn that?*

2. **Procedural Scaffolding.** SIOP teachers also incorporate instructional approaches that provide procedural scaffolding. Examples include:

- Using an instructional framework, such as GISI (Figure 5.1) that includes explicit teaching, modeling, and guided and independent practice, with an expectation of eventual student independence
- Small-group instruction, in which students practice a newly learned strategy with another more experienced student
- Social supports, such as partnering or small groups for reading and content activities, with more experienced readers assisting those with less experience
- Cooperative learning activities, such as Jigsaw

3. **Instructional Scaffolding.** SIOP teachers use instructional scaffolding to provide multilingual learners with access to content and language concepts. Examples include:

- Graphic organizers focused on text structure, such as chronological or sequential (see Vogt & Echevarria, 2022)
- Models of completed assignments: students' sample products, such as posters, booklets, or reports to give a clear picture of the goal
- Sentence frames or sentence starters, partially completed outlines, or advance organizers
- Home language texts and/or modified texts
- Electronic texts with vocabulary links to definitions
- Visuals, including pictures, diagrams, illustrations, videos, props, or picture dictionaries. See Artifact 5.1 for an anchor chart that a teacher created for helping students remember the steps in solving word problems. Note in Artifact 5.2, how the teacher used colored markers to indicate each of the "CUBE" steps.

ARTIFACT 5.1 Anchor Chart: Steps to Solve Word Problems

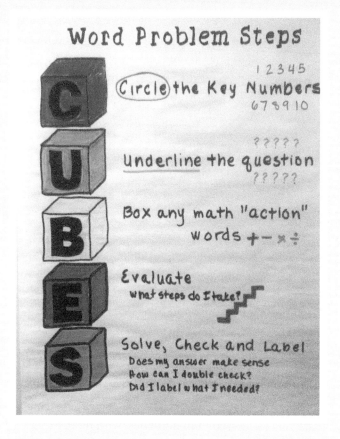

Word Problem Steps

C — Circle the Key Numbers 1 2 3 4 5 6 7 8 9 10

U — Underline the question ????? ?????

B — Box any math "action" words + − × ÷

E — Evaluate what steps do I take?

S — Solve, Check and Label
Does my answer make sense
How can I double check?
Did I label what I needed?

ARTIFACT 5.2 Example of Word Problem Indicating CUBE Steps

There are 2,274 students at Shakopee High School. They are each given one colored t-shirt to wear to the Homecoming Game. The t-shirts are red, yellow, green and blue. There is an equal number of each colored shirt. How many students received a red t-shirt?

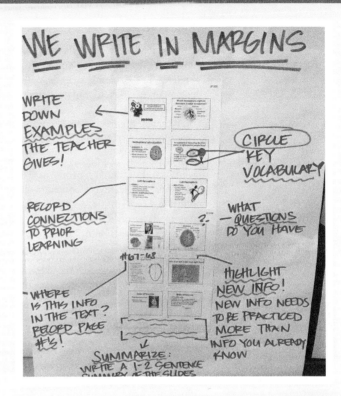

> This anchor chart idea not only provides an important scaffold for students when they are taking notes, but it also supports a teacher's think-aloud during instruction. The questions posed in the anchor chart help uncover students' thinking processes used in note-taking, determining importance, and summarizing key information, all of which are important learning strategies.
>
> Andrea Rients, District Professional Learning Coordinator, Minnesota

As you begin to write SIOP lesson plans, keep this in mind: *A scaffold is a temporary structure for helping students complete a task that would otherwise be too difficult to do alone.* The release of verbal, procedural, and instructional scaffolds is gradual until student independence has been achieved. Resist the temptation to keep scaffolding in place beyond the point that students need it. Additionally, state assessments may require that students complete assessment tasks without teacher scaffolding, so stay alert to students' increasing independence with learning tasks.

SIOP® **SIOP® FEATURE 15:**

A Variety of Questions or Tasks That Promote Higher-Order Thinking Skills

Effective SIOP teachers provide meaningful practice with learning strategies by asking questions and providing tasks that promote critical thinking. Over the years, several taxonomies have been designed to assist teachers in including higher-level questions and tasks in their lessons. Anderson and Krathwohl's (2001) taxonomy of cognition from lowest to highest includes: *Remember, Understand, Apply, Analyze, Evaluate,* and *Create* (see Table 5.2). Webb (1997) developed a similar, but more complex system and criteria for aligning standards, teaching, and assessment, called Depth of Knowledge (DOK).

TABLE 5.2	Process Verbs and Products at Varying Levels of Cognition

Level	Process Verbs	Products
Create	compose, propose, formulate, assemble, construct, set up, manage, plan, design, pretend, revise, blend, arrange, collect, create, invent, develop, hypothesize, generalize, originate, derive, compile, predict, act, modify, suppose, reorganize, role-play	film, poem, story, theatrical play, formula, machine, design, blueprint, goal, plan, play, solution, cartoon, new game, invention, video, event, newspaper, magazine
Evaluate	judge, evaluate, appraise, rate, compare, value, validate, defend, probe, assess, measure, decide, revise, conclude, determine, justify, support, prioritize, recommend, reject, referee, debate, award, score, choose, estimate	investigation, opinion, report, survey, editorial, debate, scale, conclusion, review, recommendation, critique, verdict, estimation
Analyze	distinguish, calculate, test, question, solve, analyze, research, characterize, appraise, interpret, diagram, experiment, compare, contrast, examine, scrutinize, dissect, probe, discover, categorize, investigate, order, differentiate, sift, sort, deduce	diagram, checklist, investigation, chart, graph, outline, conclusion, list, category, plan, illustration, survey, inventory, database, graphic organizer, rubric, matrix
Apply	teach, apply, employ, adapt, show, manipulate, exhibit, relate, solve, illustrate, operate, schedule, calculate, interview, collect, interpret, change, dramatize, prepare, record, construct, make, translate, use	puzzle, prediction, scrapbook, drawing, demonstration, diary, photograph, report, illustration, diorama, simulation, poster, sculpture, diagram, experiment, lesson
Understand	restate, describe, explain, paraphrase, report, tell, discuss, recognize, summarize, locate, review, list, research, locate, calculate, convert, outline, expand upon, annotate, give example, give main idea	recitation, example, summary, definition, reproduction, quiz, collection, list, explanation, test, dramatization, label, show & tell, outline
Remember	define, repeat, list, label, memorize, record, recall, relate, match, locate, show, select, group, quote, underline, recite, distinguish, cite, choose, give example, sort, describe, reproduce	quiz, label, definition, list, test, worksheet, workbook

It is important to carefully plan higher-order questions and tasks prior to lesson delivery. This is especially critical when teaching multilingual learners. As students are acquiring proficiency in English, it is tempting to rely on simple questions that result in yes/no or other one-word responses. It is possible, however, to reduce the linguistic demands of responses while still promoting higher levels of thinking.

For example, in a study of plant reproduction, the following question requires little thought: *Are seeds sometimes carried by the wind?* A nod or one-word response is almost automatic if the question is understood. However, a higher-level question coupled with a higher-order task, such as the following, requires analysis, though not a significant language demand:

- *Which of these seeds would be more likely to be carried by the wind: the rough seed or smooth seed?*
- *What do you think about this seed that has fuzzy hairs?*
- *Why do you think a particular seed would be more likely to be carried by the wind?*

Having three types of seeds available, either the actual seeds or photographs, and perhaps a small fan (or just blow air on the seeds to simulate the wind), enables students with lower English proficiency levels to have a concrete understanding of the English words, *seeds* and *wind,* so they can respond to the higher-level question and perform the higher-order task, which can be done using words with which they are familiar.

In addition, multilingual learners can also be encouraged to respond to higher levels of questions in their home languages, using translation for both the questions and the students' responses. Other students in the class who speak the same language can help translate, or you can use translation apps or websites. You might check with your district office for multilingual learners to see which translation service they recommend. Encouraging students to respond with higher levels of thinking requires teachers to consciously plan and incorporate higher-order questions and tasks, with scaffolding of course, at a variety of cognitive levels.

To assist in your lesson planning, review the examples of Process Verbs and Products as presented within varied levels of cognition (see Table 5.2). Note that you can use these active verbs in your content and language objectives, as well as in the questions you ask and the assignments you create. The highest level of cognition as depicted here is *Create*; the lowest is *Remember* (Anderson & Krathwohl, 2001).

Pearson eTextbook

Video Example 5.2

In this video, you will see two students, one of whom is a multilingual learner, working on an assignment in which they are to use signal words (Vogt & Echevarria, 2008, p. 36), to compare and contrast two characters from a story they've read. Notice the higher order thinking that both girls are engaging in, even though one of the students is at a lower level of English proficiency. https://mediaplayer.pearsoncmg.com/_bluetop_640x360_ccv2/ab/streaming/myeducationlab/ell/MN/rc/AR_ELA_Grade05_02SmallGroupA.mp4

■ Application to Your Classroom: Strategies

What follows are effective activities that teach and provide practice with learning strategies, include scaffolding techniques, and foster critical thinking.

- **Directed Reading-Thinking Activity (DR-TA)**, grades K–12 (Stauffer, 1969; Vogt & Echevarría, 2008). DR-TA is an effective activity for encouraging strategic thinking while students are reading or listening to narrative (fiction) text. The text to be read by students or as a teacher-read-aloud should be rich, interesting, and, if possible, have a surprising or unanticipated ending. Throughout the reading of the story, stop periodically in pre-designated spots and have students respond to a variety of probes, such as:
  - *With a title like . . ., what do you think this story will be about?*
  - *What do you think is going to happen next? What makes you think so?*
  - *Did . . . happen? If not, why not?* (revisit predictions)
  - *Now, what do you think is going to happen? Why?*
  - *Where did you get that idea? Does anyone else think that?*
  - *Tell me more about that . . .*

It is important that you revisit previously made predictions after chunks of text are read so that students come to understand how predictions (and their confirmation or disconfirmation) impact their comprehension. Note that an adapted DR-TA process is also effective in the upper grades for novels, with chapter-to-chapter discussions focusing on what students think will happen, what really happened, and why. (See Chapter 3, Mrs. Ornelas's lesson vignette that includes a DR-TA activity.)

Pearson eTextbook

Video Example 5.3

In this video, Dr. Vogt explains Squeepers (SQP2RS) step-by-step.
https://www.youtube.com/watch?v=KOulq0IkRSk

- **SQP2RS ("Squeepers").** This instructional framework, grades 1–10, is intended to provide practice with metacognitive strategies (predicting, self-questioning, monitoring/clarifying, evaluating, summarizing), while students read content in expository (nonfiction) texts (Vogt & Echevarría, 2022, p. 112). For young children, you can teach and practice Squeepers with informational big books, modeling the process as you read the book aloud. (See Mr. Montoya's lesson and lesson plan and Table 5.3 for Squeepers steps).

- **Canned Questions** (Vogt & Echevarria, 2022, p. 97). This idea has two purposes: (1) to provide practice in asking questions about a topic that is being studied; and (2) to provide a safe way for students to ask questions that they are reluctant to ask in front of the class. The steps to this simple idea are:

  - Decorate a large container (such as an oatmeal box) that has a plastic lid. This is your Question Can. Cut a slit in the lid big enough for pieces of paper to fit through it. With masking tape, not duct tape, secure the lid to the container. You will need to be able to open it to read students' questions.

  - Cut strips of paper for students' questions and place them in a box or envelope near the Question Can.

For free, downloadable, Squeepers posters, see:
https://assets.savvas.com/asset_mgr/current/201941/SQPRRS_posters_2019.pdf?_gl=1*1j9wzq9*_ga*Mzg1Nzcz MDIwLjE1OTk2NzIzNzY.*_ga_79FVM8Y0G4*MTY2NzIxNDQ4NS4xMTg1LjEuMT Y2NzIxNDUwMi40My4wLjA.&_ga=2.213532823.2089527723.1667214490-385773020.1599672376

TABLE 5.3	SQP2RS (Squeepers)

Steps for Squeepers Lesson	Procedures
Survey	Explore the text before reading: Look at the pictures and captions. Skim the highlighted text, bold words, headings, subheadings. Think about what you are going to learn while reading.
Question	With a partner or small group, come up with 3–4 questions that you think you'll be able to answer after reading the text. Record your questions.
Predict	Predict 2–3 things you're going to learn by reading this text. Use your questions and the lesson's content and language objectives to guide your thinking. Record your predictions.
Read	Read the text, alone, with the teacher, with a partner, or with a small group. Use sticky notes to indicate where your questions were answered and where your predictions were confirmed or disconfirmed.
Respond	Discuss with a small group or the whole class: Which questions were answered? Where in the text? Which predictions were confirmed or disconfirmed? Where? Develop new questions for the next section/chapter of text.
Summarize	Summarize, orally or in writing, what you have learned, alone, or with a partner or small group.

- Explain what the Question Can is for and model how to write questions, at varied levels (see Table 5.2 for active verbs at varied levels of cognition). Encourage multilingual learners to write questions for the Question Can in their home language, if they choose to do so.

- Plan time each day for answering students' questions; sometimes other students can answer questions, too, which can foster class discussion.

- Multilingual learners and students who struggle may benefit from question frames that they can use to ask their questions. You can create strips and go over them with students. For example, here are some possible question frames that students could use:

  - *Can you please explain _____? I still don't understand it*
  - *Will you please tell me again what _____ means?*
  - *I'm confused about _____. Will you please help me understand it better?*
  - *I need to practice _____. Can you tell how I should do that?*

■ Differentiating for Multilevel Classes

- Almost by definition, during SIOP lessons, scaffolding leads to differentiated instruction. One way to scaffold strategy practice for multilingual learners' varied language development needs is through Strategic Sentence Starters (Olson, Land, Anselmi, & AuBuchon, 2011, p. 251). Giving students sentence starters or frames provides the support many need to be able to participate in literature and content area discussions. The following examples could be printed on small "cue cards" that students select and use, as needed (see Table 5.4).

TABLE 5.4 **Strategic Sentence Starters**

Learning Strategies & Language Learning Strategies	Sentence Starters
Planning and Goal Setting	*My purpose is . . .* *My top priority (or most important job) is . . .* *I will accomplish my goal by . . .*
Tapping Prior Knowledge	*I already know . . .* *This reminds me of . . .* *This relates to . . .*
Asking Questions	*I wonder why . . .* *What if . . . ?* *How come . . . ?*
Making Predictions	*I'll bet that . . .* *I think . . .* *If . . . , then . . . .*

(continued)

TABLE 5.4	Strategic Sentence Starters *(continued)*

Learning Strategies & Language Learning Strategies	Sentence Starters
Visualizing	*I can picture . . .* *In my mind, I see . . .* *If this were a movie, I'd be seeing . . .*
Making Connections	*This reminds me of . . .* *I experienced this once when . . .* *I can relate to this because once . . .*
Summarizing	*The basic gist is . . .* *The key information is . . .* *In a nutshell, this says that . . .*
Monitoring	*I got lost here because . . .* *I need to reread the part where . . .* *I know I'm on the right track because . . .*
Clarifying	*To understand better, I need to know about . . .* *Something that is still not clear is . . .* *I'm guessing that this means _____, but I need to know . . .*
Reflecting and Relating	*So, the big idea is . . .* *A conclusion I'm drawing is . . .* *This is relevant to my life because . . .*
Evaluating	*I like/don't like _____ because . . .* *My opinion is _____ because . . .* *The most important message is _____, because . . . . . .*

> " When multilingual learners are learning new tasks during SIOP lessons, their affective filter is lower, because they understand the expectations, make connections to what they know, and have multiple ways to self-monitor their understanding.
>
> Dr. Nicole Teyechea McNeil
> Senior Learning Specialist
> Arizona "

■ The Lesson

The Rainforest (Grade 7)

The three classrooms described in the teaching scenarios in this chapter are heterogeneously mixed with native-English speakers, fluent English proficient speakers (redesignated English learners), and multilingual learners who have mixed levels of English fluency. The middle school is in a suburban community, and native-Spanish speakers make up approximately 40% of the student population.

The following teaching scenarios take place during the first day of a multi-day unit on the interdependence of organisms in an ecosystem. Mrs. Fletcher, Miss Lee, and Mr. Montoya are each using the same article about the depletion of the rainforests taken from a science news magazine designed for middle school students. The following state standards for Science, Reading, and Language Arts guided the development of the teachers' lessons:

- Construct an explanation that predicts patterns of interactions among organisms across multiple ecosystems.
- Trace and evaluate the argument and specific claims in a text, assessing whether the reasoning is sound, and the evidence is relevant and sufficient to support the claims.

■ Teaching Scenarios

To demonstrate how Mrs. Fletcher, Miss Lee, and Mr. Montoya planned instruction for their students, including their multilingual learners, we look at how each designed a lesson on the rainforest, using the magazine article to introduce the topic to students.

Mrs. Fletcher

Mrs. Fletcher began her lesson by distributing the rainforest article to the students and asking them to read together the title, "The Deforestation of our Rainforests." She then directed them to predict from the title and opening photograph what they thought the article would be about. Several students had difficulty with the word *deforestation*, so Mrs. Fletcher reminded the class that the prefix *de-* means *removal* or *take away*. Next, Mrs. Fletcher began reading the article, stopping once to ask the class, "What do you think will happen to the plants and animals in this rainforest? What evidence did you hear to support your predictions?" When she had finished orally reading the article, she asked the students if they had any questions.

One of the students asked, "Why do people burn the rainforests if it's so bad?" Mrs. Fletcher replied that the wood is very valuable, and people want to make money from the sale of it. Because there were no further questions, she asked each student to write a letter to the editor of the local newspaper explaining why we, as humans, should save the rainforest ecosystem. She also reminded students to give specific examples from the article. Several of the students began writing, while others reread the article to find information to include in their letters. A few appeared confused about how to start, and Mrs. Fletcher helped them individually. When the class had finished writing their letters, Mrs. Fletcher asked for volunteers to read their papers aloud. After a brief discussion of the letters, Mrs. Fletcher collected them and dismissed the students for lunch.

Check your understanding: On the SIOP form in Figure 5.2, rate Mrs. Fletcher's lesson on each of the Strategies features.

FIGURE 5.2	**Strategies Component of the SIOP® Model: Mrs. Fletcher's Lesson**

4	3	2	1	0
13. Ample opportunities provided for students to use **learning strategies**		Inadequate opportunities provided for students to use **learning strategies**		No opportunity provided for students to use **learning strategies**
4	**3**	**2**	**1**	**0**
14. **Scaffolding techniques** consistently used, assisting and supporting student understanding (e.g., think-alouds)		**Scaffolding techniques** occasionally used		**Scaffolding techniques** not used
4	**3**	**2**	**1**	**0**
15. A variety of **questions or tasks that promote higher-order thinking skills** (e.g., literal, analytical, and interpretive questions)		Infrequent **questions or tasks that promote higher-order thinking skills**		No **questions or tasks that promote higher-order thinking skills**

Miss Lee

Miss Lee introduced the magazine article by presenting a 15-minute lecture on the rainforest and by showing a variety of photographs of the rainforest ecosystem. She then divided the students into groups of four or five and asked one person in each group to read the magazine article to the other group members. When the students were finished reading, Miss Lee distributed worksheets. The students were first instructed to define words from the article, including *deforestation, biome, ecosystem,* and *organisms.* While Miss Lee circulated, students independently wrote answers to the following questions:

1. How much of the Earth's surface is covered by rainforests?
2. What percent of the Earth's species are found in the rainforest?
3. What are three products that come from the rainforests?
4. Why are the rainforests being burned or cut?
5. Who are the people that are doing the burning and cutting?
6. One of the birds found in the rainforest is a _____.
7. Global warming is believed to be caused by _____.
8. I hope the rainforests are not all cut down because _____.

In addition to the rainforest article, Miss Lee encouraged students to use the class computers to search the Internet for the answers to these questions. She told them to type in "rainforest" on a search engine to begin their search, and to keep track of the websites they explored.

When the students had finished writing their responses, they compared them to their group members' answers. Miss Lee directed the class to use the article to fix any answers the group thought were incorrect. She explained that they needed to come to agreement and record their group answer on a clean handout. For question #8, students were to determine the best answer of the group members' responses.

Check your understanding: On the SIOP form in Figure 5.3, rate Miss Lee's lesson on each of the Strategies features.

FIGURE 5.3 **Strategies Component of the SIOP® Model: Miss. Lee's Lesson**

4	3	2	1	0
13. Ample opportunities provided for students to use **learning strategies**		Inadequate opportunities provided for students to use **learning strategies**		No opportunity provided for students to use **learning strategies**
4	**3**	**2**	**1**	**0**
14. **Scaffolding techniques** consistently used, assisting and supporting student understanding (e.g., think-alouds)		**Scaffolding techniques** occasionally used		**Scaffolding techniques** not used
4	**3**	**2**	**1**	**0**
15. A variety of **questions or tasks that promote higher-order thinking skills** (e.g., literal, analytical, and interpretive questions)		Infrequent **questions or tasks that promote higher-order thinking skills**		No **questions or tasks that promote higher-order thinking skills**

Mr. Montoya (see Figure 5.5 for Mr. Montoya's lesson plan)

Mr. Montoya began his lesson by orally reviewing his lesson's content and language objectives, and by introducing the unit theme, Interdependence of Organisms in an Ecosystem. To connect with the previous days' lessons, Mr. Montoya wrote *ecosystem* on the whiteboard and gave students three minutes to review their notes with a partner and write their definition of *ecosystem* on an assigned spot on the whiteboard. The teacher and students then quickly checked the definitions for accuracy, and each pair was asked to identify an ecosystem that they had learned about previously.

Mr. Montoya then showed a picture of a rainforest on the smartboard, along with the vocabulary word, *rainforest.* He then separated the compound word into "*rain + forest*" and asked students to predict what might be unique about rainforests as compared to other forests. After listening to a few of the students' ideas, Mr. Montoya projected a picture of a forest with pine trees and repeated his questions about how a forest and rainforest might differ.

Mr. Montoya then went online and brought up a three-dimensional map of the world that showed countries where there are rainforests. He introduced the vocabulary word, *deforestation,* showing a picture taken from the air of a rainforest with a large area that had been deforested. He asked students what they thought the word, *deforestation*, might mean. Students grappled with the parts of the word for a few minutes before Mr. Montoya defined the prefix *de-* as meaning *away from* or *opposite of.*

Students thought for a minute before Mr. Montoya reminded them about a vocabulary word that he wrote on the whiteboard *desalinate*, that they had learned earlier in the unit. He asked the class for a definition, and several students replied with, *removing salt from sea water.* He then referred students to the definition of *deforestation* in the article: *the action of clearing a wide area of trees.* One student said, "That's the opposite of planting trees. They're cutting them down in the rainforest. Why are they doing that?"

After distributing the magazine article on the tropical rainforest to his class, he engaged his students in a SQP2RS activity (Squeepers: See Table 5.3). Students, with partners, surveyed the section of the article they were going to read, for one minute, and in small groups, they generated several questions that they thought would be answered by reading the assigned section of the article. Students then referred to the lesson objectives, their questions, and the text, and determined 4–5 main concepts they predicted they would learn about the tropical rainforest. Each group shared their questions and predictions with the class, as Mr. Montoya charted them under two columns: *Questions We Have* and *Predictions: What We Will Learn.*

Mr. Montoya then read aloud the first two paragraphs about the rainforest ecosystem while the students followed along in their copies of the text. At the end of the two paragraphs, students were asked to determine if any of their questions on the chart paper had been answered and if any of their predictions had been confirmed or disconfirmed. With partners, students were directed to indicate with small sticky notes where this information could be found in the article. Referring again to the chart, Mr. Montoya placed a plus (+) sign next to each prediction that had been confirmed by the text reading; a minus sign (−) indicated a prediction that was disconfirmed; and a question mark (?) was used for any prediction that had not been answered to this point in the article.

A few additional questions and predictions were generated by the class prior to Mr. Montoya's directions to quietly read the next section of the text (about six paragraphs) with a partner or a triad. In their small groups, students ascertained whether their earlier predictions, as posted on the chart paper, were confirmed or disconfirmed. They also shared the evidence they had found in the article while reading.

Mr. Montoya led the class in a brief discussion of any unknown terms from the article, including further clarification of *deforestation*. In their small groups or with partners, the students then reviewed the questions that had been posted earlier to see if they had found answers during their reading. They also checked their predictions according to the process Mr. Montoya had previously modeled. Next, students individually wrote summary sentences, including the key vocabulary, about what they had learned, using their generated questions and predictions as a guide.

Toward the end of the class, Mr. Montoya displayed on the whiteboard the following questions:

1. Why are we dependent on the rainforests for our survival on Earth?

2. What is the ozone layer and why is it important?

3. Compare and contrast the arguments of foresters and environmentalists, as described in the article. With which argument do you most agree? Why? What in the text convinced you of one position or the other?

After reading the questions aloud, and having students read them with their partners, in their first languages and/or in English, Mr. Montoya turned to homework. He provided students with a copy of three of the questions and encouraged students to write them in their L1 if desired. He assigned a brief written response to each question, again in the L1, if they wished to. He announced that these questions and the topic of the ozone layer would be discussed further during the next day's class, and they would eventually have a classroom debate about question #3. Before the bell, Mr. Montoya reviewed each of the three content and language objectives with his students. On a sticky note, students self-assessed the degree to which they met each of the objectives, with a: 1 = *I understand it well*; 2 = *I think I understand it, but I still have questions*; 3 = *I don't understand it yet and need some help.* They put their names on the sticky note and each gave the exit ticket to Mr. Montoya as they exited the classroom.

Check your understanding: On the SIOP form in Figure 5.4, rate Mr. Montoya's lesson on each of the Strategies features.

FIGURE 5.4	Strategies Component of the SIOP® Model: Mr. Montoya's Lesson

4	3	2	1	0
13. Ample opportunities provided for students to use **learning strategies**		Inadequate opportunities provided for students to use **learning strategies**		No opportunity provided for students to use **learning strategies**
4	3	2	1	0
14. **Scaffolding techniques** consistently used assisting and supporting student understanding (e.g., think-alouds)		**Scaffolding techniques** occasionally used		**Scaffolding techniques** not used
4	3	2	1	0
15. A variety of **questions or tasks that promote higher-order thinking skills** (e.g., literal, analytical, and interpretive questions)		Infrequent **questions or tasks that promote higher-order thinking skills**		No **questions or tasks that promote higher-order thinking skills**

FIGURE 5.5 SIOP® Lesson Plan: Tropical Rainforests (Science) Grade 7

Mr. Montoya's Lesson Plan

Key: SW = Students will; TW = Teacher will; HOTS = Higher-Order Thinking Skills

State Content and Language Standards:

- Construct an explanation that predicts patterns of interactions among organisms across multiple ecosystems.
- Trace and evaluate the argument and specific claims in a text, assessing whether the reasoning is sound, and the evidence is relevant and sufficient to support the claims.

Key Vocabulary: review *ecosystem*; introduce *rainforest; deforestation;*

Visuals/Resources: Article on deforestation of tropical rainforests; photographs of depleted rainforests and from space depicting hole in the ozone layer; chart paper and markers

HOTS: (1) Surveying, self-questioning, predicting, summarizing; (2) Determining key vocabulary meaning from the prefix (*de-*); comparing forests to rainforests

Connections: Prior Knowledge/Building Background/Previous Learning: TW review SQP2RS's previously learned steps; review *ecosystem*; review examples of ecosystems

Content and Language Objectives:

- Content Objective: SW analyze the impact of deforestation of tropical rainforests on the environment.
- Language Objectives:
  - SW ask questions and predict key concepts prior to reading about tropical rainforests.
  - SW read and write summary sentences about deforestation in the rainforests, using key vocabulary: *ecosystem, rainforest, deforestation.*

Supplementary Materials:

- Pictures of depleted rainforests from space, rainforest with deforestation, Colorado forest, map of rainforests
- Homework handout with three questions
- Chart paper/markers with Squeepers T-chart: Questions We Have; What We Will Learn
- Science magazine with rainforest article

Sequence of Instruction

Introduce Objectives:

1. TW post and orally explain content and language objectives.

Building Background/Review of Past Learning:

2. TW review term: *ecosystem*
3. TW review and ask students (with partners) to briefly describe ecosystems learned to this point.
4. TW review SQP2RS process for reading expository texts
5. TW show pictures of rainforests on smartboard with the vocabulary word; write *rain + forest*; ask students to look at the compound word and predict what is unique about rainforests as compared to other forests (show picture of forest with pine trees); show map via the Internet of countries where there are rainforests. Show picture of rainforest with a large swath that has been deforested. Introduce meaning of *deforestation* (review *desalinate* as a clue to meaning)

(continued)

FIGURE 5.5 **SIOP® Lesson Plan: Tropical Rainforests (Science) Grade 7** *(continued)*

Read the Article:

6. Partners with Squeepers: Survey article; generate 2–3 questions about deforestation; record 2–3 predictions about what will be learned in article.
7. Small group discussions about generated questions/predictions
8. Whole class: TW chart questions and predictions from each group in 2 columns (*Questions We Have* and *Predictions: What We'll Learn*)
9. TW read aloud two paragraphs; SW check questions/predictions to this point.
10. Small Groups: SW continue to read article (alone, with partners, or in small group) to answer their questions & confirm/disconfirm predictions; encourage L1 usage as needed.
11. TW circulate, monitor; read with individuals, if needed.
12. Individuals: SW use sticky notes to: (a) indicate answers found in text; (b) note where predictions were confirmed or disconfirmed
13. Whole class: Return to charted questions and predictions
14. Individuals or partners: Writing of summaries; TW monitor; summaries turned in
15. Introduce handout with three questions; go over them with class.
16. Review content and language objectives.
17. Exit tickets (sticky notes) for level of understanding for each objective: 1 = *I've got it!*; 2 = *I think I've got it, but I still have questions*; 3 = *I need more information or review*

Homework questions:

1. Why are we dependent on the rainforests for our survival on Earth?
2. What is the ozone layer?
3. Compare and contrast the arguments of foresters and environmentalists, as described in the article. With which argument do you most agree? Why? What in the text convinced you of one position or the other?

Review & Assessment Throughout Lesson

- Review of Squeepers procedures
- Review of *ecosystem* and examples
- Questions and predictions about the rainforest posted on chart paper
- Students' identification of answers to questions with sticky notes
- Students' identification of where predictions were confirmed or disconfirmed (placement of sticky notes)
- Group discussions around answers to questions
- Summary sentences and use of key vocabulary
- Selection of question for next day's debate
- Exit tickets

Discussion of Lessons

Look back at your rating form and think about the reasons you scored the lessons as you did. What evidence is in the scenarios? Read on to see our analyses.

13. *Ample Opportunities Provided for Students to Use Learning Strategies*

Mrs. Fletcher: 3

Miss Lee: 2

Mr. Montoya: 4

- **Mrs. Fletcher's** lesson received a "3" for the inclusion of learning strategies. She began the lesson by asking her students to make predictions from the title of the article. In addition to the predictions, the teacher also modeled a language strategy, using word structure (the prefix *de-*) to help determine the meaning of *deforestation*, and encouraged students to confirm and expand their understandings of the topic on the Internet.

  Mrs. Fletcher's lesson would have been more effective had she included a graphic organizer or other means for students to organize the information they were learning. She also could have periodically stopped her oral reading to reinforce important concepts, clarify confusing points, and discuss predictions that were confirmed or disconfirmed. Even though Mrs. Fletcher had the students write a letter to the editor, providing students with a chance to demonstrate their understanding, she missed the opportunity to model summarizing as a language learning strategy.

- **Miss Lee's** lesson received a "2" for the inclusion of strategies. She encouraged her students to evaluate and determine importance during the discussions of the answers to the questions on the worksheet. Students were required to support their responses, clarify misunderstandings, and reach consensus on the answers before turning in their papers. However, rather than presenting all the information orally, she could have discussed the photographs and generated student predictions and questions about the content of the pictures.

- **Mr. Montoya's** lesson received a "4" for the inclusion of strategies. He began the lesson by asking students to recall a language learning strategy he had taught them earlier, using word structure to determine word meaning. He then provided practice with five metacognitive strategies when he engaged his students in the SQP2RS/Squeepers activity. As Mr. Montoya led his students through the activity, he modeled and provided support in how to survey text, generate questions, make predictions, confirm or disconfirm predictions based on text information, and summarize.

14. *Scaffolding Techniques Consistently Used, Assisting and Supporting Student Understanding*

    Mrs. Fletcher: 2

    Miss Lee: 3

    Mr. Montoya: 4

- **Mrs. Fletcher's** lesson received a "2" for scaffolding. Mrs. Fletcher attempted to scaffold by reading the entire article to the students. This reduced the reading demands of the text, but the scaffolding could have been more effective if she had begun reading the article to the students, and then had them complete the reading with a partner or small group. Also, there may have been some students who would have benefitted from reading with the teacher in a small group. Further, Mrs. Fletcher missed opportunities to scaffold when she simply assigned the letter to the editor without showing sample letters, providing words and phrases that might be found in such letters, and allowing students to work with partners on their letters. Another scaffolding technique is to encourage students to work with an "editing partner," who can look over a piece of writing before it's shared publicly. Also, including a "silent-reading practice run" before a read-aloud helps pronunciation, increases fluency, allows for simple editing help from another student, and reduces stress for the readers.

- **Miss Lee's** lesson received a "3" for scaffolding. She effectively scaffolded student learning in three ways. First, the photographs she displayed during her brief lecture provided support for students who had little background knowledge about the topic of rainforests. Second, by having the students complete the reading in their groups, the reading demands were reduced. Depending on the length of the article, she might have encouraged the reading involvement of more than one student in each group if she had suggested, for example, a "Page, Paragraph, or Pass" approach. With this activity, each student decides whether they wish to read a page, a paragraph, or pass on the oral reading. Multilingual learners and reluctant readers may feel more comfortable having the option of choosing whether and how much they'll read aloud to their peers.

  Miss Lee also scaffolded the students' answering of the questions on the handout. They had to answer the questions independently, but then were allowed to compare their responses to those of the other students and decide on the correct answers together. This provided students the opportunity to demonstrate individual learning of the rainforest material, and also gave them the chance to negotiate their understandings with their peers (a language learning strategy).

- **Mr. Montoya's** lesson received a "4" for scaffolding. He incorporated and modeled a variety of techniques that provided support with key vocabulary and the academic content. He used several grouping configurations during the lesson, including whole class, small groups, triads, partners, independent work. Students had the opportunity to confer with each other, receiving support and assistance if necessary, including in their first language. Mr. Montoya also carefully modeled the process for the students prior to requiring application. The reading demands of the article were reduced when students were allowed to read it in pairs or triads, and to ask questions and write in the first language, if they chose to do so.

15. *A Variety of Questions and Tasks That Promote Higher-Order Thinking Skills*

Mrs. Fletcher: 1

Miss Lee: 2

Mr. Montoya: 4

- **Mrs. Fletcher's** lesson received a "1" for higher-order thinking. She missed several opportunities to use higher-order questioning to engage her students' thinking. After students made some predictions, she could have probed with questions such as, "What made you think that?" or "Tell me more about that." Toward the end of the lesson, when one student asked why people still burn the rainforests, Mrs. Fletcher might have used the student's question to develop inquiry skills, and the resulting questions could have motivated the letters to the editor. Instead, the letter-writing activity, while potentially meaningful and thought provoking, seemed somewhat removed from the article and brief discussion the class had about the rainforests. It's important to remember that assigning a higher-order thinking task is just the first step for this SIOP feature. Enabling all students to accomplish the task meaningfully is the goal.

- **Miss Lee's** lesson received a "2" for questioning. Although she incorporated questioning into her lesson by using the handout, the questions were mostly written at the literal level, with answers that could be found easily in the rainforest article. The activity would have required greater cognitive work on the part of the students if Miss Lee had written questions at various levels. Question 8 was the only one that required actual application and evaluation of the content concepts.

  In addition, although Miss Lee tried to incorporate technology into her lesson, she did not provide enough guidance to help students find the information they needed in a timely fashion. She could have worked with students who were interested in using the Internet to refine their search procedures; generate some of their own questions about the rainforest; and use several key words to yield the information they were seeking while narrowing the field of potential websites.

- **Mr. Montoya's** lesson received a "4" for questioning. He incorporated questioning throughout the lesson, first during review and instruction of key vocabulary, the SQP2RS (Squeepers) activity, when students generated their own questions based on the text information, and made predictions as to what they would learn. Note the varied levels of the homework questions: The first question requires analysis and evaluation; the second question is a literal-level question, and the third requires application, synthesis, and evaluation. Mr. Montoya effectively reduced the text's difficulty through the Squeepers activity, not by lowering the cognitive demand of the lesson (see Figure 5.5 for the lesson plan).

◼ Final Points

As you reflect on this chapter and the impact of learning strategies, scaffolding, and higher-order thinking questions and tasks, consider the following main points:

- Promoting critical and strategic thinking for all students is important, including multilingual learners. Learning is made more effective when teachers actively assist students in developing a variety of learning strategies, including those that are cognitive, metacognitive, language based, and socio-affective. Learning strategies promote self-monitoring, self-regulation, and problem-solving abilities.

- Students with developing English proficiency should be provided with effective, creative, and generative teaching while they are learning the language. Therefore, it is imperative that all teachers provide them with sufficient scaffolding, including verbal supports such as paraphrasing, frequent repetition, and opportunities to clarify in their first language; procedural supports, such as teacher modeling with think-alouds, one-on-one teaching, and opportunities to work with more experienced individuals in flexible groups; and instructional supports such as the appropriate use of graphic organizers, and content and text adaptations.

Through appropriate and effective scaffolding, multilingual learners can participate in lessons that involve strategic and critical thinking.

- We frequently remind teachers, "Just because students don't read well doesn't mean they can't think!" A similar adage to this might be said of multilingual learners: "Just because students don't speak English proficiently doesn't mean they can't think!" Therefore, SIOP teachers include in their lesson plans a variety of higher-order thinking questions and tasks.

■ Discussion Questions

1. In reflecting on the content and language objectives at the beginning of the chapter, are you able to:
   a. Identify and build on students' strategy use during content lessons: cognitive, metacognitive, language learning, and socio-affective?
   b. Select effective teaching techniques for verbal, procedural, and instructional scaffolding?
   c. Write questions or tasks that are differentiated for students' English proficiency levels and are at different levels of cognition?
   d. Include in a lesson plan, instruction and practice with one or more learning strategies, scaffolding for those who need it, and higher-level questions and tasks?

2. We know that grade-level instruction without scaffolding will probably be unsuccessful for multilingual learners. Think of a content topic that you teach to multilingual learners and other students. What types of scaffolds must you put in place for your students to successfully access the lesson's content and language objectives?

3. Here's a factual question a teacher might ask based on a social studies text: "Who was the first president of the United States?" Given the topic of the presidency, what are several additional questions you could ask that promote higher-order thinking? Why is it important to use a variety of questioning strategies with multilingual learners? Use the Process Verbs and Products (Table 5.2) to guide the development of your questions.

4. The answers to higher-order thinking questions may involve language that is beyond a student's current level of English proficiency. Discuss the advantages of encouraging multilingual learners to use their first language when answering questions at higher levels of cognition. Search for translation websites or apps to assist you and students in translating students' responses in their home languages.

5. Using the SIOP lesson you have been developing, add meaningful activities that augment learning strategies. Determine how to scaffold multilingual learners' access to your objectives. Write several higher-order thinking questions or tasks for your lesson plan.

■ Pearson eTextbook Application Videos

The purpose of the Pearson eTextbook Application Videos is to provide you with an opportunity to observe and reflect on SIOP teaching and learning practices. There are multilingual students in each of the classrooms with varying levels of English proficiency. The teachers you will observe are at different levels of their SIOP implementation, from second year SIOPers to veterans. As you observe the lessons they have created, focus on the students and the lesson objectives, keeping in mind that becoming a high-implementing SIOP teacher takes time, practice, and support to refine teaching practices. We are grateful to each of these SIOP educators for welcoming us into their classrooms, and for their dedication to SIOP, their multilingual learners, and other students.

Pearson eTextbook Application
Video Example 5.1
SIOP Lesson: Grade 10 History; Comparing and Contrasting the U.S. and the Roman Empire (Teacher 1)

6 Interaction

CONTENT OBJECTIVES

This chapter will help you to . . .

- List ways that collaborative conversations and discussions are aligned with the Interaction component.
- Design grouping structures that support a lesson's content and language objectives.
- Identify techniques to increase wait time.
- Identify resources to support students' use of their home language.

LANGUAGE OBJECTIVES

This chapter will help you to . . .

- Describe techniques to reduce the amount of teacher talk in a lesson.
- Practice asking questions that promote student elaboration of responses.
- As part of a lesson plan, add structured time for partner and small-group productive work.

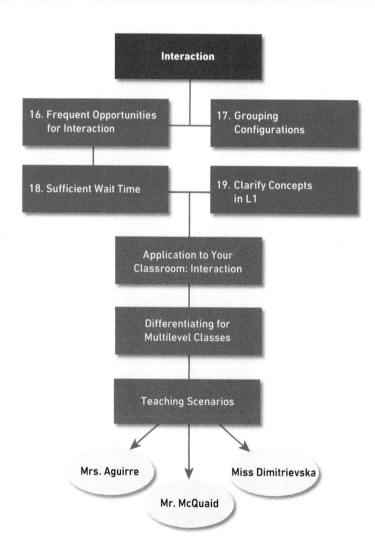

Interaction

16. Frequent Opportunities for Interaction

17. Grouping Configurations

18. Sufficient Wait Time

19. Clarify Concepts in L1

Application to Your Classroom: Interaction

Differentiating for Multilevel Classes

Teaching Scenarios

Mrs. Aguirre

Mr. McQuaid

Miss Dimitrievska

All teachers are language teachers. Content teachers have made a significant investment in preparing to teach a specific subject area such as science, math, social studies, music, and so forth, so it's natural that their focus is on teaching the content topics in their area of expertise. Elementary teachers also teach a variety of subjects and tend to focus on the topic at hand, whether it is teaching a science lesson or poetry. However, few would disagree that language permeates all topics and subject areas. Every subject has specific academic language that students need to learn and practice using, such as *identify branches of government* for social studies and *plot points on a graph* for math. In addition, general academic terms are not unique to a specific discipline but are used across content areas, such as *relative*, *surface*, and *determine*. This type of language use is challenging for all students (Scheppegrell, 2020), but especially for multilingual learners. Academic language development is the responsibility of general education teachers, even when multilingual learners have access to support from ESL/ELD specialists.

Talking, listening, and thinking are a powerful combination of processes associated with learning, and each strengthens the others (City, 2014; Vygotsky, 1978). Online learning has increased the amount of time students spend communicating with electronic devices rather than face to face and has, overall, diminished multilingual learners' oral participation. Students have limited exposure to extended discourse given that much social and school interaction takes place via devices. The style of communication used is typically abbreviated messages that lack pragmatics (linguistic context clues such as nonverbal cues, turn-taking, and nego-tiating meaning) and are delivered while multitasking rather than focusing on the discussion (Rosen, 2012). At the same time, state standards call for students to engage in substantive, collaborative discussions around text and concepts. The only opportunity many students have for quality talk around texts and topics is in the classroom.

Short and Echevarría (2016) discuss a number of benefits of collaborative academic discussions. As students talk about a topic, they have the opportunity to try out new words, grammatical structures, and language functions (see Chapter 2 for examples of language functions). They also learn from peers who have more advanced language proficiency, those "more capable others" who provide support for multilin-gual learners' understanding (Vygotsky, 1978). Participation in discussions with peers provides the language practice time that multilingual learners need. Conversation time increases significantly when working in partners or small groups since students have fewer opportunities for practice when working with the whole class.

> **"**
> SIOP teaching has shifted my practice from delivering content to facilitating experiences where students process the content by using language.
>
> Tan Hunh, Secondary Language Specialist, Thailand
> **"**

To understand and use academic English, multilingual learners need to be provided with a classroom environment that facilitates interaction by helping students acclimate to the type of interaction desired. Many multilingual learners may not be accustomed to interactive lessons where they are expected to work with a partner or in groups, briefly speaking in turn-and-talk or more extensively in preparing for a class presentation. Haneda and Wells (2012) emphasize the importance of creating an engaging environment that encourages discussion to allow multilingual learners to practice their linguistic skills.

In addition, increased student interaction and discussion requires structured opportunities for practice in all subject areas throughout the school day, not just during a designated English language development (ELD) time. The integration of language development across the curriculum is vital and is recognized by some states as part of their instructional framework (see California Department of Education, 2014). As students are learning in and through a new language, English, teachers must create ample opportunities to practice using *academic* language, not just social language. It is recommended that multilingual learners have daily opportunities to talk about content in pairs or small groups, practicing and extending material already taught (Baker et al., 2014). ■

For many teachers it may be challenging to move from presenting whole-class instruction to providing the kinds of small-group opportunities needed for students to have high-quality discussions. Sharing responsibility for learning with students working in small groups or with partners is an adjustment for many teachers, but it can make a significant impact on learning. Researchers have found that multilingual learners are more engaged academically when working in small groups or with partners than they are in whole-class instruction or individual work (Brooks & Thurston, 2010). In this chapter, we present ways that teachers can use interaction to launch students to higher levels of English proficiency, improve academic outcomes, and meet standards. Later in the chapter, you will see examples of first-grade teachers in a dual immersion program who implement the features of Interaction with varying degrees of effectiveness.

■ Background

"Use it or lose it" is a saying that conveys what we know from our own experience in learning a second language. If one doesn't practice using the language, it is difficult to maintain it. But what about learning a language in the first place—does speaking it help to develop the language? The answer is a resounding "Yes!" The role that conversation plays in the process of second language teaching and learning is clear. But discussion also offers important benefits for learning in general. As Gerald Graff puts it, "Talk—about books and subjects—is as important educationally as are the books and subjects themselves" (Graff, 2003, p. 9).

The issue is, why are there so few opportunities for students to interact in typical classrooms? Studies indicate that in most classrooms, teachers dominate the linguistic aspect of the lesson, leaving students severely limited in terms of opportunities to use language in a variety of ways (Cazden, 2001; Goodlad, 1984; Marshall, 2000). In a classroom observation study, there was evidence of "academic dialog and discussion" in only .5% of the 1500 classrooms observed (Schmoker, 2006). It goes without saying that teachers have extensive knowledge to share and discuss with students, but consistent teacher dominance reduces the opportunities students have to participate fully in lessons by discussing ideas and information, and practicing English as they express their understandings, opinions, and answers.

There are many benefits to having students actively engaged in interaction around subject matter. Some include:

> **"**
> If it never shows up in a student's oral language, it will never show up in a student's written language, therefore interaction is imperative!
> Andrea Rients, Professional Learning Coordinator, Minnesota
> **"**

- **Deeper understanding of text, including vocabulary learning.** When teachers use thoughtful questioning to promote discussion, it encourages students to think critically about the passage. In doing so, students also think more deeply about the meaning of the words they encounter (Wasik & Iannone-Campbell, 2012). Also, new understandings are co-constructed through interactions (McIntyre et al., 2010).

- **Oral language development.** Findings of the National Literacy Panel on Language-Minority Children and Youth (August & Shanahan, 2006) confirmed the important relationship between oral proficiency in English and reading and writing proficiency. Specifically, reading comprehension skills and writing skills are positively correlated with oral language proficiency in English (Geva, 2006). In a recent review of the research on the Science of Reading for multilingual learners, Goldenberg (2020) points out that explicit instruction and structured practice are needed for advancing oral language proficiency. Solid reading comprehension is the foundation for achievement in nearly every subject area in school, and writing proficiency in English is an essential skill as well.

- **Student agency.** Students become more independent, confident learners when they are active participants in the class. They benefit by taking control of their own learning process and learn to work well with others through productive groups. In the process of interacting with peers, they hone their critical thinking skills because it puts them in the position of developing their own opinions and articulating their understanding of material instead of simply receiving and restating information given by the teacher (Hendy & Cuevas, 2020).

- **Brain stimulation.** Interesting, engaging activities, including discussions, play an important role in learning. When students are engaged and their brains are activated, more of the pleasure structures in the brain fire than when students are simply asked to memorize information (Jensen & McConchie, 2020; Poldrack et al., 2001).

- **Increased motivation.** Providing opportunities for interactions with others in pairs or small groups has a positive impact on students. In fact, the more opportunities a teacher can provide for multilingual learners to use their second language safely, with a lowered affective filter, the more motivated these students will be to participate (Mellon, et al., 2018). Using a conversational approach has been found to create positive changes in multilingual learners' attitudes toward school and academic motivation (Davin, 2013).

- **Reduced risk.** The typical question-answer sessions in which teachers call on students may be threatening to some students, particularly those who are unprepared to respond or who are uncomfortable with speaking in whole-class settings. Some students have difficulty focusing on the content in this situation because it triggers the brain's "threat response" (Jensen & McConchie, 2020). Having students talk in pairs or in small groups minimizes the risk and allows ideas to flow more easily. However, some students may need support to engage in academic discussions (TESOL, 2018).

- **More processing time.** Many students benefit from having time to process information presented by the teacher, especially multilingual students who are learning new information in a new language. Some multilingual learners may be mentally translating the information, and they need time to do so. SIOP teachers purposely present information (or reading passages) in chunks, then turn the talk over to students by asking them to actively process and discuss the information, such as by summarizing it with a partner, answering questions, or jointly completing a written task. This process makes learning large amounts of information more manageable. Teachers might teach students to go through the following questions to help process the information (see Chapter 5 for a discussion of metacognitive strategies):

  ◆ *Does this make sense to me? Do I understand the language and the ideas presented?*

  ◆ *Does it connect with something I already know?*

  ◆ *What questions do I have?*

  ◆ *Am I ready to repeat what the teacher did or said or will it require a lot of practice?*

To illustrate the importance of more student participation, we find that it is both interesting and helpful to analyze actual transcripts from lessons that demonstrate the kind of teacher dominance that is common in classrooms. The transcripts in Figures 6.1 and 6.2 are from a pilot SIOP study in sixth-grade social studies classes. The teachers were videotaped teaching the same content about consumerism to multilingual learners, with the first using a traditional approach found in general education classes and the second using the SIOP Model. Both classes had approximately 25 students, and in this lesson students were learning how to read labels on clothing and directions on a bottle of antiseptic.

As you read through the transcript, note the amount of teacher talk compared to student talk in each lesson. Also, focus on the quality of student responses in each.

In examining the exchanges, what did the teacher do when students gave partial or incorrect answers? He answered the question himself. He also tended to finish sentences for the students and accept any form of comment without encouraging extended expression. In this case, there were several missed opportunities where the teacher could have encouraged a more balanced exchange between himself and

Pearson eTextbook

Video Example 6.1

Watch this video to hear about the importance of student interaction and watch students working together. What stands out for you about the way students are interacting?

https://www.youtube.com/watch?v=GjOrFN6PEDg&t=3s

TEACHER: Look at the piece of clothing at the bottom. It says *(he reads)*, "This shirt is flame-resistant," which means what?

STUDENT: Could not burn.
STUDENT: Won't catch fire.
STUDENT: *(unintelligible)*

TEACHER: It will not burn, won't catch fire. Right *(continues reading)*. "To retain the flame-resistant properties"—what does "to retain" mean?

TEACHER: To keep it. All right. *(He reads)* "In order to keep this shirt flame–resistant wash with detergent only." All right *(he reads)*. "Do not use soap or bleach. Tumble dry. One hundred percent polyester." Now, why does it say, "Do not use soap or bleach"?

STUDENT: 'Cause it'll take off the . . .
STUDENTS: *(fragmented responses)*

TEACHER: It'll take off the what?

TEACHER: It'll take off the flame-resistant quality. If you wash it with soap or bleach, then the shirt's just gonna be like any old shirt, any regular shirt, so when you put a match to it, will it catch fire?

STUDENT: No.

TEACHER: Yes. 'Cause you've ruined it then. It's no longer flame-resistant. So the government says you gotta tell the consumer what kind of shirt it is, and how to take care of it. If you look at any piece of clothing: shirt, pants, your shirts, um, your skirts, anything. There's always going to be a tag on these that says what it is made of and how you're going to take care of it. Okay. And that's for your protection so that you won't buy something and then treat it wrong. So labeling is important. All right. Let's review. I'll go back to the antiseptic. What did we say indications meant? Indications? Raise your hands, raise your hands. Robert?

STUDENT: What's it for.

TEACHER: What is it for, when do you use this? Okay. What do directions, what is that for, Victor?

STUDENT: How to use . . .
STUDENTS: *(various mumbled responses)*

TEACHER: How to use. Okay, so indications is when you use it *(holds one finger up)*, directions is how you use it *(holds another finger up)*, and warnings is what?

TEACHER: How you don't use it. This is what you don't do.

---

the students. In the segment that begins with the teacher asking, *"What do directions . . . what is that for, Victor?"* the non-SIOP teacher answered for students (Victor and others). He did not encourage students to express their thoughts completely; he accepted partial and mumbled answers. Second, he answered for the students, dominating the discussion. Note the length of teacher utterances compared to those of students.

It is easy to imagine how students could become uninterested, passive learners in a class in which the teacher accepts minimal participation and does most of the talking. Students learn that they can disengage because the teacher will continue with the "discussion."

The SIOP teacher let the students have time to express their thoughts. For example, when a student says, *"It kills . . . It kills germs"* the teacher could have completed the sentence for the student, but she waited for him to finish his thought. Also, the SIOP teacher encouraged and challenged the students more than the non-SIOP teacher did by asking twice, *"What else?"* Finally, the SIOP teacher called on students who volunteered to talk and repeated what they said so that the class could hear a full response (e.g., Veronica).

The SIOP teacher allowed for a balance of teacher-to-student talk and encouraged student participation, which can be seen visually in the student column. She asked questions, provided wait time for students to respond, and restated or elaborated on their responses. In this case, what did the teacher do to elicit answers to the question? She scaffolded the answer by encouraging the students to think about it, prompting them to give their responses.

FIGURE 6.2   SIOP Lesson

TEACHER: Most clothing must have labels that tell what kind of cloth was used in it, right? Look at the material in the picture down there *(points to picture in text)*.[1] What does it say, the tag right there?
TEACHER: The tag right there.
TEACHER: Resistant.

STUDENT: The, the, the . . .

STUDENT: *(Reading)* "Flame-resis . . . "
STUDENT: "Flame-resistant. To retain the flame-resistant properties, wash with detergent only. Do not use soap or bleach. Use warm water. Tumble dry."
STUDENT: "Polyester."

TEACHER: "One hundred percent . . . "
[The teacher then explained that they would be doing an activity in which they would read labels for information]
TEACHER: Now, most clothes carry labels, right? *(pointing to the neck of her sweater)*. They explain how to take care of it, like dry clean, machine wash, right? It tells you how to clean it. Why does this product have to be washed with a detergent and no soap or bleach?
TEACHER: Why can't you use something else?

STUDENT: Because clothes . . .
STUDENTS: *(several students mumble answers)*
STUDENT: *(says in Spanish)* Because it will make it small.
STUDENT: It's not going to be able to be resistant to fire.

TEACHER: It may shrink, or *(gestures to a student)* it may not be . . . what does it say?
TEACHER: Exactly. It's flame-resistant, right? So, if you use something else, it won't be flame-resistant anymore. How about the, uh, look at the *antiseptic (holds hands up to form a container)*—the picture above the shirt, the antiseptic?
TEACHER: Antiseptic *(Teacher reads)* and other health products you buy without a prescription often have usage and warning labels. So what can you learn from this label? Read this label quietly please, and tell me what you can learn from the label. Read the label on that antiseptic. *(Students read silently.)*
TEACHER: What can you learn from this label?
TEACHER: Steve?
TEACHER: It kills germs. You use it for wounds, right? What else?
TEACHER: One person at a time. Okay, hold on. Veronica was saying something.

STUDENT: Read it?

STUDENT: It kills, oh I know.
STUDENT: It kills germs.
STUDENT: Yeah, it kills germs.
STUDENTS: *(various enthusiastic responses)*
STUDENT: It tells you in the directions that, you could use it, that like that, 'cause if you use it in another thing, it could hurt you.
STUDENT: If you put it in your mouth, don't put it in your mouth or your ears or your eyes.
STUDENT: No more than 10 days.
STUDENT: Ten days.

TEACHER: It could hurt you. Okay, what else? Ricardo?

TEACHER: Very good. Don't put it in your mouth, ears, and eyes. Okay, for how many days should you use it? No more than what?
TEACHER: So don't use it—you have to follow what it says—so don't use it more than 10 days. Now, the next activity you're going to do . . .

[1] The teacher explained then that they would be doing an activity in which they would read labels for information.

As a novice SIOP teacher, there were other ways she could have encouraged more student participation such as by having students turn and talk. After she explains that they'll be doing an activity she says: *"Now, most clothes carry labels, right? (pointing to the neck of her sweater)."* At that point, she could have had students turn to one another and discuss the purpose of labels and what their own experience with reading labels has been. At another point, she might have had students work in small groups of three or four to generate questions about the instructions on the antiseptic bottle, then ask other groups to answer them. Nonetheless, even the level of interaction seen here prompted more student engagement and participation, evidenced by the amount of student talk as well as enthusiasm displayed. When she said, *"It kills germs. You use it for wounds, right? What else?"* many students were eager to speak and the teacher said, *"One person at a time. Okay, hold on. Veronica was saying something"* Contrast their level of participation with that of students in the non-SIOP lesson.

The features of SIOP within the Interaction component are designed to provide teachers with concrete ways of increasing student participation and developing English language proficiency.

SIOP® **SIOP® FEATURE 16:**

Frequent Opportunities for Interaction and Discussion Between Teacher/Student and Among Students, Which Encourage Elaborated Responses About Lesson Concepts

This SIOP feature includes two important aspects of oral language development. First, it emphasizes the importance of balancing linguistic turn-taking between the teacher and students, and among students. It also highlights the practice of encouraging students to elaborate their responses rather than accepting yes/no and one-word answers, even from the youngest learners and beginning English speakers.

Research supporting interactive approaches includes the following:

1. There has long been recognition that language, cognition, and reading are intimately related (Tharp & Gallimore, 1988; Verhoeven, et al., 2019). As one acquires new language, new concepts are developed. Think about your own language learning with respect to understanding computer functions. Each new vocabulary word and term you learn and understand (e.g., *grid system* and *site map*) is attached to a concept that in turn expands your ability to think about how a computer works. As your own system of word-meaning grows in complexity, you are more capable of using the self-directed speech of verbal thinking (*"Remember to add a hyperlink."*). Without an understanding of the words and the concepts they represent, you would not be capable of thinking about (self-directed speech) or discussing (talking with another) computer functions.

> We must let students verbalize in order to internalize! It is important for students to synthesize information in their own words in order to learn the material.
>
> Andrea Rients, Professional Learning Coordinator, Minnesota

2. Multilingual learners require explicit instruction in how English works coupled with structured opportunities to practice using language (Goldenberg, 2020). The level of oral English language instruction and support provided needs to match the level of challenge encountered by multilingual learners, particularly in language-intensive subjects. As Goldenberg (2020) points out, texts and words in early literacy development don't need the same level of oral language support that is required by more complex texts. As multilingual learners advance through the grades, the oral English skills required to navigate grade-level texts and the disciplinary knowledge students need to comprehend texts become increasingly complex and demanding.

3. Interactive approaches are effective in promoting meaningful language learning opportunities for multilingual learners (Cazden, 2001; Echevarría & Short, 2010). Frϕytlog and Rasmussen (2020) cite empirical research that links productive dialogues to academic achievement in math and science, logic and reasoning, English,

and reading comprehension. Teaching approaches that emphasize oral language development, active student involvement, and meaningful discussions around academic topics and texts are referred to as *collaborative discussions, academic conversations* (Zwiers & Crawford, 2011) or *instructional conversations* (ICs) (Saunders & Goldenberg, 1999). Research on ICs suggests that when learners are grappling with a question to answer, exploring a concept for understanding, or trying to solve a problem, they are more successful if there is an opportunity to engage in dialogue with another learner (Frøytlog & Rasmussen, 2020; Hendy & Cuevas, 2020). Conversational approaches such as ICs differ from typical teaching because most instructional patterns in classrooms involve the teacher asking a question, the student responding, and the teacher evaluating the response and asking another question (Cazden, 2001). In contrast, an instructional conversation uses extended expression around text and topics, which fosters text comprehension and language proficiency. Figure 6.3 illustrates the contrast in these approaches.

A rich discussion, or conversational approach, has advantages for teachers, too. Through discussion teachers can more naturally activate students' background knowledge as they are encouraged to share their knowledge of the world and their lived experiences, and to connect these to the lesson. Also, positive interactions between teachers and students foster a culturally responsive, supportive environment. Studies have shown improvements on practically every measure schools care about: higher student academic engagement, attendance, and grades; fewer disruptive behaviors and suspensions; and lower school dropout rates (Quin, 2016). When teachers connect with students, are respectful toward them, and convey genuine interest, students engage more academically because they want to please their teacher (McGrath & Van Bergen, 2015).

Finally, when working in small groups with each student participating in the discussion, teachers can listen in and are better able to determine individual levels of understanding, information that needs to be clarified, and academic language that requires review and practice. In a study with multilingual learners (Porath, 2014), the teacher learned that by talking less and listening more, she was able to gain deeper insight into her students' learning needs and strengths.

FIGURE 6.3   **Contrast Traditional Instruction with Instructional Conversations**

Traditional Instruction	Instructional Conversation
Teacher-centered	Teacher facilitates
Exact, specific answers evaluated by the teacher	Many different ideas encouraged
No extensive discussion	Oral language practice opportunities using authentic language
Skill-directed	Extensive discussion and student involvement
Easier to evaluate	Draw from prior background knowledge
Check for understanding	Student level of understanding transparent
Mostly literal level thinking and language use	Fewer black-and-white responses
	Mostly higher-level thinking and language use

Effective SIOP teachers:

1. Create a classroom environment that promotes discussion. Think about your own behavior when you're with a group of peers either at a social gathering or at work. When are you comfortable contributing to the discussion? It's less likely that you'll participate if you feel intimidated by the others, if you don't know them well, or if you're concerned that you'll misspeak, be criticized, or be ignored. Just like you, multilingual learners avoid situations where they feel vulnerable or inadequate when participating in a group discussion. SIOP teachers create an accepting, inclusive classroom environment where all students are comfortable contributing in class. Following are some tips for creating an environment that fosters discussion:

   ◆ Learn each student's name. Making students comfortable begins with knowing how to pronounce each student's name correctly and calling them by name. There is a growing awareness of the importance of honoring students' identity and fostering a sense of belonging by using their name correctly. A resource on the topic can be found at https://www.mynamemyidentity.org/ and there are children's books on the topic such as *Always Anjali* and *The Name Jar*.

   ◆ Get to know their students. Each one comes to school with interests, likes, dislikes, talents, and strengths. Find out about your students and make it a habit to ask about each one: *"How was your baseball game?" "Is your mom feeling better?" "I see that you cut your hair. It looks nice."* These interactions take only seconds, but they establish a valuable connection with each student. Also, while circulating during group work, teachers pay attention to students' comments about their interests, their experience, and so forth.

   ◆ Respect students' differences. Not all students are comfortable participating in groups. Extroverts tend to prefer the social aspects of relationships such as talking and working in collaborative groups. Introverts, those quiet or shy students, are temperamentally prone to be reflective and prefer working alone or with a partner rather than in a large group. Therefore, teachers shouldn't, for example, urge introverted students to speak up in front of the whole class or encourage them to be "more outgoing." Some of the considerations about personality differences have cultural and linguistic implications as well. Beginning multilingual and newcomer students may resemble introverts in their behaviors. For instance, newcomer students may appear shy and reticent because they are unfamiliar with American educational practices such as working collaboratively with peers and participating in discussions. Beginning English speakers will likely be reserved about speaking English aloud and shouldn't be forced to speak before they are ready, especially in front of the class. SIOP teachers respect student differences and, to the extent possible, provide opportunities for each to shine in their own way.

2. Create a safe learning environment. One of the best ways to create a caring community of learning is to teach students to interact respectfully and productively with one another (see communication norms, below). When SIOP teachers have multilingual learners and English speakers work together in small groups, it fosters mutual respect among students from different cultures and ethnicities.

Developing relationships tends to break down walls and open communication as students learn about and from one another.

3. **Communicate high expectations.** Most of us are drawn to a person who believes in us. SIOP teachers let each student know that they believe they can be successful, which enhances the teacher-student relationship: *"I see you finished that assignment. I knew you could do it," "Thank you for being on time again today. I know it's tough for you sometimes,"* or *"I see you used the sentence structure we practiced. Your English is improving!"* Let students know you are in their corner.

4. **Encourage multilingual learners to use all their linguistic and cognitive resources while working with peers.** While they speak, write, ask questions, discuss topics, and complete tasks, they may switch between English and Spanish (or another language). As discussed in other chapters, SIOP teachers acknowledge the linguistic assets multilingual learners possess.

5. **Plan and organize their lessons in ways that promote student discussion.** During planning, time is allotted for extended discussion, and during lessons SIOP teachers strive to provide a more balanced linguistic exchange between themselves and their students. It can be particularly tempting for teachers to do most of the talking when students are not completely proficient in their use of English, but these students are precisely the ones who need opportunities to practice using English the most. Being exposed to and interacting with language that is just beyond their independent speaking levels move students to higher levels of language proficiency, so grouping is part of the planning process. (See the discussion of Feature 17.)

6. **Explicitly teach communication norms.** Rules and routines for engaging in high-quality discussions are taught to students and are reviewed frequently to ensure that students engage together productively. Students take turns, stay on topic, actively listen, build on one another's comments, and are respectful of others (Short & Echevarría, 2016). Students learn to use sentence frames such as, *"I see your point but I respectfully disagree because_____"* to ensure that they consider one another's ideas and perspectives without making disparaging remarks. It's wise to start teaching rules and norms from the outset so young children learn to communicate effectively, as seen in the classroom poster in Artifact 6.1. Notice how students are strategically assigned to a partner and the poster is posted for students to see and move into pairs seamlessly.

7. **Structure groups for success.** SIOP teachers consider the purpose of the interaction and structure groups accordingly: partner work, small-group activities, or individual tasks. SIOP teachers make sure that group assignments include significant attention to oral academic language development such as creating opinion pieces, preparing to make presentations on topics, and participating in debates (Goldenberg, 2020). Teachers encourage the use of substantive language linked to the core curriculum to attain the desired outcome: gains in oral language. Too often groups are unstructured, and while there are opportunities for speaking and listening, it is not always productive talk that is moving learning forward. Make expectations for productive group work practices clear to students for best results.

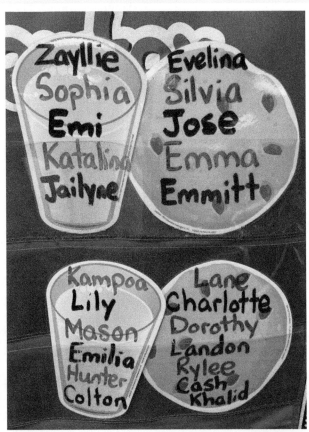

Permission from Tara Richner

8. Encourage extended expression from students when discussing the lesson's material. When SIOP teachers use techniques to elicit more elaboration from students, multilingual learners move beyond simple yes or no answers and short phrases. Some of these techniques include asking students to expand on their answers by saying *"Tell me more about that"* and by asking direct questions to prompt more language use such as *"What do you mean by . . . ?"*; *"Can you give me another example?"*; or *"I see your point. Can you cite evidence for it?"* Another technique is to provide further information through questions such as *"How do you know?" "What are the facts that support your ideas?" "Why is that important?"* SIOP teachers ask questions at students' levels of proficiency that prompt them to probe for evidence, negotiate meaning, clarify ideas, give and justify opinions, make well–reasoned statements, and more.

9. Use techniques such as offering restatements to scaffold replies: *"In other words . . . is that accurate?"* and frequently pausing to let students process the language and formulate their responses. If an English learner is obviously unsure about what to say, SIOP teachers call on other students to extend the response: *"Bibi said . . . what can you add to that?"* or *"Felix, can you help Salome with her answer?"*

10. Provide language frames to model expression. Multilingual learners can often comprehend more than they can express in English, so SIOP teachers create language frames, also called *sentence frames*, to scaffold speaking for students. Language frames are also useful for student-to-student interaction to scaffold discussion. There are a number of examples provided in Chapter 5 and later in this chapter, but it's important to use language frames effectively. Some tips to keep in mind include:

♦ **Avoid artificial use of frames.** The intent of frames is to provide students with support so that they can express their ideas more coherently, using correct sentence structure and vocabulary. After repeated use, students internalize the vocabulary and sentence structures and they become part of their linguistic repertoire. However, sometime teachers mistakenly insist that every student repeat a frame when answering questions or giving their ideas/opinions rather than letting students express themselves naturally, using frames as needed for support. It defeats the purpose of encouraging language growth when students are required to robotically repeat the same frame. For example: *I think _____ because _____. The evidence is _____.* While this frame is helpful for getting students started and for students who need the support, having every student's contribution follow this same pattern is not the way authentic discussion occurs. What is intended as a beneficial support ends up being a case of parroting sentences.

♦ **Remove frames, as needed.** Language frames are a scaffold and just as scaffolding is removed from a building once it is no longer needed, frames should be removed once students are proficient enough to use authentic language. One teacher reported that she encourages her advanced speakers and English-fluent students to use their own expressions rather than the frames she provides for others. She said she found that using frames sometimes stunted students' expression and their flow of ideas. Ultimately, all students should have the option of expressing themselves as they like.

♦ **Differentiate frames to match students' proficiency levels.** Although frames are designed to help students use appropriate academic language, they restrict students' expression and growth when they are too simple or too difficult. (See the section, Differentiating for Multilevel Classes, for examples.)

Language frames are valuable tools that support multilingual learners in expressing their ideas orally and in writing. However, they must be used strategically and for a specific purpose. Artifact 6.2 shows language frames being used specifically for practicing use of comparative adjectives. Partners work together to describe fossils using comparative adjectives, a fun way to integrate academic language practice into a science activity.

It takes time and practice for the techniques discussed in this section to become a natural part of a teacher's repertoire. The teachers with whom we've worked report that they had to consciously work at overcoming the temptation to speak for students or to complete their short responses. Effective interaction between teacher and students and among students should include significant attention to oral academic language development.

Pearson eTextbook
Video Example 6.2
Watch this video to watch 3rd grade teacher Deb Painter teach a lesson on punctuation. Notice how she organizes groups for discussion. Which of the aforementioned points are exemplified in this lesson such as a safe learning environment and having high expectations?

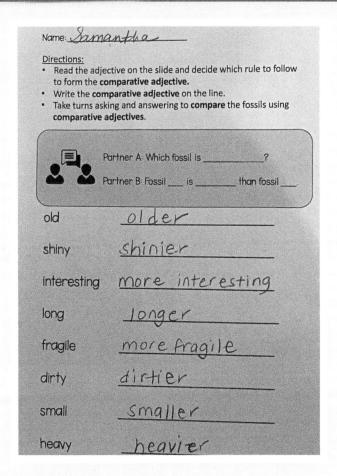

Name: Samantha

Directions:
- Read the adjective on the slide and decide which rule to follow to form the **comparative adjective.**
- Write the **comparative adjective** on the line.
- Take turns asking and answering to **compare** the fossils using **comparative adjectives.**

Partner A: Which fossil is _____?

Partner B: Fossil ___ is _____ than fossil ___.

old	older
shiny	shinier
interesting	more interesting
long	longer
fragile	more fragile
dirty	dirtier
small	smaller
heavy	heavier

SIOP®

SIOP® FEATURE 17:

Grouping Configurations Support Language and Content Objectives of the Lesson

Pearson eTextbook

Video Example 6.3

Watch this video to see an English speaker work collaboratively with a multilingual learner. Notice in the background how the teacher circulates around the room to monitor the various partners' discussion and productive work.

Learning is enhanced when teachers provide a variety of grouping configurations including whole class, partners, and small group. Most state content standards and ELD standards ask that students engage more directly in learning by having a balance of teacher presentation and productive group work. The benefits of a balanced approach include the following:

- Varying grouping configurations—by moving from whole class to small group, whole class to partners, and small group to individual assignments—provides students with opportunities to learn new information, discuss it with peers, and practice using the lesson's academic language. Organizing students into smaller groups for instructional purposes provides a setting that whole-class, teacher-focused instruction doesn't offer and has been shown to be more effective for students' learning (Gillies, 2014).

> Just like all students, ELLs have different abilities, and different needs. They need to be supported; they need to be challenged. They need to practice English; they need to build comprehension through their L1. They need to learn new information, and they need to communicate their learning. Flexible grouping arrangements allow for us to meet those varying needs. Sometimes we group same-language speakers together, and other times we intentionally separate them. Some lessons may be ideal for grouping based on language level or ability level, while other lessons are prime for heterogeneous groups, where student leaders in each group can help to move the whole class forward. At the end of the day, our students are complex individuals, so sometimes our groupings will to be equally complex. We consider what the greatest need is for each student at that moment, along with what will produce the most learning overall for all students in the class. One student may really need L1 support, while another may need to leave the L1 "nest" and be required to communicate in English. Yet another student really needs to be in a group which will help him to focus and not get distracted. We need to know our kids well

- Transitions between grouping configurations and the interaction within groups provides much-needed movement for learners. Asking students to sit still while performing their work actually <u>increases their cognitive load</u>, since it requires them to concentrate on keeping their bodies still as well as working on the academic task at hand. Sitting quietly is probably not the best condition for learning in school (Langhanns & Müller, 2018).

- Providing opportunities for students to work together in small groups has positive effects on students of all ability levels, but especially lower-ability students (Lou, 2013).

- Grouping multilingual learners with more proficient speakers builds academic and social benefits through their productive work together (Hendy & Cuevas, 2020; TESOL, 2017).

- Each grouping configuration meets specific purposes. Whole-class groups are beneficial for introducing new information and concepts, modeling processes, and review. Flexible small groups allow students to work together, express multiple perspectives, help one another, and enhance collaboration skills. Partnering provides practice opportunities, scaffolding, and assistance from classmates.

While grouping is beneficial, it's important to think about the following information as you plan lessons that include opportunities for students to work in a variety of groups.

- Grouping by ability divides students for instruction based on their perceived capabilities for learning (low group, average group, high group). The effects of ability-based grouping have been studied extensively; however, interest in the effects of ability grouping was heightened with the advent of standards-based education reform. In a review of four decades of research (Rui, 2009), the evidence concludes that heterogeneous-ability grouping was beneficial to low-ability students in terms of enhancing their academic achievement without being detrimental to the high- and average-ability students. An implication from the research is that heterogeneous grouping should be encouraged and promoted, especially in light of "the fact that for more than five decades, ability grouping has resulted in separation of students by race, ethnicity, and socio-economic status. Many studies have confirmed that minority and low-income students of all ability levels are overrepresented in the lower tracks and underrepresented in the higher tracks" (Futrell & Gomez, 2008, p. 76).

- Multilingual learners, who learn from exposure to good language models, are often shut out of the groups with rich academic learning opportunities. In fact, in some schools, it has become common practice to group multilingual learners with low-achieving students regardless of their academic ability and performance. This practice deprives multilingual learners of the opportunity to learn grade-level academic skills and language.

- When working with low-achieving groups, teachers have been found to talk more, use more structure, ask lower-level questions, cover less material, spend more time on skills and drills, provide fewer opportunities for leadership and independent research, encourage more oral than silent reading, teach less vocabulary, and allow less wait time during questioning. In addition, they spent twice as much time on behavior and management issues (Oakes, 1985; Vogt & Shearer, 2016).

Differentiating Instruction Through Groups. In small, guided instruction groups, the teacher naturally differentiates instruction as they work on focused skill instruction, language development, and/or assessment of student progress. Small-group instruction provides more opportunity to discuss text (Saunders & Goldenberg, 2007) and increases reading comprehension (Wilkenson, et al., 2015). While the teacher is working with one group, the other students can work on familiar material in small groups, with a partner, or individually, either at their desks or at workstations. Activities may include listening to recorded stories (at listening centers, on computers, or via electronic notebooks), reinforcing skills with computer games, creating graphic representations of vocabulary terms or concepts, summarizing material, practicing word sorts, or reading self-selected leveled readers.

SIOP teachers assign students to flexible groups that may be homogeneous or heterogeneous by gender, language proficiency, language background, and/or ability, and may vary depending on the intent. That is, groups are flexible, changing in composition for meeting different objectives. The decisions teachers make about how to group students should be purposeful, not arbitrary. At times, teachers allow students to choose their own groups, making sure all students are included.

A case can be made for grouping students by how well they speak English during literacy instruction (Uribe & Nathenson-Mejía, 2008), but the teacher needs to be aware of each student's individual skill profile. For example, when working on fluency, multilingual learners with strong decoding skills would not read the same text as a multilingual learner who is still working on mastering phonics. Advantages of grouping multilingual learners together are that teachers can target specific language instruction, and students are more apt to take risks in their second language. However, grouping students from very different grade levels (i.e., second through fifth grade) together based on language proficiency must be avoided because these learners have very different social and academic needs (Uribe & Nathenson-Mejía, 2008).

There are other times that grouping by language proficiency level is useful. For example, if a teacher's goal is for students at beginning levels of English proficiency to practice using a particular language structure such as the present progressive (-*ing*) form within the context of a social studies lesson, then those students may be grouped together for that lesson. Likewise, when developing the skills of students with low levels of literacy, it makes sense to have those with similar ability grouped together for a particular lesson. Assigning all multilingual learners to the same group regularly is *not* good practice. In SIOP classes, multilingual learners are given the same access to the curriculum and the teacher's expertise as English-speaking students.

It is recommended that at least two different grouping structures be used during a lesson, depending on the activity and objectives of the lesson. However, peer discussions need to be structured so that students know their roles and responsibilities, and are supervised appropriately. As more teachers move to implementing small-group structures, we've noticed that in some classes, students are put into groups for collaborative work, but little is accomplished. Groups are given a worksheet or other activity and are expected to complete it without much teacher input or oversight. Group work requires structure, with the teacher circulating, checking for understanding, prompting, questioning, and clarifying. Also, tasks should be assigned a specific amount of time so that students stay engaged and the pace of the class moves along.

SIOP® **SIOP® FEATURE 18:**

Sufficient Wait Time for Student Responses Consistently Provided

Wait time is the length of time between utterances during an interaction. In classroom settings, it refers to the length of time a teacher pauses between asking a question and soliciting a response. It is helpful to consider wait time as "think time." When SIOP teachers wait and allow learners time to respond to a question, students can better formulate their responses. The amount of time the teacher waits depends on the type of question asked. Recall questions may require about three seconds, but higher-order thinking questions could merit a wait time of seven to ten seconds (TESOL, 2018).

A review of studies on wait time revealed that after a teacher asks a question, students must begin a response within an average time of one second. If they do not, the teacher repeats, rephrases, asks a different question, or calls on another student. Further, when a student makes a response, the teacher normally reacts or asks another question within an average time of 0.9 second (Rowe, 2003). Rather than filling the silence created by wait time, teachers should see the silence as an opportunity for students to process what is being asked of them. Teachers may need to practice using wait time to become comfortable allowing students the time they need (Wasik & Hindman, 2013/2014).

Wait time varies by culture. It is appropriate in some cultures to let seconds, even minutes, lag between utterances, while in other cultures utterances can overlap one another. In U.S. classrooms, the average length of wait time is clearly *not* sufficient and doesn't provide enough think time. Imagine the impact of wait time on multilingual learners who are processing ideas in a new language and need additional time to put their thoughts into words. Research supports the idea of wait time and has found it to increase student discourse and enhance student-to-student interaction (Rowe, 2003; Tobin, 1987).

SIOP teachers are culturally responsive and consciously allow students to express their thoughts fully, without interruption. Many teachers in U.S. schools are uncomfortable with the silence that follows their questions or comments, and they immediately fill the void by talking themselves. This situation may be especially pertinent in SIOP classes where multilingual learners need extra time to process questions in English, think of an answer in their second language, and then formulate their responses in English. Although teachers may be tempted to fill the silence, multilingual learners benefit from a patient approach to classroom participation, in which teachers wait for students to complete their verbal contributions.

While SIOP teachers provide sufficient wait time for multilingual learners, they also work to find a balance between wait time and moving a lesson along. Some students may become impatient if the pace of the class lags. One strategy for accommodating impatient students is to have them write down their responses while waiting, and then check their answers against the final answer.

SIOP® **SIOP® FEATURE 19:**

Ample Opportunities for Students to Clarify and Discuss Key Concepts in Ll with Peer, Aide, Teacher, or L1 Text

There is growing awareness that one's language is tied to culture and identity, and restricting use of the student's home language (L1) sends a message that multilingual learners' language and culture are somehow "less-than" that of the United States. Using students' L1 doesn't minimize the importance of learning English. English acquisition is critical for school success, for advancing into college and careers, and for being a contributing member of society. However, using their L1 allows multilingual learners to better express themselves when working with peers, it helps clarify information they don't understand in English, and is a valuable resource for learning. Using the home language also recognizes the asset of multilingualism and honors students' heritage.

It may surprise you to know that the brain doesn't have separate compartments for each language, and development of a language such as Spanish or Farsi doesn't crowd out space for English. As Vogel & García (2017) and others have explained, multilingual students have one complex linguistic system that can have features of one, two, or more languages. Students draw on these linguistic resources to communicate and make sense of instruction. A classroom (or remote teaching) example is when the teacher reads a story aloud in English and pauses at various points in the text for students to talk together. When the students do "turn and talk," they are invited to share their thoughts in their home language or English—or a mix of both—with their paired same-home-language partner. Sometimes certain words or expressions in one language convey a precise meaning better than another, or the context may dictate a preference. For instance, if the book read aloud is about soccer, when a multilingual learner turns to their partner to discuss a portion of text, they may begin speaking in English but switch to Spanish for a description of the way a goal was scored. The student is using the full complement of their linguistic repertoire in the discussion. It is a misconception to think that combining languages indicates confusion.

Teachers should not discourage the practice of translanguaging or restrict use of students' first language at school or at home. Obvious exceptions would be, for example, tasks that require the use of English such as oral presentations or assignments designed to practice using academic English.

Although SIOP instruction involves teaching subject-matter material in English, SIOP teachers provide support for the academic learning of multilingual learners by clarifying key concepts in students' L1 if they are bilingual, or through an instructional aide or peer. There are also many resources available in students' home languages including topical materials in multiple languages, websites, and apps with translation capabilities, online bilingual dictionaries, and more.

■ Application to Your Classroom: Interaction

In the section that follows, you will find some teaching ideas to help you with preparing SIOP lessons for your class that include opportunities for Interaction.

- **Instructional Conversations (ICs).** A proven approach for advancing multilingual learners' literacy skills (Saunders & Goldenberg, 2010), ICs may be used across content areas, but most research has been conducted with literacy. A typical IC process is as follows:

  a. The teacher begins by briefly introducing the group to a theme or idea related to the text, and then relating the theme to students' background experiences: *Today we're going to talk about taking care of siblings. Do you take care of a brother or sister, or do they take care of you?* (Students share their experiences)

  b. Next, the teacher shows the text to be read and asks prediction questions: *We're going to read this book called,* A Trip to the Library. *What do you think it will be about? What do you predict will happen when the brother and sister get to the library?*

  c. As the text is read, the teacher "chunks" the text into sections to provide maximum opportunity for discussion, constantly relating the theme and background experiences to a text-based discussion: *That's an interesting turn of events. How would you feel if you were the brother? What did it say about him in the text? Let's read that part again. Have you ever had a similar experience?*

  d. Students are asked to support their comments with evidence from the text: *What do you think he'll do next? What does the book say that makes you think he'll do that? What about his sister? Show us in the book why you predict that that will happen next.*

  Questioning and discussion in the group is naturally differentiated as the teacher prompts students using language and questions they comprehend. Students in IC lessons may be grouped heterogeneously by language levels so that less proficient students are exposed to more advanced language in a context that promotes comprehension. You may also choose to group readers at lower levels with stronger readers, which provides them the opportunity to talk about ideas and use language in discussion that they may not be able to read independently. Further, some experts advocate for student-led IC groups where they create their own conversational goals, lead the conversations, and work together to create a tangible product from their discussions such as a T-chart (Mellon, Hixon, & Weber, 2019).

- **Blogging for Students.** A number of tools are available for remote teaching or homework, and blogging is one such tool. Whlie blogs may prove challenging for young children, they are tools worth exploring for a number of reasons. Class blogs offer a safe playground for preparing students to be responsible digital citizens. while offering them chances to interact, read, write, and give meaningful feedback. Platforms like *Fan.school* allow students to share their voices with a larger audience than just the teacher. Blogging platforms meant for students have multiple layers of built-in security features. The teacher can set controls to preview all posts and comments before they are published. Student information such as names and posts can be kept private behind a password. Further, a blogging platform can be used to teach students how to provide constructive feedback and how to write for a specific audience. Often, publishing for peers—whether within the same school or to an international pen pal—adds extra motivation for students to improve their writing skills.

- **Show What You Know** (Vogt & Echevarria, 2022). This activity encourages interaction among class members as they work together to become "experts" on a topic, such as MyPlate (U.S. Department of Agriculture). Working in groups, students learn about a topic, e.g., proteins, with the teacher making sure that there is a mix of English proficiency levels in each group so that more proficient students can support the reading and writing of less proficient English speakers. Students in each group use the information to create a poster that explains the food group (e.g., what proteins are, how they contribute to good health, examples of various types of protein, etc.). Each group of "experts" will Show What They Know by teaching the rest of the class about their food group. After presenting what they know to the class, their poster is added to the whole-class My Plate chart. This activity provides students with an opportunity to practice all domains of English: listening, speaking, reading, and writing. Also, they become expert in a topic as they do so!

- **Dinner Party** (Vogt & Echevarria, 2022). An activity appropriate for all grade levels and most content areas is called Dinner Party (or Birthday Party for K–2). As an example, during reading instruction, students would respond to the prompt: "Suppose you could have a dinner party for authors or poets that we have studied. Who would you invite? Why would you select them? What would be the seating order of the guests at your table, and why would you place them in that order? What do you think the guests would talk about during dinner? Include specific references to the authors' lives and works in your response." The purpose is for students to act out the questions by assuming personas, such as characters in novels, scientists, historical figures, or artists. During each Dinner Party, specific content from texts must be included and the characters must respond to each other as realistically and accurately as possible.

- **Dialogue Journals.** The time-tested activity of using Dialogue Journals provides students with an opportunity to interact through writing about topics of interest or those related to lessons. In elementary classrooms, journaling is typically between teacher and student as they share ideas. Students learn from teachers as they model appropriate written text, and teachers learn about their students' ideas and ways of expressing themselves. In secondary classes, students may be

Pearson eTextbook

Video Example 6.4

Watch this video as Dr. Jana Echevarria describes an interactive activity called Expert Stay Stray. What planning would the teacher need to do to make this activity successful?
https://www.youtube.com/watch?v=3BvIijRQMek

paired together, or students may use the journal as a diary. In either case the teacher participates in the dialogue every so often to make a connection with the student and to monitor their writing. The teacher's response also models correct writing for the student.

Differentiating for Multilevel Classes

Most classes with multilingual learners are made up of students with multiple proficiency levels. The Interaction component lends itself well to meeting the variety of instructional needs and proficiency levels of students in your classrooms. Several ideas for making instruction meaningful include the following:

- **Match language frames to students' proficiency levels.** Frames are designed to help students use academic language, and with minimal tweaking, teachers can provide a more simplified frame for beginning speakers and more complex sentence structures and vocabulary for more advanced speakers.

  In identifying scientific relationships, for example, beginning speakers benefit from a frame such as, *This is an example of _____ (predation, mutualism, competition, parasitism)*, which provides sentence structure and words from which to choose. Teachers offer more advanced speakers an open-ended frame that requires them to explain the procedure on their own or make connections such as,

  This is an example of _____. The _____ is _____ and the _____ is _____ based on _____.

  These frames provide structure that allows students to express their understanding of the lesson's content at their level of English proficiency. The sample frames for discussing scientific relationships can be easily modified for several levels of proficiency by adding or deleting words. Differentiating frames by proficiency level isn't hard or time-consuming for teachers to do, and the effort is well worth it. Practice with the right frame may advance students' English acquisition by allowing them to use language that is appropriate for their level. Be sure to use frames for practicing a variety of language functions, such as cause/effect, problem/solution, and so forth. (See Short & Echevarria, 2016, *Developing Academic Language Using the SIOP Model,* for more sample language frames and functions.)

- **Use Book Creator.** Creating e-books lends itself well to differentiating since students work at their level of proficiency. They produce e-books by adding photos, making text boxes, editing the text, and adding voice recordings. Book Creator can be used across content areas and is applied in this example to a first-grade math lesson. Practicing strategies for addition and subtraction, pairs of students use the app on a tablet to take photos of different combinations of math manipulatives, such as 8 red tiles + 8 blue tiles = 16 (double the fact strategy). They import photos and create captions for each photo, including an equation. The process of creating an e-book facilitates discussion among the students.

To extend the activity and challenge students, students may create word problems for other students to solve. For additional oral language practice, the teacher can show students how to use the voice recording option to narrate the process of solving equations. The student-created e-books can be transferred into the *iBooks* app, which allows teachers to share student work with parents during conferences.

- **Differentiate wait time.** Practice allowing more wait time for beginning English speakers and those students who require a little extra time for processing information. More advanced speakers will likely require less wait time. However, don't forget that all students benefit from think time to ponder questions or new information.

■ The Lesson

Addition and Subtraction (First Grade)

The first-grade teachers in this chapter, Mrs. Aguirre, Mr. McQuaid, and Miss Dimitrievska, work in a dual language (DL) program that offers literacy and content teaching in two languages, English and Spanish. In this suburban school, the three first-grade teachers' classes have an even distribution of Spanish-speaking students, with each class having approximately 35%. Although some of these students are at the intermediate level of English proficiency, most Spanish speakers are at the beginning stages of acquiring English. A few of the native-English-speaking students have beginning Spanish proficiency but most do not know Spanish.

The program follows a 50-50 model where native English speakers and native Spanish speakers are integrated for at least 50% of instructional time at all grade levels. All students receive instruction in the partner language at least 50% of the instructional day. English is the language of instruction in the lessons described. As is typical in dual language programs, students are strongly encouraged to use the language of instruction during the specific block of time allotted for that language, whether Spanish or English. Teachers are strict about their own consistent use of the target language so that they provide a strong language model for students; however, if students do not yet have the language to express themselves, they can respond in the other language. The teacher then often restates what the student has said in the target language.

The teachers in this school plan math units around their state math standards. In the math lessons described, all classes are working on the standard: *Add and subtract within 20, demonstrating fluency for addition and subtraction within 10. Use strategies such as counting on; making ten (e.g., $8 + 6 = 8 + 2 + 4 = 10 + 4 = 14$); decomposing a number leading to a ten (e.g., $13 - 4 = 13 - 3 - 1 = 10 - 1 = 9$); using the relationship between addition and subtraction (e.g., by knowing that $8 + 4 = 12$, one knows $12 - 8 = 4$); and creating equivalent but easier or known sums (e.g., adding $6 + 7$ by creating the known equivalent $6 + 6 + 1 = 12 + 1 = 13$).*

(continued)

Addition and Subtraction (First Grade) *(continued)*

The lessons described are part of a unit, and students have already learned and practiced the mechanics of addition and subtraction. In these lessons, the emphasis is on being aware of the most efficient strategy to use in solving word problems. The teachers co-plan lesson objectives each week so that they are teaching essentially the same content across the classes. In the scenarios that follow, the objectives are:

Content Objectives (CO): Students will solve addition and subtraction problems efficiently using strategies.

Language Objectives (LO): Students will orally express their reasoning when solving problems.

As you will see, although the objectives are the same, the teachers each have their own ways of teaching the lessons.

■ Teaching Scenarios

Mrs. Aguirre

As was her practice, Mrs. Aguirre began by reading aloud the lesson's content and language objectives that were written on the board. She told the class that they would use counting strategies to solve addition and subtraction problems. She asked them to think about how objects can be used to find solutions.

Using an interactive whiteboard, Mrs. Aguirre put up 2 rows of circles. The circles were in groups of 5, each group a different color. She began by placing 5 red circles and 3 blue circles on the top line (8). Below she placed 5 red circles and 4 blue circles (9). She asked the students how many circles there were all together (17). A number of students raised their hands and she called on two to give their answers. After showing several more problems on the board (e.g., $7 + 7$ and $9 + 6$), she asked students how they were able to figure out the answers. She drew sticks with students' names on them from a can and called on those students to explain. If a student didn't respond right away, Mrs. Aguirre didn't want to put them on the spot, especially if they were a Spanish speaker, so she drew another name. If she felt confident the student knew the answer but was reticent about speaking in English, she would allow the answer to be given in Spanish and then asked another student to translate. Most students were able to articulate in English a process such as adding the groups of 5 red circles first, then adding the blue circles (e.g., $5 + 5$, then add $10 + 3$ and $13 + 4 = 17$). She asked the class repeatedly if anyone had a question.

Once Mrs. Aguirre thought that students knew how to complete addition problems, she repeated the procedure with subtraction problems; e.g., she showed 17 circles and asked what the amount would be left if she took away 5. She demonstrated taking away on the interactive whiteboard.

Next, she called on individuals to play the role of "teacher." Four students were selected for this part of the lesson. Each took a turn putting up circles on the

FIGURE 6.4 Interaction Component of the SIOP® Model: Mrs. Aguirre's Lesson

4	3	2	1	0	
16. Frequent opportunities for **interaction** and discussion between teacher/student and among students, which encourage elaborated responses about lesson concepts		**Interaction** mostly teacher-dominated with some opportunities for students to talk about or question lesson concepts		**Interaction** teacher-dominated with no opportunities for students to discuss lesson concepts	
4	**3**	**2**	**1**	**0**	
17. **Grouping configurations** support language and content objectives of the lesson		**Grouping configurations** unevenly support the language and content objectives		**Grouping configurations** do not support the language and content objectives	
4	**3**	**2**	**1**	**0**	
18. Sufficient **wait time for student responses** consistently provided		Sufficient **wait time for student responses** occasionally provided		Sufficient **wait time for student responses** not provided	
4	**3**	**2**	**1**	**0**	**N/A**
19. Ample opportunities for students to **clarify and discuss key concepts in Ll** with peer, aide, teacher, or L1 text		Some opportunities for students to **clarify and discuss key concepts in L1**		No opportunities for students to **clarify or discuss key concepts in L1**	

interactive whiteboard and adding to or taking away a certain number to create a problem. The class had to solve the problem.

For the final twenty minutes of the lesson, students took out their math texts and solved a variety of addition and subtraction problems found in the book. At the end of the lesson, they turned in their written work.

Check your understanding: On the SIOP form in Figure 6.4, rate Mrs. Aguirre's lesson on each of the Interaction features.

Mr. McQuaid

Mr. McQuaid's classroom is arranged in pods of four desks together, which allows students to easily work with their "elbow partner" in pairs or as a small group of four in their pod. The lesson began with Mr. McQuaid having the class chorally read the content and language objectives. Mr. McQuaid asked students to turn to their partners—English speakers paired with Spanish speakers—and tell each other three counting strategies that they had learned. Then he asked several groups which ones they identified. Groups reported out the strategies using doubles $(2 + 2)$, counting by 5s or 10s, and counting on.

After reviewing strategies, Mr. McQuaid showed a counting rack on the document viewer that had two parallel rods with 10 beads, 5 red and 5 white. There was space on each rod to move the beads back and forth. He moved the beads to form groups and said, "This is how many I have on my rack (8 on top and 9 below). Talk to your partner about how many are on the rack." Then he asked how they solved the problem. One group said that they used their double facts. He asked the class, "What is this double fact?" and they replied together that $8 + 8 = 16$. He pointed out that they would then add 1 to make 17.

Mr. McQuaid continued with several more problems on the screen, showing a variety of combinations of beads. He asked the class to work in groups of four to solve the problems efficiently and explain how they arrived at their solutions. Moving from pairs to small groups provided linguistic support for the Spanish speakers in the group in case they needed clarification. With each problem Mr. McQuaid called on different groups to report out how they arrived at their solution, which provided accountability for the groups. If a group had difficulty articulating the strategy used, he asked, "Who can help your friends?" and another student would explain the strategy.

Then Mr. McQuaid told the class that they would use the racks with a partner and solve word problems together. He called a student to the front of the room, and they modeled the procedure for working together. The student held the rack, and the teacher took a card out of a plastic bag and read the problem: "I have 9 people on the bus and 10 get on. How many are there?" The student put 9 beads on the top row and 10 on the bottom and said, "19." The teacher asked her how she solved it, and she said that $9 + 9$ is a double fact so she had 18 and added 1 more. Then the teacher and student switched roles so that the teacher had the rack and the student selected a card. Mr. McQuaid reminded the students that this wasn't a winning game; it was a game for working together. They needed to share and help each other figure out the most efficient way to solve the problems.

For this activity, Mr. McQuaid again paired Spanish speakers with English speakers. If a Spanish-speaking partner had difficulty understanding something or expressing their ideas, they could ask others in their pod for support. The process of clarifying ideas in both languages deepened students' understanding of math strategies and provided practice in translanguaging for all students.

While partners worked on the game, Mr. McQuaid circulated and assisted students as needed with prompts such as "How many are on the bus? How many got on? How many total? How did you figure it out?" He used a technique of counting to himself to be sure he allowed enough wait time for students to process the question or information. Occasionally, a student asked Mr. McQuaid a question in Spanish and, although he spoke Spanish, he asked the class to translate the question into English and then answer it. At other times, he simply answered the question in English. He was careful to maintain the target language but allowed students to ask and answer questions in their L1 as needed.

After all pairs had had a chance to solve about a dozen problems between them, they followed the same process with subtraction problems. Mr. McQuaid modeled the first problem: "There are 20 on the bus and 8 get off. How many are left? What is a good way to take 8 away?" When the partners had practiced subtraction problems for a while, Mr. McQuaid called them to whole-class formation. He asked for volunteers to come up and explain their reasoning. Various students said that they counted by 5, used double facts, and used counting on.

Finally, Mr. McQuaid gave the students a worksheet that had a number chart and addition and subtraction problems to solve. Students worked individually and

4	3	2	1	0
16. Frequent opportunities for **interaction** and discussion between teacher/student and among students, which encourage elaborated responses about lesson concepts		**Interaction** mostly teacher-dominated with some opportunities for students to talk about or question lesson concepts		**Interaction** teacher-dominated with no opportunities for students to discuss lesson concepts

4	3	2	1	0
17. **Grouping configurations** support language and content objectives of the lesson		**Grouping configurations** unevenly support the language and content objectives		**Grouping configurations** do not support the language and content objectives

4	3	2	1	0
18. Sufficient **wait time for student responses** consistently provided		Sufficient **wait time for student responses** occasionally provided		Sufficient **wait time for student responses** not provided

4	3	2	1	0	N/A
19. Ample opportunities for students to **clarify and discuss key concepts in L1** with peer, aide, teacher, or L1 text		Some opportunities for students to **clarify and discuss key concepts in L1**		No opportunities for students to **clarify or discuss key concepts in L1**	

finished at their own pace. At the conclusion of the lesson, Mr. McQuaid reviewed the content and language objectives and asked students to hold thumbs up if they met the objectives.

Check your understanding: On the SIOP form in Figure 6.5, rate Mr. McQuaid's lesson on each of the Interaction features.

Miss Dimitrievska

Miss Dimitrievska, known to her students as Miss D, began her lesson by saying, "Who can tell me a strategy we know that helps us add and subtract numbers efficiently?" A few students raised their hands, and she called on each one to elicit an answer. She wrote the strategies they named on an interactive whiteboard. Also written on the board were the content and language objectives for the lesson. Miss D read the objectives and, pointing to the strategies listed, said that they would be using those strategies in the lesson.

Miss D had each table captain distribute electronic clicker responders. Then she put a line of 7 cars on the interactive whiteboard (5 yellow and 2 blue) and another line of 5 yellow cars below. She asked the class to figure out how many total cars were on the board. She reminded them to do it efficiently as she pointed to the list of strategies on the board. After a minute she told the students to enter their answers using the clickers. Each student responded and she could see who did and who did not have correct answers. She then told the students to explain to their partner how they arrived at the answer and asked for volunteers to share out. Occasionally she observed a student having difficulty expressing themselves in English, but she was gratified to see that the partners were able to work it out between themselves. Several students named strategies such as counting on and using doubles. She repeated this process a number of times until nearly every clicked answer was correct.

Then Miss D introduced subtraction in the same way. She showed two lines of balls, took some away and asked the students to solve the problem and enter their answers. Again she had partners articulate their reasoning. She continued with this process until students were solving problems with a high degree of accuracy. Although the students enjoyed using the clickers, at times Miss D asked for the response before some of the multilingual learners had processed the language associated with the problems, especially determining if it was an addition or subtraction problem. Also, they felt a bit rushed when explaining to their partner what strategy they used.

For the next part of the lesson, Miss D gave students plastic bags of beads and written addition and subtraction problems. Working with partners, each pair used the beads to represent the problems and solve them. Miss D circulated to make sure pairs were working cooperatively, solving the problems, and explaining which strategy they used. Some multilingual learners spoke in their home language with their partner and Miss D gently asked students to speak in English.

Finally, students were given a worksheet with both addition and subtraction problems to solve independently. Miss D concluded the lesson by reviewing the content and language objectives and had students respond with their clickers if they had met each one.

Check your understanding: On the SIOP form in Figure 6.6, rate Miss Dimitrievska's lesson on each of the Interaction features.

FIGURE 6.6 Interaction Component of the SIOP® Model: Miss Dimitrievska's Lesson

4	3	2	1	0	
16. Frequent opportunities for **interaction** and discussion between teacher/student and among students, which encourage elaborated responses about lesson concepts		**Interaction** mostly teacher-dominated with some opportunities for students to talk about or question lesson concepts		**Interaction** teacher-dominated with no opportunities for students to discuss lesson concepts	
4	**3**	**2**	**1**	**0**	
17. **Grouping configurations** support language and content objectives of the lesson		**Grouping configurations** unevenly support the language and content objectives		**Grouping configurations** do not support the language and content objectives	
4	**3**	**2**	**1**	**0**	
18. Sufficient **wait time for student responses** consistently provided		Sufficient **wait time for student responses** occasionally provided		Sufficient **wait time for student responses** not provided	
4	**3**	**2**	**1**	**0**	**N/A**
19. Ample opportunities for students to **clarify and discuss key concepts in L1** with peer, aide, teacher, or L1 text		Some opportunities for students to **clarify and discuss key concepts in L1**		No opportunities for students to **clarify or discuss key concepts in L1**	

■ Discussion of Lessons

Look back at your rating form and think about the reasons you scored the lessons as you did. What evidence is in the scenarios? Read on to see our analyses.

16. *Frequent Opportunities for Interaction and Discussion between Teacher/Student and Among Students Which Encourage Elaborated Responses About Lesson Concepts*

    Mrs. Aguirre: 1

    Mr. McQuaid: 4

    Miss Dimitrievska: 4

There is growing awareness about the importance of students being actively engaged in learning and having opportunities to interact productively with peers and teachers. However, many teachers struggle to relinquish the "sage on the stage" type of teaching where most often the teacher talks and students listen. In their lessons, these teachers vary the opportunities they provide to their students.

- **Mrs. Aguirre's** lesson received a "1" because the format of her lesson was teacher controlled and did not provide sufficient interaction among the students. Student participation was individual responses to teacher prompts and was largely based on volunteering. This practice tends to mask struggling students and those who do not understand since they are unlikely to volunteer. Usually the students who least need practice using the target language or help with concepts are the ones who volunteer to participate in lessons. It is very difficult to determine the needs of students and gauge their understandings when relying almost solely on volunteer responses.

    Although Mrs. Aguirre made use of technology, she used the interactive whiteboard just as she would a chalkboard. It was essentially a fancy way of writing problems on the board, calling on students individually to answer questions or to pose problems for classmates. She made the assumption that all students understood the lesson's objectives about using strategies to solve problems efficiently based on the participation of a few students.

- **Mr. McQuaid's** lesson received a "4" because he encouraged lots of student-to-student and teacher-to-student interaction. By having the students explain to one another the process they used to solve problems, their thinking was made transparent and the teacher could readily ascertain who understood the strategies and was able to apply them and who needed more support.

- **Miss D's** lesson also received a "4." She used clickers to make sure that each student was engaged and interacting with her in problem solving. It also gave her immediate feedback about how much practice was needed before moving to the next part of the lesson.

17. *Grouping Configurations Support Language and Content Objectives of the Lesson*

    Mrs. Aguirre: 0

    Mr. McQuaid: 4

    Miss Dimitrievska: 4

Whole-class instruction is necessary and effective at times, but it should not be used extensively since it limits opportunities for students to ask questions, discuss ideas, and clarify information. The stated language objective for this lesson was that students would orally express their reasoning when solving problems.

- **Mrs. Aguirre's** lesson used whole-class instruction or individual work exclusively, which did not support the objectives, especially the language objective. Therefore, her lesson received a "0." Only once during the lesson did students have an opportunity to explain the strategies they used to solve problems, and the lack of grouping configurations limited opportunities for students to identify and discuss how they solved problems efficiently. Students who are not proficient in the target language, whether English or Spanish, and those students who struggle academically may find whole-class instruction intimidating, as undoubtedly was the case with Mrs. Aguirre's lesson. Although she asked if students had questions, nobody was willing to speak up in the whole-class setting.

- **Mr. McQuaid** planned a lesson that used a balance of whole-class instruction for introducing the concepts and modeling expectations, and partner and small-group work that allowed students to create and solve problems, to articulate their reasoning, and to use translanguaging when needed. Varying grouping structures allowed for deeper understanding of the concept and also provided practice using academic English. Mr. McQuaid's lesson received a "4" for this feature.

- **Miss D's** lesson also provided optimal opportunity for interaction. She used whole-class instruction, individual response using clickers, and partner work. Miss D's lesson received a "4" on this feature.

18. *Sufficient Wait Time for Student Responses Consistently Provided*

Mrs. Aguirre: 0

Mr. McQuaid: 4

Miss Dimitrievska: 2

- The whole-class, teacher-dominated format of **Mrs. Aguirre's** lesson encouraged those students who were quick to respond (usually native speakers of English) to set the pace. Students who required more time to process information or to think of the words in English were essentially left out of the lesson, however unintentional this was on Mrs. Aguirre's part. When she called on students individually, she tried to spare them embarrassment when they didn't answer promptly by choosing someone else. It would have been more effective to scaffold the student's response with prompts and provide the wait time needed. Mrs. Aguirre's lesson received a "0" for this feature.

- **Mr. McQuaid** interacted with students in a way that allowed time for them to formulate their thoughts and express them in English. Also, working with partners and then sharing out gave additional time to students. Mr. McQuaid recognized that multilingual learners need to have a little extra time when participating in class. His lesson received a "4" for this feature.

- Although English was **Miss D's** second language and she understands multilingual learners' needs, she felt pressure to move the lesson along and didn't always provide sufficient wait time. Therefore, her lesson received a "2" for this feature.

19. *Ample opportunities for students to **clarify and discuss key concepts in Ll** with peer, aide, teacher, or L1 text*

Mrs. Aguirre: 1

Mr. McQuaid: 4

Miss Dimitrievska: 1

- Again, the format of **Mrs. Aguirre's** instructional delivery did not allow students the opportunity to clarify concepts or information with others in their home language even if it would have improved their understanding. However, she did allow students to answer in their L1 when called on and had other students translate to the target language. Therefore, her lesson received a "1" on this feature.

- **Mr. McQuaid's** lesson, on the other hand, provided lots of opportunity for student-to-student interaction, and students could use their native language when needed. Students were encouraged to discuss the math problems as well as their thinking about how they arrived at solutions. Participation in either language was accepted. Mr. McQuaid's lesson received a "4" for this feature.

- **Miss D's** lesson also provided opportunities for students to work together and they naturally used their L1 when needed. Use of the native language wasn't forbidden, however Miss D believed that she was helping students by encouraging English. Young learners, and beginning English speakers in particular, benefit from having opportunities to discuss and clarify concepts in the language they understand best. Miss D's lesson received a "1" because opportunities to use L1 were limited, and even when it was clear that students needed support, she relied on peers to "work it out." Miss D couldn't have been certain about how much the Spanish speakers understood and if they needed her to explain further in their L1.

■ Final Points

As you reflect on this chapter and the benefits of interaction for multilingual learners, consider the following main points:

- SIOP teachers create ample opportunities for multilingual learners to practice using academic English among themselves and with you, the teacher. Students are encouraged to elaborate and extend their comments and responses, not provide one- or two-word answers.

- Standards in all states require that students have opportunities to take part in a variety of rich, structured discussions—as part of a whole class, in small groups, and with a partner.

- Incorporating a number of grouping configurations into lessons facilitates using language in ways that support the lessons' objectives and develop students' English proficiency.

- For many teachers, it is challenging to wait in silence while students formulate their responses. However, it's important to allow for wait time (think time) and not speak up yourself to fill the silence.

- Teachers should use an asset-based approach, which includes valuing the use of multilingual learners' home languages. These students draw on their linguistic repertoire to make sense of information, which enhances learning. Use of their home language does not detract from the importance of learning academic English.

■ Discussion Questions

1. In reflecting on the content and language objectives at the beginning of the chapter, are you able to:

   - List ways that collaborative conversations and discussions are aligned with the Interaction component?
   - Design grouping structures that support lesson content and language objectives?
   - Identify techniques to increase wait time?
   - Identify resources to support students' use of their home language?
   - Describe techniques to reduce the amount of teacher talk in a lesson?
   - Practice asking questions that promote student elaboration of responses?
   - Include in a lesson plan structured time for partner and small-group productive work?

2. Think of a content concept that you might be teaching. Describe three different grouping configurations that could be used for teaching and learning this concept. How would you organize the students in each group? How would you monitor student learning? What would you want students to do while working in their groups? How would the grouping configurations facilitate learning for multilingual learners?

3. Either record your own classroom while you're teaching a lesson or observe another teacher's classroom for a 15-minute segment. Estimate the proportion of teacher talk and student talk. Given the ratio of teacher–student talk, what are some possible ramifications for multilingual learners in this class?

4. Productive discussions are usually the result of careful planning and preparation. What are some rules of discussion presented in this chapter that you would need to teach or reinforce with your students? What might be an appropriate language objective for a lesson on rules of discussion?

5. Using the SIOP lesson you have been developing, add activities and grouping configurations to enhance interaction.

■ Pearson eTextbook Application Videos

The purpose of the Pearson eTextbook Application Videos is to provide you with an opportunity to observe and reflect on SIOP teaching and learning practices. There are multilingual students in each of the classrooms with varying levels of English proficiency. The teachers you will observe are at different levels of SIOP implementation, from second-year SIOPers to veterans. As you observe the lessons they have created, focus on the students and the lesson objectives, keeping in mind that becoming a high-implementing SIOP teacher takes time, practice, and support to refine teaching practices. We are grateful to each of these SIOP educators for welcoming us into their classrooms, and for their dedication to SIOP, their multilingual learners, and other students.

Pearson eTextbook Application

Video Example 6.1

SIOP Lesson: Grade 10 History; Comparing and Contrasting the U.S. and Roman Empire (Teacher 2)

Practice & Application

CONTENT OBJECTIVES

This chapter will help you to . . .

- Identify a variety of ways for students to strengthen their learning through hands-on or kinesthetic practice.
- Create application activities that extend the learning in new ways and relate to content or language objectives.

LANGUAGE OBJECTIVES

This chapter will help you to . . .

- Enhance typical lesson tasks so that different language skills are integrated.
- As part of a lesson plan, write practice and application activities linked to specific lesson objectives.

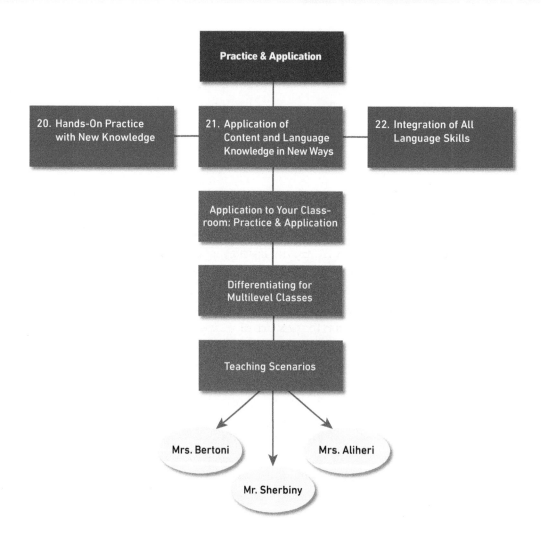

One common memory that most adults share is of learning to ride a full-sized bike. Even after riding smaller bicycles with training wheels, most of us were unprepared for the balancing act required for us to not fall down when riding a regular bike. If you had a parent or older brother or sister who talked you through the process, showed you how to balance, and perhaps even held on to the bike while you were steadying yourself, your independent practice time with the big bike was probably enhanced. Talking about the experience, listening to someone else describe it, observing other riders, and then practicing for yourself all worked together to turn you into a bicycle rider. That feeling of accomplishment, of mastering something new through practice and applying it to a bigger bike is a special feeling that most of us have experienced as learners. ■

■ Background

Up to this point in a SIOP lesson, the teacher has introduced content and language objectives, built background or activated prior knowledge, introduced key vocabulary, identified a learning strategy and higher-order questions for students to focus on, developed a scaffolding approach for teaching the new information, and planned for student interaction. In the Practice & Application component, the students have a chance to practice with the new material, and, with careful teacher oversight, demonstrate how well they are learning it. In the same lesson or a subsequent one, the teacher plans a task so students can apply this new knowledge in various ways. It is well established that practice and application help one master a skill (Dean et al., 2012; Rosenshine, 2012). For SIOP instruction, both the practice and application tasks should also aim for practice of all four language skills: reading, writing, listening, and speaking.

This stage of a SIOP lesson is very important for the academic language development of multilingual learners because learning happens in classes through the use and deliberate practice of oral and written language (Saunders & O'Brien, 2006; TESOL, 2018). Students may interact with others or independently, but in order to develop a high level of proficiency in a new language, they must have opportunities for both comprehensible input (Krashen, 1985) and targeted output (Swain, 1985), namely oral and written practice. When teachers plan these activities carefully, students benefit (Piazza, et al., 2020). So, as you develop lessons, consider the following:

Purpose of the activity. SIOP teachers need to carefully choose the activities they include in their lessons and ensure they connect to the lesson objectives.

- Some activities must strengthen the students' progress in meeting or mastering the content and language objectives. Suppose a language arts content objective calls for sixth graders to write a conclusion that supports the argument they made, and the language arts teacher instructs on ways to write a strong conclusion. After students practice writing a conclusion to some existing texts, an application activity might have them write a post for the class blog on a current event, such as ways to support refugee families in the community.

- Some activities must advance student proficiency in using English. Many SIOP teachers use sentence stems and language frames to help students articulate their thoughts and ideas while they are completing a task. These frames link to language functions, and activities can be created to encourage more sophisticated use of these frames over time. For example, students may progress from expressing an opinion simply, as in *"I believe that__"* to the more detailed *"In my opinion, __is correct/incorrect because__,"* and finally to the complex form *"The scientist cited in this article claims__, but I would argue that__."* Short and Echevarría (2016) present a range of stems organized by language function.

- Some activities may build foundational language knowledge, especially for young learners who enter school with few pre-academic experiences or secondary school newcomers to the United States who have had significant interruptions in their educational backgrounds (i.e., SLIFE newcomers). Remember that many state standards related to foundations of literacy, like phonemic awareness, are found in English language arts for grades K–5 but not for grades 6–12.

Language of the activity. In the past decade or so, research has shown that students can use their home language to support their classroom activities and deepen their knowledge, both of the content topics and the new language they may be studying (Cummins, 2016; Garcia, Johnson, & Seltzer, 2017; NASEM, 2017). The broader use of home language in the classroom as a resource for learning fits within the SIOP classroom and is an aspect of culturally responsive instruction that can take place in face-to-face and online settings (Jeong, Eggleston, & Samaniuk, 2021).

- Suppose a lesson's content objective is *"Students will be able to explain predator and prey relationships."* When the goal is to deepen content knowledge, bilingual or home language resources and translanguaging may help. Small groups or pairs organized by language background could read texts in English and/or their home language about predators and preys, perhaps focusing on a different ecosystem per group, and then share ideas and ask questions of one another in English or the home language. The groups could then report back on their learning in English.

- When the focus is on English language development, the use of the home language might be more limited or structured. We know that deliberate practice is essential for advancing proficiency in a new language. Language practice is not simply a set of vocabulary terms or substitution drills, it is "a much broader range of activities that lead to fluency, accuracy, and automaticity of specific subskills" (TESOL, 2018, p. 21). So, with a language objective such as *"Students will compare characteristics of two habitats,"* teachers would want to have students practice ways to make comparisons in English. For some students, scaffolds like word banks and sentence frames may be needed to bolster their language production. Multilingual learners might translate these supports to ensure comprehension, but they would be expected to speak or write in English to complete the task.

Differentiation of the activity. If the class includes students spanning multiple language proficiency levels, the Practice & Application component of the SIOP Model is the ideal place to differentiate instruction.

- In the language arts lesson mentioned earlier, the final application activity (writing a blog post) might be differentiated. The teacher might facilitate a whole-class brainstorming of ways to support refugee families. Students share ideas, some of which may come from their home or country backgrounds, and the teacher generates a list. If some students use their home language to suggest an item for the list, the teacher seeks a translation or asks a classmate to interpret. Next, the class selects one idea as a model and discusses reasons in favor of the idea as well as possible counterarguments they might want to oppose. The teacher might review language frames and key words to use in a conclusion. Then, some advanced-level students might write individual blog posts, intermediate-level students might write with one partner, and beginners might work with the teacher to prepare a group text.

- Teachers can incorporate project-based learning, community-service opportunities, or other differentiated activities that connect to interests, multiple intelligences, home language experiences, and cultural perspectives (Gay, 2018; Paterson, 2021; Seidlitz & Perryman, 2011; Tomlinson, 2014; Vogt, Echevarría, & Washam, 2015; Ye He, & Faircloth, 2018). As teachers plan these practice and application activities, they should consider the structure of the task and degree of difficulty for the resulting product, the grouping configurations, and the type of feedback that will be provided in light of the students' language proficiency levels and educational backgrounds.

> " Practice and Application is where differentiation takes off! Allowing students the freedom to be creative and showcase their learning in a variety of ways allows for all students in the classroom to take pride in their work and show the amazing talents and assets they bring to the classroom.
>
> Andrea Rients, Professional Learning Coordinator, Minnesota "

As you read this chapter, you will discover how sheltered language and content teachers provide multilingual learners with the types of hands-on experiences, guidance, and practice that can lead to mastery of content knowledge and higher levels of language proficiency. The teaching scenarios demonstrate how three high school ESL science teachers, who each have classes with newly arrived students with limited formal schooling, designed and delivered lessons on rotation and revolution.

SIOP® **SIOP® FEATURE 20:**

Hands-On Materials and/or Manipulatives Provided for Students to Practice Using New Content Knowledge

As previously mentioned, riding a bike is usually preceded by practicing with training wheels and working with a more experienced bike rider. Obviously, the more practice one has on the bike, the more likely one is to become a good bike rider.

Madeline Hunter (1982), a renowned expert in teaching methods, coined the term *guided practice* to describe the process of the teacher leading students through practice sessions prior to independent application. In her lesson design, new material should be divided into meaningful parts. After each part is introduced to students, they should have short, intense practice periods with the content. New material needs repeated practice at the start. Previously learned materials should be reviewed periodically with additional practice periods. Throughout, Hunter recommended, teachers should give students specific feedback so they know how well they are doing.

When SIOP teachers provide multiple lesson opportunities for students to practice in relevant and meaningful ways, they have a greater chance of mastering content skills and concepts. This is true for all learners, but is particularly important for multilingual learners who have double the work—they are learning the content at the same time they are learning English. One way to support them is by planning tasks that incorporate hands-on experiences with manipulatives or kinesthetic activities.

Pearson eTextbook

Video Example 7.1

Watch this video and see how Monica Miller's second graders use math manipulatives to practice place value. What manipulatives and kinesthetic activities can you add to your lessons?

- Manipulatives can help multilingual learners connect abstract concepts to concrete experiences. These items may be created, counted, classified, stacked, experimented with, observed, rearranged, dismantled, and so forth. They are commonly used in math and science, but are applicable across the curriculum (See Artifact 7.1.). For example, a summary of a book/chapter/video/experiment/speech or steps in any process can be written on separate strips of paper and students work together to put them in order.

- Physical movement likewise helps students put concepts into gestures and poses. Consider a lesson on the signing of the Declaration of Independence. Students could create a tableau where they sit as the members of the second Continental Congress did, at tables according to their colony, and act out the signing of the document.

Furthermore, hands-on experiences with manipulatives or kinesthetic activities that require movement reduce the language load for students and are typically more motivating. Students with beginning proficiency in English, for instance, can still participate and demonstrate what they are learning. Multilingual learners may also use their home language while engaging with the activities, although the final product of the task might require English.

Being told how to ride a bike, reading about how to do so, or watching a video of someone else engaged in bike riding is very different from riding down the bike path yourself. Whenever it is possible and appropriate, incorporate hands-on materials and movement into practice activities to boost your students' learning.

Grade 4 students in small groups pull a "canned question" from the container and respond. Group mates confirm, add on, or give a different answer.

Source: Maggie Brewer, Dual Language Elementary Teacher, Connecticut

On the SIOP rating form, a lesson may receive an N/A for feature #20 if the practice activities have happened in an earlier lesson.

SIOP® FEATURE 21:

Activities Provided for Students to Apply Content and Language Knowledge in the Classroom

We all can recall our own learning experiences in elementary, middle, and high school, and the university. For many of us, the classes and courses we remember best are the ones in which we applied our new knowledge in meaningful ways. These may have included activities such as writing a diary entry from the perspective of a character in a novel, creating a semantic map illustrating the relationships among complex concepts, or completing comprehensive case studies on learners we assessed and taught. These concrete experiences forced us to relate new information and concepts in a personally relevant way. We remember the times when we "got it," and we remember the times when we gave it our all but somehow still missed the target. Hunter (1982) recognized this: "The difference between knowing how something should be done and being able to do it is the quantum leap in learning . . . " (p. 71).

> Although multiple opportunities to practice language are critical for language development, for multilingual learners to be successful academically, they must be able to apply their new language, knowledge, and skills in a variety of ways. Since application activities lend themselves to more engagement, relevance, and higher-order thinking than practice alone, students tend to develop a deeper and more sustained understanding of the language and concepts.
>
> Helene Becker, retired EL Director, Connecticut

When SIOP teachers plan opportunities for students to apply new information to real-life situations, multilingual learners are more motivated and able to deepen their understanding because discussing and "doing" make the content concepts and the language used more relevant. Application can occur in a number of ways; and as mentioned previously, students might use their home language as they engage with the activity, while the final product could be prepared bilingually or in English. Sample activities include

- Write a book jacket synopsis, online review, or blog post for a novel or story read in class or outside of school.
- Generate solutions to real-life engineering problems, such as designing an earthquake-resistant school building or a drought-resistant garden. Encourage solutions that represent multicultural viewpoints.
- Play the role of broadcast news anchor and on-site reporters covering a current event in a country of interest.
- Discuss a scientific theory in class (e.g., "Life exists on a planet in another galaxy.") and then conduct research or write an opinion on the topic in a journal.
- Create a campaign ad, video, or social media posting for an historical leader.

Many teachers have curriculum resources with ideas for activities that apply the content topics being studied, but we must remember that multilingual learners need opportunities to apply their growing language knowledge too. For example, it is recommended that for any application task, these learners be challenged to use newly taught sentence structures, vocabulary, reading strategies, and/or other language skills to engage in and complete their work. When SIOP teachers provide supportive environments, which include scaffolds and models, multilingual learners can produce, practice, and apply new language and vocabulary successfully.

Remember that the art of teaching is guiding students to become independent learners. In Chapter 5 we presented a model for scaffolding that shows how a teacher can gradually increase the students' responsibility for learning and doing, and we argued that collaborative practice and structured conversations along with recursive teaching are important bridging steps between guided practice and independent work. Through collaborative learning, students support one another in practicing or applying information while the teacher assists as needed.

On the SIOP rating form, a lesson may receive an N/A for feature #21 if an application activity will happen in a later lesson.

SIOP® **SIOP® FEATURE 22:**

Activities Integrate All Language Skills

Reading, writing, listening, and speaking are complex cognitive language processes that are interrelated and integrated. As we go about our daily lives, we move through the processes in a natural way, reading what we write, talking about what we've read, and listening to others talk about what they've read, written, and seen. Most young children become grammatically competent in their home language by age five, and

ARTIFACT 7.2   Oral Language Sentence-Making Chart

Sentence-making chart from a first grade classroom in Oregon with visuals, prepositional phrases, and conjunctions to integrate language practice with content.

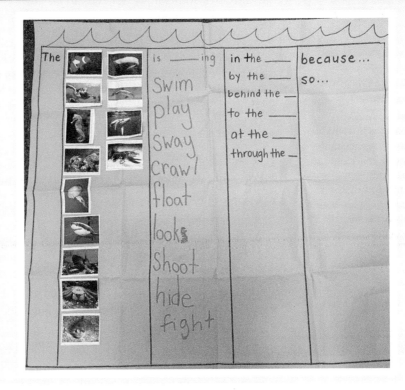

their continuing language development relates primarily to vocabulary, more sophisticated grammar usage (e.g., using relative clauses and noun phrases), and functional as well as sociocultural applications of language (e.g., adjusting one's language to a particular audience, developing rhetorical styles) (Peregoy & Boyle, 2017). Proficiency in reading and writing is achieved much later, and differences exist among individuals in levels of competence. Students especially need to learn academic language for school settings where the use of the forms and functions of social language (e.g., simple sentence and question structures) diminish while academic forms and functions (e.g., sentences with embedded clauses and abstract concepts) escalate (see Chapter 1 for a detailed discussion).

Some multilingual learners may achieve competence in the written domains of a second language earlier than in the oral language domains; others may become proficient speakers before they read and write well (August & Shanahan, 2006). But it is important to realize that the language processes—reading, writing, listening, and speaking—are mutually supportive. Although the relationships among the processes are complex, practice in any one promotes development in the others (Baker et al., 2014; Genesee et al., 2006). Research shows that oral and written language can be successfully developed in content area classrooms (Baker et al., 2014; NASEM, 2017).

We also know from research that certain knowledge, skills, and strategies can transfer from multilingual learners' home language to learning and using English. For example, phonological awareness, knowledge of print, listening and reading comprehension skills, and narrative skills that developed through the home language can be applied to English contexts (NASEM, 2017). For that reason, we want to

Pearson eTextbook

Video Example 7.2

In this video, Andrea Rients explains how the Quiz-Quiz-Trade technique integrates all four language skills and kinesthetic movement. How does the technique engage her high school history students and build academic language?

encourage multilingual learners to use their full linguistic repertoires in our classes (García, Ibarra Johnson, & Seltzer, 2017).

When SIOP teachers create opportunities for multilingual learners to practice and use all four language processes in an integrated manner, they set students up with the means to strengthen their proficiency in English. Throughout the day or class period, effective teachers offer their students varied experiences such as:

- Linking oral discussions of essential questions to reading selections
- Structuring interaction with peers
- Guiding students to use sentence starters and signal words
- Providing students with the chance to listen and react to peers' ideas
- Asking students to write about what is being learned

We do want to clarify two points about language development within the Practice & Application component:

1. Although all identified language objectives in a lesson need to be practiced and applied as the lesson advances, not all language skills that are practiced need to be tied to an objective. In other words, a language objective represents a key skill, language structure, or strategy the teacher plans to teach and intends for students to learn. There may be one domain, for example, that needs attention for a period of time. In a SIOP lesson, the teacher teaches to this objective and assesses, formally or informally, how well students are meeting it. While the objective may focus on one language domain, such as writing, in the course of the lesson, students would have additional opportunities to read, speak, and listen. These should be carefully planned, but need not be assessed in the same way an objective would be.

2. Teachers are sometimes unsure about whether to correct multilingual learners' language errors during practice time. In general, consider students' stages of English language development when deciding whether to correct them. For beginning speakers of English, errors may be developmental and reflect students' home language use (e.g., not remembering to add past tense inflected endings to English verbs). Other errors may deal with placement of adjectives, sentence structure, plurals, and so forth. Research on error correction indicates that impromptu corrections are less effective than setting aside a portion of a lesson to focus on the grammatical forms or usage issues that arise or prompting the learner to self-correct (Lyster & Saito, 2010).

   If errors impede oral communication during a class discussion, you can gently correct students by restating the sentence in proper form. Otherwise, leave the errors alone. If errors are in a written product that is to be displayed, you may want to work with the student to edit it. If you notice, however, that many students make the same error and it does not seem to be due to the language acquisition process, it is reasonable to plan a mini-lesson on the issue for a later class period or provide instruction to a small group while the rest of the class works on another task. What is most important is that you are sensitive to errors that might confuse communication; corrections usually can be modeled in a natural and nonthreatening way.

■ Application to Your Classroom: Practice & Application

In the section that follows, you will find some teaching ideas to help you develop practice and application activities for SIOP lessons:

- **Physical Timeline.** Have students move themselves instead of doing paper-and-pencil tasks for practice. For example, students can form a physical timeline about the Women's Suffrage Movement with their bodies rather than complete a worksheet. Give some students a card displaying a date; others, one displaying an event. The students would organize themselves, first pairing the dates and events, and then forming the human timeline in the front of the room. The date and event partners create a sentence using their terms (e.g., In 1848, the first Women's Rights Convention was held.) and each speaks chorally to the class. To practice more academic language, distribute a few more cards to other students with sequence terms like *"First," "Then," "After That,"* and *"A Few Years Later"* and ask them to find a reasonable spot in the timeline. Then the students in the timeline incorporate the adverbs of time into their explanations as they state their sentences aloud.

- **Games.** Educational, engaging, and fun games provide opportunities to practice or apply new content and language learning. In recent years, popular online game apps and websites, like Kahoot! and Jeopardy have let teachers build game boards to manage the content and language demand. Many allow for differentiation, so less proficient or less knowledgeable students can choose easier questions. More traditional games like Bingo can be used too. For example, students hear a number or word said aloud and then mark its written form on the bingo card; or definitions, synonyms, or antonyms could be read aloud and students would find the corresponding word on the card.

- **Foldables and Cut Paper Shapes.** Folding and/or cutting paper offers a hands-on way for students to organize information. Foldables can be made in various ways. With one foldable type, a sheet of paper is held in a landscape orientation and then folded in half lengthwise (hot dog fold). The front half is then cut into a number of flaps (e.g., three), with the cut going up to the fold. On the outside front, a key word (e.g., *element, compound, mixture*) may be placed on each flap. When each is lifted, a definition may be written on the top half and a picture may be placed on the bottom half. (For examples, see Zike, 2011, 2013.) Teachers can also cut shapes into pieces and distribute them to students who complete a task on their piece and then work with others to make the whole shape. (See, for example, Piece O'Pizza, in Vogt & Echevarria, 2022).

- **Reader's Theater, Role-Plays, and Simulations.** Students can build oral fluency, reinforce content knowledge, and practice language structures and academic vocabulary through Reader's Theater (Short, Vogt, & Echevarría, 2011, pp. 58–60). Teachers create scripts on particular topics to be performed by small groups of students. The teacher may model the script before the students are assigned roles and perform. Role-plays are more informal, with students taking roles and deciding what they want to say while acting out a fictional, historical, or current event. Simulations may place students in real-life situations and have them work together to solve problems or attain a goal.

Character Diary model
from a SIOP Science
Workshop, Virginia.

> Dear Diary,   Oct. 15
> It's cold outside. Today Mama told me
> we are going on a journey. I needed to stretch
> my wings.
>
> Dear Diary,   Oct. 16
> We flew south today with our cousins and friends.
> My wings are very tired!
>
> Dear Diary,   Oct. 20
> We kept flying. Sometimes we stopped by a lake
> Some nights we slept in trees. Now we are in a
> sunny, warm place. My new home!

Pearson eTextbook

Video Example 7.3

Watch this video to see
how Lynelle Larson brings
technology into her Grade 7
classroom. What audio and
video programs and apps do
your students use to practice and apply their content
and language learning?
https://www.youtube.com/
watch?v=1hxO7627maY

- **Character Diaries.** Students take the role of a character from a novel, an historical figure, a person in the news, or an object, such as a piece of legislation
  seeking to become a law. They create several entries in a diary, writing in the
  voice of that person/item, and including key events. See an example in Artifact
  7.3. Teachers may add other requirements to apply specific language objectives
  such as use of descriptive language, use of past tense or if-then clauses, or use of
  a key language frame.

- **Audio and Video Software.** Practice and application tasks can be done in the
  classroom or at home with a variety of software applications like Flipgrid, Voice
  Thread, and Screencast-o-matic. These tools allow the teacher and students
  to make a brief video or audio recording and share with another person who
  can listen, respond, give feedback, or add on. A major benefit for multilingual
  learners is the opportunity to practice: a recording can be re-recorded easily if a
  learner wants to make a change.

Differentiating for Multilevel Classes

The Practice & Application component offers teachers a relatively easy way to meet
the needs of students with different abilities or proficiency levels in their classrooms.
Consider the six options below when you want to adjust activities for your multi-level
classes (Echevarría, Short, & Vogt, 2008; Tomlinson & Imbeau, 2010).

1. **Group with a purpose.** Arrange students by language proficiency, home language,
   learning style or multiple intelligences, demonstrated ability, perceived ability,
   or another reasoned way that suits the goal of the activity. Mix groups from

time to time. Rotate roles so the more proficient students produce work or perform first and thus act as peer models for others.

2. **Differentiate the tasks.** Give each group a similar, yet specifically designed and equivalent task, or design one activity at multiple levels of difficulty, such as the scaffolded cloze shown in Figure 7.1, a vocabulary worksheet with a word bank and a companion one without, or a writing assignment with different required lengths or research sources consulted. Explain each group's assignment clearly, making sure it is as demanding as the others. An "easy" task may be as cognitively demanding to multilingual learners with lower English proficiency as a "hard" task is to English speakers. Remember some tasks can be partially or completely done in the students' home languages.

3. **Provide choice of task.** Allow students to use their strengths and preferences in assignments. Understanding of concepts and information can be expressed through art, drama, poetry, oral or video presentation, creating an e-book, and so forth. Some students may opt for a digital or oral presentation to demonstrate their knowledge rather than a written assignment. Less proficient students may be more comfortable with a mode of expression that involves less speaking or extended writing.

4. **Use motivational strategies.** Learn what will motivate your students to perform to their ability. The following may be considered:

   ◆ *Extrinsic:* Actual, physical rewards (points, homework passes, etc.) for accomplishing a task

   ◆ *Intrinsic:* The mental and emotional "reward" for accomplishing a task

   ◆ *Task engagement:* Positive feeling from being part of something that is stimulating, interesting, and do-able

   ◆ *Cooperative, competitive, individualistic:* The three most common classroom goal structures; each has a role, but cooperative goal structures tend to be the most motivational for students

   ◆ *Ego involvement:* Positive feeling about self when able to complete a task

5. **Use leveled questions to engage all learners.** As mentioned previously in Chapter 5, teachers tend to ask higher-level questions more frequently to high-performing students, and more literal-level questions to low-performing students. Instead, know your students' language levels (beginning, intermediate, etc.). Prepare a hierarchy of questions so that students of all proficiency levels are able to participate—simplify word choice and structure in questions for newcomers and beginners. Allocate turns, monitor turn-taking, and make sure you allow enough wait time for less proficient students to respond. Be sure all students are given the chance to be involved and display language supports like sentence frames to aid students in responding.

6. **Select resources for differentiation.** Find texts at different reading levels or in students' home languages on the same or related topics. Use wordless books or photo journals with newcomers. Bookmark websites in English and home language. Although translation websites are not 100% accurate, they are often

FIGURE 7.1 Scaffolded Listening Cloze Dictation Forms

More Proficient Students

Fill in the blanks with the missing words while the teacher reads a passage aloud. You will hear the passage twice.

Gregor Mendel _____ _____ from parent to _____. This _____ is called _____. Mendel used _____ in his _____ experiments. _____ always _____ with the same form of a _____. In one of his experiments, _____. He put the _____ of tall pea plants on the _____ _____ of the short pea plants. He discovered that _____.

Less Proficient Students

Fill in the blanks with the missing words while the teacher reads a passage aloud. You will hear the passage twice.

Gregor Mendel studied how _____ are passed on from parent to _____. This passing on of traits is called _____. Mendel used _____ pea plants in his heredity experiments. _____ plants always produce _____ with the same form of a trait as the parent. In one of his experiments, he _____ _____ pea plants. He put the pollen from the _____ of tall pea plants on the _____ of the flowers of the short pea plants. He _____ that none of the _____ were short.

useful resources. Family and community members may be able to recommend appropriate home language resources.

Two examples of activities follow:

- **Scaffolded Cloze Activities.** Consider a mixed class with students who speak English and multilingual learners. They are studying genetics. The lesson content objective is *"Students will distinguish between dominant and recessive traits"* and the language objective is *"Students will listen and take notes about Mendel's experiments."* For an activity to practice the language objective, a teacher might plan a listening cloze dictation. The English speakers might record what the teacher says as a regular dictation, but the multilingual learners might have two different dictation forms with more or fewer words already written down. (See Figure 7.1.) All the students listen to the paragraph the teacher reads on Gregor Mendel and the study of genetics, and all participate in the listening task, but the task format is differentiated to the students' English abilities. (Note that cloze activities can be a written activity, too, where students fill in words they generate or draw from a word bank.)

- **Information Gap Activities.** These activities, which include Jigsaws, problem solving, and simulations, are set up so each student (generally in a group) has one or two pieces of information about a topic or event, or to help solve a puzzle, but not all the necessary information to get the full picture. Students must work together, sharing information while practicing their language, negotiating, and critical thinking skills. Teachers differentiate by assigning the amount and complexity of the specific pieces of information to students according to their language proficiency, background knowledge, and interests.

The Lesson

Solar System (Ninth Grade Newcomers)

This lesson takes place over two days in an ESL Science Concepts class for newcomer SLIFE students. The students have experienced limited formal schooling in their home countries (less than six years of instruction), have limited literacy in varieties of English and Arabic, and range in age from 15 to 18. They are immigrants and refugees to the United States from Yemen, Lebanon, Sudan, South Sudan, Syria, and Iraq. They have entered high school but have been placed in a specialized, full-day newcomer program for one year. The goal of this class is to develop science academic language and basic middle school science concepts found in the state science standards so that they can take a high school lab science class next year. They are all considered ninth graders because they have no high school credits yet.

The unit being studied this week is the Solar System. On day one, students learned about the planets and the sun in our solar system. This two-day lesson focuses on the locations and movement of the moon and Earth, particularly revolution and rotation. The final lessons extend this basic understanding so students will be able to explain how the Earth's and moon's motions affect the seasons and the tides. The state science standard is "Describe the cyclic pattern of moon phases, eclipses of the sun and moon, and the seasons, using a model of the Earth-sun-moon system."

Teaching Scenarios

Mrs. Bertoni

Mrs. Bertoni had written the lesson agenda on the board: (1) Check homework. (2) Vocabulary: *moon, revolution, revolve, rotation, rotate, axis*. (3) Read chapter pages 83–84. (4) Discussion. (5) Homework assignment. As the students entered the classroom, she asked them to take out their notebooks so she could check their homework. As she circulated, the students talked quietly to one another in Arabic.

The teacher then turned off the lights in the room. She asked students what this made them think of. Several students said "night." She agreed and asked them what they see at night. They said "stars" and "moon"; some in English, others in Arabic. She explained that today they would learn how the moon moves and how the Earth moves. "If it is night, point to the sky and show me where you see the moon." Most students pointed straight up. She asked if the moon was always there, gesturing up too. One student responded in Arabic and a classmate interpreted, "No, it goes around."

Mrs. Bertoni drew a semicircle arc on the board. She drew a full moon at the end on the left side and added arrows to the arc to show the moon moving to the right. She drew a circle to represent the Earth centered below the semicircle. She said, "The moon moves around the Earth" while pointing to the moon and Earth. She asked the class to repeat the sentence and they did. Then she said, "This movement is called *revolution.* The moon *revolves* around the Earth." She pointed to the words *revolution* and *revolve* written on the board and asked the students to repeat "The moon revolves around the Earth." She asked one student with more English proficiency to interpret the sentence into Arabic so all would understand. She then drew a sun on the board and made a circle around it that began and ended with Earth. "The Earth revolves around the sun," she said and students repeated.

Next, she drew a line down the middle of the circle representing Earth to indicate the axis (from 1 o'clock to 7 o'clock if this figure were a clock). She explained the Earth leans to the side a little bit (leaning herself as she said this) and turns around an axis. She gestured to the line and indicated the written word *axis* on the board. As she pirouetted, she said, "This turning is called *rotation.*" She had the students repeat the word *rotation* while she pointed to it on the board. She said, "So the Earth rotates around its axis" and pointed to the word *rotate* as well. Students repeated, "The Earth rotates around its axis." She again asked the student with more English proficiency to interpret this sentence into Arabic so all would understand.

Next Mrs. Bertoni asked the students some comprehension questions like "What revolves around the Earth?" and "What does the Earth do?" She accepted brief answers from her newcomer students, like "moon" and "goes around sun." She added the key vocabulary as labels to the drawings on the board and asked the students to copy the annotated illustrations into their notebooks.

After several minutes, Mrs. Bertoni told the students to open their Earth Science textbooks to page 83. She described the photo of the moon and Earth on the page to them. She then read the first paragraph aloud and explained it more simply to the class. She read the next six paragraphs in the same manner. When done with the text, she posed comprehension questions and called on students who raised their hands to answer.

For homework, she asked the students to reread pages 83 and 84 in the text and write down in their notebook one thing they learned.

When students entered the next day, the agenda was posted: (1) Check homework. (2) Write sentences with new vocabulary. (3) Answer comprehension questions. (4) Discussion. (5) Homework assignment. The students opened their notebooks to show Mrs. Bertoni their homework. She asked two students to read aloud what they had learned. She corrected their pronunciation as they spoke.

Next, students were told to write three or four sentences independently using any of the key vocabulary words from this unit. As students worked, she circulated and corrected their sentences. After 10 minutes, she asked four students to write their sentences on the board. One by one they read them aloud, and Mrs. Bertoni pointed out ways she had helped each student improve the grammar or spelling.

For the next activity, she passed out questions related to sun, Earth, and moon movements and had students write responses. They could use their textbook. She again circulated, pointed to paragraphs in the textbook for students to reread, made corrections, and relied on classmates to interpret for struggling students. This activity took longer than she planned so she asked students to finish the task for homework.

Check your understanding: On the SIOP form in Figure 7.2, rate Mrs. Bertoni's lesson on each of the Practice & Application features.

FIGURE 7.2 **Practice & Application Component of the SIOP® Model: Mrs. Bertoni's Lesson**

4	3	2	1	0	N/A
20. **Hands-on materials and/or manipulatives** provided for students to practice using new content knowledge	**Few hands-on materials and/or manipulatives** provided for students to practice using new content knowledge		**No hands-on materials and/or manipulatives** provided for students to practice using new content knowledge		

4	3	2	1	0	N/A
21. Activities provided for students to **apply content and language knowledge** in the classroom	Activities provided for students to **apply either content or language knowledge** in the classroom		No activities provided for students to **apply content and language knowledge** in the classroom		

4	3	2	1	0
22. Activities integrate all **language skills** (i.e., reading, writing, listening, and speaking)	Activities integrate some **language skills**		Activities do not integrate **language skills**	

Mr. Sherbiny (see Figure 7.3 for the full lesson plan)

At the beginning of class, Mr. Sherbiny read aloud the lesson's objectives that were written on the board in English and the class chorally repeated them. He explained them in Arabic, his home language.

> **Content Objective:** I will be able to enact, model, and draw examples of revolution and rotation using the Earth, sun, and moon.
>
> **Language Objective:** I will be able to explain the movement of the Earth and moon orally and in writing using the language frames: "The _____ revolves around the _____." And "The _____ rotates on its axis."

Mr. Sherbiny then introduced key terms on the word wall: *revolve* (v)/*revolution* (n), *rotate* (v)/*rotation* (n), *axis* (n), *move* (v)/*movement* (n), *tilt* (n/v), and *moon* (n). Each word or word pair was written in Arabic and English with the part of speech on a large card, and there was a picture associated with each one as well. Using the visuals, he explained the meaning of the words and had students pronounce them aloud. He then asked students for real-life examples of *revolve, rotate*, and *move*. Some offered examples in English, others in Arabic. He next explained why three of the cards listed both a verb and a noun, pointing out the suffixes -*tion* and -*ment* and the root connection between the words. He associated *axis* to math graphs they had studied. He asked students to think-pair-share what they knew about how the Earth moves and how the moon moves. As was the classroom culture, the students could discuss their ideas in their home language or English.

Using three different sized balls labeled Sun, Earth, and Moon, he guided three students in demonstrating revolution and rotation. First, one student held the sun at the front of the room and a second revolved around the sun, as Earth. The class chorally repeated: "The Earth revolves around the sun. One trip around is a revolution." Then, a third student revolved around Earth as the moon. The class chorally repeated, "The moon revolves around the Earth. One trip around is a revolution."

Next Mr. Sherbiny showed the class how the Earth rotates on its axis and introduced the term, *tilt*. The class chorused, "The Earth rotates on its axis. The Earth is tilted. One turn around the axis is a rotation." He had the moon revolve while the Earth rotated with the axis at a slight angle. Finally, he guided the moon to revolve around the Earth while it rotated and revolved around the sun. The students repeated the demonstrations one at a time, and Mr. Sherbiny asked some comprehension questions of the class, some of which tapped prior knowledge. For example, he asked how long it takes for the Earth to revolve around the sun, and how long for the Earth to rotate. The three students performed each demonstration a final time while the teacher led the class in choral explanations, such as "The moon revolves around the Earth," to model the language frames.

Mr. Sherbiny gave each student group a plastic bag with cut-out pictures of the sun, moon, and Earth. He told the groups to manipulate the objects to show revolution and rotation. He asked students to take turns saying the explanation aloud to their group. He circulated and listened in, sometimes asking comprehension questions, sometimes asking students to stand and act out the movements.

The class next read about rotation and revolution from a section of a science textbook written for low literacy students. Before they started, Mr. Sherbiny asked them to raise their hand when they said or heard *revolution, revolve, rotation,* or *rotate*. One student read the first paragraph aloud. A second student read that same paragraph a second time. The teacher asked a question or two after each second reading. Most of the students remembered to raise their hands when the key words were read aloud.

After that, the teacher asked each group to create a drawing to show the sun and the movement of the Earth and moon and to write some sentences using the frames in the language objective. He circulated to check their work, and when he approved it, the students copied the drawing and sentences into their notebooks.

To wrap up, students were then asked to think of things in real life that rotate or revolve. They talked in their groups in English and Arabic. After several minutes, Mr. Sherbiny asked the students to draw their example on the board or act it out. They needed to explain it aloud, and some used English, others Arabic. Some examples that students shared were dances, race cars, running around the gym, and an electric fan. The class then revisited the objectives and students indicated how well they had learned each one, rating them by showing 1, 2, or 3 fingers (1 = *I know the concept well*).

At the start of the next day, Mr. Sherbiny asked student pairs to read the objectives to each other: Partner A would read the content objective, Partner B the language one. As a review, students volunteered to act out the key concepts and terms. The other students guessed what was being demonstrated and shared with a partner.

Mr. Sherbiny wrote the question "Why do we have day and night?" on the board. He paired students and asked them to apply what they learned the day before as they discussed the response. After three minutes, he had students share their ideas with the frame *"We have day/night because . . . "* He then asked for volunteers to try to demonstrate day and night on Earth with the different sized balls.

Next, Mr. Sherbiny distributed the classroom iPads and headsets to the student pairs. He introduced the screencasting app on the classroom iPads. He showed students how to screencast, using a photo he had taken of the sun, moon, and Earth cut-outs and playing audio he had recorded about revolution and rotation. He told the students they would take photos, too, and would record their oral explanations using the app to describe the Earth's and moon's movements. He encouraged them

FIGURE 7.3 Mr. Sherbiny's SIOP® Lesson Plan for Grade 9 Newcomer Science Class

STANDARDS:

Science: Develop and use a model of the Earth-sun-moon system to describe the cyclic patterns of lunar phases, eclipses of the sun and moon, and seasons.

ELD: Multilingual learners communicate information, ideas, and concepts necessary for academic success in the content area of Science.

LESSON TOPIC: Solar System—Earth, Sun, & Moon

OBJECTIVES:

Content Objective: I will be able to enact, model, and draw examples of revolution and rotation using the Earth, sun, and moon.

Language Objective: I will be able to explain the movement of the Earth and moon orally and in writing using the language frames: *"The ____ revolves around the ____."* and *"The ____ rotates on its axis."*

LEARNING STRATEGIES: Think-pair-share, double reading, active listening, summarizing

KEY VOCABULARY: *revolve* (v)/*revolution* (n), *rotate* (v)/*rotation* (n), *move* (v)/*movement* (n), *axis* (n), *tilt* (n/v), *moon* (n), -*tion*, -*ment* (post in English and Arabic)

MATERIALS: vocabulary cards; balls to represent sun, Earth, moon; cut-out pictures of the sun, moon, and Earth, iPads with screencast app, headsets, teacher-made screencast

Day 1

MOTIVATION:

Review objectives with class in English and Arabic.

Introduce science vocabulary on cards with visuals and explain parts of speech. Point out suffixes. Have students think-pair-share ideas about Earth and moon movements and generate examples of new vocabulary in English or Arabic.

PRESENTATION:

Have students hold balls representing sun, Earth, moon to demonstrate revolution and rotation. Start with Earth revolving around sun, then moon revolving around Earth. Have students practice the language frame, *"The ____ revolves around the ____."* Also ask students to repeat *"One trip around is a revolution."*

Show *tilt* and *axis* on Earth and demonstrate rotation. Have students practice the language frame, *"The ____ rotates on its axis."* Ask students to repeat *"The Earth is tilted. One turn around the axis is a rotation."*

Demonstrate rotation and revolution together. First, Earth rotating while circling sun, then add moon revolving around Earth. Check student comprehension and knowledge of Earth and moon movements.

PRACTICE:

Distribute cut-out pictures of Earth, moon, and sun and have student groups practice rotation and revolution at their tables. Encourage use of the language frames. As needed, have students act out movements to show comprehension.

Have class read science text, using the double reading strategy. Select one student to read a paragraph aloud and then another to reread it. Ask all students to raise a hand when they say or hear *revolution, revolve, rotation,* or *rotate*. Ask some comprehension questions after each second reading.

Have students draw and label diagrams in their notebooks of rotation and revolution. Students write some sentences using the language frames.

REVIEW & ASSESSMENT:

Have students talk with table mates in English or Arabic and generate real-life examples of things that rotate and revolve. Students draw their examples on the board or act them out.

Review objectives. Have students self-assess 1, 2, 3 for each objective. (1 finger I know it well, 3 fingers I don't understand.)

Day 2

MOTIVATION:

Have partners review objectives with each other in English or Arabic.

Ask student volunteers to stand and act out the key concepts and terms. The other students guess what is being demonstrated and share with a partner.

(continued)

FIGURE 7.3 **SIOP Lesson: Mr. Sherbiny's Lesson Plan for Grade 9 Newcomer Science Class** *(continued)*

PRESENTATION:

Ask student pairs to apply their knowledge of Earth's movements and explain how day and night occur. Use the language frame: *We have day/night because _____.*

Confirm or elaborate student understanding of the day/night phenomenon.

APPLICATION:

Distribute iPads and headsets, and Earth, sun, and moon cut-outs. Model how to use the iPad camera and the screencast app to make a video recording. Play the teacher-made sample recording. Explain purpose is to summarize what students have learned about revolution, rotation, day, and night.

Have student pairs work on making screencasts. Some may want to record once in Arabic and then again in English.

REVIEW & ASSESSMENT:

Exit Ticket: Have students write one thing they still wonder about.

to use the sentence frames still posted from the day before and add more to their oral explanations about day and night. He explained that they could listen to the recording and re-record if they wanted to improve their speech. Students could record in Arabic but he also wanted them to record in English.

The pairs arranged the cut-outs on the table and began taking photos of them with the iPads. The photos saved automatically to the devices and were easily accessed later within the screencasting app. After the photos had been taken, the pairs then spread out across the room and into the hallway to record their explanations. Mr. Sherbiny circulated and encouraged the students, helping with the app's functions if requested and reminding students of the task.

At the lesson's close, the class reviewed the lesson objectives. Before the students left the classroom, they wrote one thing they still wondered about on a notecard.

Check your understanding: On the SIOP form in Figure 7.4, rate Mr. Sherbiny's lesson on each of the Practice & Application features.

FIGURE 7.4 **Practice & Application Component of the SIOP® Model: Mr. Sherbiny's Lesson**

4	3	2	1	0	N/A
20. **Hands-on materials and/or manipulatives** provided for students to practice using new content knowledge		Few hands-on materials and/or manipulatives provided for students to practice using new content knowledge		No hands-on materials and/or manipulatives provided for students to practice using new content knowledge	

4	3	2	1	0	N/A
21. Activities provided for students to **apply content and language knowledge** in the classroom		Activities provided for students to **apply either content or language knowledge** in the classroom		No activities provided for students to **apply content and language knowledge** in the classroom	

4	3	2	1	0
22. Activities integrate all **language skills** (i.e., reading, writing, listening, and speaking)		Activities integrate some **language skills**		Activities do not integrate **language skills**

Mrs. Aliheri

After the students entered Mrs. Aliheri's classroom, she turned on the interactive whiteboard and projected a video clip. The students watched the Earth revolve around the sun and the moon revolve around the Earth while a voice explained what they were seeing. Mrs. Aliheri paused the clip and wrote *revolve* and *revolution* on the side of the smartboard. She then continued the clip and the students watched the Earth rotating and listened to the explanation. After that, the teacher wrote *rotate* and *rotation* on the board. Next, the video showed scenes depicting the four seasons and day and night while the voiceover explained how these phenomena are the result of the Earth's revolution and its rotation. Mrs. Aliheri added *seasons, day*, and *night* to the board as well.

"I'm going to play this clip again without the sound," Mrs. Aliheri said. "When you see a revolution, I want you to raise one finger. When you see a rotation, raise two fingers." She replayed the clip and students indicated their understanding. Several were confused between rotation and revolution so she played the clip again with the sound on.

Next, the class opened their textbooks to read the section on the topic. Mrs. Aliheri used a book from the elementary school because the reading level was lower. Although some illustrations depicted young children, she believed the text was better for the students who lacked literacy. She asked students to read the assigned pages with a partner. She circulated, listened, and occasionally corrected pronunciation. After 15 minutes of the partner reading, she asked some comprehension questions. Mostly the same three students raised their hands to respond.

To wrap up the lesson, she distributed one word card each to nine students: *moon, Earth, sun, rotates, revolves, seasons, day, night, around.* She asked them to come to the front of the room and use some of their cards to make a sentence. This proved confusing, so she had certain students put their cards on the board: *Earth, sun, revolves, around.* She moved the cards into the following order: *Earth, revolves, around, sun* and modeled how to turn that into a sentence orally: *"The Earth revolves around the sun."* She then wrote out the sentence. She called up more students to place cards: *night, day, rotates, Earth.* She asked the class for help forming a sentence, but no one was able to perform the task. She asked one student to move the cards into an order she dictated: *Earth, rotates, day, night.* She stated, *"Because the Earth rotates, we have day and night."* She wrote this and had the class copy both sentences into their notebooks.

As class started the next day, Mrs. Aliheri acknowledged that the writing activity the day before did not work well so she had another activity. She passed out a cloze paragraph about the Earth, moon, and sun with a word bank. She asked students to individually complete the paragraph on the worksheet by adding the missing words. After five minutes she called on a few students in turn to read a sentence from the paragraph aloud. She corrected their terms and pronunciation whenever she perceived a mistake.

Mrs. Aliheri then told the class they would do a pop quiz via Kahoot!. The students enjoyed the online tool's game atmosphere. They signed in on class iPads and began the quiz that she had prepared. At the end, she viewed an online form that indicated how students performed on each question. Of her 10 questions, most of the class only had 3 or 4 correct. She told the students to reread the pages in the textbook. They could work with a partner if they liked.

To wrap-up the class, the students took the pop quiz again using Kahoot! More than half of the class still had fewer than 6 questions correct.

FIGURE 7.5	Practice & Application Component of the SIOP® Model: Mrs. Aliheri's Lesson

4	3	2	1	0	N/A
20. **Hands-on materials and/or manipulatives** provided for students to practice using new content knowledge		Few **hands-on materials and/or manipulatives** provided for students to practice using new content knowledge		No **hands-on materials and/or manipulatives** provided for students to practice using new content knowledge	

4	3	2	1	0	N/A
21. Activities provided for students to **apply content and language knowledge** in the classroom		Activities provided for students to **apply either content or language knowledge** in the classroom		No activities provided for students to **apply content and language knowledge** in the classroom	

4	3	2	1	0
22. Activities integrate all **language skills** (i.e., reading, writing, listening, and speaking)		Activities integrate some **language skills**		Activities do not integrate **language skills**

Check your understanding: On the SIOP form in Figure 7.5, rate Mrs. Aliheri's lesson on each of the Practice & Application features.

Discussion of Lessons

Look back at your rating form and think about the reasons you scored the lessons as you did. What evidence is in the scenarios? Read on to see our analyses.

20. *Hands-On Materials and/or Manipulatives Provided for Students to Practice Using New Content Knowledge*

Mrs. Bertoni: 0

Mr. Sherbiny: 4

Mrs. Aliheri: 1

- Although **Mrs. Bertoni** visually modeled the movements of rotation and revolution, she did not have the students use manipulatives or do a kinesthetic task. The one time they used a gesture (pointing to the ceiling to indicate the moon's location) was actually a connection to their prior knowledge. The students were mostly passive while they copied her illustration from the board. Listening to a teacher read is not a practice activity. The first day they had no opportunities to practice using the new words orally, and writing vocabulary sentences and answers to reading comprehension questions on the second day did not meet the goal of this feature. Mrs. Bertoni tried to scaffold the information for the students, using the diagram on the board and paraphrasing the text, but she failed to give them any guided or independent work to strengthen their content learning. For newcomers with limited English skills, hands-on activities would have made the new information more concrete and more meaningful. This lesson received a "0" for providing hands-on materials or manipulatives for practice.

- **Mr. Sherbiny** planned and implemented several hands-on practice activities in this lesson. For example, students used manipulatives in small groups to demonstrate revolution and rotation and practiced language frames to explain the concepts. Later, each group made a drawing to show the movements and shared it with the class. Mr. Sherbiny also asked students to listen for key words and raise their hands when they heard them. They used the manipulatives again the second day for their screencast photos. Therefore, Mr. Sherbiny's lesson received a "4" for this feature. Through multiple repetitions and informal assessments, Mr. Sherbiny was able to determine whether students mastered the content and key vocabulary concepts. Such meaningful practice made concrete what could have been abstract for the multilingual learners.

- **Mrs. Aliheri** tried to involve students through movement by having them signal with fingers when they recognized *rotation* and *revolution* in the video clip. She also tried to have students manipulate word cards to make sentences, but her planning was poor, the explanation of the task was unclear, and so the task was fruitless. If she had narrowed the focus, included cards for all the words needed to make a sentence, distributed cards for only one sentence at a time, and modeled for the students from the start, these newcomers might have had a chance at success. Instead, she assumed too much. These low literate students were not ready to form sentences that she alone had in mind with only a partial set of words and the need to add words, such as *because*. Completing the worksheet the next day did not meet this feature either. Her lesson was rated a "1" for providing hands-on materials or manipulatives for practice.

21. *Activities Provided for Students to Apply Content and Language Knowledge in the Classroom*

Mrs. Bertoni: 0

Mr. Sherbiny: 4

Mrs. Aliheri: 0

- Because this was a multiday lesson and the concepts of rotation and revolution were fairly straightforward, time was available for both practice and application. Despite this, **Mrs. Bertoni's** lesson did not include an application activity. As a result, the lesson also received a "0" on the SIOP protocol for applying content and language knowledge. It is doubtful that the multilingual learners had a clear understanding of concepts or that they could apply what they had learned in any meaningful way on their own. The Day 1 homework assignment—to read the chapter independently and to write one thing they learned—is not an application activity. The Day 2 assignment was a continuation of classwork— answering reading comprehension questions. Both tasks were better suited to in-class work so the teacher could support the emerging English literacy skills of these newcomers. No task applied the language or content knowledge from this lesson to a new concept, real-life situation, or their personal experiences.

- **Mr. Sherbiny's** lesson received a "4" for applying content and language knowledge. After the students demonstrated their understanding of the newly learned concepts through practice, he had them apply that knowledge in several ways. They had to think of real-life examples where something rotates or revolves, they had to explain the day and night phenomenon using their newly acquired knowledge, and they had to apply their knowledge in making a screencast recording. With these underschooled newcomers, it was fitting as well as culturally responsive to have them work in groups and discuss their ideas, in English and their home language. By permitting the use of the home language, Mr. Sherbiny allowed for translanguaging, especially since students could use words and phrases they had not learned in English yet. He often restated in English what a student had said in Arabic, thus acting as a language model for the class, which advanced the students' language skills.

- **Mrs. Aliheri's** lesson did not have an application activity during this 2-day lesson and so received a "0" for this feature. There were very few opportunities for students to practice their language knowledge orally and none to apply it. The video clip introduced the concepts and the reading reinforced them, but students were not asked to apply the concepts in any new manner. Playing Kahoot! as a quiz was an assessment, not an application activity.

22. *Activities Integrate All Language Skills*

Mrs. Bertoni: 2

Mr. Sherbiny: 4

Mrs. Aliheri: 1

- **Mrs. Bertoni's** lesson on rotation and revolution was teacher directed and focused on information presentation. For the most part, the multilingual learners listened to the teacher—when she was drawing on the board, asking questions, reading aloud, or correcting their work. Some students answered her questions, but she did not make sure each multilingual learner had an opportunity to talk about the new concepts. On neither day did they have an academic discussion, just a teacher-dominated Q & A. The first day, students may have followed along with the reading silently, but since she summarized each paragraph, they did not need to practice reading comprehension skills. The second day they read independently to answer questions, but several struggled and did not finish in the class period. The vocabulary sentence activity gave students a chance to write their own sentences, but they worked alone with only her input. Her lesson received a "2" on the SIOP protocol for integrating all language skills.

- **Mr. Sherbiny's** lesson received a "4" on the SIOP protocol for this feature. Throughout this lesson, multilingual learners were listening, speaking, reading, and writing about rotation and revolution. Mr. Sherbiny gave his newcomers with limited formal schooling repeated practice hearing the new words, using the words and language frames while manipulating representative objects, listening for and reacting to key words when heard (raising their hands), reading the text, writing sentences, and making a screencast recording to summarize what they had learned. The language processes were well integrated into the delivery of the space systems content. He used Arabic to explain and clarify information for these newly arrived adolescents, and he made sure they practiced the English words and sentence frames. The teacher facilitated student-to-student interaction and modeled and checked on appropriate language use.

- **Mrs. Aliheri's** lesson on paper included activities that practiced language skills, but the execution was weak. Students watched and listened to a video about rotation and revolution, but the input was confusing to many. They did some partner reading from the textbook both days, but did not comprehend the material well, as evidenced by the Kahoot! quiz results. She wanted students to manipulate word cards and make some sentences, but she did not scaffold the process, and so none of them were able to complete the task. On Day 1, they copied two sentences into their notebooks and on Day 2 they completed a cloze exercise; both were minimal writing tasks for newcomers. This lesson received a "1" for integrating all language skills.

■ Final Points

As you reflect on this chapter and the impact that practice and application has on learning, consider the following main points:

- With any type of new learning, students need practice and application of newly acquired skills to ensure mastery of content concepts.
- Activities should be designed to help multilingual learners meet or master the content and language objectives. Use of the home language during practice and application activities can act as a scaffold for completing a task or as a resource for acquiring information. Activities can be differentiated to take into account students' proficiency levels, needs, and interests.
- You should plan a variety of activities and materials that include manipulatives or movement to enable students to forge connections between abstract and concrete concepts in a less language-dependent way.
- When you create application activities to extend learning, be sure to relate the activities to both the language and the content objectives.
- Because students have different preferred learning styles, when teachers use different modalities for instruction and encourage students to practice and apply new knowledge through multiple language processes, they have a better chance of meeting students' needs and furthering both their language and content development.

■ Discussion Questions

1. In reflecting on the learning outcomes in the content and language objectives at the beginning of the chapter, are you able to:
   a. Identify a variety of ways for students to enhance their learning through hands-on or kinesthetic practice?
   b. Create application activities that extend the learning in new ways and relate to language or content objectives?
   c. Enhance typical lesson tasks so that different language skills are integrated?
   d. As part of a lesson plan, write practice and application activities linked to specific lesson objectives?

2. Compare and contrast the following two teachers' approaches to teaching a lesson on coordinate planes and slope.

   a. One teacher's approach involves a lecture, graphs of lines with differing slopes, and a formula to calculate slope. Students are then tested about their knowledge of slopes by drawing lines on graphs after being given a slope and *y*-intercept.

   b. The other teacher's approach begins with students angling their textbooks to different heights and rolling their pencils down to determine how the angle affects speed. She introduces the word *slope* and asks students to describe bike riding up and down hills. Groups generate ideas as to why knowing a slope is important. She then has the students practice drawing some lines on graphs and explains the formula, $y = mx + b$. Groups then use mapping software to view 3D images of a ski resort and determine the slopes of several ski runs.

   Which approach to teaching this content concept is most appropriate for multilingual learners? How do you know? Be as specific as you can.

3. One way to ensure practice and application of new knowledge is through project-based learning. Develop a unit project that students in one of your courses can build incrementally as the series of lessons progresses over several days or weeks. Identify the steps to completion that students will accomplish in each lesson of the unit. Try to collaborate across departments, such as ESL and history or physical education and science. Plan a culminating presentation or performance that will enhance language practice.

4. Multilingual learners benefit from the integration of reading, writing, listening, and speaking during a lesson. What adjustments and techniques can a teacher use to provide successful experiences for students with limited English language proficiency while they read, write, listen, and speak about new information they are learning? Include specific activities and examples in your answer.

5. English language arts, mathematics, and science teachers are responsible for incorporating rigorous state standards in their instruction. How is it possible to provide direct application and hands-on practice for lessons? What can teachers do to alleviate the conflict between "covering the content" and giving multilingual learners time to practice the language along with the content?

6. Using the SIOP lesson you have been developing, write some activities for students to practice and then apply the key language and content concepts.

■ Pearson eTextbook Application Videos

The purpose of the Pearson eTextbook Application Videos is to provide you with an opportunity to observe and reflect on SIOP teaching and learning practices. There are multilingual students in each of the classrooms with varying levels of English proficiency. The teachers you will observe are at different levels of SIOP implementation, from second-year SIOPers to veterans. As you observe the lessons they have created, focus on the students and the lesson objectives, keeping in mind that becoming a high-implementing SIOP teacher takes time, practice, and support to refine teaching practices. We are grateful to each of these SIOP educators for welcoming us into their classrooms, and for their dedication to SIOP, their multilingual learners, and other students.

Pearson eTextbook Application
Video Example 7.1
Grade 5 Compare and Contrast with Signal Words Segment 1

Lesson Delivery

CONTENT OBJECTIVES

This chapter will help you to . . .

- Monitor lesson delivery to determine if it is supporting the lesson objectives.
- Determine how lesson preparation influences lesson delivery.
- Generate activities to keep multilingual learners engaged.

LANGUAGE OBJECTIVES

This chapter will help you to . . .

- Discuss characteristics of effective SIOP lesson delivery.
- Explain how a focus on a lesson's objectives can aid in pacing.
- Review your lesson plan to make sure the information and activities support the students in meeting the language and content objectives.

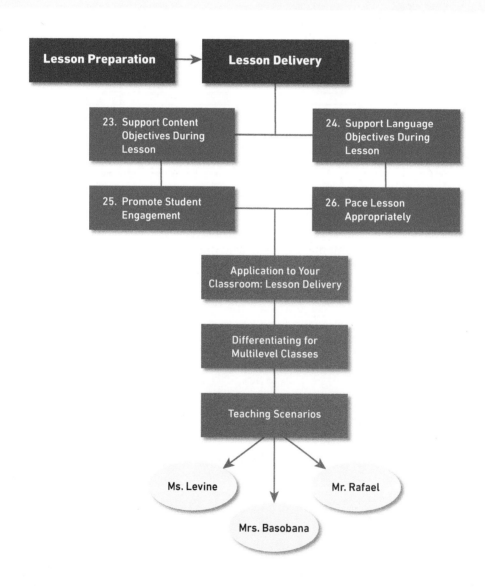

Have you ever planned a lesson that you looked forward to teaching, only to be disappointed by the students' response? Maybe after you presented some new information or process and explained the activity, your student groups could not get to work. They were distracted, chatted with one another, got out of their seats to sharpen pencils, couldn't type the password into the class website—any manner of off-task behavior. Or maybe they were trying to work, but raised their hands to call you over every three minutes to ask a question about the instructions, materials, or purpose. Or they worked diligently but couldn't complete the task in the time you had allocated. You may have been puzzled as to what went wrong. Using the SIOP protocol, you can reflect on and determine ways to improve this lesson and others in the future. ∎

■ Background

In Chapter 2, we explained the importance of carefully designing lessons with multilingual learners in mind. Good preparation is the first step in delivering a lesson that leads to student learning, but those lessons need careful implementation as well. In the Lesson Delivery component, we monitor the success of a lesson in helping students meet objectives. Some lessons unfold as planned; however, some go awry, even if the plan is well written. Activities might be too easy or too difficult for the students. The lesson might be too long or too short. A student might ask an interesting but marginally related question, and the ensuing class discussion consumes ten unexpected minutes. The Lesson Delivery component of the SIOP Model reminds teachers to stay on track, and in this chapter we provide some guidance for doing so.

This chapter addresses the way a lesson is delivered, how well the content and language objectives are supported during the lesson, to what extent students are engaged in the lesson, and how appropriate the pace of the lesson is to students' ability levels. You will see that this chapter parallels Chapter 2, Lesson Preparation, because the two components are closely related. The effectiveness of a lesson's delivery—the level of student participation, how clearly information is communicated, students' level of understanding reflected in the quality of their work—often can be traced back to the preparation that took place before the students entered the classroom.

Pearson eTextbook

Video Example 8.1

Watch two Grade 2 math teachers, Emily Schmidt and Charmin Erickson, describe the value of the SIOP lesson template for planning and delivering lessons. Which features of SIOP do you need to add to your lesson plans and implement regularly in your class?

In this component, Lesson Delivery, we go beyond having the content and lesson objectives written in lesson plans and on the board. Rather, the focus here is on whether the actual lesson delivery matches the stated objectives. We will meet the teachers from Chapter 2 again (Ms. Levine, Mrs. Basobana, and Mr. Rafael) in the Teaching Scenarios and discuss how their level of preparation was executed in their lesson delivery.

SIOP® **SIOP® FEATURE 23:**

Content Objectives Clearly Supported by Lesson Delivery

As we discussed in Chapter 2, content objectives must be stated orally, written in student-friendly language, and displayed for students and teachers alike to see. The objectives serve to remind everyone of the focus of the lesson and to provide a structure to classroom procedures.

Educational reforms and federal legislation over the past two decades have raised the level of academic rigor and accountability in elementary and secondary classrooms. Teachers are expected to post objectives tied to state standards, and administrators expect to see them. However, listing the standard in an abbreviated form, like M.Al-APR.1 (for an algebra standard), as an objective would be meaningless to the students. For young learners, it may appear as gibberish; for older students, it is something to ignore. Further, as we discussed in Chapter 2, a standard is conceptualized at the level of knowledge broader than that taught in an individual lesson plan.

We know that written objectives guide learning and help teachers and students stay on task. SIOP teachers who attend to their lesson objectives make sure there are times during the lesson when some explicit instruction takes place that targets the

ARTIFACT 8.1 **Using Technology for Sharing Objectives**

Source: Kelsins Santos, ESL/Bilingual Instructional Facilitator, Tyler ISD, Texas

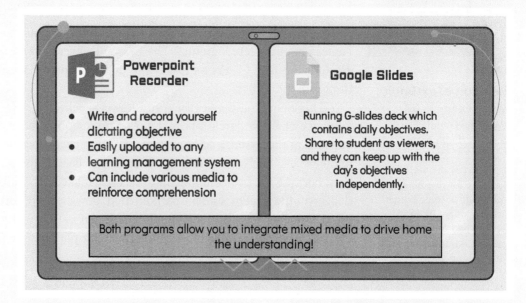

objectives and other times when students have the opportunity to practice and make progress toward meeting those objectives. Lessons can therefore be organized into meaningful segments that allow for instruction, guided practice, and comprehension checks (Schmoker, 2018). Throughout the lesson and at its conclusion, the teacher and learners can evaluate the extent to which the lesson delivery supported the content objectives.

SIOP® **SIOP® FEATURE 24:**

Language Objectives Clearly Supported by Lesson Delivery

Language objectives are an important element of effective SIOP lessons. Teachers and students benefit from having a clear language objective that is written for them to see, discussed at the outset of a lesson, and reviewed during and at the conclusion of the lesson. The objective may be drawn from a state standard for language arts or English as a new language, a scope and sequence of language skills found in a district curriculum framework or instructional text series, or a teacher's observation of student language development needs for a particular discipline.

> " When teachers make a point of addressing the language needed to access and manipulate the content, they become language teachers. This makes the biggest difference in the students' path to language acquisition.
> Ana Segulin, Bilingual/ESL/LOTE Director, Texas "

No matter which language objective is written for a lesson, this feature reminds teachers that they need to address it explicitly during instruction. For example, if first graders in a language arts lesson have to "retell a story" as their language objective after listening to *Lon Po Po* (Young, 1996), then we expect the teacher will spend some time teaching or reviewing *how to retell* with the children, perhaps using a different but familiar story, and also reviewing sequence terms. Similarly, if high schoolers have to "defend a position" as their language objective in a lesson on *To Kill a Mockingbird* (Lee, 2015) and the task is to argue in favor of Atticus's decision to act as the lawyer for Tom Robinson, then we expect the teacher will spend some of the period discussing what makes a good argument and modeling persuasive speech. Without explicit instruction in elements of academic language and without students having multiple opportunities to practice and use the language in a variety of contexts, we will fail to advance our students' academic language development.

SIOP® **SIOP® FEATURE 25:**

Students Engaged Approximately 90% to 100% of the Period

The student engagement feature calls on teachers to engage learners 90% to 100% of the class period. By this we mean that the students are paying attention and on task. It does not mean they need to be highly active (writing, reading, moving) the entire time, but they are following the lesson, responding to teacher direction, and performing the activities as expected. When students are in small groups, all are participating. When they are assigned individual tasks, they get to work.

Multilingual learners are the students who can least afford to have valuable time squandered through boredom, inattention, socializing, and acting up. Lessons where students are engaged less than 50% of the time are unacceptable. This situation tends to occur when teachers are ill prepared, have poor classroom management skills, spend excessive amounts of time making announcements or passing out and collecting papers, have not provided clear explanations of the assignment, or have not scaffolded the process well. If students don't know what to do, they will find something else to do, and then misbehavior or inattention ensues.

The most effective teachers minimize these off-task behaviors and maximize time spent actively engaged in instruction. Multilingual learners who are working to achieve grade-level competence benefit from efficient use of class time. If they have had limited or uneven schooling experiences or a high degree of absenteeism, they particularly need instruction that builds on their assets and interests to encourage participation and direct their focus.

As teachers plan and then deliver lessons, they often estimate the amount of time an activity will take (e.g., show and discuss video clip—ten minutes). While this practice can improve the pacing of a lesson (see SIOP feature 26), we suggest teachers also ask themselves when and how student engagement will lead to learning. As we have discussed throughout this book, effective SIOP teachers plan for and deliver lessons that are balanced between teacher presentation of information and opportunities for students to practice and apply the information in meaningful ways. Creative, fun activities are not effective if they are unrelated to the content and language objectives of the lesson. Equally, "skill and drill" exercises on discrete points (e.g., past tense verb endings) and endless multiple-choice practice tests are not engaging, and they reduce academic learning time as students "tune out."

We know that engagement, motivation, and cultural responsiveness are important factors in successful lessons—for all students (Gay, 2018; Nieto & Bode, 2017; TESOL, 2018). When learners are actively engaged, they are involved in tasks that challenge them and allow them to gain confidence. So what promotes student engagement? Simply, instruction that is understandable to the learners and tasks that are motivating and relevant. Younger learners may prefer activities with objects they can manipulate or movements they can perform, as well as puzzles and learning games. Adolescents are motivated by lessons that connect school topics to their current or future lives and by projects that give them agency. All learners will engage with text above their reading level if it is of interest to them. We know that technology-infused lessons also create inviting, accessible, and interactive classrooms (Pawan et al., 2022). Engagement happens when students have opportunities to talk, read, or write about the lesson's concepts through a variety of activities that reinforce learning and capture students' attention.

It is important to remember that as we plan engaging activities, we must also set students up for success. In order to do that, SIOP teachers:

- optimize the academic learning time for their students by being explicit in their expectations for student performance and by connecting tasks to the learning objectives;
- build background schema so students have knowledge to apply to a task;

Pearson eTextbook

Video Example 8.2

Watch Dr. MaryEllen Vogt reflect on how teacher expectations can enhance or hinder instruction. Do you and your colleagues teach multilingual learners as high achievers or gifted and talented students? If not, what steps can you take to do so? https://www.youtube.com/watch?v=4M-5Xpx-B5c

- plan activities that leverage students' assets, such as their home language skills, favored communication modalities, out-of-school experiences, cultural traditions, and passions;

- structure activities around familiar routines or procedures;

- provide clear directions and modeling;

- design linguistic and instructional scaffolds to help students read, write, and talk about the lesson's concepts;

- allow students to discuss and take notes in their home language (translanguaging practices) to support completing an assignment in English;

- offer choices—in tasks, texts, and/or partners; and

- conceive of outcomes, products, or performances that can be achieved through a variety of modalities.

SIOP® **SIOP® FEATURE 26:**

Pacing of the Lesson
Appropriate to Students' Ability Levels

Pacing refers to the rate at which information is presented during a lesson and the time allotted for completing activities. The pace of the lesson depends on the nature of the lesson's content, as well as the level of students' background knowledge. When working with multilingual learners, it can be challenging to find a pace that doesn't present information too quickly yet is brisk enough to maintain students' interest, especially when a range of English proficiency levels is represented in the same classroom. Finding an appropriate pace requires practice, but becomes easier as teachers develop familiarity with their students' language and academic skills.

Pearson eTextbook

Video Example 8.3

In this video, high school English teacher, Gust Abdalla, explains how focusing on his lesson objectives has improved his planning and pacing. Think about your pacing. How can you maximize learning time for your students?

- *Elementary teachers* know, for instance, that the attention span of a kindergartener or first grader is much shorter than that of a fifth grader, so they adjust their lessons accordingly. A practice activity may last only five minutes in the primary grades, whereas in the upper grades it could last 15–20. Elementary teachers also chunk important information in smaller conceptual units and allot time for processing the material taught in the new language between the chunks. In many elementary classrooms, students do not typically switch teachers or rooms, so on some days, teachers may extend certain lessons beyond the normal time frame to cover the material.

- *Middle and high school subject-area teachers* may be constrained by the school's bell schedule and district curriculum pacing guides. However, teachers cannot move so quickly through the curriculum that they leave their multilingual learners behind. Therefore, they carefully select the important concepts to focus on, provide a range of scaffolds and supports, and adjust their planning accordingly.

- *ELD teachers* can help augment instructional time. When a grade-level or subject-area teacher collaborates with the ELD teacher, both language development and content instruction benefit. The ELD teacher might introduce key vocabulary and build background on topics before they are covered in the content classroom, or provide additional practice and application activities afterward. This supports multilingual students' content learning. It also supports the acquisition of academic English and motivates learners because when they address grade-level material in the ELD class, the result is that they understand more in the content class. (See Chapter 11 for a discussion of teacher collaboration.)

In classes with both students who are proficient in English and those who are multilingual learners, it can take some effort and experience to pace the lessons well. Investing in a slower pace in the first quarter of the year to teach instructional routines and task procedures, along with related language frames, reaps dividends later because students then know the classroom practices and have better academic language skills. Most students enjoy working with peers, so collaborative learning projects with tasks geared to proficiency level and interest are beneficial. On occasion, interdisciplinary projects could be planned, such as a project on the Harlem Renaissance that involves U.S. history (e.g., the migration of African Americans from the South to the North), English literature (e.g., poems by Langston Hughes and Zora Neale Hurston), and music (e.g., the Jazz Age). Such projects not only spiral the content but also introduce and reinforce key language terms, functions, and sentence structures, allowing multilingual learners time over the course of a unit and across several content areas to develop the academic English skills they need for success.

In addition, simple routines can help the pacing:

- Put a basket by the door where students deposit homework when they enter or class work when they leave.
- Assign a materials manager for each group of desks who distributes books or worksheets to everyone in the group.
- Establish routinized activities that do not need directions explained each time.
- Set a classroom timer to ring when an activity should end.
- If students ask questions that are off-topic, refer back to the objectives and help students stay on track.
- Prepare a student choice board of independent task options that students can work on if they finish early (see Figure 8.1 on next page).

One important fact to remember is this: If a teacher wastes five minutes of a class period daily, perhaps by starting the lesson late or finishing early, over the course of 180 days, 15 hours of instructional time will be lost! So, if you finish a lesson before the allocated time ends, don't let students chat or do homework; instead, play a game to review vocabulary or key concepts. We need to maximize the way we use time when we have multilingual learners in the classroom.

FIGURE 8.1 Choice Board for Science Class

Find two recipes that use the same plant in different ways. Tell a partner about them.	Write a story about a seed becoming a plant.	Record a poem you like on Flipgrid.
Read a book for fun.	Prepare 4 questions to ask an organic farmer.	Work on a crossword puzzle.

■ Linking Lesson Preparation and Lesson Delivery

Pearson eTextbook

Video Example 8.4

Watch Myrlene Schenk discuss the importance of planning and teaching to your objectives and assessing student progress toward meeting them. What new ways have you learned so far to monitor your students' understanding of your lesson objectives?

Now that you have read about the features of this component, you can see that strong, thoughtful lesson preparation is critical to effective lesson delivery. Without the planning necessary to make the content truly comprehensible for the diversity of learners in your class and without considering which aspects of academic English they need to learn or practice in a given lesson, your lesson may fly over their heads, and a day during which they could be learning may be wasted. Figure 8.2 shows how the features of Lesson Preparation influence the features of Lesson Delivery.

FIGURE 8.2 The Relationship Between Lesson Preparation and Lesson Delivery

Lesson Preparation	Lesson Delivery
Plan for content objectives ⟶	Support learning of content objectives
Plan for language objectives ⟶	Support learning of language objectives
Address grade-level content	
Use supplementary materials	Promote student engagement
Use adapted content	Pace the lesson appropriately
Plan meaningful activities with language practice	

Supporting Content and Language Objectives.   We advocate for teachers to include content and language objectives in every lesson, and our research supports their value, especially when multilingual learners have a clear, explicit understanding of what the teacher's expectations are for a lesson (Guzman, 2015; Hayden, 2019; Short, Fidelman, & Louguit, 2012). The content and language objectives written on a lesson plan need to be presented and practiced in a way to support student learning (Balconi & Spitzman, 2021). Not all students may master the objectives the first day they encounter them, but all students should make progress toward mastery. Just writing a content and a language objective on your lesson plan is not sufficient; you have to "deliver" on those learning goals in class.

When presenting a SIOP lesson, remember the objectives should be:

- **Observable**—an observer can see or hear students participating in activities related to the learning targets.
- **Measurable**—there is a way to determine whether students met the objectives, or made progress toward meeting them.
- **Assessable**—the objectives are reviewed at the end of the lesson, and the class determines if they were met.

Some teachers fail to write out and discuss the objectives with the students because the process is time consuming. We acknowledge that it takes time to determine good objectives for every lesson, but the investment in writing them and then teaching to them pays off in student achievement (cf. Short, Fidelman, & Louguit, 2012).

Other teachers complain they can't write objectives in a manner that students will understand or are worried that they will not complete all of the objectives for the full lesson. Both of these arguments are easily addressed by practice and support. A SIOP coach or a fellow SIOP teacher can give guidance on writing student-friendly objectives. The students themselves will confirm if they understand the objective when it is presented in class. And as teachers get to know their students, writing for their age and proficiency levels becomes easier.

If the problem is that the objectives are not being met by the end of the lesson, then the teacher and students can determine why as they review them. It may be that the activities took longer than planned or class discussions veered off track, but the presence of objectives can actually impose discipline on the pacing of each lesson. If a teacher consistently does not meet objectives, however, it may also be that too many objectives have been planned for the allocated time of the lesson, or that time is lost during activity transitions or at the start or end of the period.

The following suggestions may help:

When planning,

- Estimate the time each portion of the lesson will take to ensure it fits in your allocated time.
- Reduce the number of objectives.

During the lesson,

- Reread the objective chorally with the class to re-focus the students.
- Ask students what they have done up to that point in the lesson that relates to the objective.

Pearson eTextbook

Video Example 8.5

In this video, Samantha Kanzler demonstrates several techniques for engaging her high school English language arts students. Which techniques might you try? Does increasing student engagement pose any challenges for you?

https://www.youtube.com/watch?v=dgP8sgTVZsw

● Pause periodically and have students rate how well they are meeting the objective (e.g., Thumb up ~ *I got it.* Thumb down ~ *I am lost.* Thumb horizontal ~ *I'm getting there*).

Promoting Student Engagement.   In Figure 8.2, you can see how student engagement depends in large part on what content you teach, how you adapt that content, what supplementary materials you include, and what activities you ask students to perform. Multilingual learners are motivated to learn what their English-speaking peers are learning. Sometimes, in order to provide that grade-level content in a comprehensible way, you will have to adapt it. You will decide whether the adaptation is through the texts they are reading (e.g., utilizing a book with more reading supports) or the tasks they are being asked to do, but if the material is at or a little above their level of understanding, they can be engaged with it. And of course, the planned lesson tasks play a critical role in student engagement. "Skill and drill" exercises turn everyone off—English speakers and multilingual learners alike. Creative activities related to the objectives that include plenty of language practice do not.

> We know even the best lesson plans tend to hit a speed bump! I like to record my lessons in order to watch for pace and engagement! Try first recording with the camera on you to see your instruction, then try changing the camera to record just the students so that you can watch the kids to see if/when confusion kicks in!
>
> Andrea Rients, Professional Learning Coordinator, Minnesota

Pacing SIOP Lessons.   We can't discount how the choices we make when planning a lesson affect the pacing. Planning makes a difference. If students use supplementary materials and the content has been adapted to their levels, they are better able to move through the materials with occasional support from the teacher. If, however, those materials are above their level, the class discussions and activities may get bogged down. More time will be spent explaining what something means than applying or extending the information. Likewise, if the activities are not meaningful or clearly explained, students may exhibit off-task behavior or dawdle while trying to complete the assigned work. Yet if objectives are clear and guide in-lesson decision making, if scaffolds have been prepared in advance, if familiar procedures are used, if student roles are clear, and if new content has been taught in manageable portions with comprehensible supports, then learning can take place more readily.

■ Application to Your Classroom: Lesson Delivery

Effective techniques such as the following can help a teacher check on student progress toward meeting content and language objectives, manage pacing, and promote student engagement.

● **Padlet or Jamboard.** Padlet and Jamboard function as online bulletin boards that teachers and students can access in class and out. Teachers create a shared wall with a unique Web address (or in a Google classroom website) and users can add or pin different links, images, and text that other users can see. Some teachers create one wall for each unit of study. It is a place to post exit tickets, ongoing group work, relevant research links, and more. Teachers may have one section with language supports, such as sentence frames, signal words, and key vocabulary. In addition to the benefit of having students work collaboratively and share knowledge, teachers wind up with a useful artifact that can be used for reference, reflection on student learning, guidance for further instruction, and review of key concepts.

- **Chunk and Chew.** To help with pacing and knowledge acquisition, this technique encourages teachers to pause after every ten minutes of input (i.e., a "chunk" of new information) to give students time to talk or reflect (i.e., "chew") with a partner or in a small group about what they have just learned. Effective SIOP teachers carefully structure this student talk with specific prompts, sentence starters, and small-group discourse routines (see WIDA, 2017 for examples of discourse moves).

- **Roam and Review.** At the end of a lesson, the teacher may pose a reflection question (e.g., *"What was the most important thing you learned today?"* or *"What surprised you in our lesson today?"*) and have students think silently, then stand and roam the classroom, discussing their ideas with classmates. This is unstructured; students can roam and talk to whomever they choose.

- **Hand Up-Stand Up-Pair Up.** This is a similar technique that can be used as well. In this case, students write a response on a sheet of paper, stand up holding it, raise their hand, pair up with another who has a raised hand, and then both lower hands. Pairs share ideas, then raise hands again, look around the room for another partner, and repeat the process.

- **Podcasts and Screencasts.** Students prepare a two to three-minute oral summary on a topic that they have selected or that the teacher has assigned. They rehearse and then record it on their tablet or phone and use it as a podcast. Screencasts are similar but allow students to record over images or other content on a screen.

- **TV Talk Show.** A culminating project that addresses content and language objectives (particularly listening and speaking ones) and engages students is the TV talk show (Cloud et al., 2010). In groups, students plan a talk show on a topic of study that includes multiple parameters. One student serves as the host and interviewer; others are the guests. For example, after the class has studied extreme weather phenomena, one guest might be an expert on hurricanes, another on blizzards, a third on earthquakes, and a fourth on tornadoes. The talk shows could be videotaped for later viewing and analysis by the teacher or the students. The analysis might look at how well the students spoke, used key vocabulary, responded to host questions, and so forth.

- **Writing Headlines.** By writing a newspaper headline, students try to capture the essence of a day's lesson, section of a text read, video watched, or information presented orally. Teachers can encourage students to use descriptive language and focus on word choice to create compelling headlines.

- **E-Journals, E-blogs, Vlogs, and Wiki Entries.** The teacher can have students write in an e-journal daily or once a week to reflect on what they have been learning or contribute to a class blog or vlog. At the end of a unit, the teacher might ask students to write an online entry for a class wiki that presents key information on a topic being studied.

■ Differentiating for Multilevel Classes

As teachers deliver their lessons, they need to be cognizant of the learning process all of their students experience. The following ideas will help teachers differentiate instruction among multilevel students at various levels of English proficiency as well as gauge which students are meeting the objectives and which students need more assistance.

- **Pro-Rate the Task.** The product of a task need not be exactly the same across all students. The more advanced students are in their knowledge or language skills, the more they can be asked to do. In classes with both multilingual learners still developing proficiency in English and other learners who are proficient, a teacher might assign a task for the multilingual learners that seemingly has less required output, but can be as cognitively challenging as a different task for students proficient in English. It may be helpful to remind the proficient students that the multilingual learners are doing the work in a language they are still mastering.

- **Radio Advice Line.** The teacher can select two or three of the more advanced learners to be the radio show host. Other students can draft questions they have on a topic, perhaps as review questions for a unit or clarification questions on a lesson topic. They "call in" to pose the questions to the radio hosts, who take turns responding. The teacher can monitor what questions are being asked and which students seem to be making good or weak progress in meeting the lesson's objectives.

- **Projects.** One of the best ways for students to work at their own ability level, language level, and interest level is through projects. Projects offer a meaningful way to determine whether students can apply information they are learning, and they enable students to tap into their creativity and home language, too.

- **Leveled Questions.** Teachers can modulate the questions they ask students according to their levels of language proficiency. It is recommended that they plan the range of questions in advance, so that the questions will generate higher-order thinking but the language of the questions will be accessible.

- **Homogeneous Small-Group Rotations.** From time to time, teachers may want to cluster their students into homogeneous small groups based on their ability with the skill or topic (e.g., solving math problems, reading grade-level text) to provide targeted support. One way is to set up three centers in the class: one for teacher-directed instruction, one for independent work, and one for small-group or partner activities. The teacher always starts with the group of students who need the most support, and the instruction provides the foundation for their later small-group and independent work. The other groups, when working with the teacher, might have their independent and small-group work reviewed, might have a skill clarified, or might have an enrichment opportunity. In this set-up, the teacher can offer more assistance to those who are struggling or need language scaffolds while letting the others work on their own. (See Vogt, Echevarría & Washam, 2015, pp. 158–159, for a detailed description of how the rotation process can be designed.)

■ The Lesson

Solving Local Problems (Fourth Grade)

We revisit the teaching vignettes described in Chapter 2 in this chapter. The fourth-grade classrooms of teachers Ms. Levine, Mrs. Basobana, and Mr. Rafael, you may remember, are located in a suburban elementary school. Multilingual learners represent approximately 30% of the student population, and the children speak a variety of languages. The majority of the multilingual learners are at the intermediate stage of English proficiency, and native English speakers and multilingual students who have exited the English language development program are also present.

As part of the fourth-grade social studies curriculum, Ms. Levine, Mrs. Basobana, and Mr. Rafael planned the unit "Making a Difference" on solving a problem in their local community. The lessons and culminating project about solutions and outcomes to a local issue were guided by the Big Question, "What is a problem at school or in our community? How could changing it make a difference?" The teachers approached the unit topic each in their own manner.

■ Teaching Scenarios

We reflected on the teachers' lesson preparation in Chapter 2. Here we will summarize the lesson from the first two days of the unit on local problems and solutions that Ms. Levine, Mrs. Basobana, and Mr. Rafael taught. (See Chapter 2, Teaching Scenarios, for a complete description of the three lessons.) As you read the summaries, consider the SIOP Model features for Lesson Delivery: meeting content objectives, meeting language objectives, engaging students 90% to 100% of the time, and pacing the lesson appropriately for students' ability levels.

Ms. Levine

Ms. Levine began the lesson on local problems by reading aloud the content and language objectives for the day and reminding students that they find solutions to problems in math class and they have talked about cause and effect in science.

> Content: SW identify problems and their causes, solutions, and outcomes in texts.
>
> Language: SW read a text and write a summary of the problem, solution, and outcome.

She introduced the Big Question and new vocabulary terms, *activist*, *effective*, and *outcome*. The class looked at word parts and made connections among *act*, *action*, and *activist*; *effect* and *effective*; and *outcome* as a compound word. Students had some time to add new terms to their vocabulary notebooks, including an illustration, definition, and/or a translation.

Ms. Levine then led a class brainstorming session about a local problem they might try to solve. Partners generated ideas that she recorded. To model how a solution might be accomplished, she briefly explained Bellen Woodard's activism, introduced the story via picture walk, and read it aloud twice, once to give students an overview and a second time to help students focus on the problem, solution, and outcome. The lesson continued with the class creation of a summary of the story using the SWBST (Somebody Wanted But So Then) organizer[1]. The first day ended with student reflection on how Bellen made a difference.

The second day began with the "Oh Yesterday" technique in which several students told what they remembered from the previous lesson. Most of the time, however, involved student group work with texts about other youth activists, building on the tasks conducted as a whole class the day before, and showcasing for the students a variety of approaches that could be taken to solve problems. Multilingual learners who were not yet proficient in English were assigned to heterogenous groups with stronger readers and they used the reciprocal teaching technique to read and analyze the texts and complete their own SWBST organizer. Ms. Levine worked with three students at the lowest English proficiency levels. Two groups with the strongest readers had the modified SWBBST (Somebody Wanted Because But So Then) organizer. The lesson concluded with each group sharing their summary statement, discussions of other possible solutions and effective outcomes, a physical "vote" on the most effective activism, and a student self-assessment review of the lesson objectives.

Check your understanding:

On the SIOP form in Figure 8.3, rate Ms. Levine's lesson for each of the features in Lesson Delivery.

FIGURE 8.3	Lesson Delivery Component of the SIOP® Model: Ms. Levine's Lesson

4	3	2	1	0
23. **Content objectives** clearly supported by lesson delivery		**Content objectives** somewhat supported by lesson delivery		**Content objectives** not supported by lesson delivery
4	**3**	**2**	**1**	**0**
24. **Language objectives** clearly supported by lesson delivery		**Language objectives** somewhat supported by lesson delivery		**Language objectives** not supported by lesson delivery
4	**3**	**2**	**1**	**0**
25. **Students engaged** approximately 90% to 100% of the period		**Students engaged** approximately 70% of the period		**Students engaged** less than 50% of the period
4	**3**	**2**	**1**	**0**
26. **Pacing** of the lesson appropriate to students' ability levels		**Pacing** generally appropriate, but at times too fast or too slow		**Pacing** inappropriate to students' ability levels

---

[1] Sample organizers can be found in Vogt & Echevarria, 2022 (pp. 177–180).

Mrs. Basobana

Mrs. Basobana was eager to teach the unit, but she did not define content or language objectives. Recall that she only loosely planned activities for the lessons:

> Day 1: SW review the local newspaper for issues in the community and discuss with class.
>
> Day 2: SW generate a list of community and school problems.

She brought newspapers to class for student groups to look through to identify local problems, but did not introduce the unit topic or Big Question, pre-teach any vocabulary, or select articles that might be at the students' reading levels. Realizing the activity was not working as she envisioned it, she tried to regroup the class and read one article aloud and led a discussion with questions written on the board. Few students participated.

Mrs. Basobana explained the unit project orally to the class the next day. She stated the class would generate ideas for a problem and solution that they would then write a newspaper article about, in a group, or individually if a student preferred. Next, she asked students to brainstorm ideas of a school or community problem and to rank their top three choices. The tallying was time consuming and students had no tasks while she did so, which led to some misbehavior. To close the lesson, Mrs. Basobana asked students to sketch a solution to the problem with the most votes, *People sleeping on the ground.*

Check your understanding:

On the SIOP form in Figure 8.4, rate Mrs. Basobana's lesson for each of the Lesson Delivery features.

FIGURE 8.4 Lesson Delivery Component of the SIOP® Model: Mrs. Basobana's Lesson

4	3	2	1	0
23. **Content objectives** clearly supported by lesson delivery		**Content objectives** somewhat supported by lesson delivery		**Content objectives** not supported by lesson delivery
4	3	2	1	0
24. **Language objectives** clearly supported by lesson delivery		**Language objectives** somewhat supported by lesson delivery		**Language objectives** not supported by lesson delivery
4	3	2	1	0
25. **Students engaged** approximately 90% to 100% of the period		**Students engaged** approximately 70% of the period		**Students engaged** less than 50% of the period
4	3	2	1	0
26. **Pacing** of the lesson appropriate to students' ability levels		**Pacing** generally appropriate, but at times too fast or too slow		**Pacing** inappropriate to students' ability levels

Mr. Rafael

Mr. Rafael planned a lesson that was true to the social science discipline, and he hoped it would be motivating for his students. He defined content and language objectives by paraphrasing the standards identified for the unit:

> Content: SW explain individual approaches people have taken, or could take in the future, to address local or national problems, and predict results of those actions.

> Language: SW write about problems and solutions using reasoning, correct sequence, examples, and details with relevant information in a play.

Mr. Rafael invested time in finding a video of Harriet Tubman to illustrate the theme of "Making a Difference" and turned on closed captioning to help the multilingual learners. Unfortunately, he did not pre-load it and lost time on Day 1 getting it to work. As a result, he had to quickly introduce key vocabulary terms and the problem-solution concept and he postponed sharing the content and language objectives until the second day. He prepared a worksheet (with a word bank) to focus student attention on the video and also found and uploaded an additional text about her life for students to read on their tablets. With his support and these two sources of information, the students completed the worksheet.

He shared the Big Question for the unit with the class the second day and tried to reach consensus on a problem the class could solve. The students participated in the brainstorming and voting, but no idea received the majority of votes. Mr. Rafael had to spend more time with a second round of votes for the top three choices. He then tried to explain his ambitious unit project plan of writing and performing a play and assigned students to specific groups, but students had so many questions that he realized he needed to work with the whole class to outline the plot sequence across three acts. He did not review elements of a play with the students either. The ensuing discussion was inconclusive and would have to be continued the following day.

Check your understanding:

On the SIOP form in Figure 8.5, rate Mr. Rafael's lesson for each of the Lesson Delivery features.

| FIGURE 8.5 | Lesson Delivery Component of the SIOP® Model: Mr. Rafael's Lesson |

4	3	2	1	0
23. **Content objectives** clearly supported by lesson delivery		**Content objectives** somewhat supported by lesson delivery		**Content objectives** not supported by lesson delivery
4	3	2	1	0
24. **Language objectives** clearly supported by lesson delivery		**Language objectives** somewhat supported by lesson delivery		**Language objectives** not supported by lesson delivery
4	3	2	1	0
25. **Students engaged** approximately 90% to 100% of the period		**Students engaged** approximately 70% of the period		**Students engaged** less than 50% of the period
4	3	2	1	0
26. **Pacing** of the lesson appropriate to students' ability levels		**Pacing** generally appropriate, but at times too fast or too slow		**Pacing** inappropriate to students' ability levels

■ Discussion of Lessons

Review your rating form and think about the reasons you scored the lessons as you did. Look for evidence in each scenario. Read on to see our analyses.

23. *Content Objectives Clearly Supported by Lesson Delivery*

> Ms. Levine: 4
>
> Mrs. Basobana: 1
>
> Mr. Rafael: 2

- From the beginning of the lesson, **Ms. Levine** had a clearly defined content objective, which she posted and read aloud so students knew what they were supposed to learn. On both days, the activities helped students determine problems and solutions in texts. She modeled the analysis with the whole class on the first day and student groups worked to identify them on the second day. When they reported out, she could informally assess their learning. The lesson was rated a "4" for supporting content objectives.

- In contrast, **Mrs. Basobana's** lesson received a "1" on this feature. She had no content objective, just a general plan of activities. A content objective was implied (e.g., *"Students will identify problems in the community and school"*) but the students did not have a clear idea of the learning goal. Moreover, the lesson did not support this implied objective very well. Mrs. Basobana jumped into the unit topic with little background building for her students. She did not define vocabulary terms, and although she brought in authentic materials, newspapers, the first day, she failed to consider whether they were at a reading level appropriate to her fourth graders, nor did she pre-select articles the students might review, instead overwhelming them with the variety in the paper. The second day brought a bit more focus to the implied objective with the brainstorming activity, but the connection to the unit theme and Big Question was never made.

- Mr. Rafael understood the importance of having and sharing objectives with the students, but due to technical difficulties, he did not do so until Day 2. His content objective was too broad for the lesson, but he did support it partially through the lesson activities. The video clip, text, and worksheet enabled students to report on Harriet Tubman's approach to solving a problem. However, he erroneously assumed that his students could easily select a problem and determine a solution for a three-act class play without more support. Had he narrowed his objective, presented it on the first day, and offered more guidance for the class project, his lesson would have received a higher score for this feature. Because he did not, his lesson received a "2."

24. *Language Objectives Clearly Supported by Lesson Delivery*

> Ms. Levine: 4
>
> Mrs. Basobana: 0
>
> Mr. Rafael: 1

- **Ms. Levine's** lesson was rated "4" on this feature. Language objectives were clearly written and stated, and students had several opportunities to meet them. Ms. Levine taught key terms so they could discuss the topic and read the texts. She helped them complete the SWBST summary for the Bellen Woodard story and then organized reciprocal teaching groups so they could read, discuss, and summarize a new text. She supported the multilingual learners at beginning levels of English, too.

- **Mrs. Basobana** did not write or state any language objectives. As with the content objective, one might have been implied (perhaps *"Students will read a newspaper article for specific details"*), but none were explicitly shared with the students. No instruction was provided to help students master that objective and no supports were offered for her multilingual learners. Although she did assign a reading activity and told students there would be a writing project, the newspaper articles were inaccessible for many of the students and the writing activity, as briefly explained, was very complicated linguistically (students had to define a problem and imagine a solution, but write the article in past tense as if it had already happened). Further, as we pointed out in Chapter 2, a language activity is not the same as a language objective. Her lesson received a "0" for supporting language objectives.

- **Mr. Rafael** presented his language objective on the second day, but did little to support the students in meeting it. In addition, it was too broad for the lesson. He wanted the students to practice reading, writing, listening, and speaking, and while there was some listening and writing practice on the first day, the language objective for writing a class play was not met. He did not provide a model script, review the elements of the play, or discuss how dialogue differs from prose. He failed to connect the video clip they had seen to a play and had no written directions for the project. His lesson was rated a "1."

25. *Students Engaged Approximately 90% to 100% of the Period*

Ms. Levine: 4

Mrs. Basobana: 1

Mr. Rafael: 2

- In **Ms. Levine's** lesson, students were very engaged. She planned the unit lessons carefully, included a range of activities, and maximized academic learning time. Although Day 1 was more whole class-oriented, she encouraged partner discussions and individual vocabulary work. Students brainstormed ideas and had time for reflection and self-assessment. On Day 2, every student participated in the reciprocal teaching task with texts about youth activists of interest to young learners and in groups that Ms. Levine had pre-arranged to provide support to the multilingual students. Because modeling occurred the first day, student interaction with the text and summary writing on the second day was accomplished in a straightforward manner. Students were active and on task throughout, and the material was relevant to the standards and objectives, so the lesson received a "4" for this feature.

- The students in **Mrs. Basobana's** class were not very engaged over the two days. The lesson bounced from activity to activity without any meaningful learning goals for the students. The newspaper articles were too difficult for them to read, in terms of both the background schema needed to understand them and the sheer number of articles to look through. The lack of student participation even after she read one news article aloud indicated lack of comprehension and engagement. The second day some students misbehaved and distracted others; no task was assigned during the minutes that votes were tallied. She did not plan for student-to-student interaction and relied on teacher talk as the means for conveying information. Overall, Mrs. Basobana did not maximize academic learning time and students were engaged only about half of the allotted instructional time. This lesson was rated a "1" for this feature.

- **Mr. Rafael's** students were engaged from time to time during the two days. While Mr. Rafael fiddled with the video on the first day, the students had nothing to do. He did refocus them, however, and they watched the video about Harriet Tubman, read the text, and completed the worksheet. The closed captions and word bank provided some scaffolding for the multilingual learners. During Day 2, the selection of a class problem and the playwriting task were not well structured and may have been confusing for some of the students with beginning levels of English, but the students were not unruly, nor did they exhibit off-task behavior. This lesson received a "2" for student engagement.

26. *Pacing of Lesson Appropriate to Students' Ability Levels*

Ms. Levine: 4

Mrs. Basobana: 1

Mr. Rafael: 1

- **Ms. Levine's** lesson was well-paced and rated a "4" for this feature. The preparation done in advance of the unit helped the activities run smoothly and avoided any wasting of time for students to get materials or ask questions about the assignments. The texts and videos were selected to appeal to the students' interests, the graphic organizer (SWBST) was familiar to students, the reciprocal teaching groups were pre-arranged with peer support for multilingual learners, and instructions were clear. The modeling and whole-class practice done on the first day paved the way for group success on the second. The students were not bored, they interacted with partners and small groups, there was physical movement, and students' ideas and opinions were sought and validated.

- The pacing of **Mrs. Basobana's** lesson was problematic. Very little was accomplished in the first two days of the unit and her lack of adequate planning was the reason. By not providing an overview or building background for the unit, she did not motivate the students. By not defining and presenting objectives to the students, she did not help them see a purpose for the activities nor give them a goal for their learning. The newspaper activity was unsuccessful because no vocabulary development, modeling, or pre-selection of the articles took place. As a result, she had to pivot to an impromptu reading of one article aloud, but without comprehension checks or supports for the students learning English.

This took up most of the remaining time on Day 1. On the second day, time was wasted with the tallying of votes and with students sketching ideas to solve the problem of homelessness. The learning time could have been utilized in a more productive way. This lesson received a "1" for pacing.

- **Mr. Rafael's** lesson was not well-paced because he made assumptions in his planning that did not bear fruit. It started on Day 1 with the video clip that would not load and led to his curtailing the vocabulary development portion of the lesson and the introduction of the unit's Big Question and lesson objectives. He also assumed students would agree on a class problem and write a play in a few days without any models or scaffolds. Because he did not build a foundation for the students to do the writing, the initial outlining of the play's three acts had to be carried over into Day 3. This lesson was rated a "1."

Final Points

As you reflect on this chapter and the impact of effective lesson delivery, consider the following main points:

- The importance of setting and meeting objectives cannot be overemphasized. Many teachers may feel comfortable having a general objective in mind and moving along with a lesson's flow, but that approach is not helpful for multilingual learners.
- If you plan objectives, you have to teach to them. Delivering a lesson geared to objectives allows the teacher to stay on track and lets the students know what is important to focus on and remember.
- By incorporating a variety of techniques that engage students throughout the lesson, teachers not only give students opportunities to learn, practice, and apply information and language skills, but also help to ensure the students meet the lesson's objectives.
- An appropriate pace for a lesson is critical for multilingual learners. Information that is presented at a pace suitable for native English speakers may render that information meaningless, especially for students at beginning stages of English acquisition. Finding the right pace for a lesson depends in part on the content of the lesson, students' prior knowledge about the topic, and differentiation. Effective SIOP teachers use instructional time wisely.

Discussion Questions

1. In reflecting on the content and language objectives at the beginning of the chapter, are you able to:
   a. Monitor lesson delivery to determine if it is supporting the lesson objectives?
   b. Determine how lesson preparation influences lesson delivery?
   c. Generate activities to keep multilingual learners engaged?
   d. Discuss characteristics of effective SIOP lesson delivery?
   e. Explain how a focus on a lesson's objectives can aid in pacing?
   f. Review your lesson plan to make sure the information and activities support the students in meeting the language and content objectives?

2. Reflect on a lesson that you taught or observed that did not go well. What happened? When did it go awry? Can you identify a feature in Lesson Delivery that might have caused the lesson to be less successful? Or a feature from another SIOP component? In retrospect, how might the delivery of the lesson have been improved?

3. Suppose three new students, all with limited English proficiency, joined your eighth-grade class midyear. The other students in the class include a few former English learners and native English speakers. You are studying the Bill of Rights. Think of one task that you might include that helps students apply the content concepts and also practice academic language. Now, how might you pro-rate that task to meet the different academic language needs of the students?

4. How do teachers or supervisors determine whether a majority of students, including multilingual learners, are engaged during a lesson? What techniques could be used to sustain engagement throughout the period? What should the teachers do if they sense that students are off task? Why is sustained engagement so critical to multilingual learners' academic progress?

5. Look over the SIOP lesson you have been working on. Check that you have explicit instruction and practice opportunities included for your objectives. If not, add to the lesson. Then write down the amount of time you expect each section (or activity) of the lesson to take. Teach the lesson and reflect. When did student learning occur? Did you have a good handle on pacing? If not, review your lesson for tightening or extending. What can you add or take away? Were students as engaged as you anticipated? Share with a colleague your ideas for maximizing time-on-task and student engagement.

■ Pearson eTextbook Application Videos

The purpose of the Pearson eTextbook Application Videos is to provide you with an opportunity to observe and reflect on SIOP teaching and learning practices. There are multilingual students in each of the classrooms with varying levels of English proficiency. The teachers you will observe are at different levels of SIOP implementation, from second-year SIOPers to veterans. As you observe the lessons they have created, focus on the students and the lesson objectives, keeping in mind that becoming a high-implementing SIOP teacher takes time, practice, and support to refine teaching practices. We are grateful to each of these SIOP educators for welcoming us into their classrooms, and for their dedication to SIOP, their multilingual learners, and other students.

Pearson eTextbook Application
Video Example 8.1
Co-Teachers Teach Grade 2
SIOP Math Lesson on Place
Value

Review & Assessment

CONTENT OBJECTIVES

This chapter will help you to . . .

- Identify challenges in assessing content and language learning of students with limited English proficiency.
- Plan formative and summative assessments for multilingual learners that will provide information to make sound instructional decisions during lesson planning.
- Determine opportunities for reviewing and assessing students' use of academic language, key vocabulary, and content concepts throughout a lesson.

LANGUAGE OBJECTIVES

This chapter will help you to . . .

- Provide effective academic, oral, and written feedback to multilingual learners during a lesson.
- Define each of the following assessment terms: *informal assessment, formal assessment, formative assessment, summative assessment, performance-based assessment, multidimensional indicators,* and *multiple indicators.*

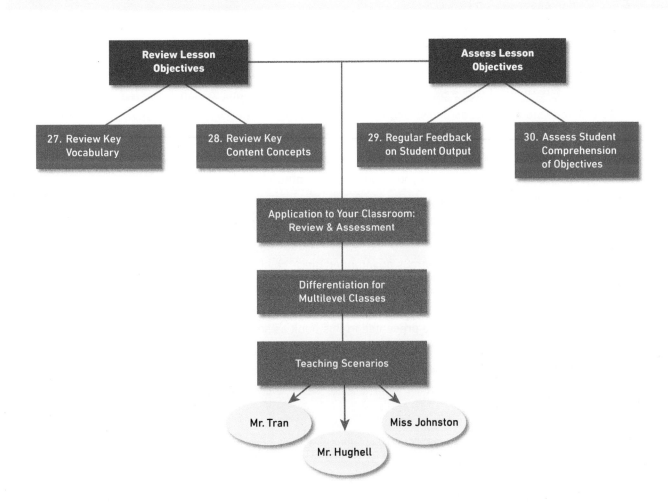

In years past, it was not unusual for a teacher to introduce a unit on Monday, teach lessons pertaining to the unit throughout the week, and then administer an end-of-unit test on Friday. This routine was considered a normal instructional process, especially in the upper elementary grades through high school. In fact, in the 1970s in some schools, it was expected that students' results on unit and informal tests would fall along the Bell curve (personal experience). For example:

- A small number of students should attain high grades (A) for a test.
- A small number of students should nearly fail or fail the test (D or F).
- The largest number of students' test results should fall somewhere in the middle of the curve (B or C).

You may be scratching your head as to why creating a test with the goal of having some students fail it, with only a few students doing well, were the expectations for students' academic performance. That was then.

Today, we view assessment of student performance in the classroom through a very different lens. The goal is that all students, including multilingual learners, will meet rigorous standards, learn academic language and content, and be as successful as is possible on assessments of learning. Effective SIOP teachers use assessment findings to plan lessons according to students' needs and strengths, review students' progress toward meeting content and language objectives throughout each lesson, and evaluate how effectively their lessons have been delivered. Therefore, in this chapter, we focus on an important aspect of teaching: assessing your students' strengths, needs, experiential backgrounds, and language proficiencies.[1]

Sometimes, SIOP teachers ask why the Review & Assessment component comes at the end of the SIOP protocol, if reviewing and assessing are to occur throughout a lesson. Keep in mind that there is no intended hierarchy in the order of the SIOP components, nor is any one component more important than another. Instead, the SIOP components are integrated, interrelated, and inextricably linked. For the sake of discussion, they are presented in this book as separate components and features. However, during SIOP lessons, teachers incorporate the eight components and 30 features seamlessly. ■

> " The best part about the last SIOP component is that it is the FIRST thing I think of when planning a SIOP lesson! What are the content and language goals I want to see my students excel at by the end of this lesson or unit?
>
> Andrea Rients, District Professional Learning Coordinator, Minnesota "

---

[1] Note that it is beyond the scope of this book to provide detailed information about formal or commercial language, literacy, and academic assessments that are appropriate for multilingual learners.

■ Background

Throughout the book, we have discussed the instructional features of the SIOP Model that positively impact the achievement and language development of multilingual learners. These features, along with classroom management and teaching effectiveness, determine the learning environment for multilingual learners and other students.

The SIOP component of Review & Assessment shifts the focus from instruction to assessment, so that teachers can ascertain the degree to which their students are meeting a lesson's content and language objectives. Informal assessment throughout a lesson provides information for relevant, on-the-spot feedback. Through informal assessment, SIOP teachers determine who is ready to move on and who needs further reteaching, review, and practice (see Chapter 5, Figure 5.1). Just as students need to know what the objectives are for a lesson, they also need to be informed about how they will be assessed on them. Both formative and summative assessments of students' progress provide important information. You will see in the scenarios that follow later in the chapter how three teachers implement the Review & Assessment features into their lessons.

Formative and Summative Assessment

In the classroom, teachers generally use two types of assessments, formative and summative:

Pearson eTextbook

Video Example 9.1

In this video, Dr. Vogt discusses various ways to collect formative assessment information during lessons.
https://www.youtube.com/watch?v=8xpYxnPbat0

- *Formative Assessment*: Formative assessments include tools and approaches that help identify students' understandings, misunderstandings, misconceptions, and gaps in knowledge as related to academic content and language use. For multilingual learners, formative assessment affords students the opportunities to practice their new language and learning in a safe environment. For example, monitoring small-group discussions can be a formative assessment opportunity when you are observing students' content knowledge and academic language production. Furthermore, regular, targeted feedback about students' content knowledge and language use during formative assessment is essential. Students can learn to provide feedback to peers in a constructive and helpful manner after it has been modeled. Formative assessments occur throughout a lesson (see Table 9.1 for examples of formative assessments).

- *Summative Assessment*: In contrast to formative assessment, summative assessments appraise students' knowledge and understandings of newly taught content at the end of a lesson and/or unit. In addition, students' language proficiency can also be assessed more formally at the conclusion of a lesson. Summative assessments may be graded (points or letter grades), and/or they can be used in tandem with formative assessment (see Table 9.1 for examples of summative assessments).

Assessment and Evaluation

Historically, educators have blurred somewhat the line between assessment and evaluation, generally using the term *evaluation* for both formative and summative judgments.

TABLE 9.1	Examples of Formative and Summative Assessments

Examples of Formative Assessments	Examples of Summative Assessments
Discussions and instructional conversations	End-of-unit tests created by teacher
Electronic quizzes (e.g., Quizlet)	Final projects
Low-stakes group work	Essays
Self-checked pop quizzes	Oral presentations
Quick Writes (1–2 minute reflections)	Tests with multiple-choice or open-ended questions
Homework assignments	Written reports
Quiz-Quiz Trade (partners quiz each other with a question/answer on a card; partners trade cards, quiz new partners; repeat trading)	Final grading for projects or units

In the past, the teacher's role in evaluation was primarily as an "evaluator," one who conveyed a value on the completion of a given task. This value was frequently determined from the results of assessments that served as the basis for report card grades in elementary and secondary schools.

Today, however, educators distinguish between assessment and evaluation (Lipson & Wixson, 2013; Shearer, Carr, & Vogt, 2019), as follows:

- *Assessment* is defined as the gathering and synthesizing of information concerning student learning.
- *Evaluation* is defined as making judgments about students' learning based on assessment results.

The processes of assessment and evaluation can be viewed as progressive: first, assessment; then, evaluation. Formative and summative assessments that are multifaceted provide relevant and practical information to the teacher about how to design appropriate and culturally relevant content and language instruction for linguistically and culturally diverse students.

Informal Assessment

The formative assessment measures generally used by teachers to gather data about their students' academic and language performance in the classroom tend to be *informal*. Qualities of informal, effective classroom assessments include:

- They are *authentic,* such as portfolios and performance-based projects that are characterized by their application to everyday living, where students are engaged in meaningful tasks that take place in real-life contexts.
- They are *multidimensional* because teachers use different ways of determining student performance, including written pieces, student and parent interviews, video clips, observations, creative work and art, discussion, performance, oral group responses, and so forth.

- They include *multiple indicators* that reflect student learning, achievement, motivation, and attitudes. Indicators are related to a lesson's content and language objectives, such as homework, class notes, discussion, and/or the use of home language to answer questions and participate in academic discussion. They provide a teacher with varied ways of looking at a multilingual learner's language proficiency and content knowledge. The teacher thus has more than one piece of evidence indicative of progress toward mastery of lesson objectives.

Informal assessment involves on-the-spot, ongoing opportunities for determining the extent to which students are learning content and academic language. These opportunities may include teacher observations, anecdotal reports, teacher-to-student and student-to-student conversations, or any number of tasks that occur within the regular instructional period and are not intended to be graded or evaluated according to set criteria.

Formal Assessment

Pearson eTextbook

Video Example 9.2

Two kindergarten teachers discuss how they use formative assessment with the children they teach in Canberra, Australia. Notice how the children are continually self-assessing their learning of the "intentions" (goals or objectives) and how they communicate it following lessons. Note also the collaborative partnership of the teachers (see Chapter 11 for more information about collaboration and SIOP).

https://www.youtube.com/watch?v=9FZR3-l8Y5Y&list=RDCMUC2zniDSpDbJ7u2rqO6aShTg&index=1

Formal assessments can be *formative* (to achieve a baseline or beginning point) or *summative* (to determine progress over time). One type is standardized and norm-referenced, and it ranks students' scores in comparison to a normed group of students. Another type of standardized measure is criterion-referenced. These tests measure students' performance as compared to a set of academic skills or objectives. Generally, formal assessments are used by schools and districts to look at academic trends over time and to identify subgroups of students who are performing extremely well or unsatisfactorily.

Considerations for Multilingual Learners

Many, but not all multilingual learners are at a disadvantage when they are taking a standardized or other formal assessment that presumes the test taker is English proficient. Depending on where you live, many states allow a variety of accommodations for state tests. Further, these accommodations can and should also be implemented in the SIOP classroom. Doing so helps you get a more accurate picture of your multilingual students' learning. In addition, for multilingual learners and struggling students, SIOP teachers should explicitly teach, model, and provide practice with the general academic words and terms that are described in Chapter 3. These are frequently the types of vocabulary that are used in standardized tests.

When planning assessments for multilingual learners, distinguish between informal language assessments for the purpose of determining a student's level of English proficiency and a summative assessment of skills and content knowledge. For example, suppose a student writes an essay that shows understanding of the academic content of a lesson or unit, but the paper is criticized by the teacher because of the quality of the writing, such as grammar and spelling errors that are not unusual for students at earlier stages of English development. Therefore, be certain that when multilingual learners are learning content, that's what you are assessing—their knowledge and understandings of the content. When you are targeting Academic

English in your lesson, then assessing English usage and academic language proficiency is necessary and appropriate. Keep in mind that translanguaging, as defined throughout this book, can enable multilingual learners to demonstrate their understanding of academic content through both their primary language and English, depending on their proficiency levels.

SIOP® **SIOP® FEATURE 27:**

Comprehensive Review of Key Vocabulary

An important aspect of ensuring students' retention of key vocabulary is providing a comprehensive vocabulary review at the end of each lesson. During a lesson, multilingual learners may receive 20 to 30 minutes or more of input in a new language. Unless the teacher takes the time to highlight and review key vocabulary, multilingual learners and other students may not understand the lesson's focus. Students, especially those at the early stages of English acquisition, devote considerable energy to figuring out at a basic level what the teacher is saying or the text is telling them. These students are much less able to evaluate which academic vocabulary words, terms, and phrases are important to remember, given all the oral input they receive, so it is important that SIOP teachers take the time to review pertinent vocabulary during and at the end of a lesson.

Moreover, we know that students with robust vocabularies are more successful in school (Duke & Cartwright, 2021). Therefore, it stands to reason that teachers would want to regularly revisit and review key words and terms to ensure that students are adding to their vocabulary knowledge. Researchers differ on the number of exposures that students need to internalize words at a deep level, but they agree that introducing a new word, reviewing it once or twice, and then expecting students to remember and internalize the word is not going to work. Multiple exposures to academic vocabulary, with opportunities to practice with new words, terms, and phrases in a variety of contexts (listening, speaking, reading, writing) is necessary. Encourage students to use the key words, terms, or phrases in their discussions, and validate their efforts when they do so.

There are several ways that SIOP teachers meaningfully review vocabulary toward the end of a lesson. For example:

- Students orally share understandings with a partner while the teacher spot-checks their explanations.
- Students write a quick definition in their own words on individual whiteboards and hold them up for the teacher, and perhaps other students, to see.
- Students do a quick match of words and definitions on an interactive whiteboard.
- Students write two or three Outcome Sentences on exit cards (see this chapter) that include the lesson's vocabulary. The teacher collects the cards at the end of the instructional period and uses them to review relevant vocabulary at the beginning of the following lesson.

Remember that effective review of vocabulary does not include the "dreaded word list" approach—assigning a list of miscellaneous words on Monday, giving a pretest on the words on Wednesday, and a final test on the words on Friday. Nor should we include the equally ineffective assignment of having students write vocabulary or spelling words 10 (or more) times each. Research findings are clear—isolated word lists and dictionary definitions alone do not promote vocabulary and language development. Rather, provide as many exposures as possible to new, important words, terms, and phrases through meaningful tasks that incorporate multiple modalities: reading, writing, illustrating, discussing, acting out, charting, and so forth. What is also important is that teachers plan for the final review of key vocabulary just as they plan for the other activities in their lessons.

SIOP® **SIOP® FEATURE 28:**

Comprehensive Review of Key Content Concepts

Just as it is important to review key vocabulary at the end of a lesson, it is also essential that multilingual learners have key content concepts reviewed at the same time. An effective end-of-lesson review technique of SIOP teachers is Outcome Sentences. A teacher posts 2–3 sentence starters on the whiteboard or chart paper, such as:

Pearson eTextbook

Video Example 9.3

In this video, Dr. Echevarría discusses an idea for having students review and reflect on their understandings of key vocabulary and key concepts in math through journal writing, which occurs during the first few minutes of the next day's lesson. How might you use this technique in other content areas, as well?

https://www.youtube.com/watch?v=3ZUlXzy8Vyw

I wonder . . .

I discovered . . .

I still want to know . . .

I learned . . .

I don't understand . . .

I have a question about . . .

Something I will remember is . . .

Students take turns selecting and completing an outcome sentence orally, or in writing on an exit ticket (a small piece of paper or sticky note). They can also confer with a partner before responding. Students' responses to Outcome Sentences provide information about their understandings of key concepts, including questions, misconceptions, and errors. SIOP teachers frequently begin the next day's lesson by using the students' responses to the Outcome Sentences as a kick-off for discussion, clarification, answering students' questions, and so forth.

A more structured review might involve students summarizing with partners, writing in a journal, doing a quick check via Quizlet, or discussing key points that are listed on the interactive white board. Toward the end of the lesson, a final review helps multilingual learners and other students assess their own understandings and clarify their misconceptions. Students' responses to a review can guide a teacher's decisions about what to do next, such as administering a summative assessment or, if needed, additional reteaching and assessing.

SIOP® **SIOP® FEATURE 29:**

Regular Feedback Provided to Students on Their Output

Periodic review of language, vocabulary, and content enables teachers to provide specific oral and written academic feedback to students to clarify confusing points and to correct misconceptions and misunderstandings. Effective feedback for multilingual learners:

- **Supports and validates.** For multilingual learners to receive teacher feedback, they must be able to provide output of some kind. Keep in mind that we can provide feedback when multilingual learners draw, use gestures, act out, and more. Quiet, shy, and unconfident students can go unnoticed, and sometimes their coping strategies mask weaknesses in language production. Perhaps the most important way to provide feedback is through being supportive, providing validation when students do interact, participate, and engage meaningfully. We also show support through validating what students know by providing feedback that corroborates their content knowledge, while advancing their use of the target language, such as English.

- **Is specific and academically oriented.** While support and validation are certainly important, how we do both is critical. For some teachers, it's almost a habit to say, *"Good job!"* or *"Nice work!"* or *"Well done!"* While these comments feel good when students hear them, they don't provide much information about what was good about the job or nice about the work. Multilingual learners and students who struggle need very specific academic feedback, and for some, it is best if it is given in private. They need to know exactly what they did that's right so they can do it again and/or build upon it.

  For example, compare the praise phrase, *Good job!* to the following feedback from a SIOP teacher: *Enrique, I noticed that you had a question about one of the items on the study guide. I saw you look back at the chapter for help, and then I noticed you turned to Felipe with a question. Those were good strategies to try! And, thanks, Felipe, for helping Enrique with his question!*

  Of course, not all comments need to be this detailed. It might be as simple as, *Good use of upper case letters!* Just remember to be specific about what you have observed and communicate it directly to the student(s) involved. Also, remember that immigrant students who have attended school with a classroom context different from their current school benefit greatly from specific feedback as they are learning to negotiate their new educational environment.

- **Is appropriate to students' language proficiency levels.** As an example, SIOP teachers do not criticize a beginning English speaker's poor sentence structure or misuse of conjunctions. Instead, the teacher's feedback focuses on the academic content and language that are being taught via the content and language objectives. This point also reiterates the need for knowing your students' levels of English proficiency (see the Glossary: Levels of Language Proficiency).

- **Focuses on both content and language.** Many multilingual learners plateau at the intermediate level of English proficiency, in part because they are exited prematurely from ESL programs, but also because when they are exited they don't have teachers who continue to develop academic language while they're teaching content. Therefore, as a SIOP teacher, encourage these students to use increasingly sophisticated words, phrases, and sentences by modeling their use in your teaching and during teacher-student conversations. Remember to continue to provide temporary scaffolds, as needed, as you did when these students had lower levels of English proficiency.

- **Includes modeling.** Teachers can model correct English usage when restating a student's response: *"Yes, you're correct that the scientists were confused by the skull lying next to the mummy."* Overly correcting multilingual learners' grammar and pronunciation may shut them down. Therefore, simply restating the sentence with correct form, while validating, provides feedback that is instructive and helpful. However, if you want the students to start using the correct pronunciation or sentence structure, you need to dedicate some time to teaching and having students practice these particular skills. An explicit focus on form makes more of a difference than a teacher-corrected restatement of a student's response (Saunders & Goldenberg, 2010).

- **Includes paraphrasing.** Paraphrasing also supports students' understandings and validates answers when we add, *"Is this what you were thinking/or saying?"* after a paraphrase. If you know that some students are only able to respond to questions in one or two words, you can extend their responses in complete sentences: *"Yes,* embalming *is the process of preserving bodies and it was used for mummification."* Always give students a chance to elaborate on their own first, with phrases such as *"Tell me more about that."*

- **Includes facial expressions and body language.** A nod, smile of support, or encouraging look can take away fear of speaking aloud, especially for students who are beginning to develop English proficiency. At the same time, a teacher's facial expressions and body language that convey frustration, impatience, or ambivalence speak volumes to a student who is trying to learn challenging content and a new language at the same time.

- **Can be provided by students for each other.** Partners or groups can discuss among themselves, giving feedback on both language production and content understanding to each other, and then report back to the whole class. The teacher can facilitate effective feedback by providing appropriate modeling of how it is done. Sentence frames or Talk Moves, also assist students in getting started: *"What you said was very interesting, because _____"*; *"One word that you used that helped me understand your point was _____"*; *"One question I have about what you said is _____."*

`SIOP®` **SIOP® FEATURE 30:**

Assessment of Student Comprehension and Learning of All Lesson Objectives Throughout the Lesson

The purpose of this feature is to ensure that SIOP teachers assess the degree to which individual students meet or are making progress toward meeting a lesson's content and language objectives. In SIOP lessons, assessment takes place at any time during a lesson, and teachers are encouraged to assess students whenever they have an opportunity. Examples include:

- The lesson begins with an activity that activates students' prior knowledge and experience, providing the opportunity to build background for those who need it. This also enables the teacher to assess those who may lack background information about the topic and/or have difficulty with the content and language concepts in the forthcoming lesson.

- During the lesson, while students are practicing and applying the lesson's key vocabulary and concepts, there is another opportunity to see who may need more review or reteaching. SIOP teachers use informal assessments including teacher observation, spot-checking with individuals, conversations with students about their progress, and group response techniques, such as those suggested later in this chapter.

- At the end of the lesson, SIOP teachers assess which students have met the content and language objectives by reviewing them both with individuals and with the class. This final review of all content and language objectives is critically important. It provides you with information to guide the planning of your subsequent SIOP lessons.

Some teachers who are learning to implement the SIOP Model express concern about having varied assessments throughout a lesson, in part because of the perceived amount of work it takes to create them and because some believe it is unfair if students are not assessed equally. While acknowledging these concerns, we also believe that for multilingual learners, assessment adaptations must be made if teachers are to ascertain accurately the extent to which lesson objectives and standards are met. Often, multilingual learners do know the information on which they are being assessed, but because of English language proficiency issues, including vocabulary, reading, and writing, they are unable to demonstrate their knowledge fully.

In SIOP classes, where students may have different levels of language proficiency, the value of assessment becomes readily apparent (Vogt, 2022). If you gather baseline data on what your students know and can do with the content information before instruction occurs, and then assess what they know and can do during a lesson and after its conclusion, you can identify student growth more accurately.

End-of-Lesson Review of Content and Language Objectives

A critically important part of this final SIOP feature is that you orally review with your students the posted content and language objectives of each SIOP lesson. This needs to be more than simply asking for a "yes" or "no" response to the question, *Did you meet your content and language objectives?* Students are likely to respond to this question without analyzing whether they, indeed, met the lesson's objectives. To foster student reflection and self-assessment, SIOP teachers ask students to indicate on an exit ticket, piece of paper, individual whiteboard, and/or Group Response Techniques (see later in this chapter), the degree to which they met each objective. Young children can self-assess by circling or pointing to a smiley face, a question mark, or a sad face. An example of a Self-Assessment Rubric for review of each content and language objective for a lesson, follows (Vogt & Echevarria, 2022, p. 235):

1 = I don't understand.

2 = I think I understand.

3 = I understand but I still have questions.

4 = I understand but I can't really explain (the concept) to others.

5 = I understand and can explain (the concept) to others.

> When teachers establish routines for planning and monitoring their own lessons using SIOP, then students can consistently access grade-level instruction to apply new learning, interact with classmates, self-monitor, and provide feedback. SIOP provides a roadmap for teachers to plan effective lessons that foster student ownership through choice, responsibility and autonomy.
>
> Dr. Nicole Teyechea McNeil, Senior Learnng Specialist, Arizona

■ Application to Your Classroom: Review & Assessment

Review and assessment can be accomplished with individual, partner, small-group, or whole-class activities, such as the following:

- **Jeopardy Labs** (jeopardylabs.com). Jeopardy Labs is an easy-to-use, free website that enables teachers to quickly create game boards for playing Jeopardy, just like the popular television show. Rather than the teacher always preparing the Jeopardy questions and categories, small groups of students can come up with them for the whole class. Depending on their level of English proficiency, multilingual learners may find it easier to speak or write answers and questions in their home language first, before they are translated into English. Also, instead of using a traditional buzzer or bell, students in teams can use individual whiteboards, one per team, to play the game. The teams can choose categories and dollar amounts on a rotating basis, with each student having an opportunity to review the material, perhaps in their home language, including key vocabulary and content concepts. In addition to creating your own Jeopardy game boards, the site allows users to search many games created by other educators.

- **75 Digital Tools and Apps to Support Formative Assessment in the Classroom** (Kathy Dyer, 2021). This amazing resource was compiled through the auspices of a nonprofit research organization, the Northwest Evaluation Association (NWEA), in Oregon. The categories of the tools and apps, and an example from each, follow. See the References for the link to the complete list of 75 digital tools.

- Record Audio and Video: *Animoto*
- Create Quizzes, Polls, and Surveys: *Poll Everywhere*
- Brainstorming, Mind Map, and Collaborate: *Dotstorming*
- Present, Engage, and Inspire: *BrainPop*
- Generate Word or Tag Clouds: *EdWordle* (For an example of a word cloud, see Chapter 3, Artifact 3.4.)
- Get Real-Time Feedback: *Plickers*
- Foster Family Communication: *Seesaw*
- Strengthen Teacher-to-Student and Student-to-Student Communication: *ForAllRubrics*
- Keep the Conversation Going with Live Chats: *Backchannel Chat*
- Create and Store Documents or Assessments: *Piazza* (for secondary)

- **Vocabulary or Word Study Journals.** Vocabulary or Word Study Journals are intended for specific subject areas. One section of the journal might focus on multiple-meaning words. For example, a math journal might have four columns labeled with:

  - Word: *prime*
  - Common Definition: *The best*
  - Math Definition: *A number that can only be divided by itself and one (1)*
  - Where I Found It: *In our textbook*.

  Students' Vocabulary or Word Study Journal provide students with the opportunity to review words at any time.

- **Rubrics.** Often, rubrics are used to ascertain a developmental level of performance for a particular goal, objective, or standard. For example, on a developmental rubric, student performance may be characterized as *emergent, beginning, developing, competent, or proficient*. Other rubrics may communicate evaluative information, such as *inadequate, adequate, thorough*, or *exceptional*. The Internet has made it possible to easily find examples of teacher-created rubrics for a variety of content areas or purposes. When creating rubrics for your assignments, it is important to share the specific criteria for each rubric designation with students beforehand, so they can aspire to high levels of success. Depending on the assignment, age of students, and language proficiency levels, showing actual examples for each designation on a rubric can provide additional scaffolding. Rubrics are not necessary for all assignments, but for major projects, reports, or research papers that receive a grade, a rubric can provide scaffolding for what constitutes satisfactory (and above) performance. Whichever rubric is used, the results of assessment and evaluation are often shared with other interested stakeholders, such as parents and administrators, as well as with the students themselves.

- **Group Response Techniques (GRT).** GRT enable you to immediately determine each individual student's understanding during an assessment activity with the whole class. Here are some examples of ways to generate group responses:

  - *Handheld Devices.* There are a number of electronic resources that can be used with informal review and assessment. Handheld devices, such as clickers and classroom performance tools, can be used in many ways, including recording student responses, learning about concepts in measurement, practicing multiplication tables, and taking notes, to name a few. Teachers can use clickers for a group review: students hold their clickers and respond to a prompt with multiple-choice options. The computer records and displays the class results, along with the correct answer. Teachers can pose yes/no, true/false, or multiple-choice questions, and students respond anonymously. The data are quickly collated and displayed so the teacher and students can see the number of correct responses and determine how many students might need reteaching.

- *Thumbs Up/Thumbs Down (or Pencils Up/Down for older students).* This is a low-tech and quick alternative to handheld devices. Students signal using their thumbs or pencils to *agree/disagree*, say *yes/no*, or indicate whether the statement is *true/false*. They can indicate *I don't know* by making a fist or holding a pencil, in front of the chest, and wiggling it back and forth.

- *Number Wheels.* Another low-tech alternative is Number Wheels, which provide the teacher with immediate information about students' comprehension of content concepts. A number wheel is made from card stock strips held together by a metal ring fastener. Each strip has a number printed on it, with ✻ to 5 or ✻ to 10, or a–d, depending on your needs and students' ages. Students use their individual number wheels to indicate their answers to questions or statements that offer multiple-choice responses. Possible answers are displayed on the smartboard, chart paper, or pocket chart, and the teacher asks the questions or gives the statements orally. The ✻ is intended to signify *I don't know* or *I'm confused* about an answer to the question. When students determine their answers, they hold the number wheels close to their chests, and cover the answer with their other hand. Use the cues, "Think" (allow time to process); "Get Set" (find the correct number/letter and cover it with a hand); and "Show Me" (students display their answers, again in front of their chests for only the teacher to see). They repeat the process as you ask the remaining questions.

- *Response Boards.* Popular dry-erase boards and dry-erase pens are great to have on hand for group responses. Ask a question and students respond on their boards and then turn them to face you when you say, *Think, Get Set, Show me!* Laminated card stock or plastic insert sleeves also can be used in the same way as group response boards.

- **Batter Up!** (Vogt & Echevarria, 2022, p. 214). This is a fun, interactive, and high-energy activity for students of all ages that provides an informal review and assessment of students' understandings of key concepts and vocabulary prior to a unit test or other more formal assessment. Depending on age, students can be involved in writing questions based on the unit concepts and vocabulary, or the teacher can write and include some, if not all, that may be on the unit test. Prepare questions written on four levels:

  - First Base: Easiest questions
  - Second Base: More challenging questions

◆ Third Base: Even more challenging questions

◆ Home Run: The most challenging questions

If possible, move desks/tables out of the way to make room for creating a "baseball diamond" on the classroom floor (painters tape works well), or play the game in a hallway, or outside. Divide students into two heterogeneous teams (very important that they're heterogeneous, so students can help each other). The game is played like baseball without a ball or bats: One at a time, students are up to bat, and they choose which level of question they want to try to answer. The teacher selects and reads a question, and the batter answers it. You can decide whether the batters get help from their team members, or whether pairs of students, rather than individuals, are up to bat. An incorrect answer is a "strike out" and the other team is up to bat after three strikes. A point is earned for every student who makes it "home." Incorrect answers provide information about which content concepts may need further review (see Artifact 9.1 Batter Up).

ARTIFACT 9.1   Batter Up! A game to assess student readiness for a unit test

This is an illustration for how to tape or provide an outline of a baseball diamond on the classroom floor, hallway, or even outside. It can also be projected if there's not room for students to move from one base to the other.

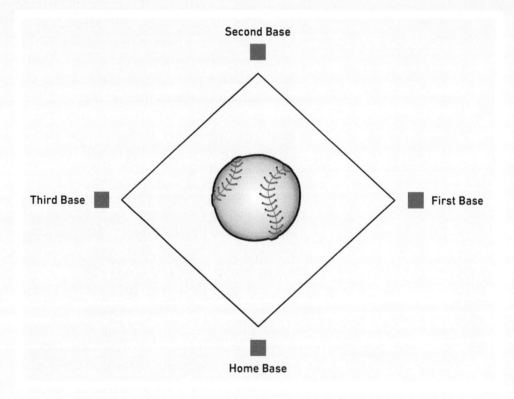

■ Differentiating for Multilevel Classes

In the previous chapters, you have read about instructional changes you can make in your SIOP lessons to differentiate for multilingual learners' individual needs. What follows are ways that you can differentiate formative and summative assessment for students with varied levels of English proficiency.

- Adapt **the number of items** a multilingual learner is expected to complete, such as even or odd numbers only, or the first five of ten questions (see Leveled Study Guides in Chapter 2 as another example). Determine percentages of correct responses based on the number of items assessed. Of course, if the student chooses to do more, that is fine.

- Adapt **the amount of time** the multilingual learner has for completing a task, such as providing more processing time and/or breaking tasks into manageable chunks. Unless there is a requirement to have a timed test, allowing additional time should not impact a student's score or grade.

- Adapt the **amount of scaffolding** provided to a multilingual learner during assessments by asking an aide, peer assistant, or parent volunteer to read and/or explain the task, or even read aloud in the student's home language, translating, if necessary and possible, the items for the assessment. Remember the difference between assessing a multilingual learner's ability to *read* and follow *written* directions, and their ability to complete a task or answer questions about a content topic. If you are assessing students' content knowledge, not their ability to read directions, it is fine to have someone else help with reading or clarifying what the expectation for the task is.

- Adapt the **skill level, type of problem or task**, and the process for how a multilingual learners can approach the task, such as allowing calculators, English-Spanish (or another language) electronic translator, or simplified instructions. Once again, you are not reducing the expectation that students should know the material—you're just making it easier for them to demonstrate understanding.

- Adapt the **type of response** multilingual learners are allowed to provide, such as permitting drawings, working with manipulatives, allowing verbal responses, or responding in the student's home language. Whereas native speakers may be required to write a paragraph summary or essay, it may be reasonable for multilingual learners, and other students who need the scaffold, to submit an illustration, poster-board explanation, or other kind of product that demonstrates understanding of key concepts.

- Adapt the **degree of active involvement** of students in assessment, such as encouraging individual self-assessment, assistance in creating rubrics, and cooperative group self-assessment. As you have read often in this book, content learning is enhanced for all students, but especially for multilingual learners, through interaction and group work. Students can certainly be involved in assessing their own progress, particularly in the upper grades, but also in the lower grades, when using group response techniques, pictures, or hand-held devices.

- **Adapt the procedures** used in each lesson. When students are working in collaborative groups, they often assume roles, such as recorder, timekeeper, reader, discussant, and so forth. While it is important for multilingual learners to be able to participate fully, some roles, such as timekeeper, require less language. Of course, when students gain language proficiency, they should be encouraged to take on roles that require more reading, writing, and speaking.

◼ The Lesson

Egyptian Mummies (Eighth Grade)

The classrooms described in the teaching vignettes in this chapter are all in a large urban middle school with a heterogeneously mixed student population. Multilingual learners are approximately 45% of the students who are in the teachers' eighth-grade classes, with the majority speaking Spanish as their home language. The multilingual learners represent a variety of levels of English proficiency; there are no beginning English speakers in these classes.

The three, eighth-grade, language arts/social studies core teachers, Mr. Tran, Mr. Hughell, and Miss Johnston, are teaching an extended unit on Egypt. The lessons illustrated here are on the topic of Egyptian mummies. Each of the teachers has planned a two-day lesson using an article about Mummy No. 1770, maintained at the Manchester Museum in England. Because very little was known about this mummy, the museum made it available to a group of scientists who wanted to use modern techniques to determine its age, its mummification process, and how the person had lived. The article describes what the scientists learned, including when the 13-year-old lived (A.D. 260), what she had eaten, what her life was like, how she died, and how her body was preserved.

The following ELA and Social Studies Standards (grades 6–8) were used to guide the development of the following lessons:

- *Evaluate specific claims in a text, assessing whether the reasoning is sound and the evidence is relevant and sufficient; recognize when irrelevant evidence is introduced.*
- *Determine central ideas or conclusions of a text; provide an accurate summary of the text distinct from prior knowledge or opinions.*

The following teaching vignettes represent the second day of the mummy lessons taught by Mr. Tran, Mr. Hughell, and Miss Johnston.

◼ Teaching Scenarios

Mr. Tran

In his lesson plan and on the whiteboard, Mr. Tran listed the following objectives for this lesson:

Content Objectives

Students will explain how scientists learned about Mummy No. 1770.

Students will identify major discoveries scientists made during the autopsy of the mummy and compare them to news reports published at the time of the discovery.

Language Objective

Students will define and correctly use the following vocabulary words from the text: mummy, mummification, autopsy, evidence, embalming, tissue.

During day 1 of the lesson, working in small groups, Mr. Tran's class created a word wall with words students knew, along with words from the first section of the article that they read. They began work on a sequence chain graphic organizer, listing steps taken by the scientists, and using words from the word wall.

On the second day of the lesson (the one observed for the SIOP rating), Mr. Tran reviewed the content and language objectives from the previous day and introduced a new language objective for day two's lesson:

Students will orally compare the scientists' description of Mummy No. 1770 in the original article to a Wikipedia article about Mummy 1770.

Mr. Tran then referred students to the word wall and the class read together the words in sequence and again in random order. He then asked for volunteers to give informal definitions for a few of the words, focusing on the key vocabulary he had selected to emphasize:

mummy, mummification, autopsy, evidence, embalming, tissue

He reviewed the section of the article read on the previous day and asked students to recall with a partner the most important information they had learned about Mummy No. 1770. As needed, Mr. Tran clarified definitions, assisted students with pronunciations, and gently corrected errors.

Mr. Tran then asked students to share the sequence chains they had begun the previous day with their partners. Students provided feedback to their peers about their sequence chains' content, and all were prompted to add words from the word wall, as appropriate. Mr. Tran circulated and listened to the discussions of several pairs, again assisting as needed.

Next, the entire class briefly reviewed the major discoveries of the scientists described to this point in the reading, and two were listed on the board. The teacher referred to illustrations on pages five through seven of the article and asked students to predict what they thought happened to the teenage girl and how scientists might have reached conclusions about her death. He wrote on the board, *"What* evidence *did the scientists discover during the* autopsy *of the* mummy?" as a focal question for the rest of the lesson.

Students were directed to look for additional scientific discoveries as they read the next four pages with partners. They were asked to complete a T-chart with the following column headings: "Evidence scientists discovered about No. 1770's life" and "Evidence scientists discovered about No. 1770's death." As a matter of practice, Mr. Tran walked around the room while students were working. He frequently smiled, voiced encouragement, answered questions, and provided feedback and support for his students' efforts.

The lesson continued as students reviewed their T-charts and the text to find additional words for the word wall. Among the words added were *embalmers, painted pictures,* and *tissue* (see Artifact 9.2). Mr. Tran wrote *embalm, embalmer,* and *embalming* on the board and discussed the differences in meaning. Similarly, he wrote

People	Mummification	Evidence
archaeologists	autopsy	artifacts
embalmers	drying out process	coffin
mummy	embalm	gold
pharaohs	linen	jewels
Tutankhamen	preservation	oils
	tissue	painted pictures
	wrappings	perfumes
	X-ray	pyramids
		sarcophagus

mummy, mummified, and *mummification* on the board and asked students to discuss differences in meaning with a partner. Students then completed the second section of their sequence chains, indicating the subsequent steps the scientists had taken to gather evidence from the mummy.

Mr. Tran next distributed and read aloud a brief article (14 sentences) about Mummy 1770 found on Wikipedia. Using their sequence chains, T-charts, and the word wall vocabulary, students worked with partners to compare the scientific evidence gathered from the Mummy 1770 article, and from the 14-sentence Wikipedia article, noting similarities and differences. Based on the comparison, the class voted on which source was more reliable, providing specific examples as evidence.

Mr. Tran concluded the lesson by highlighting in yellow on the word wall the key vocabulary words, and these were reviewed one last time. He reviewed each of the lesson's content and language objectives to determine whether the students thought they had been met.

Check your understanding: On the SIOP form in Figure 9.1, rate Mr. Tran's lesson for each of the Review & Assessment features.

Mr. Hughell

Mr. Hughell's lesson plan noted the following objectives:

Write a paragraph about what mummies teach scientists about how Egyptians lived.
Explain how mummies were preserved.
Match 20 vocabulary words with their definitions.

FIGURE 9.1   Review & Assessment Component of the SIOP Model: Mr. Tran's Lesson

4	3	2	1	0
27. Comprehensive **review of key vocabulary**		Uneven **review of key vocabulary**		No **review of key vocabulary**

4	3	2	1	0
28. Comprehensive review **of key content concepts**		Uneven **review of key content concepts**		No **review of key content concepts**

4	3	2	1	0
29. Regular **feedback** provided to students on their output (e.g., language, content, work)		Inconsistent **feedback** provided to students on their output		No **feedback** provided to students on their output

4	3	2	1	0
30. **Assessment** of student **comprehension and learning of** all lesson objectives (e.g., spot checking, group response) throughout the lesson		**Assessment of student comprehension and learning** of some lesson objectives		No **assessment of student comprehension and learning** of lesson objectives

The plan for the first day of the lesson included the following: Distribute a list of 20 words and definitions related to mummies along with page numbers on which the words could be found in the assigned article; read aloud half of the article while students follow along; have students find the first group of 10 vocabulary words in the chapter and write an original sentence related to the topic of mummies for each word.

Mr. Hughell began the second day of the lesson by asking volunteers to read several of the vocabulary sentences they had written the previous day. As students read, Mr. Hughell corrected language errors when needed. He clarified content misconceptions, modeled appropriate pronunciation, and reminded students of the correct definitions for the vocabulary. He then gave students five minutes to review what had been read the previous day. He asked volunteers to orally summarize what they had learned about Mummy No. 1770 and how mummies were prepared. Several students responded briefly, and Mr. Hughell prompted others to elaborate. He highlighted key points by writing them on the board and made additions to the students' summaries.

He then asked for volunteers to read the next set of 10 words and definitions from the vocabulary list. He informed students that they would have a vocabulary matching quiz on these words the following day. Students were then directed to read the rest of the article silently and were encouraged by Mr. Hughell to ask for help if they found words they did not understand. Following the reading, students worked with partners to write 10 more sentences for the remaining words on the vocabulary list.

At the end of the period, Mr. Hughell called on a few volunteers to read their sentences aloud and asked if anyone had questions. Because not everyone had finished writing the sentences, he assigned the remaining ones for homework and reminded students of the vocabulary quiz planned for the next day. He suggested that students review the entire article at home because, in addition to the vocabulary quiz, they were going to be writing a paragraph in class on what scientists have learned from mummies. He would evaluate the students' comprehension of the article with the written paragraph and quiz the following day.

Check your understanding: On the SIOP form in Figure 9.2, rate Mr. Hughell's lesson for each of the Review & Assessment features.

Miss Johnston

Miss Johnston's lesson plans revealed one content objective for the two-day lesson on mummies: *"The learner will understand how mummies were made."* The plan included the following for both days: *"Read article about Mummy No. 1770 and complete the worksheet questions."*

Miss Johnston began the second day of the lesson by calling on a student to summarize the article that had been read aloud the previous day. The student responded, *"We took turns reading about how some guys in a museum unwrapped an old mummy."* Another student added, *"And scientists learned the mummy was a girl with no legs."* Miss Johnston offered no further explanation or review.

FIGURE 9.2 **Review & Assessment Component of the SIOP Model: Mr. Hughell's Lesson**

4	3	2	1	0
27. Comprehensive **review of key vocabulary**		Uneven **review of key vocabulary**		No **review of key vocabulary**
4	**3**	**2**	**1**	**0**
28. Comprehensive **review of key content concepts**		Uneven **review of key content concepts**		No **review of key content concepts**
4	**3**	**2**	**1**	**0**
29. Regular **feedback** provided to students on their output (e.g., language, content, work)		Inconsistent **feedback** provided to students on their output		No **feedback** provided to students on their output
4	**3**	**2**	**1**	**0**
30. **Assessment of student comprehension and learning of** all lesson objectives (e.g., spot checking, group response) throughout the lesson		**Assessment of student comprehension and learning** of some lesson objectives		No **assessment of student comprehension and learning** of lesson objectives

Miss Johnston then distributed a worksheet to students that had multiple-choice and fill-in-the-blank questions covering information in the article, along with two short essay questions. Students worked individually but were allowed to use their books while completing the worksheets. If they finished early, Miss Johnston gave them a word search including a variety of words related to mummies. This task would become a homework assignment if the period ended before students were finished. The teacher circulated through the room, answering questions and keeping students on task.

Toward the end of the period, to assess their learning, Miss Johnston asked students to exchange the worksheet papers. She read the correct answers for the multiple-choice and fill-in-the-blank questions aloud, and students marked their peers' papers. When she asked how many students had one or two wrong answers, no one raised a hand. The lesson concluded with students turning in their papers so Miss Johnston could assign a grade. She reminded students to finish the word searches and to bring in shoe boxes and craft materials the next day so that each student could make a diorama as a culminating activity for the lessons.

Check your understanding:

On the SIOP form in Figure 9.3, rate Miss Johnston's lesson for each of the Review & Assessment features.

| FIGURE 9.3 | Review & Assessment Component of the SIOP Model: Miss Johnston's Lesson |

4	3	2	1	0
27. Comprehensive **review of key vocabulary**		Uneven **review of key vocabulary**		No **review of key vocabulary**
4	3	2	1	0
28. Comprehensive **review of key content concepts**		Uneven **review of key content concepts**		No **review of key content concepts**
4	3	2	1	0
29. Regular **feedback** provided to students on their output (e.g., language, content, work)		Inconsistent **feedback** provided to students on their output		No **feedback** provided to students on their output
4	3	2	1	0
30. **Assessment of student comprehension and learning** of all lesson objectives (e.g., spot checking, group response) throughout the lesson		**Assessment of student comprehension and learning** of some lesson objectives		No **assessment of student comprehension and learning** of lesson objectives

■ Discussion of Lessons

Look back at your rating form and think about the reasons you scored the lessons as you did. Read on to see our analyses.

27. *Comprehensive Review of Key Vocabulary*

> Mr. Tran: 4
>
> Mr. Hughell: 1
>
> Miss Johnston: 0

The emphasis on vocabulary and content instruction, practice, review, and assessment varied across the three classrooms.

- **Mr. Tran's** lesson received a "4" for this feature. He had clearly defined content and language objectives, one of which focused specifically on vocabulary. Throughout the lesson, his instruction and activities were congruent with these objectives. He built upon what students already knew about mummies, incorporated student selection of important terms, and ensured the key vocabulary words were included on the word wall. He pointed out similarities in word structure and differences in word meanings (e.g., *embalm/embalmer/embalming* and *mummy/mummified/mummification*).

    Mr. Tran's multilingual learners were challenged to articulate the key vocabulary both orally and in writing. Although many terms and phrases related to mummies were introduced, discussed in the text, and included on the word wall, sequence chain, and T-chart, Mr. Tran limited the words students were expected to master to six. It is important to note that he repeatedly reinforced these words, at the beginning, in the middle, and again at the end of the lesson. By using the vocabulary in context, repeating the words orally, and writing the question on the whiteboard (*"What* evidence *did the scientists discover during the* autopsy *of the* mummy?"*), Mr. Tran reviewed the pronunciation, meanings, and usage of the words. In addition, because the word wall was organized and alphabetized by topics (*People, Mummification, Evidence*), students were better able to find the words or phrases they were seeking.

    Finally, Mr. Tran expected students to use the new key vocabulary orally and in their writing during partner, small-group, and whole-class discussion. While listening to their conversations and observing their writing, he could readily determine who had met or partially met the vocabulary objectives.

- **Mr. Hughell's** lesson received a "1" for this feature. He reviewed the vocabulary sentences from the first day's lesson, provided definitions and page numbers, and allowed students to write their sentences with partners. However, it is unrealistic to expect multilingual learners, as well as struggling readers, to master such a large number of vocabulary words (i.e., 20 words) using the approaches he selected. He did not assist students in learning the words through analogy, pictorial representations, or exploration of language structure, and provided very few exposures to the words. The sentences that the partners were writing were not expected to result in connected text; thus, the students only used the words in isolated instances. Moreover, many students did not complete the assignment in class, so Mr. Hughell was unable to review or assess student understanding of the words.

Mr. Hughell ran out of time at the end of the period and expected students to conduct their own review of the article at home. Obviously, this did not provide the type of scaffolding that multilingual learners need and did not represent effective review of language, vocabulary, and content.

- **Miss Johnston's** lesson received a "0" for this feature. She had no language objectives for the lesson plan and did not introduce, teach, or review any key vocabulary to assist students in completing the worksheet. There may have been words in the multiple-choice questions that students were unfamiliar with, reflecting "test language," but she gave them no opportunity to ask about them, nor did she explain the words to the students in advance. Some students (those who finished the worksheets early) practiced finding vocabulary on a word search, and the rest were assigned the word search as homework. It is important to note that word searches, while engaging, do not constitute effective review of vocabulary because students are expected to simply match spellings without knowing pronunciations and meanings.

28. *Comprehensive Review of Key Content Concepts*

Mr. Tran: 4

Mr. Hughell: 1

Miss Johnston: 1

Most teachers, if they review at the end of a lesson, focus on the content concepts. In these three scenarios, the teachers did so to varying degrees.

- **Mr. Tran's** lesson received a "4" for this feature. Throughout the lesson, he consciously and consistently reviewed content directly related to his objectives that were derived from the ELA/Social Studies standards for this lesson. Students reviewed the information they learned the previous day, as well as the new information from this lesson, with partners and the entire class. Mr. Tran created opportunities for students to correct errors or add information to the sequence chains and T-charts and had them compare the Wikipedia information to the original article. During each of these activities, the teacher could clarify misunderstandings. At the conclusion of the lesson, Mr. Tran had students review the major discoveries, along with the lesson's content and language objectives.

- **Mr. Hughell's** lesson received a "1" for this feature. He began by providing a basic review of the previous day's reading. He gave students time to focus on their previous learning and had volunteers summarize what had been read. He asked others to elaborate and wrote the information on the board so all students could follow along. Most important, he clarified points and added information to their summaries. These efforts were primarily reviewing the previous day's work. Thus, the lesson may have received a "3" on SIOP feature 8 in Building Background (link to past learning). While this is important to do, especially for multilingual learners, this review was not followed by previewing the present day's key concepts. Unfortunately, Mr. Hughell ran out of time at the end of the period and consequently failed to review content concepts adequately before the lesson concluded. It was inappropriate to require multilingual learners to review at home an entire article that had specialized terminology. The teacher is the one to provide this review or at least scaffold student efforts to review by themselves, prior to assessment and evaluation.

- **Miss Johnston's** lesson received a "1" for this feature. She took a different approach in reviewing content concepts with the students, but it yielded little success with multilingual learners. Initially, she asked students to summarize the article they had read. Although two students made an attempt, each stated only one sentence, which included a fact but did not summarize the information. Miss Johnston's concept review was through an individualized paper-and-pencil assignment. This was, however, an assessment of student knowledge and reading comprehension, not a true review of content concepts. Students could peruse the article to find information, but neither the class as a whole nor students in groups had an opportunity to discuss and clarify understandings about the content material. Moreover, Miss Johnston's only objective was vague (*"Students will understand how mummies were made"*) and did not provide clearly defined content concepts for the students. This was in large part because the objective was not derived from content standards as described in the lesson overview.

29. *Regular Feedback Provided to Students on Their Output*

    Mr. Tran: 4

    Mr. Hughell: 2

    Miss Johnston: 1

Mr. Tran, Mr. Hughell, and Miss Johnston had different ways of providing feedback to the students during their lessons.

- **Mr. Tran's** lesson received a "4" for this feature. He scaffolded students' learning by clarifying, discussing, and gently correcting responses. He encouraged peer support and feedback when the graphic organizers were shared, and he used explanation and discussion to help students understand how to evaluate the importance of the scientists' discoveries. He moved around the classroom during the lesson, offering support and academic feedback. Mr. Tran clearly used review, assessment, and feedback to develop his students' language proficiency and content knowledge throughout the lesson. His final review was of the lesson's content and language objectives.

- **Mr. Hughell's** lesson received a "2" for this feature. He frequently clarified misconceptions and gave clear corrections for students' errors. However, his feedback would have been more effective had it better scaffolded students' developing language proficiency and content knowledge. That is, Mr. Hughell's feedback was primarily corrective rather than instructive. He essentially told students their answers were incorrect and then gave them the correct answers, rather than assisting them in formulating the correct responses themselves. Mr. Hughell also directed students to read the article independently and ask for help if needed. Many students, multilingual learners especially, may be reluctant to ask for help for fear of appearing inattentive and/or because they don't know how to formulate the questions they need to ask. Also, because Mr. Hughell's classroom was quite teacher-centered (he delivered instruction mostly by standing at the front of the room), students had little opportunity to work together to provide each other with helpful feedback. His teaching would be more effective for multilingual learners if he created a more supportive classroom environment. He could begin by providing more meaningful academic feedback to his students.

- **Miss Johnston's** lesson received a "1" for this feature. She attempted to help students by answering questions while they were completing their worksheets. She also corrected the papers in class, providing the answers for the questions. However, the amount of feedback she provided students was very limited, and not particularly supportive. When she gave the correct responses to the worksheet questions, she provided little or no explanation, and she did not consider student output on an individualized basis during the lesson. In all, multilingual learners received very little supportive feedback during the observed lesson.

30. *Assessment of Student Comprehension and Learning of All Lesson Objectives*

Mr. Tran: 4

Mr. Hughell: 2

Miss Johnston: 1

Assessing student learning is a critical step in the teaching and learning cycle. The three teachers in these vignettes all conducted some assessment but in different ways.

- **Mr. Tran's** lesson received a "4" for this feature. As his lesson unfolded, Mr. Tran's assessment opportunities included group response, partner, and whole-class reporting, as well as individual written work. His assessments occurred throughout the lesson and were authentic, multidimensional, and included multiple indicators. Most important, his assessments were directly linked to his content and language objectives.

- **Mr. Hughell's** lesson received a "2" for this feature. His assessments of student understanding in the observed lesson were only somewhat effective. He called upon a few students to read their vocabulary sentences aloud, so for those students he was able to assess their sense of the words' meanings, but he had no way of knowing whether the rest of the students, particularly the multilingual learners, understood the vocabulary terms. When students read the article silently, he did not assess their reading comprehension of the content. He planned some summative assessments, namely the vocabulary matching test and the written paragraph, and tried to match assessment to his objectives: "*Write a paragraph on what mummies teach scientists about how Egyptians lived. Explain how mummies were preserved. Match 20 vocabulary words with their definitions.*" However, these assessments were scheduled for the following day, too late to guide necessary review, feedback, and reteaching during the period of instruction. By the time he discovered who had met the language and content objectives and who had not, the lesson would be completed.

- **Miss Johnston's** lesson received a "1" for this feature. The factual recall sentences elicited responses from only two students. Although the worksheet constituted summative evaluation, there was no ongoing assessment throughout the lesson. Students responded to the worksheet individually, and only after she collected the papers, looked at the scores, and issued grades—after the class had ended— would she have a sense of what students had learned. As with Mr. Hughell, this information would arrive too late to guide review and reteaching. Without a rubric or criteria upon which the diorama projects would be assessed, it is doubtful they would inform Miss Johnston about the students' understanding of key vocabulary and content concepts. Finally, the one objective ("The students will understand how mummies were made") was too general, not directly measurable, not observable, and not derived from standards.

■ Final Points

As you reflect on this chapter and the impact and role of review and assessment of vocabulary and content and language objectives, consider the following points:

- Review and assessment are integrated processes, essential for all students, but they are critical to the success of multilingual learners.
- Informal assessment is attentive to the classroom context, is authentic and multidimensional, and includes multiple indicators of students' performance.
- Effective SIOP teachers carefully plan for review and informal assessment of key vocabulary throughout a lesson and at its conclusion.
- Formal assessments (e.g., standardized tests) require that students understand and apply content knowledge on tests that have high stakes. Therefore, it is important to teach, review, and assess multilingual learners' understandings of the cross-curricular/process/function words and terms that are often found in test questions.
- At the conclusion of a SIOP lesson, teachers assess the degree to which students have met all content and language objectives.
- Most important, review and assessment guide teaching and reteaching, inform decision making, lead to supportive and academic feedback, and provide for fair and comprehensive judgments about student performance.

■ Discussion Questions

1. In reflecting on the content and language objectives at the beginning of the chapter, are you able to:
   a. Identify the challenges in assessing content and language learning of multilingual students?
   b. Create a plan for formative assessment for the linguistically diverse students in your classroom that will provide you with the information you need to make sound instructional decisions during lesson planning?
   c. Determine opportunities for reviewing and assessing students' use of academic language, key vocabulary, and content concepts throughout a lesson?
   d. Provide effective academic, oral, and written feedback to multilingual learners during a lesson?
   e. Define each of the following assessment terms: *informal assessment, formal assessment, formative assessment, summative assessment, performance-based assessment, multidimensional indicators,* and *multiple indicators*?

2. Many teachers introduce key vocabulary at the beginning of the lesson, but often neglect to revisit the new terms systematically throughout the lesson and review them at its conclusion. Describe a variety of ways you would review key vocabulary and terms, as well as the techniques you could put in place to include vocabulary review in each lesson. Which of the activities introduced in this chapter would you select? Why?

3. Research has shown that gratuitous compliments to students, such as *"Good job"* or *"Keep up the good work"* do little to motivate them or assist with their learning. Instead, effective SIOP teachers give regular, substantive feedback to students on their verbal contributions and on their academic work. What are some ways to provide constructive, specific academic feedback to students? Consider class size and the English proficiency levels of your students as you answer this question.

4. Reflect on the ideas presented in this chapter, as well as other activities you have used to assess student learning of specific lesson objectives. How much time do you think you should allocate for review and assessment during each lesson? What if you discover (as is often the case) that some students are ready to move on, while others need more review and/or reteaching?

5. Using the SIOP lesson you have been creating, provide specific provisions for students at varying levels of English proficiency. Plan multiple indicators throughout the lesson that will enable you to assess on-the-spot progress toward meeting the lesson's content and language objectives. Then determine what you will do for (1) independent or partner work for students who are ready to move on; and (2) a reteaching or review minilesson for those who need additional assistance. This is probably the most challenging aspect of providing differentiated instruction, not only for multilingual learners, but for all students. How will you assess who is ready to move on? How will you assess the students in the reteaching/review group to determine if, and when, they're ready to move on? What will you do if a few students are still struggling? These are the *big* questions to ask (and answer) when planning for a lesson's review and assessment.

■ Pearson eTextbook Application Videos

The purpose of the Pearson eTextbook Application Videos is to provide you with an opportunity to observe and reflect on SIOP teaching and learning practices. There are multilingual students in each of the classrooms with varying levels of English proficiency. The teachers you will observe are at different levels of SIOP implementation, from second-year SIOPers to veterans. As you observe the lessons they have created, focus on the students and the lesson objectives, keeping in mind that becoming a high-implementing SIOP teacher takes time, practice, and support to refine teaching practices. We are grateful to each of these SIOP educators for welcoming us into their classrooms, and for their dedication to SIOP, their multilingual learners, and other students.

Pearson eTextbook Application
Video Example 9.1
SIOP Lesson: Grade 10 History; Comparing and Contrasting the U.S. and Roman Empire (Teacher 2)

Multi-Tiered System of Supports for Multilingual Students

CONTENT OBJECTIVES

This chapter will help you to . . .

- Explain how instruction provided in Tier 1 differs from that in Tier 2.
- Describe in-class supports or modifications that content teachers can provide to multilingual learners.
- Identify a legal provision that ensures appropriate services for multilingual learners.

LANGUAGE OBJECTIVES

This chapter will help you to . . .

- Discuss with a group the first four steps in MTSS for multilingual learners who are underperforming academically.
- Write a lesson plan for a multilingual learner with the same characteristics as the student, Adriana (described in Case Study #2).

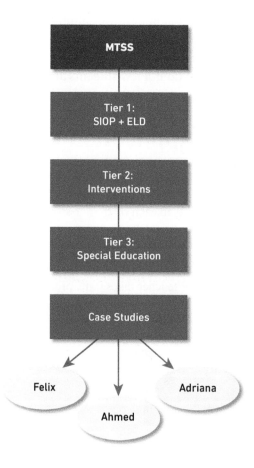

In our work with teachers and administrators throughout the United States, a persistent question concerns appropriate instruction for multilingual learners who exhibit difficulties with reading and learning. Teachers often feel ill prepared to provide content instruction for these students because they're not sure whether a student's difficulty is due to a reading problem, a learning disability, a lack of schooling, limited English proficiency, or another reason. In this chapter, we provide a discussion of the process used in schools to systematically address these issues.

Although it is not the intent of this chapter to provide a comprehensive treatment of the topic of struggling learners, we hope it will stimulate your thinking and discussions with colleagues about multilingual learners. We begin with a brief discussion of research on literacy development for multilingual learners since more than 80% of referrals for additional services are related to reading. We also examine the importance of having an effective tiered system of supports in place, referred to as Multi-Tiered System of Supports (MTSS), also called Response to Intervention (RTI) in some schools. (For a full discussion of multitiered supports, see *Response to Intervention (RTI) and English learners: Using the SIOP Model* [Echevarría, Richards-Tutor, & Vogt, 2015]. For a discussion of special education and multilingual learners, see [Echevarría & Graves, 2015].) ■

Teachers face many challenges related to the literacy development of multilingual learners, due in part to students learning to read and write in a new language that they do not fully understand. In a discussion of the Science of Reading and multilingual learners, Goldenberg (2021) reports that most multilingual learners in schools in the United States are enrolled in English-only programs, and they are learning to read at the same time they are learning a new language. If multilingual learners don't learn to read in their home language (L1), they're unable to carry over their knowledge of reading in the L1 to reading in English. As a result, these students may have difficulty with attending to the distinct sounds of English, letter identification, and vocabulary as well as comprehending text because they lack familiarity with the purposes and mechanics of reading. Furthermore, many multilingual learners lack the oral proficiency to help them recognize words and internalize grammar. Thus, many multilingual learners are behind before the onset of school (Snow, Burns, & Griffin, 1998).

Literacy research, studies that comprise the Science of Reading, suggests that multilingual learners, like native English speakers, need systematic, high-quality literacy instruction from the start (Goldenberg, 2020; Goldenberg, 2021). According to the Report of the National Literacy Panel on Language-Minority Children and Youth (August & Shanahan, 2006), teachers of multilingual learners should provide substantial instruction in the key components of reading as identified by the National Reading Panel (NICHD, 2000). These include phonemic awareness, phonics, fluency, vocabulary, and comprehension. As important as these are, they are not sufficient for multilingual learners.

Oral language development, for example, often overlooked during literacy instruction, is also critical. Researchers suggest modifications to instruction, such as repetition and rehearsal, adjusted rate of teacher speech, and building on prior knowledge, all of which are found in SIOP's features (Cardenas-Hagan, 2020; Goldenberg & Coleman, 2015).

■ Multi-Tiered System of Supports (MTSS)

MTSS is a service delivery model used to identify at-risk learners early and to provide appropriate supports including effective instruction in general education (typically called Tier 1), followed by targeted intervention as needed (Tier 2), and, when appropriate, more intensive support through special education services (Tier 3). It's important to mention that there isn't a prescribed number of tiers or levels of support. For example, Tier 3 may involve more intensive interventions, with special education being Tier 4 in some schools. The point is to provide the level and intensity of supports students need to be successful.

Generally, MTSS consists of skill screening for all students, close monitoring of student progress, and the use of interventions to bolster student achievement. The process is founded on the principle that *all students can learn* and is designed to catch learning problems early, thus reducing the number of students eligible for and in need of special education services. Early identification and intervention can help prevent reading difficulties altogether (Torgesen, 2012).

One of the advantages of a multitiered model is its emphasis on ensuring appropriate learning opportunities for all students, beginning in the general education classroom. All students receive instruction in the core curriculum, even those who receive additional services. In other words, Tiers 2 and 3 do not compensate for ineffective or inadequate Tier 1 instruction. By focusing on the instruction and interventions students need to be successful rather than their "problems," more students' needs will be met in the least restrictive (and less costly) environment, and decisions about student placement will be based on documented evidence over time.

MTSS provides educators with a system for supporting struggling multilingual learners in general education instead of considering referral to special education as the first or only option. As mentioned, many reading difficulties can be ameliorated when they are identified early and when appropriate support is provided to the student. Some multilingual learners need time and exposure to become familiar with the sounds of English and to associate words with the concepts they represent. MTSS, when implemented well, systematically documents student progress, and the areas

> " The SIOP is a model that can be used across all tiers in an MTSS framework. The eight components in the SIOP align to critical elements of intervention and provide the additional instructional supports that multilingual learners need to be successful.
>
> Dr. Cara Richards-Tutor, Professor of Special Education "

FIGURE 10.1 **Multi-Tiered System of Support for Multilingual Learners**

Tier 1: Core Content Instruction Using SIOP + ELD

Increasing intensity →

Continue with effective instruction ← **YES** ─ (1) General Education: Is student reaching benchmarks and no parent or teacher concerns are expressed? **NO** → Proceed to Step 2

(2) Tier 1 Site-Based Team Plan: Meet with grade-level teams or site team to analyze instruction & make adjustments. *Ask: Is instruction linguistically appropriate?*

Continue with instructional plan ← **YES** ─ (3) Is student responding to the adjustments/plan? **NO** → Proceed to Step 4

(4) **Tier 2: Targeted small-group interventions & progress monitoring**

Exit intervention ← **YES** ─ (5) Is student responding to interventions? **NO** → Proceed to Step 6

(6) Adjust interventions & monitor progress

Exit intervention ← **YES** ─ (7) Is student responding to interventions? **NO** → Initiate referral for special education services*

* Secure parent permission for evaluation. Provide forms in parent's home language.

Tier 3: Special Education and Related Services

(8) Tier 3: Administer psychoeducational evaluation; conduct some assessments in L1, as appropriate.

(9) Conduct IEP team meeting with parent participation & interpreter provided. Determine extent of services provided and create the IEP.

(10) Student receives special education services which involves:

High quality, linguistically appropriate instruction (SIOP)

\+

Ongoing progress monitoring & review of performance at annual IEP meeting

IEP – Individualized Education Plan
- Annual measurable goals
- Language supports specified

\+

Testing accommodations, as needed (e.g., directions read to student in L1)

\+

ELD/ESL instruction

that require focused instruction become apparent. Thus, multilingual learners are more likely to receive the kind of instruction they need to advance academically and in their English proficiency.

It is important to note that students with disabilities in our schools have the right to an appropriate individualized education through special education, and multilingual students with disabilities have the right to both appropriate individualized education and English language development services. So, it is equally important to identify those students for services. In some cases, a student's learning issues are significant enough to warrant more intensive services without spending valuable time going through each step of the school's MTSS process (Fuchs, Fuchs, & Compton, 2012). In any case, intervention strategies cannot be used to delay or deny evaluation of students suspected of having a disability (USED, 2016).

For the purposes of this chapter, our discussion is framed around the flowchart pictured in Figure 10.1, which depicts a step-by-step process for schools to use in supporting students' academic achievement. First, we describe the steps involved and then relate three multilingual students' journeys through the MTSS process. The steps can and should be adapted to make the support system relevant to your school setting. However, the information presented here represents a *minimum* level of support required for multilingual learners. In other words, many other levels and types of support may be needed in each setting such as counseling, social worker services, tutoring, after-school programs, and the like.

Tier 1: Core Content Instruction Using SIOP + ELD

Step 1: Is the student reaching the benchmarks?

The importance of high-quality Tier 1 (General Education) instruction cannot be overstated:

> Within [MTSS], the frontline of prevention is Tier 1, or the general education classroom, where every student regardless of ability is to receive *high-quality* instruction. Thus, the preventive possibilities of [MTSS] are only as good as the Tier 1 supports classroom teachers provide students (Brozo, 2010, p. 147).

As we've discussed throughout this book, effective instruction for multilingual learners takes place in classrooms where teachers hold high expectations for all students, respect students' language and cultural backgrounds, consider families as valued partners in their children's education, and actively assist multilingual learners with their language development. Instruction will not be effective if students are disengaged, distressed, or feel disrespected (Echevarría, Frey, & Fisher, 2015).

SIOP's features offer the Tier 1 supports that classroom teachers provide multilingual students. They use evidence-based practices that work for the individual student and monitor each student's progress. Since the SIOP Model has been found to be effective with all learners—and is essential for multilingual learners—its features should be implemented consistently to provide high-quality instruction for all students.

Pearson eTextbook

Video Example 10.1

Watch this expert practitioner, Mary Casto, describe what classroom teachers need to know about multilingual learners in Tier 1. https://www.youtube.com/watch?v=YY2KeMQcYec

English Language Development (ELD).   Coupled with effective SIOP instruction, multilingual learners receive daily English language development, also called ESL, ESOL, and content-based ESL. ELD is a legally mandated language support delivered by a teacher with certification or an endorsement in English learner education (Kangas, 2018). It takes place during a specific time each day when multilingual learners have an opportunity to focus on learning English. Students are grouped with others at or near their level of English proficiency so that lessons can be tailored to their needs.

During ELD, teachers provide explicit instruction and structured practice in using English. When given opportunities to practice speaking, students have a chance to use words and other features of the language in a specific order to create logical, meaningful sentences or phrases. They experiment with the language and better understand how English works. With practice they become more comfortable using terms that initially might have seemed unfamiliar or abstract.

Lessons may have an age-appropriate theme such as "Our neighborhood" for young learners, while older learners may discuss whether screen time should be limited. Texts may provide the basis for discussion, but the emphasis is on acquiring English—its forms, functions, and vocabulary—and on how to become a more proficient user of the language. ELD instruction is based on state ELP standards, which ensures that all four skills (reading, writing, speaking, and listening) are taught, practiced, and tested.

Instruction and practice with academic English becomes increasingly important as students move through the grades. For multilingual learners to become successful readers of English, attention needs to focus on accelerating their oral English proficiency so that they can participate and engage fully in academic discussions and other literacy activities. ELD is an opportune time to work on accelerating students' English proficiency. Goldenberg (2020, p. S136) concludes:

> First, if [multilingual learners] become more proficient in English, they become more efficient readers and more similar to native English speakers in their reading abilities. Second, to the extent that [multilingual learners] do not become sufficiently proficient in English, their reading skills remain inefficient and their reading more effortful, which in turn are likely to have mutually reinforcing negative effects on achievement and motivation.

When a student isn't reaching benchmarks in general education or if a parent or teacher has expressed concern about the student's academic progress, Step 2 would be implemented.

Step 2: Tier 1 Site Team Plan

This step in the process is typically informal, but is essential for multilingual learners. Any number of variables may contribute to underperformance including ineffective teaching, absenteeism or transiency, inadequate English language development (ELD) teaching, or the simple fact that these students are learning new information and skills in a new language. Step 2 provides an opportunity for colleagues to discuss a plan for supporting struggling students guided by the question: Is the instruction linguistically appropriate?

When we consider the principles of MTSS, we realize that learning difficulties are often the result of instructional issues, not an inherent problem in the learner. Since all students *can* learn, the team seeks the best ways to reach and teach each learner. Language and literacy are interdependent, so it's common to question the cause of multilingual learners' struggles with developing literacy skills. Steps 2 and 3 are designed to help decipher the cause of underperformance.

In Step 2, collaborative teams offer support for struggling students—and their teachers—by seeking to uncover what instructional adjustments need to be made. The team assists the teacher in analyzing instruction and offers suggestions. If you teach in a school with SIOP-trained staff, the process might be fairly easy; even veteran SIOP teachers enjoy the benefit of other teachers' suggestions and ideas for helping their students do well. If not, it's critical that at least one person on the team have knowledge about second language acquisition and experience with effective teaching for multilingual learners. Primarily, the team's purpose is to ensure that instruction is linguistically appropriate for the student and to offer ideas to scaffold or support student learning. Using the features of SIOP as a guide, the team may specifically recommend:

- assignments that capitalize on students' lived experiences, cultural practices, strengths, and interests.
- increased opportunities to develop oral language in a setting that is anxiety-free.
- explicit English language teaching followed by practice in small groups or with partners to increase confidence in using the language.
- culturally relevant materials including multimedia and computer programs.
- foundational skills, including decoding, taught using multimodal experiences and sufficient practice.
- meaningful reading experiences, accompanied by discussion and writing opportunities, where students' perspectives and opinions are valued.
- multiple exposures to targeted words in meaningful contexts.
- small-group or individualized instruction, which tends to be less intimidating for multilingual learners than whole-class instruction.
- family involvement/partnership, which demonstrates respect for and acceptance of students' background, family, and community.
- strategic use of home language support to make lessons more understandable.
- modification of assignments or materials to match students' educational experience (i.e., newcomer) and English proficiency.
- counseling services to address social-emotional issues that may be interfering with learning.
- Saturday school or after-school sessions that are geared to the needs of multilingual learners.

It is worth reiterating that the focus in Step 2 is making a plan to change variables such as teaching methods, materials, level of language support, and/or student behaviors so the learner can be successful. A passive, reluctant learner may become engaged in learning given the right setting, interesting materials, and teaching that is comprehensible, meaningful, and relevant for students. Comprehension is enhanced with supports or scaffolds including those that make connections between the learner and the lesson content. In other words: highly implemented SIOP teaching.

Step 3: Is the student responding to the plan?

After a specific period of time, the team revisits the student's progress. For many students, the extra attention to language and facilitating learning will be enough to see that they are making sufficient progress in acquiring language and literacy skills. The teacher continues implementing the strategies and techniques that have been beneficial, documenting progress along the way, so that the student continues to make progress.

For those students whose performance doesn't improve with additional classroom supports, interventions are necessary, which is Tier 2 (Step 4).

■ Tier 2: Targeted Small-Group Interventions and Progress Monitoring

Step 4: Interventions

In addition to the high-quality core instruction that students receive in general education, a subset of students (approximately 20% to 30%) may require more intensive interventions to remediate gaps in foundational literacy skills. Interventions supplement core instruction and are continued as long as there is evidence that they are needed. Some characteristics of interventions include:

- Instruction is focused and targeted, and is delivered by the general education teacher, reading specialist, or other specialist.
- Groups consist of 3 to 5 students and interventions include key features important for multilingual learners (e.g., oral language practice and vocabulary development).
- Students are grouped according to the specific component or components of reading identified as needing focused teaching, such as decoding or fluency.

Studies have shown that effective, beginning reading interventions for native-English speaking students have been deemed effective for multilingual students as well, with the addition of intensive, interactive oral language instruction and practice (Goldenberg, 2020). The focus on oral language use will strengthen vocabulary and other oral language skills, making it more likely that students' reading and writing skills will also improve.

As part of the MTSS process, teachers document changes in student behavior or performance as a result of interventions and assessments. Some students may need only one short-term intervention cycle while others may move in and out of interventions over time in order to reach grade-level performance, seen in Figure 10.1. That is, students receive interventions for a specific amount of time and progress-monitoring data are analyzed continually to determine appropriate next steps.

Step 5: Tier 2 Is the student responding to interventions?

Progress-monitoring data are an essential part of MTSS. Does the student need the same level of intervention for a longer period of time, or more intense interventions? Have Tier 2 interventions been sufficient, and thus are they no longer needed? Students aren't "stuck" in intervention indefinitely; their progress is closely monitored, and data are used to make decisions based on student needs.

The MTSS team responsible for decision making must include experts knowledgeable about multilingual learners and second language acquisition such as an ELD/ESL specialist, bilingual speech/language pathologist (SLP), or bilingual teacher/coordinator. Too often referral processes fail to take into consideration multilingual learners' cultural and linguistic backgrounds (Klinger & Eppolito, 2014).

Based on progress monitoring, the MTSS team may find that the student has responded well to interventions and no longer needs to receive additional services. In contrast, students like Felix (Case Study #1, below) may need to continue with another cycle of interventions that are adjusted based on his documented performance.

Step 6: Tier 2 Adjust interventions

A characteristic of Tier 2 is the individualized nature of the instruction (based on the student's specific need), the intensity of the interventions (student/teacher ratio, frequency and duration of sessions), and the frequency of assessments. When students require another cycle of interventions, adjustments may include increased language supports (e.g., more connections made to home language or use of visual aids).

Step 7: Analyze student progress

Some students are ready to exit Tier 2 services after two cycles of interventions, while others who make some progress may benefit from continued support for a specified period of time. However, other students have had systematic, effective, linguistically appropriate interventions, but do not make satisfactory progress. If a student continues to underperform with interventions, they would be referred for more intensive interventions, typically evaluation for special education services. The information in Figure 10.2 may be useful as the team considers next steps.

Once a team decides to pursue more intensive interventions, the question of language or disability often comes up. Research indicates that it is difficult for school personnel to distinguish between the challenges associated with acquiring a second language and those related to a language-based learning disability (Klinger & Eppolito, 2014) and the is-it-language-or-disability question is prominent in discussions about multilingual learners who underperform academically (For a full discussion of the issue, see Kangas, 2021.)

The distinctions can be fairly subtle, as you can see in Figure 10.2. The linguistic characteristics in the Language Differences column are to be expected and reflect the normal second language acquisition process. Behaviors in the Language Learning Disabilities column are "red flags" and merit further examination.

FIGURE 10.2 Distinguishing Language Differences from Language Learning Disabilities

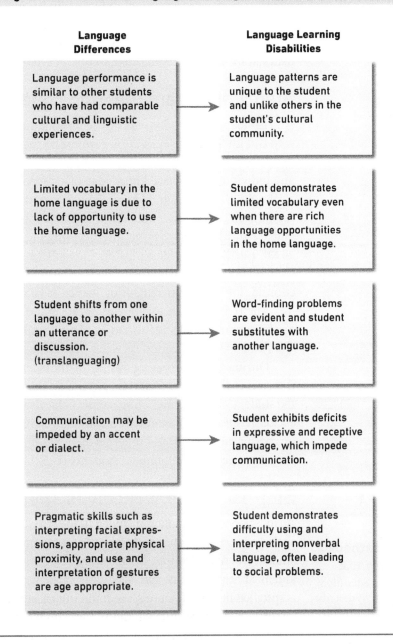

Language Differences → Language Learning Disabilities

Language Differences	Language Learning Disabilities
Language performance is similar to other students who have had comparable cultural and linguistic experiences.	Language patterns are unique to the student and unlike others in the student's cultural community.
Limited vocabulary in the home language is due to lack of opportunity to use the home language.	Student demonstrates limited vocabulary even when there are rich language opportunities in the home language.
Student shifts from one language to another within an utterance or discussion. (translanguaging)	Word-finding problems are evident and student substitutes with another language.
Communication may be impeded by an accent or dialect.	Student exhibits deficits in expressive and receptive language, which impede communication.
Pragmatic skills such as interpreting facial expressions, appropriate physical proximity, and use and interpretation of gestures are age appropriate.	Student demonstrates difficulty using and interpreting nonverbal language, often leading to social problems.

■ Tier 3: Evaluation for Special Education Services

Step 8: Evaluation

Once the team determines that evaluation for special education services is appropriate, the student's parents are contacted and written permission to conduct assessments must be given. All contact with parents, spoken or written, should be in their home language so that they are fully informed and give consent prior to an evaluation.

When an effective MTSS process is in place, documented failure to respond to intensive intervention may suffice for qualification for services. More commonly, after parent permission is secured, a battery of assessments is completed to determine eligibility for special education services. Some assessments would be administered in the student's home language, as needed, to obtain accurate, comprehensive assessment results.

Step 9: IEP team meeting conducted

An IEP team, by law, consists of the multilingual student's parents, an individual who can interpret the evaluation results and facilitate parents' participation in the discussion, an administrator, general education teacher, special education teacher, and individuals who have knowledge of or special expertise about the student such as a school psychologist and speech/language pathologist (SLP). Parent participation is essential since they offer valuable insight into their child's development and home life and are entitled to have input into deciding the language of instruction (Cioé-Peña, 2020). Further, IEP teams must include at least one professional with expertise in second language acquisition such as an ELD/ESL teacher or bilingual teacher/ coordinator (U.S. Department of Justice & U.S. Department of Education, 2015).

The IEP team takes into consideration the fact that multilingual students with disabilities are "dually identified" and are legally entitled to both English learner services and special education services, per IDEA and federal civil rights laws.

During the IEP meeting, results of the evaluation are presented, and the team determines the extent of services provided. The team documents on the IEP form the student's present level of academic achievement and functional performance and establishes goals that are measured annually. Goals address what the student will work on, both academically and in terms of functional development. IEPs must include the language needs of multilingual students (U.S. Department of Education, 2022).

Step 10: Student receives special education services

Pearson eTextbook

Video Example 10.2

Listen to special education teacher John Davis describe why he uses SIOP with his students with disabilities. https://www.youtube.com/ watch?v=aSCSS_R9o2I

As mentioned, information included in the IEP drives instruction and services. The special education teacher uses the IEP as a roadmap to guide the specific supports each student will receive as they work toward achieving their goals. It is highly recommended and most helpful for the special education teacher when the language of instruction is specified in the IEP, since some multilingual learners have the benefit of bilingual instruction. Also identified in the IEP are modifications and accommodations the student will receive, such as testing accommodations. Some students may need more time to complete testing or may have the testing directions read to them in their home language.

Daily ELD continues to be part of a dually identified student's instructional program. Multilingual learners are legally entitled to daily ELD teaching, regardless of disability status. Assignment to special education services must not result in the elimination of English learner (EL) services (Kangas, 2017).

■ Case Studies

To illustrate the MTSS process, we present case studies of three students who will navigate this system step-by-step. The process described here is only one of a number of ways schools use multitiered systems to support students.

Case Study #1: Felix.

Step 1: Is Felix reaching benchmarks?

Felix is a third grader whose teacher, Mr. William, is a veteran SIOP teacher. He consistently provides scaffolds for his students using features of SIOP. He collaborates with the ESL teacher who spends 30 minutes each day with Felix and a small group of other students working on listening and speaking skills to improve their English proficiency. Typically, they discuss the story being read in class, highlighting key vocabulary terms necessary for understanding the story, explicitly teaching sentence structure by analyzing sentences in the story, making connections between the story and the students' own experiences, and eliciting language from the students. Mr. William provides lots of opportunities for students to practice using English. Even though Felix can decode words fairly well, over time he remains significantly behind grade level and Mr. William turns to his colleagues for assistance.

Step 2: Site team plan for Felix.

The team suggests that Mr. William do a preview/review with each story being read. For example, he might use a graphic organizer to outline the way the story unfolds so Felix has a general understanding of what the story is about before it is read, translating terms as needed and pointing out cognates. After reading the story in class, Mr. William works with Felix to summarize the story, asking him to retell the story using clues from the graphic organizer and listed vocabulary words. After several weeks of this kind of effort and documented progress monitoring, Mr. William found no appreciable improvement in Felix's comprehension or recognition of words previously taught.

Step 3: Is Felix responding to the plan?

The grade-level team took into consideration Felix's language and cultural background. In Step 2, the team had suggested practices such as translating words as needed, making connections between Spanish and English by pointing out cognates, and linking elements of stories to Felix's own experiences to make stories more meaningful and relevant to him, but since Mr. William's additional efforts did not help Felix make much progress, it was time to seek assistance from the Tier 2 Intervention team.

Step 4: Targeted small-group interventions for Felix and monitoring his progress.

The intervention team collectively examined data and recommended a focus on intensive word recognition and comprehension strategies since Mr. William reported that Felix can haltingly decode words but doesn't comprehend them. Mr. William felt that Felix's progress should be monitored every four weeks to gauge learning, and the team agreed.

Step 5: Is Felix responding to the interventions?

The team found that Felix made slight progress but did not respond sufficiently to the intervention after eight weeks. Mr. William reported that Felix continued to fall behind his peers in literacy development.

Step 6: Adjusting the interventions for Felix.

Based on data and Mr. William's comments, the team decided to modify the interventions, continue for eight more weeks, and monitor progress every two weeks. Mr. William agreed that Felix might benefit from more time with the interventions.

Step 7: Analyzing Felix's progress.

At the end of the second cycle of interventions, Mr. William reported to the team and showed data that revealed Felix had not made the level of progress that would have been expected. The team initiated a referral for evaluation for special education services. Parent notification was sent to his family in Spanish, and they agreed to an evaluation for special education services.

Step 8: Evaluating Felix for special education services.

Felix took part in a battery of assessments. The SLP conducted an evaluation in Spanish and English to establish his level of proficiency in each language. Felix demonstrated auditory processing difficulties in both languages.

Step 9: Conducting Felix's IEP team meeting.

The IEP team met, including Felix's parents and an interpreter, and an instructional program was agreed upon. Since Felix qualified for speech/language services, the various IEP goals included one for accelerating oral language proficiency in English. In addition, it was noted that he would continue daily English language development with the ESL teacher.

Step 10: Felix received special education services.

Staff at Felix's school implemented SIOP teaching, including the special education teachers. Felix received high-quality SIOP instruction as he worked on his specific IEP goals. SIOP lesson planning ensured that instruction was comprehensible and meaningful for him and provided opportunities to practice and apply new knowledge, skills, and vocabulary. He also benefitted from speech therapy to improve his auditory processing and daily ELD class.

Case Study #2: Adriana

Step 1: Is Adriana reaching benchmarks?

As a recent immigrant from Brazil, Adriana is reluctant to participate in her fifth grade class. Her teacher, Ms. Beltran, has not had training in the SIOP Model but does her best to help Adriana understand lessons. She uses visuals and partners Adriana with another Portuguese-speaking student for support. Adriana receives about 20 minutes of ELD three times per week. The ELD teacher creates her own materials, many downloaded from the Internet. Since these materials are separate from the core curriculum, Adriana is being taught English skills that aren't tightly linked to what Ms. Beltran does in her classroom. Adriana's parents have expressed concern that she isn't happy in school and doesn't seem to be learning. Ms. Beltran suspects that she needs Tier 2 intervention to improve literacy in English.

Step 2: Site team plan for Adriana.

Ms. Beltran met with the site-based support team for suggestions. The bilingual teacher on the team assessed Adriana's reading skills in Portuguese and found that she has the foundational skills necessary to read in her home language. She suggested that Ms. Beltran use practices promoted in the SIOP Model such as providing opportunities for Adriana to practice hearing and using English in small-group settings where she feels comfortable participating in discussions about lessons. The team also suggested that ELD time increase to 30 minutes each day, with the teacher focusing on explicitly teaching English vocabulary and syntax from the core curriculum with opportunities for practice.

Step 3: Is Adriana responding to the plan?

With Ms. Beltran's additional focus on making core content comprehensible coupled with more intensive and intentional English language development in class and during ELD time, Adriana's English proficiency began to accelerate, and Adriana began participating more in class as her English language skills expanded. No further intervention was needed.

Case Study #3: Ahmed

Step 1: Is Ahmed reaching benchmarks?

Ahmed, age 14, is in grade 9 at a high school in the Midwest. He immigrated with his family to the United States when he was 13 years old. While growing up in Dubai, he had learned to speak some English at his school. When he arrived in the United States, he was placed in the ELD program, with an assessed level of English at Beginning, Level 2. During the past year, Ahmed's use of conversational English has blossomed. He speaks confidently with friends and his teachers, and by all accounts, he is an average teenage boy. However, his language development with academic English has stalled, and Ahmed is close to failing several of his classes. Those teachers report that he hasn't submitted assignments, all of which have involved reading in the content areas. In Algebra, Ahmed is doing quite well, and he readily admits that the class is his favorite. He receives 30 minutes of ELD, but the teacher uses the time as "tutoring" to help her multilingual learners complete assignments for classes or prepare for tests.

Step 2. Site team plan for Ahmed.

The site-based team referred Ahmed to the school counselor because of his grades and "attitude." With some prodding by the counselor, Ahmed finally admitted that he isn't able to read the assignments from his classes. He blames his inability to do the assignments on his lack of English and a job that he has every afternoon after school. The counselor reported his findings to the site-based team.

Step 3. Is Ahmed responding to the plan?

The team concluded that they needed to ascertain Ahmed's first language literacy skills. A bilingual paraprofessional determined that not only is Ahmed unable to read English other than very simple words, he is also unable to read Arabic. Ahmed is illiterate in both languages. His conversational ease with English has, to this point, covered up what might be a reading disability, but it also might be that Ahmed was never taught to read. The team also met with the ELD teacher and since Ahmed had strong listening and speaking ability, they recommended that the focus of instruction be on academic English, explicitly teaching some of the oral language skills required in his classes such as argumentation and summarization. Although it is important for multilingual learners to pass their classes, the most critical goal for long-term success is academic language proficiency. The ELD teacher also worked on foundational literacy skills to reinforce the instruction Ahmed received in Tier 2.

Step 4: Targeted small-group interventions for Ahmed and monitoring his progress.

Because of Ahmed's age and the fact that there are no Arabic-speaking teachers on staff, the team referred him to Tier 2 intervention to receive intensive work in the foundational literacy skills he needs in English: alphabetic principle, phonemic awareness, and phonics. Ahmed has the advantage of oral English proficiency so he can make sense of the words he learns to decode. He knows the meaning of many words he has begun to learn to "sound out" so his comprehension of text is relatively strong. In addition, his ELD teacher collaborated with his English language arts teacher to work on the same skills and vocabulary needed to do well in his general education class.

Step 5: Is Ahmed responding to the interventions?

Progress-monitoring data showed that Ahmed made steady progress in developing literacy skills, but eight weeks was not sufficient to exit intervention.

Step 6: Adjusting the interventions for Ahmed.

It was determined that Ahmed would benefit from another cycle of intervention to continue building academic vocabulary and comprehension of grade-level text.

Step 7: Analyzing Ahmed's progress

The team determined that Ahmed had developed sufficient foundational literacy skills to exit Tier 2 services. He became enthusiastic about his newly acquired skills. The team encouraged Ahmed to continue to build his skills by consistently reading for pleasure as well as doing repeated readings of assigned text for his classes to gain practice with more challenging text and increase his comprehension and fluency.

■ Final Points

As you reflect on this chapter on MTSS for multilingual learners, consider the following points:

- All multilingual learners receive SIOP instruction for core content plus daily English language development to enhance English proficiency. Oral language proficiency is particularly critical for academic achievement and is emphasized during content teaching as well as during ELD.
- Before a multilingual learner is assigned to interventions, a site-based team analyzes classroom instruction to make sure it is linguistically appropriate for that student. Suggestions are implemented to improve the student's performance.
- Interventions for literacy development are targeted to the specific components of reading that need focused teaching.
- Students aren't "stuck" in interventions indefinitely. They move in and out based on their instructional needs determined by frequent analysis of data.
- Those multilingual learners who require special education services have IEPs that include specific language goals, supports to which they are legally entitled. In addition, they continue to receive daily ELD.
- Effective instruction and interventions offer supports to struggling students. The goal is to provide them with the most appropriate and effective instructional program possible.

■ Discussion Questions

1. In reflecting on the content and language objectives at the beginning of the chapter, are you able to:
   a. Explain how instruction provided in Tier 1 differs from that in Tier 2?
   b. Describe in-class supports or modifications that content teachers can provide to multilingual learners?
   c. Identify a legal provision that ensures appropriate services for multilingual learners?
   d. Discuss with a group the first four steps in MTSS for multilingual learners who are underperforming academically?
   e. Write a lesson plan for a multilingual learner with the same characteristics as the student, Adriana (described in Case Study #2)?
2. Select an English learner in your class who is having difficulty with reading and/or content learning. Reread Steps 1-3 and their corresponding questions on page 261 (Figure 10.1). Begin with the first question: Is the student meeting benchmarks?
3. Based on your reading of this chapter, how can MTSS help ensure that multilingual learners are receiving an appropriate education and that proper services are offered as needed?

4. How would you respond to a teacher who says, "Well, if I follow the SIOP Model and make sure my multilingual learners are able to access content using these activities, techniques, and approaches, my on-level kids and English speakers will be bored." Do you agree with this statement? Why or why not?

Collaborative Practices for Implementing the SIOP Model

CONTENT OBJECTIVES

This chapter will help you to . . .

- Identify different approaches to take when beginning to implement the SIOP Model.
- Investigate ways educators can collaborate to understand and implement SIOP.
- Determine how to leverage content and language expertise to build collective efficacy in implementing the SIOP Model.

LANGUAGE OBJECTIVES

This chapter will help you to . . .

- List action steps for initiating collaborative partnerships.
- Describe how the SIOP Model components connect to each part of the collaboration and co-teaching cycle.
- Write lesson plans in partnership with colleagues using the SIOP Model.

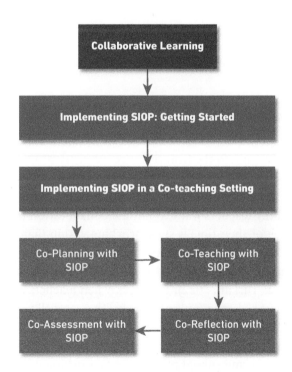

Introduction

The previous chapters of this book aim to support teachers in becoming familiar with the eight components and 30 features of the SIOP Model. The information, lessons, and examples affirm the value of teaching language in conjunction with content instruction. For decades, studies have shown that comprehensive use of the SIOP Model accelerates language development for multi-

lingual learners. Rather than isolating language to teach disconnected linguistic concepts and vocabulary, SIOP instruction uses content as a conduit for teaching meaningful language and academic communication in highly comprehensible ways.

The purpose of this chapter is to provide examples of how teachers work in collaboration to learn and implement the SIOP Model. Whether you are new to the SIOP Model or an experienced SIOP educator, we offer ways that you can join forces with other teachers to grow, advance, and refine your implementation of SIOP to better support the multilingual learners you teach. ■

■ Collaborative Learning

A notable shift in the field of language instruction is the building of momentum for collaboration as a means to achieving greater success for multilingual learners (Dove & Honigsfeld, 2019).

Many teachers want to initiate collaboration to feel more supported because so much of their time is spent working within their own classrooms. Insufficient communication and collaboration between colleagues can lead to language teachers feeling isolated and subject to power differentials in which they feel undervalued (Wong & Turkan, 2022). However, when teachers engage regularly with colleagues, they have access to multiple perspectives as well as opportunities for all to benefit from the collective knowledge among group members. Additionally, "Our collective motivation to create equitable opportunities for learning is driven by cooperative experiences and shared resources and workload" (Hollins-Alexander & Law, 2022). When teachers who are beginning to implement SIOP work with colleagues, they enhance their professional growth around serving multilingual learners because they can collectively navigate how to best incorporate the different features. Dove and Honigsfeld (2019) suggest the following collaborative practices for teachers to engage in as part of an ongoing commitment to supporting multilingual learners (pp. 80-81):

- joint planning
- curriculum mapping and alignment
- parallel teaching
- co-developing instructional materials
- collaborative assessment of student work

> **"**
>
> Our students don't have the luxury of viewing language and content separately. And yet, our systems often create unnecessary barriers that result in an exclusive, incoherent experience for multilingual students. Collaboration between teachers and specialists leads to identifying language development opportunities in an inclusive way, ensuring that our students have the language they need for success in school.
>
> Tim Blackburn, Title III Administrator, Oregon
>
> **"**

When the SIOP Model serves as a foundation for these collaborative endeavors, the impact of collaboration extends to students as well. Hattie's (2008) research, for example, affirms that the collective efficacy achieved through collaboration positively and strongly correlates with student achievement.

Honigsfeld and Dove (2019) offer a compelling list of reasons why students benefit when teachers collaborate including:

- more differentiated instruction due to collaborative teacher planning,
- more varied instructional materials and resources,
- more carefully crafted lessons,
- more authentic and meaningful assessments that are adapted to the needs of students who are struggling or at risk, and
- more appropriate instructional adaptations for students who are struggling or at risk.

Some teachers who want to bring SIOP to their school or district, initiate SIOP implementation by inviting a colleague, or several colleagues, to join them in their learning. An invitation to collaborate is a promising way to learn and reflect together. Conducting a book study with this text is one way to engage with others throughout the process of implementing the components when the model is new. Reading chapter by chapter and subsequently implementing components and features in the order they are laid out is one possible approach teams can take. Another option is to read the chapters out of order to focus first on components that might be familiar to teachers such as Comprehensible Input or Building Background, and then move on to less-familiar practices such as writing language objectives in the Lesson Preparation component.

Establishing a culture of collaboration helps maintain the momentum of continually adding more components and features because colleagues can support and encourage each other. Teachers provide feedback to one another when creating content and language objectives, collaboratively planning lessons, and sharing lesson ideas and outcomes in order to learn from each other.

Teachers who are new to the SIOP Model, but entering a context where implementation is already underway or already an established part of the sitewide instruction, can seek out mentorship from SIOP-trained colleagues who have more experience. SIOP mentor teachers can offer support and insight to other educators at the beginning stages of implementation through sharing their own personal anecdotes about using the SIOP Model, including tips and ideas as well as insights they've gained over time. When possible, teachers observe a colleague who is fully implementing the SIOP components, or a recording of one of their lessons, to see the features in action. Pairing an observation with a SIOP teacher's written lesson plan that identifies how the features will be incorporated into the lesson can help solidify understanding of how lessons incorporate all of the components and features.

Alternatively, if there isn't an expert SIOP teacher down the hall, or within their building, teachers can look outside their personal context to find someone with the competencies they seek. Utilizing social media and technology is a great way to connect to a professional learning network (PLN) in order to communicate, collaborate, and reflect with a wider net of colleagues (Toppel, Huynh, & Salva, 2021). Additionally, the Savvas Learning Company (www.savvas.com) offers a variety of ways to engage in professional learning about the SIOP Model, including instructional videos, blog posts, and virtual institutes.

Implementing SIOP: Getting Started

When beginning to implement the SIOP Model, teachers often wonder where to start. There are many different ways to approach implementing SIOP, and the choices teachers make will likely differ depending on their experience with teaching multilingual learners, knowledge of linguistic and learning needs of multilingual learners, as well as their teaching context (e.g., years of teaching experience, instructional role, extent of SIOP implementation schoolwide). It is not necessary, or recommended, to implement the entire model all at once when beginning. In fact, our recommendation is to go slowly and methodically so teachers focus on refining their practices to make instruction more comprehensible, purposeful, and relevant to their students. Implementing all of the features consistently does yield demonstrated results for multilingual learners; however, attempting too much at once can feel daunting and may inhibit success for both teachers and students.

Teachers can build up to full implementation by starting with one component and adding additional components one by one, at a rate that feels reasonable. With sufficient support in place (e.g., coaching, planning time, ongoing professional learning), some teachers implement one new component each month throughout a school year. Other teachers stagger the introduction of each new component further by implementing one new component each academic quarter throughout a school year. The latter pace introduces and provides substantial practice with four components during the first year of implementation and the remaining four components the second year of implementation. Starting slowly provides teachers opportunities to gain a thorough understanding of each component and the features that support it.

The 30 features are numbered; however, the numbers do not dictate a sequential order for implementation. As mentioned previously, some teachers begin with Building Background or Comprehensible Input and make great strides in sheltering instruction for the benefit of multilingual learners before adding additional components. Even though there is flexibility around what component to start with, many SIOP educators do recommend Lesson Preparation (Chapter 2), or more specifically writing content and language objectives, as a good place to begin when implementing the SIOP Model.

Crafting clear content and language objectives for lessons is a building block for successful implementation of other components and features, so it makes sense that learning how to write both types of objectives is a meaningful initial step. Clear objectives create a very specific focus for lesson planning, and consequently help teachers stay focused when deciding how best to infuse other features as they incorporate additional components into lessons. For example, a well written language objective will support teachers in clarifying what language is expected and should be practiced during the part of the lesson when students interact. If a teacher instead tries to set up opportunities for students to interact, without the foundation of clear and explicit lesson objectives, student interactions may not result in the practicing of particular linguistic forms, vocabulary, or academic language.

We recommend taking the time to explore and experiment to understand the purpose and value of the different options within a component or feature before moving to another. For example, Feature 4, Supplementary Materials, calls for a variety of resources that help to support student understanding of content concepts. While it may be quick and easy to utilize more pictures or realia in lessons, it takes a greater investment of teacher time to find, create, and introduce other kinds of supplementary materials such as related literature that is culturally responsive or adapted texts that are differentiated for levels of language proficiency. Some types of supplementary materials, such as math manipulatives for younger students or lab equipment for older students, may require additional instruction around expectations for use. Investing time to thoroughly understand each feature and explore different possibilities for implementation provides teachers opportunities to fine tune their ability to use tools for supporting multilingual learners strategically and intentionally.

> "
> Start slowly and implement one component at a time. Even within the components, set realistic small goals on a weekly basis. If possible, work with a colleague who teaches in a different classroom; try out the same strategies so that you can debrief your experiences and assist each other with successful implementation.
> Helene Becker, retired EL Director, Connecticut
> "

With gradual implementation, teachers can thoughtfully consider how the SIOP features are impacting students and how they can further adjust instruction so their students achieve even greater levels of success. This incremental process will help to promote quality instruction for multilingual learners while also providing teachers professional learning opportunities as they reflect on how their instructional choices affect student outcomes. Applying the SIOP Model one component at a time can be an iterative process of trying something new, reflecting and refining, then adding slowly to eventually achieve full implementation.

Another approach to implementing the SIOP Model is to apply the components and features to one content area, time of day, or period at a time. Elementary teachers might choose one subject, such as science or social studies, to focus on, then reflect on how to best apply the features to an upcoming unit of study. Secondary teachers might take a similar approach with a course they teach within their content area. Teachers can identify content standards, key content concepts, and vocabulary, then layer in SIOP components as they think through how to (a) make the content comprehensible, (b) ensure students have opportunities to practice and apply the new content, (c) organize tasks so students will interact with one another, and so forth.

Another beneficial way to apply the SIOP Model to a unit of study is to start by determining which language standards best align with the content standards, writing content and language objectives for the unit, then breaking the overarching goals down into manageable chunks for individual lessons. Once the long-term unit planning is organized, teachers can apply additional SIOP features to individual lessons.

If teachers choose to begin with a single content area, they should gradually add additional subjects or courses until their entire instructional day has been aligned with, and enhanced by, the SIOP components and features. SIOP teachers report that once they learn lesson planning with the model for one subject area, it is relatively easy to apply the process to other subjects.

Implementing SIOP in a Co-Teaching Setting

> **"**
> The power of effective co-teaching is limitless. When thinking about 8 components and 30 features feels overwhelming, co-teaching gives teachers the opportunity to intentionally share the work. While teachers benefit in sharing the workload in this day and age, students benefit too. They intentionally receive both language and content instruction by two experts instead of one. Effective instruction never stops when co-teachers are invested in their practice. If a co-teacher is out, no substitute is needed because the effective co-planning that comes with co-teaching can ensure the highest quality of instruction continues for both language and content for all students.
>
> Carlota Holder, Director of academic language, Indiana
> **"**

In the previous section we provided suggestions for general education teachers, language specialists, special education teachers, and co-teaching teams to get started with SIOP implementation. Some of the suggestions included ways to engage in learning alongside others. Collaboration, as mentioned previously, benefits teachers who often feel isolated and offers many advantages including opportunities to share strengths, collectively create new ideas, provide and receive feedback, and reflect on instruction (Cohan, Honigsfeld, & Dove, 2019). Collaborative practices are multidimensional and can fall on a continuum ranging from informal, unstructured, and infrequent connections between colleagues to formal, structured, and sustained professional interactions in the context of ongoing partnerships.

Co-teaching is an example of a more inclusive instructional model for serving multilingual learners that relies on collaborative practice. Co-teaching is commonly defined as a general education teacher collaborating with a specialist to deliver effective instruction to identified students. As an instructional model, it was originally designed for working with students in special education (Cook & Friend, 1995; Pappamihiel, 2012), but it has more recently been applied to multilingual learners (Dove & Honigsfeld, 2017).

Dove and Honigsfeld (2019) describe co-teaching as equal instructional partners who "combine their expertise and talents to make instruction comprehensible" (p. 81). They credit the success of co-teaching to "ongoing meaningful professional dialogue among teachers in well-established collaborative teams" (Dove & Honigsfeld, 2017, p.1). Friend (2008) explains co-teaching as a learning environment in which two or more certified professionals share the responsibility of lesson planning, delivery of instruction, and progress monitoring, while making instructional decisions as a team. Co-teaching embodies the shared sense of community and responsibility for multilingual learners and affirms the necessity of collaboration between content teachers and language teachers to meet students' linguistic needs in all aspects of their schooling (TESOL, 2018). Co-teaching partnerships exemplify formal, structured, and sustained professional interactions that lead to increased efficacy in serving multilingual learners.

Dove and Honigsfeld (2017) offer a framework that is specifically for multilingual learners and is compatible with the SIOP Model because of the fundamental shared goals, vision, and purpose around the integration of content and language instruction. The collaborative instructional cycle includes the following:

- co-planning
- co-teaching
- co-reflection
- co-assessment

FIGURE 11.1 Collaborative Instructional Cycle with SIOP Components

SIOP Components	Co-Planning	Co-Teaching	Co-Assessing	Co-Reflecting
	Lesson Preparation	Lesson Preparation	Review & Assessment	Lesson Delivery
	Building Background	Building Background		Review & Assessment
	Comprehensible Input	Comprehensible Input		
	Strategies	Strategies		
	Interaction	Interaction		
	Practice & Application	Practice & Application		
	Lesson Delivery	Lesson Delivery		
	Review & Assessment	Review & Assessment		

Together, these "maximize teacher effectiveness" (Dove & Honigsfeld, 2017, p. 9) and positively support multilingual learners with language acquisition, literacy learning and content attainment. Despite the growing prominence and interest in co-teaching, establishing and maintaining all of the steps in the collaborative instructional cycle is not an easy feat; however, "the 8 components and 30 features of the SIOP Model serve as the perfect blueprint for co-creating lessons" (Holder, Bell, & Toppel, 2019).

For teachers who are establishing co-teaching partnerships, utilizing the SIOP Model as a framework to guide the collaborative instructional cycle ensures that teams are working from a common model to better support the needs of students (Dove & Honigsfeld, 2017; Pratt, et al., 2017; Yoon, 2021). To illustrate how the components and features of SIOP can support successful co-teaching partnerships, we will discuss which SIOP components and features fit within each of the four parts of Dove and Honigsfeld's collaborative instructional cycle (see Figure 11.1).

■ Co-Planning with SIOP

The first part of Dove and Honigsfeld's collaborative instructional cycle is collaborative planning, also referred to as *co-planning*. Thoughtful lesson planning is essential for quality lessons, particularly lessons that support the varying language strengths and needs of multilingual learners. It stands to reason that collaborative planning, drawing on different talents, skill sets, and strengths of team members, results in better outcomes for multilingual learners. For SIOP co-planning, the team would have a content teacher (i.e., a grade-level classroom teacher or secondary subject area teacher) and a language teacher (i.e., ELD specialist). In order to have sufficient time for this collaboration to happen, we highly recommend that schools provide designated, protected co-planning time for co-teachers. The following discussion shows some ways the co-teaching partnership can lead to effective SIOP implementation.

Let's begin with the Lesson Preparation component. Content teachers and ELD teachers leverage the skills they bring to the team by contributing to co-planned

> Co-teaching is better for the kids. I have always loved having two adults in the room, but co-teaching really elevates every aspect of my teaching. It begins with explicit and thoughtful planning and leads to quality teaching where we are both working on getting every student to speak as much as we can. During the lesson we are building on each other's cues to the students. After, we are able to debrief and tweak things moving forward. Effective communication throughout each step of the process makes it run smoothly.
>
> Molly Haag, first grade teacher, Oregon

lessons. As discussed in Chapter 2, Lesson Preparation emphasizes the use of content and language objectives to identify what students need to learn about the content topic and what students need to learn about English to demonstrate knowledge and perform academic tasks connected to the content. Having input from both a content teacher and a language teacher in the planning process leads to better content objectives and language objectives in co-taught lessons.

The content teacher has in-depth knowledge of the content standards, will be able to identify appropriate content concepts in order to create content objectives, and has an understanding of how best to sequence the content targets and accompanying information. Meanwhile, the ELD specialist brings an understanding of the language demands associated with the target content including the components of language that will be necessary to model and teach along with the content instruction as well as the necessary language forms and functions to consider when writing language objectives. ELD specialists can also apply knowledge of language development to adapt materials and scaffolds to reach the needs of students at different levels of language proficiency. Co-teachers blend their ideas to plan for many of the remaining elements that need attention during lesson preparation such as using effective visuals, identifying supplementary materials that will support students in understanding content concepts, creating meaningful activities, and differentiating based on student needs.

Because teachers need to think through all of the SIOP Model components and features while planning for lessons, using a SIOP lesson plan template is a helpful tool during co-planning conversations. A lesson plan template that addresses each SIOP component provides teachers with a guide for what to discuss and how each component will be reflected in the lessons. Teachers can also identify specific elements of the lesson plan that can be completed prior to meeting, because, "if both content and language teachers engage in preplanning (i.e., preparation in advance of the co-planning meeting), the team will be better prepared to make the most of collaboration time" (Toppel, 2022). Utilizing a SIOP lesson plan helps co-teachers determine how they can each contribute to lesson planning and assists them in "dividing and conquering" some of the post-planning responsibilities. Post-planning refers to the independent completion of lesson planning tasks (e.g., scaffolding activities, differentiating materials, finding alternative resources), which teachers do after they have completed collaborative planning together (Dove & Honigsfeld, 2017). The completed SIOP lesson plan is also a resource to revisit during co-reflection.

Linking concepts to students' backgrounds and creating links between past learning and new learning are two features of the Building Background component discussed in Chapter 3. Hammond (2014) affirms the importance of supporting students to connect new content to what they already know and believes that teachers must intentionally plan how to cue the brain to pay attention. While co-planning, teams also join forces to support students in making connections to what is familiar to "ignite" (Hammond) the brain's readiness for new learning. The content teacher's knowledge of students' past learning, whether it was in the same class, in prerequisite courses, or in previous school years, helps teams consider how to connect what students know to new learning. The ELD specialist may have more in-depth knowledge of students' cultures, home languages, or lived experiences based on prolonged relationships with students across multiple school years. By taking students' funds of knowledge into consideration, teams can write lessons that connect the new content

Pearson eTextbook

Video Example 11.1

Watch this video to see co-teachers discussing features connected to Building Background during their co-planning session. Notice how they work together to identify key vocabulary and create a plan to link their lesson on place value to students' experiences helping at home.

to students' backgrounds and make instruction relevant for multilingual learners (Hammond, 2014; Moll, Amanti, Neff, & Gonzalez, 1992).

The third Building Background feature is developing key vocabulary. Content teachers and ELD specialists plan vocabulary instruction together. Content teachers bring knowledge of content vocabulary that is essential for understanding the target topic or concepts. ELD specialists contribute by adding general academic terms and by planning to teach word parts, such as prefixes and suffixes, that will help students develop capacity to use and comprehend variations of the vocabulary words in speaking and writing (Lems, Miller, & Soro, 2017).

During the co-planning process, content and language teachers also consider the features of Comprehensible Input (Chapter 4), Strategies (Chapter 5), Interaction (Chapter 6), Practice and Application (Chapter 7), and Lesson Delivery (Chapter 8) to ensure lesson plans sufficiently attend to the needs of multilingual learners. For these components, there are features that will not apply until the lessons are taught (e.g., Feature 10: Appropriate Speech; Feature 18: Sufficient Wait Time; and Feature 26: Pace Lesson Appropriately); however, they incorporate many features that need to be discussed during co-planning, in order to agree how teachers will navigate them together when they co-teach. When addressing these components during co-planning, teams reciprocally and collectively enhance lesson plans through discussion and active engagement in working together to plan for instruction. Having multiple perspectives and different kinds of teaching experience among teams is an asset that benefits co-planning.

Content teachers identify key concepts and how big ideas can be broken down into a meaningful sequence or smaller chunks. ELD specialists are well suited to sharing a variety of techniques to make content concepts clear for multilingual learners, such as specific paralinguistic supports like gestures or body language, visuals, relatable analogies, and the like.

To address the Strategies component, teams plan for procedural and instructional scaffolds as well as questions or tasks that will promote higher-order thinking. Together, co-teachers decide on other elements that need to be planned or created in advance such as a completed model of a task, an appropriate graphic organizer, or multimedia to supplement teacher instruction. It is important to remember that co-planning time is often limited. Frequently, teachers make decisions about what is needed for the lesson together and then independently prepare materials or complete tasks on their own during individual post-planning.

Based on experience delivering the target lesson material, content teachers identify appropriate points in the lesson when student interactions can take place. ELD specialists share ideas to make sure students at lower proficiency levels can meaningfully interact with peers, with suggestions for visuals or verbal scaffolds that would be helpful. Together, teachers choose which of the co-teaching models will work best during the lesson, a choice that goes hand in hand with decisions about grouping configurations. It is a good idea to plan grouping configurations ahead of time because there are many factors to consider (see Chapter 6 for details).

While co-planning, teams will want to discuss what meaningful activities students will engage in, so they have a chance to practice what they've learned and apply the material in new ways. Discussions around practice and application of new content are essential to ensure that content and language are integral to student activities. Content teachers identify activities that provide good opportunities to practice and apply content knowledge. ELD specialists suggest additional lesson ideas and enhancements to activities that integrate all of the language domains. Making decisions around lesson activities can also influence decisions around grouping configurations and opportunities for students to interact.

Even though Lesson Delivery seems best aligned with the co-teaching part of the collaborative instructional cycle, co-teachers still consider the features associated with Lesson Delivery during co-planning in order to be sufficiently prepared to carry them out during their co-taught lesson. To ensure that both the content and language objectives are supported, teachers plan for times during the lesson when they will provide explicit instruction connected to the content and language objectives they have written. They also use their shared knowledge of the individual students as well as the whole-class dynamic to identify how to maintain student engagement so that when they are delivering the lesson, students are engaged for 90% to 100% of the time. The plan for student engagement connects to the specific activities the teachers will use to provide opportunities for practice and application and how they will have students interact. When planning lessons, co-teachers also attend to the needs of students when making decisions about pacing both within single lessons and also across multiple lessons or instructional units. In the planning stages, attending to pacing could mean mapping out what the teachers hope to accomplish each day or across the week as well as deciding how long an activity should take or how to divide up their time teaching the whole class.

Finally, co-teachers consider Review & Assessment practices that help them identify and align instructional expectations as well as criteria for success for both content and language objectives. The ELD specialist offers input on what language output can be expected for students at each language level and determines ways to differentiate assessments by language proficiency. It is imperative that co-teaching partners engage in "collaborative conversations that create a common frame of reference" (Dove & Honigsfeld, 2017, p. 214) for assessing multilingual learners. Co-teaching partners can also plan how to incorporate assessment as, for, and of learning (Gottlieb, 2016) throughout larger instructional timelines or units. For multilingual learners at varying levels of proficiency in English, alternative assessments offer a range of opportunities for students to show what they know, which can include the use of their home language to demonstrate understanding of the content.

■ Sample Lesson

As we continue discussing how the SIOP Model can be used as a blueprint for the collaborative instructional cycle, we will tie in descriptions of how Ms. Solares, a fourth grade teacher, and Mr. Wright, an ELD specialist, collaboratively planned and co-taught a series of lessons about volcanoes for Ms. Solares' class (See Figure 11.2 for the SIOP Model components they address during co-planning). Both Ms. Solares and Mr. Wright received professional development focused on the SIOP Model and they use a SIOP lesson plan template for their weekly co-planning sessions. The lessons described are the first lessons they co-planned and taught together as part of a larger unit on natural disasters. Ms. Solares has taught this unit for several years, but it will be her first time collaborating to teach the unit as a team. Ms. Solares' class of 27 students include seven multilingual students at different levels of proficiency in English.

FIGURE 11.2 Collaborative Instructional Cycle: Co-Planning with SIOP Components

SIOP Components	Co-Planning	Co-Teaching	Co-Assessing	Co-Reflecting
	Lesson Preparation	Lesson Preparation	Review & Assessment	Lesson Delivery
	Building Background	Building Background		Review & Assessment
	Comprehensible Input	Comprehensible Input		
	Strategies	Strategies		
	Interaction	Interaction		
	Practice & Application	Practice & Application		
	Lesson Delivery	Lesson Delivery		
	Review & Assessment	Review & Assessment		

Mr. Wright and Ms. Solares' Pre-Planning

Prior to their weekly co-planning session, Ms. Solares sent Mr. Wright a link to their shared Week at a Glance template (Artifact 11.1). She had already added the science standard they would focus on and content objectives for the lesson series. Ms. Solares also listed 12 key vocabulary words for the unit and drafted some language objectives for the lessons. When Mr. Wright received the SIOP lesson template, he added the language functions (express cause and effect, persuade) as well as the language forms needed to complete the language objectives (see bold words in the Week at a Glance plan). Mr. Wright also filled in the language standards connected to their lessons.

ARTIFACT 11.1 Week at a Glance Planning Document

Volcanoes

	Lesson 1	Lesson 2	Lesson 3	Lesson 4	Lesson 5
Content Standard	4-ESS3-2 Earth and Human Activity: Generate and compare multiple solutions to reduce the impacts of natural Earth processes on humans.				
ELP Standards	ELP 10: make accurate use of standard English to communicate in grade appropriate speech and writing. ELP 4: construct grade appropriate oral and written claims and support them with reasoning and evidence.				
Content Objective	Identify how and why volcanoes erupt	Identify how and why volcanoes erupt	Investigate how volcanic eruptions positively and negatively affect humans	Use evidence about the impacts of volcanic eruptions to evaluate if volcanoes are helpful or harmful	Create a plan with solutions to reduce the negative impacts volcanic eruptions have on humans
Language Objective	Draw/annotate illustrations showing what factors lead to eruption using key vocabulary words	Explain the cause and effect relationships of volcanic eruptions using **compound or complex sentences**	Describe orally the positive and negative effects volcanoes have on humans using **key vocabulary and compound or complex sentences**	Make a written claim that volcanoes are helpful or harmful using **key vocabulary and transition words**	Orally share solutions to reduce the negative impacts volcanoes have on humans using **command verbs and transition words**
Key Vocabulary	lava, magma, ash, vent, pressure, chamber, erupt/eruption			destroy/destruction, catastrophic, evacuate	
Language Form	Specific Nouns / Verbs	Sentence Complexity	Specific Nouns / Sentence Complexity	Specific Nouns / Transition Words	Command Verbs, Transition Words
Language Function	Cause & Effect			Persuade	

ARTIFACT 11.2   Completed Week at Glance Planning Document

	Lesson 1	Lesson 2	Lesson 3	Lesson 4	Lesson 5
Content Standard	4-ESS3-2 Earth and Human Activity: Generate and compare multiple solutions to reduce the impacts of natural Earth processes on humans.				
ELP Standards	ELP 10: make accurate use of standard English to communicate in grade appropriate speech and writing. ELP 4: construct grade appropriate oral and written claims and support them with reasoning and evidence.				
Content Objective	Identify how and why volcanoes erupt	Identify how and why volcanoes erupt	Investigate how volcanic eruptions positively and negatively affect humans	Use evidence about the impacts of volcanic eruptions to evaluate if volcanoes are helpful or harmful	Create a plan with solutions to reduce the negative impacts volcanic eruptions have on humans
Language Objective	Draw/annotate illustrations showing what factors lead to eruption using **key vocabulary words**	Explain destructive effects of volcanic eruptions using **compound or complex sentences**	Describe orally the positive and negative effects volcanoes have on humans using **key vocabulary and compound or complex sentences**	Make a written claim that volcanoes are helpful or harmful using **key vocabulary and transition words**	Orally share solutions to reduce the negative impacts volcanoes have on humans using **command verbs and transition words**
Key Vocabulary	**lava, magma, ash, vent, pressure, chamber, erupt/eruption, destroy/destructive, catastrophic, evacuate**				
Language Form	Specific Nouns / Verbs	Sentence Complexity	Specific Nouns / Sentence Complexity	Specific Nouns / Transition Words	Command Verbs, Transition Words
Language Function	Cause & Effect			Persuade	
Supplementary Materials	Differentiated Text Set	Leveled Article- A huge volcano erupted in Guatemala. Why was it so destructive?	Article: Volcanic Eruptions: Positive and Negative Effects	Volcanoes: Helpful or Harmful?	HOW TO STAY SAFE WHEN A VOLCANO THREATENS

Mr. Wright and Ms. Solares' Co-Planning

When they met for their weekly session, Ms. Solares and Mr. Wright reviewed the information they had already added to the shared Week at a Glance plan. They used their SIOP lesson plan template to guide them through the remaining SIOP components and details they needed to discuss. Artifact 11.2 shows the completed Week at a Glance plan. Ms. Solares suggested using a repeated structure to review each day before adding new information in the lessons. They selected Play It Again (Vogt & Echevarría, 2022) and planned to create a visual sequence on the classroom wall with an image or archive from each lesson to support students in recalling the previous day's content. They engaged in conversation about the activities the students would do to practice and apply new learning, how students would be grouped for each activity, and when in the lessons the students would have opportunities to interact in order to share their thinking. This helped them think about which co-teaching model(s) would be a good fit for the lesson because students would be working in the whole group, with partners, in small groups, and independently throughout the week and the teachers needed to plan their roles accordingly.

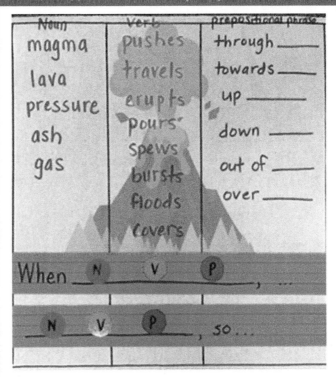

Next, Mr. Wright suggested some verbal scaffolds they could use, including sentence starters for partner talk, a sentence pattern chart to support students in using key vocabulary (see Artifact 11.3), some cause and effect sentence frames, and a table tent listing discourse moves with visuals that students could use when they shared their learning in small groups. He also suggested explicitly addressing how the vocabulary words *destroy* and *erupt* have variations using the suffix *-tion*. Ms. Solares had many visuals showing key vocabulary terms, and Mr. Wright offered to enhance the visuals to include word variations.

When Mr. Wright and Ms. Solares discussed their plans for assessment, they tried to find ways to incorporate student voice and choice. Rather than giving a multiple-choice test on vocabulary or volcano facts, they wanted to include more engaging ways for students to show what they know. They decided to offer different choices for the culminating activity, so students could decide how they wanted to demonstrate their understanding. They created three different options that would allow students at different language levels to be successful, and they also took into consideration different modalities that would be engaging for their students (i.e., drawing, technology, informational video).

To finish up their co-planning time, Ms. Solares and Mr. Wright reviewed the lesson plans and double checked to make sure students had opportunities to read, write, listen, and speak each day. They made a quick list of the materials needed for the lessons, including materials needed to scaffold for different levels of language proficiency. They took a few minutes to decide which teacher would be in charge of getting the different items and each teacher left the meeting with a list of their post-planning responsibilities and tasks.

Co-Teaching with SIOP

The second part of the collaborative instructional cycle is collaborative instructional delivery, or co-teaching. SIOP co-teachers utilize the Lesson Delivery features to monitor how successfully the lesson helps students meet the objectives. Co-teachers work together to make sure the instruction stays focused on the intended lesson objectives, the students are engaged in the instruction, and the pacing of the lessons allows progression through the entire lesson sequence that teachers co-planned. As mentioned in Chapter 8, the effectiveness of lesson delivery (and co-teaching) traces back to the lesson preparation and co-planning teachers did previously. In addition to Lesson Delivery, co-teachers rely on other SIOP features to support student learning during instruction.

At the beginning of a co-taught lesson, teachers share the content and language objectives they planned. Teams may decide to have the content teacher read the content objectives and the ELD specialist share the language objectives, or they might find a different way to jointly participate. Some teachers like to annotate content and language objectives by underlining or circling academic vocabulary included in the objectives and writing more familiar terms to help students understand the lesson targets. In this case, one teacher might take the lead in reading the objectives with students while the other teacher annotates and then explains. To demonstrate balance in the co-teaching partnership, teachers may alternate roles or switch roles at the end of the lesson when content and language objectives are revisited during lesson review.

During co-planning, teams took time to discuss how to connect new content to past learning and students' experience. During co-teaching, teams introduce the lesson by sharing examples or references to situate students and prepare them to learn the new content. Depending on need, it might involve a quick reminder of previous learning or a simple statement of how the content connects to students. Alternatively, teachers might invest a longer amount of time to tell a story or review previous material to lay the foundation for the new content. Co-teachers teach the agreed upon vocabulary words using the visuals, affixes, and other supplementary materials they planned for and prepared prior to the lesson. They also monitor their speech and provide clear directions during co-teaching in addition to other techniques to ensure that students understand the information being shared.

A significant advantage of having co-teachers is that they can take on different roles during instruction. When one teacher is talking, the other teacher might scan the room to monitor student understanding. If students seem confused or disengaged, the second teacher might repeat, rephrase, or signal for a slower rate of speech. The language teacher might filter the instruction through the lens of a student at emerging or beginning proficiency and use supplementary materials such as visuals or gestures to help make content comprehensible as the content teacher is explaining. These teaching techniques are also used when academic tasks are being explained. While one teacher verbally explains the tasks, the other teacher might write and/or draw the steps on the board or display visuals to help students understand expectations. Another useful way for the language teacher to support instruction is by anticipating points of confusion and asking clarifying questions about the content being taught.

Co-teachers also support one another by monitoring the balance between when the teacher talks and opportunities for students to talk. It can be a challenge for teachers to self-monitor how long they have been talking, so having a co-teacher keep track can be extremely helpful. One teacher can also take on the responsibility of monitoring wait time so students can think about how they will respond prior to interacting with peers or sharing their ideas to the group. For portions of the lesson where students will interact with one another, co-teachers model academic conversations by engaging in dialogue with each other about the content to demonstrate what language output will be expected of students. This includes modeling how to use vocabulary in context or academic moves like elaborating, asking for clarification, supporting ideas with examples, building on a partner's idea, paraphrasing what someone else said, and synthesizing conversation points (Short & Echevarria, 2016; Zwiers & Hammerla, 2017).

Co-teaching partnerships will have different dynamics and levels of active collaboration during instruction, but over time co-teachers develop a rhythm and greater ability to seamlessly support students and one another as they share responsibilities during instruction. An essential mindset for successful co-teaching partnerships is the recognition of partners as equals as opposed to one being the teacher and the other being a helper or assistant in the classroom. There can be an ebb and flow of classroom responsibilities performed by each co-teacher during a co-taught lesson. The bottom line is that the teachers are respected as equals by one another and the students. To illustrate how two teachers navigate joint instruction during a lesson, we will focus on Lesson 4 co-taught by Mr. Wright and Ms. Solares. Their completed SIOP lesson plan is shown in Artifact 11.4 (See Figure 11.3 for the SIOP Model components they address during their co-taught lessons).

Pearson eTextbook

Video Example 11.2

Watch this video to see co-teachers Molly Haag and Dr. Katie Toppel review vocabulary words with first grade multilingual learners and their peers. Notice how they share responsibility for supporting students with hand signals, examples, and opportunities to respond. https://youtu.be/SyTrfaTvIgg

---

FIGURE 11.3   **Collaborative Instructional Cycle: Co-Teaching with SIOP Components**

	Co-Planning	Co-Teaching	Co-Assessing	Co-Reflecting
SIOP Components	Lesson Preparation	Lesson Preparation	Review & Assessment	Lesson Delivery
	Building Background	Building Background		Review & Assessment
	Comprehensible Input	Comprehensible Input		
	Strategies	Strategies		
	Interaction	Interaction		
	Practice & Application	Practice & Application		
	Lesson Delivery	Lesson Delivery		
	Review & Assessment	Review & Assessment		

ARTIFACT 11.4   Completed SIOP Lesson Plan

Grade/Subject: Grade 4 Science

Standard(s):
- 4-ESS3-2 Earth and Human Activity: Generate and compare multiple solutions to reduce the impacts of natural Earth processes on humans.

ELP Standards:
- ELP 10: make accurate use of standard English to communicate in grade appropriate speech and writing.

Content Objective(s):
- Students will be able to use evidence about the impacts of volcanic eruptions to evaluate if volcanoes are helpful or harmful

Language Objective(s):
- Students will be able to make a written claim that volcanoes are helpful or harmful using **key vocabulary and transition words**

Key Vocabulary	Supplementary Materials
Essential Vocabulary Concepts: **erupt/eruption, destroy/destruction, catastrophic, evacuate** Key Vocabulary: **lava, magma, ash, vent, pressure, chamber**	• Key Images from previous lessons • Anchor chart from previous lesson (helpful/harmful) • Differentiated graphic organizers to support writing

Included in this lesson...

Lesson Preparation	Scaffolding	Group Options
✓Adaptation of content	✓ Modeling	✓Whole class
___Links to background	✓ Guided practice	___ Small groups
✓ Links to past learning	✓Independent practice	✓ Partners
___Learning strategies incorporated	✓ Comprehensible input	✓ Independent

Integration of Language Domains	Application	Assessment
✓Reading	___ Hands-on	✓ Individual
✓Writing	✓ Meaningful	___ Group
✓Speaking	✓ Linked to objectives	✓ Written
✓Listening	✓ Promotes engagement	✓ Oral

Building Background
Connection to past learning:
Play It Again-Review using images/archives from each previous 3 lessons.
On {day}, we focused on _____.
Something I learned was _____.

Lesson Sequence:

1. Content/language objectives
2. Play It Again to review previous content using diagram of a volcano, volcano eruption sentence pattern chart, and T-chart listing positive and negative effects of volcanoes-(partners)
3. Explain task using graphic organizer to model
4. Guided practice-think aloud to model evaluating impacts of volcanoes
5. Independent/Small-group writing
6. Share writing (partners feedback)
7. Wrap-up–review objectives with fist-to-five self evaluation

Practice & Application:
Students complete a graphic organizer-write a claim that volcanoes are helpful or harmful and 3 reasons to support the claim.

Review & Assessment:
Partner feedback
Review objectives at the end w/self evaluation

Extension:
Students consider what someone might say who opposes their opinion about volcanoes and make a short list. Students then find someone who wrote about the opposing viewpoint, listen to their writing, then check off any opposing points from their list they heard from their classmate.

Reflection:
Some students could benefit from more time in order to see completed work from their classmates. Mr. Wright's group could benefit from some examples of compound/complex sentences to incorporate into their writing.

Mr. Wright and Ms. Solares' Co-Teaching

To begin the lesson, Ms. Solares led the students in chorally reading the content and language objectives, which were written on the whiteboard at the front of the room.

Content Objective: Use evidence about the impacts of volcanic eruptions to justify if volcanoes are helpful or harmful.

Language Objective: Make a written claim that volcanoes are helpful or harmful using **key vocabulary and transition words.**

Afterward, Mr. Wright annotated the objectives to show more commonly used synonyms for the academic terms to ensure all students understood the purpose of the lesson.

Next, Ms. Solares reminded the students they would start each lesson with the Play It Again activity to review what they had previously learned. She pointed to three visuals on the board (a diagram of a volcano, the volcano eruption sentence pattern chart, and the T-chart listing positive and negative effects of volcanoes), which represented the content from each of the previous three lessons, and asked the students to take turns sharing with their partners using two sentence frames:

On {day} we focused on _____. Something I learned was _____.

Because the routine was familiar, students began talking and both teachers circulated around the room listening to students share. Mr. Wright checked in with students identified as English learners, while Ms. Solares listened to as many students as she could within the three minutes they allocated for the review activity. When they called the class back together, Ms. Solares randomly called on three students to share something they had learned during the previous lesson.

Student 1: Something I learned is when the ash goes on the soil, it can actually make the soil good for growing plants.

Student 2: Something I learned was the ash covers everything so it can be bad for people to breathe.

Student 3: People leave home.

Mr. Wright: Try that again and use the Play It Again frame.

Student 3: Something I learn is the lava flow a lot so people leave home.

Mr. Wright connected the review to the new lesson by saying students would use ideas like the ones just shared to decide if they think volcanoes are helpful or harmful and why. He used a document camera to project the graphic organizer for the task. Ms. Solares modeled a "think aloud" as she walked through the steps of the assignment. As Ms. Solares explained the assignment, Mr. Wright pointed out the labels on the boxes of the graphic organizer, repeating the academic terms like **claim**, **reason**, and **transition words** and reminding students of the more familiar terms from the annotated objectives.

Following the introduction to the task, students worked independently on their own writing. Mr. Wright gathered a small group of students to write at a larger table so he could support them with their assignment. He repeated the directions for the task and provided the group a list of transition words and a paragraph frame depending on their need (see Artifact 11.5). Meanwhile, Ms. Solares circulated around the classroom answering questions and supporting other students.

Name: _____

Volcanoes:
Helpful or Harmful?

Claim

In my opinion, volcanoes are: helpful / harmful.

Reason 1

First, volcanoes are _____ because

_____

Reason 2

Another reason volcanoes are _____

is _____

_____

Reason 3

Finally, volcanoes are _____

because_____

_____

■ Co-Assessment with SIOP

The third part of the collaborative instructional cycle is collaborative assessment of student learning, or co-assessment. Co-Assessment aligns with the SIOP Component Review & Assessment (see Figure 11.4). Teachers culminate co-taught lessons by reviewing key vocabulary (Feature 27) as well as key content concepts (Feature 28), and use informal assessment measures to gauge student comprehension of the lesson objectives (Feature 30). Co-teachers might provide on the spot feedback to students about their output (Feature 29) or provide feedback independently or collaboratively after they have reviewed a lesson artifact, by using an exit slip or class assignment. Additionally, teachers might ask students for feedback on how the lesson went and how well students think they understand the lesson objectives. This can be done in conjunction with reviewing the content and language objectives at the closing of the lesson. Two teachers informally assessing student learning affords the opportunity for each teacher to check in with half the class or for one teacher to work more closely with a small group or individual students to gauge their understanding and points of confusion.

FIGURE 11.4	Collaborative Instructional Cycle: Co-Assessing with SIOP Components

	Co-Planning	Co-Teaching	Co-Assessing	Co-Reflecting
SIOP Components	Lesson Preparation	Lesson Preparation	Review & Assessment	Lesson Delivery
	Building Background	Building Background		Review & Assessment
	Comprehensible Input	Comprehensible Input		
	Strategies	Strategies		
	Interaction	Interaction		
	Practice & Application	Practice & Application		
	Lesson Delivery	Lesson Delivery		
	Review & Assessment	Review & Assessment		

Mr. Wright and Ms. Solares' Co-Assessment

When students completed their writing, Ms. Solares called for everyone's attention and asked Mr. Wright to be her partner so they could model how to give a partner feedback. Ms. Solares read her claim and three reasons while Mr. Wright listened and filled out the peer feedback checklist. He then used the sentence frame on the bottom of the feedback checklist to model how to give a partner verbal feedback. Students then worked with their assigned partners to give each other feedback.

Finally, Mr. Wright called the class's attention back to board to review the content and language objectives. Ms. Solares asked students to signal "fist to five" to indicate how successful they felt in meeting the objectives for the lesson.

Co-Reflection with SIOP

The final part of the collaborative instructional cycle is reflection on action and in action, which is also referred to as *co-reflection*. Co-reflection is a powerful practice co-teachers and teams use to engage in dialogue about many aspects of their collaborative instructional cycle, particularly Lesson Delivery and Review & Assessment (see Figure 11.5). Reflection can be done both formally and informally and is a flexible process that can be broad or specific in nature. Teachers can also engage in co-reflection at different points in the collaborative instruction cycle in order to inform subsequent co-planning, co-teaching, or co-assessment.

Many teachers find it helpful to reflect after completing co-taught lessons to consider what to keep the same or change going forward. This can be particularly helpful for an ELD specialist who teaches similar lessons with multiple content teachers, multiple class periods with the same teacher, or more than one teacher on the same grade-level team. Reflection and feedback can inform subsequent lessons' iterations of the same lesson with additional classes.

Quick, informal debriefs can give co-teachers an opportunity to express their thoughts on what aspects of a co-taught SIOP lesson went well and what aspects did not. Teachers might reflect on how particular lessons or tasks went for individual

FIGURE 11.5	Collaborative Instructional Cycle: Co-Reflecting with SIOP Components

	Co-Planning	Co-Teaching	Co-Assessing	Co-Reflecting
SIOP Components	Lesson Preparation	Lesson Preparation	Review & Assessment	Lesson Delivery
	Building Background	Building Background		Review & Assessment
	Comprehensible Input	Comprehensible Input		
	Strategies	Strategies		
	Interaction	Interaction		
	Practice & Application	Practice & Application		
	Lesson Delivery	Lesson Delivery		
	Review & Assessment	Review & Assessment		

students, a sub-population of students, or for the class as a whole. Within a trusting co-teaching partnership, opportunities to debrief are also opportunities to give one another feedback on some of the SIOP features that connect to co-teaching (e.g., pacing, student engagement).

Co-reflection also occurs more formally in conjunction with co-planning where co-teachers begin by sharing thoughts on the most recent co-taught lessons or how upcoming lessons went when they were taught in the past. Teams may choose to reflect on implementation of specific SIOP components or features, a single part of the collaborative instruction cycle, or anything else that seems pertinent within their collaborative practices. Teachers might want to establish routines for reflecting to ensure that feedback is regularly part of the process and not something to be taken personally.

Finally, co-reflection goes hand in hand with engaging student voices as part of the collaborative instructional cycle. Safir and Dugan (2021) speak to the necessity of "street data," which disrupts the assumptions that teachers know what is best for students by "bringing student voice to the forefront of our discussions and providing more trusted, heartfelt, and personalized information" (p. 58). When teachers invite students into conversations in order to listen to their perspectives and experiences, they must reflect on what students have shared and revise instruction accordingly. Prioritizing student voice then impacts co-planning.

Co-Reflection with Mr. Wright and Ms. Solares

The day after Lesson 4 ended, Mr. Wright and Ms. Solares had a brief conversation before school about how the lesson went. Ms. Solares commented that there was a good mix in terms of how many students claimed volcanoes are helpful and how many claimed volcanoes are harmful. She noted that students were very successful using transition words. Mr. Wright shared that the students he worked with really liked the graphic organizer and it helped them organize their ideas. He felt some students struggled with incorporating the compound and complex sentences into their reasons, but their information was accurate. The teachers decided to postpone their final activity in order to spend more time fixing up their claim writing. They chose several papers to show on the doc camera to point out what they did well and additionally offered an extension for students who were finished with their writing.

■ Final Points

As you reflect on this chapter and the impact that teacher collaboration has on learning, consider the following main points:

- Initiate collaborative relationships to learn, implement, and refine the SIOP Model in your instructional context.
- Consider which colleagues or mentors you would seek out who can join your professional learning, and establish structures that allow you to support one another in a strategic rollout of the SIOP components.

The SIOP Model is an effective roadmap for the collaboration and co-teaching cycle.

- Calibrating the SIOP components and features with the collaboration and co-teaching cycle brings the benefit of common language and shared expectations for co-planning and co-teaching lessons focused on meeting the needs of multilingual learners.

■ Discussion Questions

1. In reflecting on the content and language objectives at the beginning of the chapter, are you able to:
   a. Identify different approaches to take when beginning to implement the SIOP Model?
   b. Investigate ways educators can collaborate to understand and implement SIOP?
   c. Determine how to leverage content and language expertise to build collective efficacy in implementing the SIOP Model?
   d. List action steps for initiating collaborative partnerships?
   e. Describe how the SIOP Model components connect to each part of the collaboration and co-teaching cycle?
   f. Write lesson plans in partnership with colleagues using the SIOP Model?

2. In what ways does collaboration positively impact practitioners? In what ways does collaboration between practitioners positively impact multilingual learners?

3. In this chapter, we discussed different approaches for strategically implementing the components of the SIOP Model. Which approach is the best fit for your instructional context? In what ways can you interact with colleagues to expand your learning as you begin implementing the SIOP Model?

4. Choose one part of the collaboration and co-teaching cycle. How will the SIOP components we've aligned with that part of the cycle support and enhance collaborative practices?

SIOP® Protocol

Observer(s): _____   Teacher: _____

Date: _____   School: _____

Grade: _____   Class/Topic: _____

Language proficiency level: _____   Lesson: Multi-day   Single-day   (*circle one*)

Total Points Possible: 120 (Or subtract 4 points for each N/A given: _____)

Total Points Earned: _____   Percentage Score: _____

Directions: Circle the number that best reflects what you observe in a SIOP lesson. You may give a score from 0–4 (or N/A on selected items). Cite under "Comments" specific examples of the behaviors observed.

▪ Lesson Preparation

4	3	2	1	0
1. **Content objectives** clearly defined, displayed, and reviewed with students		**Content objectives** for students implied		No clearly defined **content objectives** for students

Comments:

4	3	2	1	0
2. **Language objectives** clearly defined, displayed, and reviewed with students		**Language objectives** for students implied		No clearly defined **language objectives** for students

Comments:

4	3	2	1	0
3. **Content concepts** appropriate for age and educational background level of students		**Content concepts** somewhat appropriate for age and educational background level of students		**Content concepts** inappropriate for age and educational background level of students

Comments:

(Echevarría, Vogt, & Short, 2000, 2004, 2008, 2013, 2017, 2023)

4	3	2	1	0

4. **Supplementary materials** used to a high degree, making the lesson clear and meaningful (e.g., computer programs, graphs, models, visuals)

Some use of **supplementary materials**

No use of **supplementary materials**

Comments:

4	3	2	1	0	N/A

5. **Adaptation of content** (e.g., text, assignment) to all levels of student proficiency

Some **adaptation of content** to all levels of student proficiency

No significant **adaptation of content** to all levels of student proficiency

Comments:

4	3	2	1	0

6. **Meaningful activities** that integrate lesson concepts (e.g., interviews, letter writing, simulations, models) with language practice opportunities for reading, writing, listening, and/or speaking

Meaningful activities that integrate lesson concepts but provide few language practice opportunities for reading, writing, listening, and/or speaking

No **meaningful activities** that integrate lesson concepts with language practice

Comments:

■ Building Background

4	3	2	1	0	N/A

7. **Concepts explicitly linked** to students' background experiences

Concepts loosely linked to students' background experiences

Concepts not explicitly linked to students' background experiences

Comments:

4	3	2	1	0
8. **Links explicitly made** between past learning and new concepts		**Few links made** between past learning and new concepts		**No links made** between past learning and new concepts

Comments:

4	3	2	1	0
9. **Key vocabulary** emphasized (e.g., introduced, written, repeated, and highlighted for students to see)		**Key vocabulary** introduced, but not emphasized		**Key vocabulary** not introduced or emphasized

Comments:

■ Comprehensible Input

4	3	2	1	0
10. **Speech appropriate** for students' proficiency levels (e.g., slower rate, enunciation, and simple sentence structure for beginners)		**Speech** sometimes inappropriate for students' proficiency levels		**Speech** inappropriate for students' proficiency levels

Comments:

4	3	2	1	0
11. **Clear explanation** of academic tasks		**Unclear** explanation of academic tasks		**No** explanation of academic tasks

Comments:

4	3	2	1	0
12. **A variety of techniques** used to make content concepts clear (e.g., modeling, visuals, hands-on activities, demonstrations, gestures, body language)		Some techniques used to make content concepts clear		No **techniques** used to make concepts clear

Comments:

■ Strategies

4	3	2	1	0
13. Ample opportunities provided for students to use **learning strategies**		Inadequate opportunities provided for students to use **learning strategies**		No opportunity provided for students to use **learning strategies**

Comments:

4	3	2	1	0
14. **Scaffolding techniques** consistently used, assisting and supporting student understanding (e.g., think-alouds)		**Scaffolding techniques** occasionally used		**Scaffolding techniques** not used

Comments:

4	3	2	1	0
15. A variety of **questions or tasks that promote higher-order thinking skills** (e.g., literal, analytical, and interpretive questions)		Infrequent **questions or tasks that promote higher-order thinking skills**		No **questions or tasks that promote higher-order thinking skills**

Comments:

■ Interaction

4	3	2	1	0
16. Frequent opportunities for **interaction** and discussion between teacher/student and among students, which encourage elaborated responses about lesson concepts		**Interaction** mostly teacher-dominated with some opportunities for students to talk about or question lesson concepts		**Interaction** teacher-dominated with no opportunities for students to discuss lesson concepts

Comments:

4	3	2	1	0

17. **Grouping configurations** support language and content objectives of the lesson | | **Grouping configurations** unevenly support the language and content objectives | | **Grouping configurations** do not support the language and content objectives

Comments:

4	3	2	1	0

18. Sufficient **wait time for student responses** consistently provided | | Sufficient **wait time for student responses** occasionally provided | | Sufficient **wait time for student responses** not provided

Comments:

4	3	2	1	0	N/A

19. Ample opportunities for students to **clarify and discuss key concepts in L1** with peer, aide, teacher, or L1 text | | Some opportunities for students to **clarify and discuss key concepts in L1** | | No opportunities for students to **clarify or discuss key concepts in L1** |

Comments:

■ Practice & Application

4	3	2	1	0	N/A

20. **Hands-on materials and/or manipulatives** provided for students to practice using new content knowledge | | Few **hands-on materials and/ or manipulatives** provided for students to practice using new content knowledge | | No **hands-on materials and/ or manipulatives** provided for students to practice using new content knowledge |

Comments:

4	3	2	1	0	N/A

21. Activities provided for students to **apply content and language knowledge** in the classroom | | Activities provided for students to **apply** either **content or language knowledge** in the classroom | | No activities provided for students to **apply content and language knowledge** in the classroom |

Comments:

	4	3	2	1	0

22. Activities integrate all **language skills** (i.e., reading, writing, listening, and speaking) — Activities integrate some **language skills** — Activities do not integrate **language skills**

Comments:

■ Lesson Delivery

	4	3	2	1	0

23. **Content objectives** clearly supported by lesson delivery — **Content objectives** somewhat supported by lesson delivery — **Content objectives** not supported by lesson delivery

Comments:

	4	3	2	1	0

24. **Language objectives** clearly supported by lesson delivery — **Language objectives** somewhat supported by lesson delivery — **Language objectives** not supported by lesson delivery

Comments:

	4	3	2	1	0

25. **Students engaged** approximately 90% to 100% of the period — **Students engaged** approximately 70% of the period — **Students engaged** less than 50% of the period

Comments:

	4	3	2	1	0

26. **Pacing** of the lesson appropriate to students' ability levels — **Pacing** generally appropriate, but at times too fast or too slow — **Pacing** inappropriate to students' ability levels

Comments:

■ Review & Assessment

4	3	2	1	0
27. Comprehensive **review of key vocabulary**		Uneven **review of key vocabulary**		No **review of key vocabulary**

Comments:

4	3	2	1	0
28. Comprehensive **review of key content concepts**		Uneven **review of key content concepts**		No **review of key content concepts**

Comments:

4	3	2	1	0
29. Regular **feedback** provided to students on their output (e.g., language, content, work)		Inconsistent **feedback** provided to students on their output		No **feedback** provided to students on their output

Comments:

4	3	2	1	0
30. **Assessment of student comprehension and learning** of all lesson objectives (e.g., spot checking, group response) throughout the lesson		**Assessment of student comprehension and learning** of some lesson objectives		No **assessment of student comprehension and learning** of lesson objectives

Comments:

(Reproduction of this material is restricted to use with Echevarría, Vogt, and Short (2023), *Making Content Comprehensible for Multilingual Learners: The SIOP® Model.*)

SIOP Protocol
(Echevarría, Vogt, & Short, 2000, 2004, 2008, 2013, 2017, 2023)

Observer(s): _____ School: _____
Date: _____ Teacher: _____
Grade: _____ Class/Topic: _____
ESL Level: _____ Lesson: Multi-day Single-day (circle one)

Total Points Possible: 120 (Subtract 4 points for each N/A given) _____
Total Points Earned: _____ Percentage Score: _____

Directions: Circle the number that best reflects what you observe in a SIOP lesson. You may give a score from 0–4 (or N/A on selected items). Cite under "Comments" specific examples of the behaviors observed.

Lesson Preparation	Highly Evident 4	3	Somewhat Evident 2	1	Not Evident 0	
1. **Content objectives** clearly defined, displayed, and reviewed with students	❏	❏	❏	❏	❏	
2. **Language objectives** clearly defined, displayed, and reviewed with students	❏	❏	❏	❏	❏	
3. **Content concepts** appropriate for age and educational background level of students	❏	❏	❏	❏	❏	
4. **Supplementary materials** used to a high degree, making the lesson clear and meaningful (e.g., computer programs, graphs, models, visuals)	❏	❏	❏	❏	❏	
						N/A
5. **Adaptation of content** (e.g., text, assignment) to all levels of student proficiency	❏	❏	❏	❏	❏	❏
6. **Meaningful activities** that integrate lesson concepts (e.g., interviews, letter writing, simulations, models) with language practice opportunities for reading, writing, listening, and/or speaking	❏	❏	❏	❏	❏	

Comments:

Building Background	4	3	2	1	0	N/A
7. **Concepts explicitly linked** to students' background experiences	❏	❏	❏	❏	❏	❏
8. **Links explicitly made** between past learning and new concepts	❏	❏	❏	❏	❏	
9. **Key vocabulary emphasized** (e.g., introduced, written, repeated, and highlighted for students to see)	❏	❏	❏	❏	❏	

Comments:

Comprehensible Input	4	3	2	1	0
10. **Speech appropriate for students' proficiency levels** (e.g., slower rate, enunciation, and simple sentence structure for beginners)	❏	❏	❏	❏	❏
11. **Clear explanation of academic tasks**	❏	❏	❏	❏	❏

	4	3	2	1	0	
12. **A variety of techniques** used to make content concepts clear (e.g., modeling, visuals, hands-on activities, demonstrations, gestures, body language)	❑	❑	❑	❑	❑	

Comments:

Strategies	4	3	2	1	0	
13. Ample opportunities provided for students to use **learning strategies**	❑	❑	❑	❑	❑	
14. **Scaffolding techniques** consistently used assisting and supporting student understanding (e.g., think-alouds)	❑	❑	❑	❑	❑	
15. A variety of **questions or tasks that promote higher-order thinking skills** (e.g., literal, analytical, and interpretive questions)	❑	❑	❑	❑	❑	

Comments:

Interaction	4	3	2	1	0	
16. Frequent opportunities for **interaction** and discussion between teacher/student and among students, which encourage elaborated responses about lesson concepts	❑	❑	❑	❑	❑	
17. **Grouping configurations** support language and content objectives of the lesson	❑	❑	❑	❑	❑	
18. Sufficient **wait time for student responses** consistently provided	❑	❑	❑	❑	❑	
						N/A
19. Ample opportunities for students to **clarify and discuss key concepts in Ll** with peer, aide, teacher, or L1 text	❑	❑	❑	❑	❑	❑

Comments:

Practice & Application	4	3	2	1	0	**N/A**
20. **Hands-on materials and/or manipulatives** provided for students to practice using new content knowledge	❑	❑	❑	❑	❑	❑
						N/A
21. Activities provided for students to **apply content and language knowledge** in the classroom	❑	❑	❑	❑	❑	❑
22. Activities integrate all **language skills** (i.e., reading, writing, listening, and speaking)	❑	❑	❑	❑	❑	

Comments:

Lesson Delivery	4	3	2	1	0
23. **Content objectives** clearly supported by lesson delivery	❑	❑	❑	❑	❑
24. **Language objectives** clearly supported by lesson delivery	❑	❑	❑	❑	❑
25. **Students engaged** approximately 90% to 100% of the period	❑	❑	❑	❑	❑
26. **Pacing** of the lesson appropriate to students' ability level	❑	❑	❑	❑	❑

Comments:

Review & Assessment	4	3	2	1	0
27. Comprehensive **review of key vocabulary**	❏	❏	❏	❏	❏
28. Comprehensive **review of key content concepts**	❏	❏	❏	❏	❏
29. Regular **feedback** provided to students on their output (e.g., language, content, work)	❏	❏	❏	❏	❏
30. **Assessment of student comprehension and learning** of all lesson objectives (e.g., spot checking, group response) throughout the lesson	❏	❏	❏	❏	❏

Comments:

Effective Use of the SIOP® Protocol

The SIOP Model and its protocol have been used in school districts and universities for teacher development since 1998 with measurable success. Over the years we have interviewed many school personnel who told us their stories of SIOP implementation. Some descriptions were reported in *Implementing the SIOP Model for Professional Development and Coaching* (Echevarría, Short, & Vogt, 2008); other accounts have been presented at professional conferences and/or have appeared in professional journal articles. The protocol is regularly used as a classroom observation tool and in empirical research studies because it is one of the few reliable and validated observation instruments designed for classes with multilingual learners (Guarino, et al., 2001). To ensure its continued efficacy for SIOP professional development, we offer the following suggestions and guidelines.

Purpose of the SIOP Protocol

The SIOP protocol provides a tool for gauging the quality of teaching for multilingual learners. Qualitative and quantitative information recorded by an observer on the protocol itself documents lesson effectiveness and shows areas that need improvement. It is typically completed by a coach, administrator, or university supervisor (for student teachers) while observing a lesson, or immediately thereafter if detailed notes have been taken. The observation data recorded on the protocol may be used by teachers, coaches, administrators, university faculty, and researchers.

Teachers find the SIOP protocol useful for improving their own practice through self-reflection and/or peer coaching. The protocol is ideal for co-planning in a co-teaching situation because it provides a guide for effective lesson planning as well as a tool for debriefing lessons. Some teachers and co-teachers regularly use the protocol to reflect on their lessons, completing the protocol after they have taught a specific lesson. More effective is when teachers videotape their lessons and use the protocol to score the lessons on SIOP's features. The objectivity the camera provides is valuable to teachers in helping them to recognize their strengths as well as areas that need attention.

In Appendix A, you have seen a long form and short form of the protocol. The long form is typically used for observing and scoring lessons, discussed in the next section. The short form is useful for lesson planning and serves as a checklist to ensure that SIOP's features are included in your planning. You may also want to use the short version for self-reflection after having taught a lesson.

Scoring and Interpreting the SIOP® Protocol

On the protocol, there is a box for the total score the teacher received based on implementation of SIOP's features. It is most useful to represent a teacher's score as a percentage because N/A (not applicable) affects a total score number (see the next section for an explanation of scoring).

When scoring a lesson, an observer may assign scores in several ways: (1) during the observation itself, as individual features are recognized; (2) after the observation, as the observer reflects on the entire lesson, referring to observational field notes; or (3) after the observation while watching a videotape of the lesson. The third option is often useful so that the teacher and observer are able to share the same point of reference when discussing the lesson.

It is important to stress that not all features on the SIOP will be present in every lesson. An introductory lesson, for example, may not have Practice & Application activities. However, some features, such as items under Lesson Preparation, Comprehensible Input, Interaction, and Review & Assessment, are essential for each lesson. Over the course of instruction (several lessons a week), all features should be represented.

There will be times that you use only specific portions of the protocol. As discussed in Chapter 11, SIOP professional development may focus on implementing one component for a period of time, in which case lessons are rated on that one component. As other components are learned and practiced, lessons would be rated on those components as well.

Assigning Scores

We suggest that an observer determine the level of SIOP implementation by using the scenario descriptions in this book as a guide. Each chapter's scenarios were designed to show a clear example for each feature, with scores ranging from 0 to 4. The SIOP protocol provides a five-point scale as well as space for qualitative data. Use the "Comments" section to record examples of the presence or absence of each feature. That way, both the observer and the teacher have specific written information, in addition to a score, to use in their post-lesson discussion.

To assist in more accurate scoring, ask the teacher for a copy of the lesson plan in advance of observing the class. Ideally, the teacher and observer would meet for a pre-observation conference to discuss the lesson plan and provide the observer with background about the lesson. In this way, the observer is better able to rate the lesson, especially the Lesson Preparation section and N/A items.

The Not Applicable (N/A) rating is important because it distinguishes a feature that is "not applicable" to the observed lesson from a score of "0," which indicates that the feature should have been present but was not. Consider, for example, the following. Mr. Leung taught a five-day unit on atomic structures. During the first few lessons of the unit, Mr. Leung concentrated on making the rather dense information accessible to his students. He adapted the text to make it understandable for them and provided ample opportunities for students to use strategies. On the final day of the unit, an observer was present. Mr. Leung wrapped up the unit by having the students complete an enjoyable hands-on activity in which they applied the concepts they had learned. It was obvious that the students had learned the content and were able to use it in the activity. However, because of the nature of that particular lesson, there was no observed adaptation of content (Feature #5). Mr. Leung was not penalized by receiving a score of "0" because the final lesson did not lend itself to that item and he had covered that item on another day. A rating of N/A would be correct in this case.

In contrast is Ms. Striker's lesson. She taught the same five-day unit as Mr. Leung; however, she used the grade-level text chapter on atomic structures and didn't provide any adaptation or supports to help multilingual learners comprehend the text. It was clear that the students struggled considerably to understand the material. She received a "0" on Feature #5.

The distinction between a "0" and "N/A" is an important one because a rating of "0" adversely affects the overall score for the lesson, while an "N/A" does not because a percentage is used to indicate a lesson's score.

Calculating Scores

There are 30 features on the SIOP, each with a range of possible scores from 0 to 4, although five features have an N/A option as well. After scoring each feature, the observer tallies all numeric scores. The score is written over the total possible score, usually 120 (30 features times a score of 4). So, an example of a total score would be written 115/120. An exception is made when there are one or more N/A scores. Because of one N/A or more, the total possible score will be less than 120.

The Step-by-Step Process for Tallying Scores

1. Add the lesson's scores from all features.
2. Count the number of N/As, multiply by 4, then subtract this number from 120.
3. Divide the number from step 2 into the number from step 1 (the adjusted possible score into the lesson's score).

In our research studies using the SIOP protocol for measuring level of implementation, we established the following guidelines:

High implementation—lessons that receive a score of 75% or higher
Low implementation—lessons that receive a score of 50% or lower

■ Using SIOP® Scores and Comments

When lessons are rated, comments supporting the scores are essential. A completed protocol can be used as a starting point for a collaborative discussion between a teacher and a supervisor or coach, or among a group of teachers. We have found that videotaping a lesson, rating it (or writing comments without scores), and then viewing and discussing it with the teacher provides an effective forum for professional growth. We also get valuable information when teachers explain a student's behavior or discuss why something may not have taken place despite the element being included in the lesson plan, for example. The discussion may take place between the teacher and the observer, or a group of teachers may meet on a regular basis to provide feedback to one another and assist in refining their teaching.

While the SIOP protocol is a useful tool for professional development, scores should be used with caution. Many variables affect the success or failure of a given lesson, such as time of day, time of year, dynamics among students, and numerous other factors. Rather than just doing one observation and scoring a lesson, an observer should rate several lessons over time for a more complete picture of the teacher's implementation of SIOP.

■ Using the Protocol Without Numeric Scoring

You may find it useful to change the rating scale from numeric 0-4 to Novice–Expert as seen below.

Expert		Novice
1. **Content objectives** clearly defined, displayed, and reviewed with students	**Content objectives** for students implied	No clearly defined **content objectives** for students

Comments:

Expert		Novice
2. **Language objectives** clearly defined, displayed, and reviewed with students	**Language objectives** for students implied	No clearly defined **language objectives** for students

Comments:

Expert		Novice
3. **Content concepts** appropriate for age and educational background level of students	**Content concepts** somewhat appropriate for age and educational background level of students	**Content concepts** inappropriate for age and educational background level of students

Comments:

In this case, the observer would mark an X along the continuum to indicate if the feature was demonstrated at the expert level, novice level, or somewhere in between. When using the protocol with numbers, some teachers equate a 4 as an A grade, a 3 as a B grade, and so forth. Understandably, most teachers want to receive an A, or 4, on every feature. When you discuss that 4 is expert level, teachers begin thinking more realistically about their practice and may be more open to thinking deeply about how they might improve their teaching. The goal is for observers and teachers to have more substantive and productive post-observation discussions.

■ Conclusion

The SIOP Model and protocol provide concrete examples of the features of effective instruction for multilingual learners. The protocol provides a lesson planning guide as well as a lesson reflection and/or rating instrument.

The use of scenarios in Chapters 2–9 allows readers to "see" what each feature might look like in a classroom setting and how each feature is rated using the protocol. The features of the SIOP Model represent best practice for teaching multilingual learners and have been shown to benefit English-speaking students as well.

SIOP® Lesson Plan Template 1

Date: _____ Grade/Class/Subject: _____

Unit/Theme: _____ Standards: _____

Content Objective(s): _____

_____

Language Objective(s): _____

_____

Key Vocabulary	Supplementary Materials

SIOP® Features

Lesson Preparation
___ Adaptation of Content
___ Links to Background
___ Links to Past Learning
___ Strategies incorporated

Integration of Processes
___ Reading
___ Writing
___ Speaking
___ Listening

Scaffolding
___ Modeling
___ Guided practice
___ Independent practice
___ Comprehensible input

Application
___ Hands-on
___ Meaningful
___ Linked to objectives
___ Promotes engagement

Grouping Options
___ Whole class
___ Small groups
___ Partners
___ Independent

Assessment
___ Individual
___ Group
___ Written
___ Oral

Lesson Sequence

Reflections:

(Reproduction of this material is restricted to use with Echevarría, Vogt, and Short (2017), *Making Content Comprehensible for English Learners: The SIOP® Model.*)

SIOP® Lesson Plan Template 2

STANDARDS:

LESSON TOPIC:

OBJECTIVES:
Content

Language

LEARNING STRATEGIES:

KEY VOCABULARY:

MATERIALS:

MOTIVATION:
(Building background)

PRESENTATION
(Content and language objectives, comprehensible input modeling, strategies, interaction, feedback)

PRACTICE & APPLICATION:
(Meaningful activities, interaction, strategies, practice/application, feedback)

REVIEW & ASSESSMENT:
(Review objectives and vocabulary, assess learning)

EXTENSION:

SIOP® Lesson Plan Template 3

Topic:	Class:	Date:

Content Objectives:

Language Objectives:

Key Vocabulary:

Materials (including supplementary and adapted):

Higher-Order Questions:

Time:	**Activities**
	Building Background
	Links to Experience:
	Links to Learning:
	Key Vocabulary:

(*Continued on next page*)

Time:	**Student Activities** (Check all that apply for activities throughout lesson):

Scaffolding: ❏ Modeling ❏ Guided Practice ❏ Independent Practice

Grouping: ❏ Whole Class ❏ Small Group ❏ Partners ❏ Independent

Processes: ❏ Reading ❏ Writing ❏ Listening ❏ Speaking

Strategies: ❏ Hands-on ❏ Meaningful ❏ Links to Objectives

Review & Assessment (Check all that apply):

❏ Individual ❏ Group ❏ Written ❏ Oral

Review Key Vocabulary:

Review Key Content Concepts:

Review content and language objectives at end of lesson.

(Reproduction of this material is restricted to use with Echevarría, Vogt, and Short (2017), *Making Content Comprehensible for English Learners: The SIOP® Model.*)

(Developed by John Seidlitz. Used with permission.)

SIOP® Lesson Plan Template 4

SIOP® Lesson Grade:	Subject:
Standards:	

Key Vocabulary:

Higher order questions and tasks:

Multimedia/Materials:

Building Background:

Objectives	Lesson Sequence	Review & Assessment
Content Objectives: **Language Objectives:**		

Wrap-up (including review of content and language objectives):

Lesson Reflection/Extension:

(Reproduction of this material is restricted to use with Echevarría, Vogt, and Short (2017), *Making Content Comprehensible for English Learners: The SIOP® Model.*)

Frequently Asked Questions: Getting Started with the SIOP® Model

The purpose of this Appendix is to provide you with additional information and suggestions for beginning your work with SIOP. From many conversations with SIOPers over the years, we have culled some of the most frequently asked questions about implementing SIOP and you'll find our answers below.

■ General SIOP Questions

1. Who can implement SIOP?
   - Keep in mind that SIOP is an instructional framework, not a program, not a lock-step way of teaching, or a curriculum. Therefore, as a guide for lesson planning and delivery, it can be used in many educational contexts where students are diverse, and learning is the goal. Pre-K, elementary, and secondary subject-area teachers, reading/language arts and English teachers, resource teachers, coaches, ESL/ELD specialists, special educators, community college instructors, and university professors implement the SIOP Model in a variety of educational program designs.
   - Any teacher whose students are learning academic content through a language that differs from the language of instruction can use SIOP effectively as part of any educational program, including general education, ESL or ESOL, bilingual, late-exit bilingual, two-way bilingual immersion, newcomer, sheltered, foreign language immersion, special education, gifted and talented, and so forth.

2. How can you use SIOP in a dual language program?
   - Regardless of the educational context, SIOP teachers plan lessons that have a dual focus on teaching academic content and academic language, consistently and concurrently in the target language. Therefore, regardless of the language of instruction in a dual language program, the teacher's lessons are equally effective when the SIOP protocol is used consistently for planning content lessons.

3. How can you use SIOP with SLIFE/SIFE students?
   - Multilingual leaners and other students with interrupted or limited formal education benefit from scaffolded instruction that accelerates their learning of academic content and academic language. High-implementing SIOP teachers provide both through their instruction that provides substantial scaffolding through SIOP's 30 instructional features.

4. Is SIOP only for multilingual learners?
   - No. SIOP has been validated also with native-English speaking students, general education and special education students, and students who were formerly in ESL programs. When teachers implement the 30 features consistently, all

subgroups of students, including students receiving special education services, have been shown to demonstrate academic gains.

5. Isn't SIOP just good instruction?

- SIOP is excellent instruction, with research-based features that have been proven effective with multilingual learners and other students. What distinguishes SIOP is the systematic, consistent, and simultaneous teaching of both content concepts and academic language through its 30 features. In addition, as of the time of this writing, SIOP is the only empirically validated model of sheltered instruction for multilingual learners that exists.

6. What is the relationship between SIOP and Culturally Responsive Teaching?

- Almost by definition, when teachers implement SIOP to a high degree, they're engaging in culturally responsive teaching. For example, through their lessons, SIOP teachers show respect for students' home languages and cultures by incorporating their background knowledge and experiences into lessons, and by valuing their students' home languages (L1), by encouraging translanguaging and use of the L1 for clarification and other purposes (see Glossary for a definition of translanguaging).

- Effective SIOP teachers also create groups where students work together on relevant activities, ensuring that multilingual learners are equal participants during group work.

- With SIOP, teachers hold high expectations for all students and adjust instruction and materials to provide access to the grade-level curriculum. Compare the tenets of culturally responsive teaching and the features of SIOP and you will see that they intersect naturally, and thus are not separate or competing instructional approaches.

7. Is SIOP aligned with the Science of Reading (SOR)?

- SOR represents a body of research spanning many decades, that focuses on how individuals learn to read. Several of the SOR studies focus on mulitlingual learners. SIOP teachers use published research to guide their instruction, including SOR research findings.

- In Chapters 3, 5, and 6, you will find citations for references pertaining to relevant SOR research studies supporting the points that are being made in the chapter.

- For further information, see the *Reading Research Quarterly* SOR articles from 2020-2021 (www.literacyworldwide.org); and the National Literacy Panel Report on Language Minority Children and Youth.

8. What if there are only a few multilingual learners in my classroom?

- We now have empirical evidence that all students benefit academically when teachers implement SIOP to a high degree. Therefore, all teachers who have multilingual learners in their classrooms should become SIOP teachers, regardless of the number. SIOP isn't something that teachers "turn on" and "turn off," depending on the makeup of their classes. Rather, it becomes the way they teach from period to period, subject to subject, throughout the day, whether there are many or few multilingual students.

9. What is the most important thing I should keep in mind (whether a teacher, coach, or administrator)?

  ● Recognize that learning to implement SIOP is a process of refining your teaching practices. Not all features will be observed to a high degree in the beginning stages. Use the SIOP protocol for planning lessons and for reflecting on the lessons after you teach them. Work through SIOP systematically to ensure it will become internalized and part of your regular classroom practice.

10. Can SIOP be used with inquiry lessons?

  ● Yes, SIOP is compatible with inquiry-based learning, an approach in which students learn by doing, thus enabling them to build knowledge through discovery, experience, and discussion.

  ● Consider the following content objective: *Students will investigate what factors influence plant growth.* This is appropriate with an inquiry lesson because it doesn't reveal what students will discover. Similarly, an accompanying language objective such as, *Students will complete an observation report using complete sentences,* focuses on necessary language skills without revealing anything about what the report will include. Other language objectives could focus on academic vocabulary related to inquiry, such as *investigate, observe, evidence,* and *factors.*

  ● Some SIOP teachers have their students do an introductory activity or experiment at the start of the lesson and then present the objectives after that. The exploration aspect is preserved while the purpose of the lesson and learning outcomes are clarified for students.

■ Questions About Getting Started with SIOP in the Classroom

1. How do I get started using SIOP in my classroom?

  ● Read the section titled "Implementing SIOP: Getting Started" in Chapter 11. The nuts and bolts of getting started with SIOP are discussed there.

  ● With the SIOP protocol, assess your areas of strength as well as those that need improvement. You can do this by recording a lesson with your phone, followed by a careful analysis of your instructional practices, using the protocol. You'll probably find that you're already including many of the SIOP features in your lessons. But are they present in your lessons on a daily basis, or just occasionally? Are there some SIOP features that are seldom or never part of your instructional plans? Engaging in this process with a colleague who is also new to SIOP can be beneficial to both of you.

  ● Begin with one component at a time, gradually adding the others over time. We suggest that unless you'll be working alone to implement SIOP, you and your subject-area or grade-level colleagues should discuss and decide together which SIOP component will be your starting point.

  ● As you attain proficiency in one SIOP component, gradually add others to your teaching repertoire. Again, working with your colleagues on lesson planning, observing each other's lessons (in person or via video), and sharing techniques and ideas are all beneficial.

2. Can I combine the content and language objectives into one objective?

- For many teachers, writing and orally explaining language objectives to students is something entirely new, especially for secondary, content teachers. Their specialty is their content, and they may not be aware of or have experience with the dual instructional focus of teaching academic content and academic language in every lesson. Encouraging two types of objectives, content and language, for each lesson maintains this dual focus.

- From our experience, combining the objectives results in teachers dropping the language piece at some point, mostly because it's more challenging. When that happens, we're back to a single focus on teaching content and not only multilingual students will lose out. The second reason we discourage combining the objectives is because students get used to seeing both objectives posted in their classrooms, with teachers going over the content and language goals during every lesson. Keep in mind that the purpose of the objectives is for the students to know what they are to learn and be able to do as related to both academic content and academic language within the lesson. They're not just for teachers to include in lesson plans.

- Sometimes for language arts, English, and ESL teachers, it's difficult to figure out which objective is for content and which is for language, so there's a temptation to put them together into one objective. Please don't. As language and literacy teachers, we do have academic content to teach (think affixes, elements of a short story, parts of speech, grammar, and so forth), so maintaining a dual focus is important for language teachers, as well.

3. Do I have to implement the eight components in the order they're presented in the book?

- No. There's no intended hierarchy or order of the components, with the exception, perhaps, of Lesson Preparation. However, teachers may choose to begin with another component first if that's more comfortable. We recommend that Lesson Preparation not be delayed beyond the second or third component because of the necessity of including content and language objectives in lessons.

4. Do I have to incorporate all 30 SIOP features in every lesson?

- Eventually, that's the goal. We recommend that elementary teachers begin implementing one component at a time in one subject area until all components are implemented in that subject area. The ultimate goal is to add other subjects until all are SIOPized. However, there might be occasional lessons where not all features are present, such as in a review lesson at the end of a unit. If you're able to speed up this process (adding new components and subject areas or periods), so much the better!

- For middle and high school teachers, your pacing schedule will differ from that of your colleagues in the elementary grades. Select one preparation period to begin implementing SIOP, along with one component, such as Period 2, Biology. If this is your same prep for additional periods, then, obviously, you can begin SIOPizing lessons in more than one period.

- The recommended time frame for adding new components differs somewhat depending on the level of support teachers receive. With SIOP coaching and opportunities for professional learning, adding a new component each month of the school year can work. However, the most common time frame is adding a new component each 9-week quarter of the school year, so at the end of year 1 of SIOP implementation, teachers will be incorporating four components consistently in their lessons. By the end of year two, they will be implementing, consistently, all eight of the SIOP components.

- Keep in mind that the definition of "a lesson" varies somewhat depending on the age of students you're teaching and the way the classroom day is organized. For example, pre-K, kindergarten, and first-grade teachers present many lessons in 15- to 20-minute (or less) blocks of time, while elementary teachers of older students may plan lessons ranging from 30–45 minutes. A rule of thumb is: *What can you teach, have students practice and apply, and assess, in a given period of instructional time?* That's what constitutes a "lesson" with SIOP.

5. What if I have students who can't speak any English? Will SIOP help?

   - SIOP will certainly help, but it's not enough. Beginning speakers, or newcomers, need intensive English instruction provided by an ESL or ELD teacher, in addition to effective SIOP instruction the rest of the day.

   - If newcomer programs are not available, SIOP instruction provides students with the best opportunity to comprehend lessons, because teachers are teaching content and academic English concurrently. During SIOP lessons, newcomer students can also benefit from partnering occasionally with a student or aide whose home language is the same as theirs.

6. How long will it take for me to become an effective SIOP teacher?

   - It depends on the support you receive. Our research has shown teachers can become effective SIOP teachers in one year with coaching, observations, workshops, and planning time. Realistically, we generally say it takes two to three years with consistent focus on the eight components and 30 features to become a high implementer of the model. And, of course, follow-up professional development, observations, and coaching certainly help.

7. How should I use the SIOP protocol?

   - Use it as a lesson plan checklist, self-assessment tool, and conversation starter with colleagues. You may wish to record yourself teaching and use the protocol to check the degree to which you are implementing specific features. SIOP teachers have found that sharing and discussing video lessons is very beneficial for deepening their understandings of effective teaching. See Appendix B for additional information about uses of the SIOP protocol.

   - Once you are familiar with the features in the individual components, use the protocol as a tool for post-teaching reflection. Two resources that may be helpful while planning lessons are books that offer a multitude of teaching ideas and activities for enhancing SIOP components and features in your lessons (see Vogt & Echevarría, 2022; Vogt, Echevarría, & Washam, 2015).

- Observe a peer's lesson and use the protocol to determine the degree to which SIOP features were present in the lesson you observed. You can then discuss together which SIOP features were highly evident, somewhat evident, or not evident in the lesson you observed.

8. Now that I've read the book and tried out some components, how do I deepen my SIOP knowledge?

- Collaborate with and observe other educators who are committed to excellent SIOP teaching.
- Observe other SIOP classrooms and frankly discuss what is working, what is problematic, and what a teacher can do to overcome problems.
- Read the other SIOP books that are cited in this text (see Appendix F for a list of Professional Resources). Also, there are a number of research articles written about the SIOP Model that may be helpful (see the Reference list for more information). Form a cohort of SIOPers and have a study group with these resources.
- Connect with other SIOP schools and districts.

■ Questions About School-Wide Implementation of the SIOP Model

1. How should we get started in our school-wide implementation?
   - It's critically important that you have a plan in place, including who will receive professional development, who will provide it, where the funding will come from, and so forth. See Echevarría, Short, and Vogt (2008) for details about how to create a plan, and how other schools and districts have rolled out their plan once it was created.
   - Get your school administrator on board with the SIOP Model as a school-wide initiative.

2. Who should receive SIOP professional development?
   - Anyone who will be working with multilingual learners, including teachers, support personnel, special educators, reading specialists, instructional assistants, and administrators, should participate in SIOP professional development.
   - In addition, an overview of SIOP is beneficial for school board members and district-level administrators so everyone is starting on the same page, with the same ultimate goals.

3. What should SIOP professional learning include?
   - Ideally, it should be a combination of workshops, coaching, observations with one-on-one conferences, book study with this text, reflecting on video clips (e-book edition), and follow-up workshops focusing on individual SIOP components.
   - While we know of schools, districts, and states that have rolled out effective SIOP implementation using their own classroom teachers, ESL teachers, and

curriculum administrators as trainers, many districts have chosen to work with Savvas Learning, the only company sanctioned by the SIOP authors to provide training for teachers, paraprofessional, coaches, ESL specialists, administrators, and so forth. For further information, see savvas.com/SIOP and join us and other SIOPers on Twitter: @SIOPModel.

4. How should SIOP be used school-wide?

   - SIOP provides a common language to use when discussing best practices for teaching English learners.

     ◆ The SIOP protocol can be used as an informal observation instrument for peers, mentors, coaches, and administrators. It is a tool for observing teachers' growth in implementing SIOP features, over time. The protocol is also an observation tool for fidelity of SIOP implementation, but it is not intended to be an instrument for teacher evaluation. To change their regular lesson planning style to the SIOP Model, teachers must be able to take some risks. Because the process takes time and is challenging, lessons should not be rated early in the process of learning SIOP.

     ◆ The SIOP protocol is a source for targeted and productive discussions among preservice student teachers, master teachers, and university supervisors, and between a teacher and coach.

5. What should we do about resistant or reluctant teachers during SIOP implementation?

   - Don't begin SIOP implementation with resistant or reluctant teachers. Instead, begin with those who want to improve their instruction of multilingual learners and other students.

   - That said, if resistant teachers have multilingual learners in their classrooms, eventually they will need to receive and be held accountable for SIOP professional learning. From our experience, when resistant teachers hear their colleagues talk about SIOP successes, they eventually come around and want to be part of the story, particularly if their multilingual learners are not experiencing academic success, but the students of the SIOP teachers are.

6. With whom should we collaborate during SIOP implementation?

   - Collaborate with anyone who works with multilingual learners, including the classroom teacher, ESL teacher, SIOP coaches, special educators, paraprofessionals, and administrators.

   - Use a collaborative approach with teachers, including conferencing about observations, setting goals for implementing other features of the model, reflecting on progress in using SIOP, and so forth. (See Chapter 11 for more information about collaboration and co-teaching with SIOP.)

7. What does it mean to be a high-implementing SIOP teacher?

   - The SIOP protocol, with the 0–4 rubric, can be used to measure levels of implementation of SIOP instructional features. From our research and that of others, we have learned that fidelity (level of implementation) to SIOP makes a difference in student performance. High implementers are those teachers whose lessons consistently score 75% or higher on the SIOP protocol as measured during classroom observations (mostly 3's and 4's for high-quality inclusion of the SIOP features).

8. Is SIOP compatible with state content and language standards?

- Yes. State content and language standards are used to guide the development of SIOP teachers' content and language objectives for their SIOP lessons.

- The state standards do not directly address *how* multilingual learners (and struggling students) are to attain standards. For many teachers, SIOP provides a pathway for these students to attain higher levels of academic language proficiency so they can meet or make progress toward meeting the academic state standards.

9. SIOP is a lesson planning and delivery system for teachers, but what about student outcomes?

- Our research has focused almost exclusively on the impact of SIOP on student achievement (see Appendix E). In the classroom, the features of the SIOP Model translate directly into student outcomes when implemented well.) At the conclusion of an effective SIOP lesson, students should be able to demonstrate the outcomes as listed in Figure D.1. This checklist may be used as a spot check to gauge the effectiveness of SIOP lessons.

FIGURE D.1 **Checking Learner Outcomes**

High Quality SIOP Lessons

Students of High-Implementing SIOP Teachers . . . .

- demonstrated that they understood the purpose and objectives of the lesson.
- used the differentiated materials available and participated in meaningful activities.
- were actively encouraged to make links between their own background and the lesson's concepts and activities.
- had multiple opportunities to use new vocabulary in meaningful ways.
- responded to the teacher's modified speech and comprehensible input techniques.
- used learning strategies in completing tasks and assignments.
- were supported while completing tasks and assignments at their level of academic and language proficiency.
- were able to respond to a variety of questions including higher-order questions.
- demonstrated that they could work both independently and collaboratively, using academic English and their home language.
- participated in a variety of grouping configurations that facilitate interaction and discussion.
- used their home language and translanguaging opportunities to discuss, read, and write about key concepts, ask clarification questions, and demonstrate their learning.
- contributed to the lesson by using manipulatives or other resources to practice and apply content knowledge.
- were engaged and working at their potential throughout the lesson.
- adjusted the pace of the lesson.
- demonstrated understanding of the lesson's key vocabulary and content concepts.
- received appropriate and regular feedback on their output (e.g., language, content, work).
- were aware of their progress through assessment of the lesson's objectives.

10. As an administrator, where can I get some assistance?

   - Additional information about school-level implementation of the SIOP Model from an administrator's perspective can be found in *The SIOP® Model for Administrators* (2nd ed., Short, Vogt, & Echevarría, 2017).

   - Become familiar with the additional SIOP resources that support lesson planning and delivery. Books of lesson techniques, SIOP lessons and units for English-language arts, mathematics, history/social studies, and science, and of the SIOP's use in Response to Intervention programs are available. (See Appendix F for Professional Resources.)

11. How can the SIOP protocol be used by researchers and program evaluators to measure teachers' level of SIOP implementation?

   - Use the SIOP protocol for observations of lessons to help determine if a school's or district's investment in SIOP staff development is returning dividends.

   - Analyze student performance in conjunction with teachers' level of implementation, as measured by rating the degree to which SIOP features are present consistently in lessons.

   - Researchers can use the protocol to graph teachers' growth with SIOP, as measured by the consistency of SIOP features found in lesson plans and observed lessons.

Research on the SIOP® Model

The SIOP Model has been developed and refined through 25+ years of sustained research and development studies. The discussion below highlights the first three major investigations. More details on these research projects can be found in Short, Echevarria, and Richards-Tutor (2011) as well as the articles cited in each description.[1]

■ Large-Scale Studies

CREDE Research: Initial Development of the SIOP® Model, Protocol, and Professional Development Program

- The first version of the SIOP began in the early 1990s as an observation tool to determine if observed teachers incorporated key sheltered techniques consistently in their lessons.

- The protocol evolved into a lesson planning and delivery approach, known as the SIOP Model (Echevarría, Vogt, & Short, 2000), through a seven-year, quasi-experimental research study, *The Effects of Sheltered Instruction on the Achievement of Limited English Proficient Students* that was sponsored by the Center for Research on Education, Diversity, & Excellence (CREDE) and funded by the U.S. Department of Education. It began in 1996.

  - The goals of the research project were to (1) develop an explicit model of sheltered instruction; (2) use that model to train teachers in effective sheltered strategies; and (3) conduct field experiments and collect data to evaluate teacher change and the effects of sheltered instruction on LEP students' English language development and content knowledge.

  - This original SIOP study involved collaborating middle school teachers in four large metropolitan school districts—two on the East Coast and two on the West Coast—who worked with researchers to identify key practices for sheltered instruction and develop a professional development model that would enable more teachers to use sheltered instruction effectively in their classrooms. Dr. Jana Echevarría of California State University, Long Beach, CA, and Dr. Deborah Short of the Center for Applied Linguistics in Washington, DC, were co-project investigators.

  - Together, we reviewed the professional literature on best practices for English learners in the areas of ESL, bilingual education, reading, second language

---

[1] Please note that in discussing the research in this appendix we refer to terms that were used during the studies, such as *limited English proficient* and *English learner*, to adhere to the published reports.

acquisition, discourse studies, special education, and classroom management and found many techniques that showed promise but hadn't been empirically investigated. We decided to test combinations of these techniques and thus built our initial model.

◆ During four years of field testing, we analyzed teacher implementation and student effects as teachers tried out variations in their classrooms.

◆ In 2000, we finalized the format—30 features of instruction grouped into eight components essential for making content comprehensible for English learners—Lesson Preparation, Building Background, Comprehensible Input, Strategies, Interaction, Practice & Application, Lesson Delivery, and Review & Assessment (Echevarría, Vogt, & Short, 2000). These components emphasize the instructional practices that are critical for second language learners as well as high-quality practices that benefit all students. The eight components are:

  – The six features under *Lesson Preparation* initiate the lesson planning process, so teachers include content and language objectives, use supplementary materials, create meaningful activities, and more.

  – *Building Background* focuses on making connections with students' background experiences and prior learning, and developing their academic vocabulary.

  – *Comprehensible Input* considers how teachers should adjust their speech, model academic tasks, and use multimodal techniques to enhance comprehension.

  – The *Strategies* component emphasizes teaching learning strategies to students, scaffolding instruction, and promoting higher-order thinking skills.

  – *Interaction* prompts teachers to encourage students to elaborate their speech and to group students appropriately for language and content development.

  – *Practice & Application* provides activities to practice and extend language and content learning.

  – *Lesson Delivery* ensures that teachers present a lesson that meets the planned objectives and promotes student engagement.

  – The *Review & Assessment* component reminds teachers to review the key language and content concepts, assess student learning, and provide specific academic feedback to students on their output.

◆ We created a 5-point scale for each feature on the observation protocol so we could measure the level of implementation in any lesson (4—closest to recommended practice, 0—no evidence of the use of the practice). A separate study confirmed the SIOP protocol as a valid and highly reliable measure of sheltered instruction (Guarino et al., 2001). Experienced observers of classroom instruction (e.g., teacher education faculty who supervise student teachers) who were *not* specifically trained in the SIOP Model were able to use the protocol to distinguish between high and low implementers of the model. A statistical analysis revealed an inter-rater correlation of 0.90 or higher.

- Most of the English learners in the research districts were exempted from the standardized testing process because this CREDE study predated the No Child Left Behind Act of 2001, which mandated assessments. Therefore, to investigate whether the model yielded positive results in terms of student performance, we used pre- and post-measures of the Illinois Measurement of Annual Growth in English (IMAGE) writing test as an outcome measure of academic literacy. The IMAGE was the standardized assessment of reading and writing used by the state of Illinois to measure annual growth of these skills in their English learners in Grades 3–12. It was correlated to and a predictor of scores on the IGAP (the state standardized test of achievement) that was given to all students in Illinois, except those exempted for linguistic development reasons or learning disabilities. The IMAGE Writing Test provided separate scores for five features of writing: Language Production, Focus, Support/Elaboration, Organization, and Mechanics, as well as an overall score.

- Two distinct, but similar, cohorts of English learners in sheltered classes participated: students whose teachers were trained in implementing the SIOP Model (the treatment group), and students whose teachers had no exposure to the SIOP Model (the comparison group). The students in both groups were in Grades 6–8 in the same districts and represented mixed proficiency levels. We found that students who participated in classes taught by teachers trained in the SIOP Model improved their writing skills significantly more than students in classes with non–SIOP-trained teachers. They also made greater gains from the fall to spring administrations of the test. These findings were statistically significant (Echevarría, Short, & Powers, 2006).

- We found that this model can be applied in ESL classes as well as all content area classes because it offers a framework for instruction that incorporates best practices for teaching both language and content.

- From 1999 to 2002, we field-tested and refined the SIOP Model's professional development program that incorporates key features of effective teacher development as recommended then by Darling-Hammond (1998) and still recommended (Darling-Hammond, Hyler, & Gardner, 2017). The program includes professional development institutes and online courses, videotapes of exemplary SIOP teachers, facilitator's guides, and other training materials. See www.siop.savvas.com for more information.

NJ SIOP® Research: Improvement in English Language Proficiency

- From 2004–2007 we replicated and scaled up the SIOP research in a quasi-experimental study. *Academic Literacy through Sheltered Instruction for Secondary English Language Learners* was conducted by researchers at the Center for Applied Linguistics in two districts in New Jersey and funded by the Carnegie Corporation of New York and the Rockefeller Foundation from 2004–2007. The treatment and comparison districts each had one high school and two middle schools with ESL programs and had multilingual student populations.

- In the treatment site, math, science, social studies, language arts, ESL, and technology teachers participated in ongoing SIOP Model training: approximately 35 teachers for two years (Cohort 1) and an additional 25 for one year (Cohort 2). The professional development program included summer institutes, follow-up workshops, and on-site coaching. The teachers in the comparison site did not receive any SIOP Model training.

- We collected teacher implementation data (two classroom observations each year, one in the fall, the other in the spring) using the SIOP protocol at both sites. We found that 56% of the treatment teachers in Cohort 1 became high implementers of the SIOP Model after one year and 71% were high implementers after two. Seventy-four percent of the Cohort 2 teachers who joined the Cohort 1 teachers at their schools reached the high implementation level in just one year. At the comparison site, fewer teachers implemented the SIOP features to a high level: 5% of the teachers in the first year; 17% by the second year (Short, Fidelman, & Louguit, 2012).

- We also collected student data from the state English language proficiency assessment at that time, the IPT (Idea Proficiency Tests), for all English learners in Grades 6–12 in both districts. Students with SIOP-trained teachers made statistically significant gains in their average mean scores for oral language, writing, and total proficiency on the state assessment of English language proficiency, compared to the comparison group of English learners (Short, Fidelman, & Louguit, 2012).

CREATE Research: Fidelity Matters and All Students Benefit—English Learners and English Speakers Alike

- From 2005–2011, researchers from California State University, Long Beach, and the Center for Applied Linguistics participated in the program of studies at the National Center for Research on the Educational Achievement and Teaching of English Language Learners (CREATE), funded by the U.S. Department of Education. The study, *The Impact of the SIOP® Model on Middle School Science and Language Learning*, first examined the SIOP Model in middle school science classrooms (Himmel, Short, Richards, & Echevarría, 2009) and later applied the SIOP Model as the professional development framework for a school-wide intervention (Echevarría & Short, 2011). In this set of studies, we used an experimental design and English learners, former English learners, and native English speakers were part of the treatment and control student populations.

  - A pilot study was conducted to develop SIOP science curriculum units, where local standards and curricula were enhanced with SIOP features, and to design and field-test science language assessments that would measure student scientific vocabulary, reading comprehension, and writing skills.

  - In 2006–2007, an experimental study was conducted in eight middle schools for one semester. Five received the treatment, which was SIOP professional development, classroom-based coaching, and four SIOP science units developed by researchers and teacher consultants. Three schools were control sites where teachers taught in their regular fashion with their own lessons. Treatment and control teachers were observed and their lessons were rated using the SIOP protocol.

♦ Results showed that students in the treatment classes outperformed control students (Echevarría, Richards-Tutor, Canges, & Francis, 2011) and the higher the level of SIOP implementation, the better the students performed on assessments (Echevarría, Richards-Tutor, Chinn, & Ratleff, 2011). This result held true for English learners, former English learners, and native English speakers.

♦ During the 2009–2010 school year, another experimental study took place. A two-year intervention focused schoolwide on Grade 7 and the SIOP Model was the overarching professional development framework (Echevarría & Short, 2011). Other content-specific curriculum interventions tested through earlier years of the CREATE program were implemented as well. Eight schools were randomly assigned to treatment or control. The four treatment schools had SIOP professional development and classroom-based coaching for SIOP implementation, and where applicable, for the content-specific curriculum intervention. The teachers in the four control schools delivered regular instruction without curriculum units or SIOP training. Their instruction was observed for research purposes, but they did not receive feedback.

♦ In the 2010–2011 school year, teachers in three of the prior year's control schools became treatment teachers and received the SIOP professional development and curriculum interventions as well. A new treatment school joined the study that year, bringing the number of schools to four.

♦ Researchers collected data in the treatment and control sites during both years. Teacher implementation levels were measured with the SIOP protocol and other tools. Student performance was measured with standardized tests and curriculum-based assessments. Analyses showed that this school-wide intervention improved outcomes in content knowledge and academic English for both English learners and native English speakers in the treatment classes. Specifically, students in SIOP curriculum groups outperformed control students to a significant degree on criterion-referenced vocabulary, science, and social studies measures (Short & Himmel, 2013).

■ Focused SIOP Studies

Since the initial SIOP Model studies were published in the early 2000s, other researchers have investigated the SIOP Model in a number of ways, ranging from experimental research designs to case studies. At the time of this writing we know of more than 50 studies and dissertations that have been published.[2] Furthermore, in recent years, more and more researchers have looked at the SIOP Model in a non-US context, such as English as a foreign language (EFL), English as a medium of instruction (EMI), and Content and Language Integrated Learning (CLIL) classes, in primary, secondary, and university settings.

---

[2] We appreciate the assistance of Susan Hurt in identifying and reviewing some of these studies.

SIOP Model and the Impact on Student Achievement

A number of studies examined the effectiveness of the SIOP Model in terms of student outcomes. These studies sought to discover whether students taught using the SIOP Model would experience greater growth in English proficiency or higher achievement on standardized test scores than students who were not taught using SIOP. Most found that the SIOP Model had a positive effect on the achievement of English learners. Several mentioned that fidelity to the model was important to improve student performance. (See, for example, Alnusayan & Al-Salouli, 2020; Ebedy, 2019; Friend, Most, & McCrary, 2009; Guzman, 2015; Hayden, 2019; Ingram, 2018; McIntyre et al., 2010; Merritt et. al., 2016; Rivera, 2019; Vidot, 2011; Watkins & Lindahl, 2010; Whittier & Robinson, 2007; and Wong, Meadows, & Ober, 2021).

SIOP Model Professional Development and Classroom Instruction

Other researchers have used the SIOP Model as a basis for professional development (PD). They have found SIOP to be effective in promoting teacher learning. Many of these studies used the SIOP protocol to measure transfer and implementation of the SIOP instructional practices. Some also explored changes in teachers' attitudes and expectations of their multilingual students, or increases in teacher knowledge about language instruction, or the ability to embed linguistically and culturally responsive practices in lessons. One consistent recommendation is to give teachers time and support to implement the SIOP well. Several studies made suggestions for modifying the PD to suit specific programmatic needs, such as by adding a coaching component. (See, for example, Aldakhil & Alfadda, 2021; Bárcena-Toyos, 2022; Batt, 2010; Chen, Kyle, & McIntyre, 2008; Coppersmith, Slapac, & Song, 2019; Daniel & Pray, 2017; Gonzalez, 2016; Gruver & Bowers, 2020; Hanson-Thomas, Langman, & Farias, 2018; Honigsfeld & Cohan, 2008; Kim, Song, & Coppersmith, 2018; Koura & Zahan, 2017; O'Neal, Ringler, & Lys, 2009; Piazza et al., 2020; Shi, Zaier, & Maina, 2019; Short, Cloud, Morris, & Motta, 2012; Song, 2016a, 2016b; Song & Samimy, 2015; Üzüm, Petrón, & Berg, 2014; Welsh & Newman, 2010; and Ye He & Faircloth, 2018).

SIOP and Program Evaluation

School districts have conducted a number of program evaluations on their implementation of the SIOP Model that can be reviewed in *Implementing the SIOP® Model Through Effective Professional Development and Coaching* (Echevarría, Short, & Vogt, 2008). Some other studies that evaluated school or district programs that have implemented the SIOP Model include Calderon & Zamora (2014), Chandler (2020), and Li et al. (2016).

■ Conclusion: SIOP® Research to Date

By looking at these research studies as a whole, we see that SIOP instruction is making a positive learning difference for multilingual learners and other students who are in the classrooms. Teachers can learn to implement the model to a high degree with ongoing PD and support. No one is disadvantaged by SIOP instruction; rather, the focus on academic literacy and scaffolded instruction helps all students learn academic English and grade-level, content curricula better.

SIOP® Professional Development Resources

■ Savvas SIOP® Website

Various SIOP® resources are on the Savvas Learning website at SIOP.Savvas.com. Resources include video clips, podcasts, SIOP® Lesson Plan Templates, and information on SIOP® events and workshops.

■ Books

Core SIOP Texts

Echevarría, J., Vogt, M.E., & Short, D. (2023). *Making content comprehensible for multilingual learners: The SIOP® Model* (6th ed.). Pearson.

Echevarría, J., Short, D., & Peterson, C. (2012). *Using the SIOP® Model with pre-K and kindergarten English learners*. Pearson.

Echevarría, J., Vogt, M.E., & Short, D. (2018a). *Making content comprehensible for elementary English learners: The SIOP® Model* (3rd ed.). Pearson.

Echevarría, J., Vogt, M.E., & Short, D. (2018b). *Making content comprehensible for secondary English learners: The SIOP® Model* (3rd ed.). Pearson.

Additional SIOP Texts

Echevarría, J., Short, D., & Vogt, M.E. (2008). *Implementing the SIOP® Model through effective professional development and coaching*. Pearson.

Echevarría, J., Vogt, M.E., & Short, D. (2010). *The SIOP® Model for teaching mathematics to English learners*. Pearson.

Short, D., & Echevarría, J. (2016). *Developing academic language using the SIOP® Model*. Pearson.

Short, D., Echevarría, J., & Vogt, M.E. (2017). *The SIOP® Model for administrators* (2nd ed.). Pearson.

Short, D., Vogt, M.E., & Echevarría, J. (2011a). *The SIOP® Model for teaching history-social studies to English learners*. Pearson.

Short, D., Vogt, M.E., & Echevarría, J. (2011b). *The SIOP® Model for teaching science to English learners*. Pearson.

Vogt, M.E., & Echevarría, J. (2022). *99 ideas and activities for teaching English learners with the SIOP® Model* (2nd ed). Pearson.

Vogt, M.E., Echevarría, J., & Short, D. (2010). *The SIOP® Model for teaching English-language arts to English learners*. Pearson.

Vogt, M.E, Echevarría, J., & Washam, M. (2015). *99 more ideas and activities for teaching English learners with the SIOP® Model*. Pearson.

Teaching Multilingual Learners with Learning Challenges

Echevarría, J., & Graves, A. (2015). *Sheltered content instruction: Teaching English learners with diverse abilities* (5th ed.). Pearson.

Echevarría, J., Richards-Tutor, C., & Vogt, M.E. (2015). *Response to intervention (RTI) and English learners: Using the SIOP® Model* (2nd ed.). Pearson.

Research Briefs (Downloadable)

Echevarría, J. (2012). *Effective practices for increasing the achievement of English learners.* https://eric.ed.gov/?id=ED549139

Echevarría, J., & Hasbrouck, J. (2009). *Response to intervention and English learners.* https://files.eric.ed.gov/fulltext/ED549176.pdf

Echevarría, J., & Short, D. (2011). *The SIOP® Model: A professional development framework for comprehensive school-wide intervention.* https://eric.ed.gov/?id=ED549149

Himmel, J., Short, D.J., Richards, C., & Echevarría, J. (2009). *Using the SIOP® Model to improve middle school science instruction.* https://eric.ed.gov/?id=ED549177

■ Blogs

A number of current and archived blog posts about teaching multilingual learners and using the SIOP Model can be found at www.JanaEchevarria.com and at tinyurl.com/SavvasSIOPBlogs.

■ SIOP Research

Al-Aloom, L.B. (2019). *Effective sheltered instruction observation protocol (SIOP) model strategies among Arab ELLs.* Capella University, ProQuest Dissertations Publishing, 27544311.

Aldakhil, A., & Alfadda, H. (2021). The implementation of Sheltered Instructional Observation Protocol (SIOP) Model in Saudi schools: A study of EFL teache

Al Fadda, H. A. (2020). Implementation of the Sheltered Instructional Observation Protocol (SIOP) Model in the Saudi classroom: EFL teachers' perspectives. *Arab World English Journal, 11*(2) 339–360. DOI: https://dx.doi.org/10.24093/awej/vol11no2.24

Alfaro, Y. (2020). *The effect of elementary teachers trained in the SIOP Model on the achievement of English language learners in the English reading domain.* University of St. Francis, ProQuest Dissertations Publishing, 28149422.

Alnusayan, I. S., & Al-Salouli, M.S. (2020). The effectiveness of Sheltered Instruction Observation Protocol (SIOP) Model of developing mathematical achievement in preparatory year female students at Al-Imam Mohammad Ibn Saud Islamic University. *Journal of Educational and Psychological Sciences, 4*(25), 93–113. DOI: https://doi.org/10.26389/AJSRP.E180220

Bárcena-Toyos, P. (2022). CLIL and SIOP: An effective partnership? *International Multilingual Research Journal.*

Batt, E. (2010). Cognitive coaching: A critical phase in professional development to implement sheltered instruction. *Teaching and Teacher Education 26,* 997–1005.

Bertram, R. L. (2011). *Sheltered instruction: A case study of three high school English teachers' experiences with the SIOP Model* (Doctoral dissertation). Available from ProQuest Dissertations and Theses database. (UMI No. 3486471)

Bose, D. (2012). *Effects of just-in-time online training on knowledge and application of the Sheltered Instruction Observation Protocol (SIOP) model among in-service teachers.* Available from Idaho State University, ProQuest Dissertations Publishing, 3536205.

Boughoulid, M. (2020). The SIOP Model as an empowering teaching method for English language learners: A study case. *European Journal of English Language Teaching, 6*(2), 39–53.

Calderon, C. T., & Zamora, E. (2014). Factors affecting the implementation of sheltered instruction observation protocols for English language learners. *National Forum of Educational Administration & Supervision Journal, 31*(3), 20–32.

Chandler, P. T. (2020). *Implementing the SIOP Model to support English language learners.* All Theses And Dissertations. 315. https://dune.une.edu/theses/315

Chen, C-T, Kyle, D., & McIntyre, E. (2008). Helping teachers work effectively with English language learners and their families. *The School Community Journal, 18*(1), 7–20.

Chen, G., Ling, W., Li, L., & Shi, Y. (2020). A research of digital integrated circuit design curriculum's bilingual education based on methodology of SIOP. *Advances in Social Science, Education and Humanities Research,* 412, 484–488.

Choi, W., Kim, W.H., Wright, W., & Morita-Mullaney, T. (2022). Improving English language arts instruction in Indiana dual language bilingual education classrooms. *Language and Education,* DOI: 10.1080/09500782.2022.2032731

Daniel, S., & Pray, L. (2017). Learning to teach English language learners: A study of elementary school teachers' sense-making in an ELL endorsement program. *TESOL Quarterly, 51*(4), 787–819.

de Jager, T. (2019). Are principles of the Sheltered Instruction Observation Protocol Model promoting ESL teaching and learning? *The International Journal of Pedagogy and Curriculum, 26*(1), 43–58. DOI:10.18848/2327-7963/CGP/v26i01/43-58

Dodici, A. (2011). *The relationship between teachers' multicultural attitudes and their instructional practice with English language learners: A mixed method study.* (Doctoral dissertation). DOI 10.15760/etd.141

Ebedy, H.G. (2019). Developing reading comprehension skills using Sheltered Instruction Observation Protocol (SIOP) among EFL students. *Journal of Research in Curriculum, Instruction and Educational Technology, 5*(2), 197–220.

Echevarria, J., Richards-Tutor, C., Canges, R., & Francis, D. (2011). Using the SIOP Model to promote the acquisition of language and science concepts with English learners. *Bilingual Research Journal, 34*(3), 334–351.

Echevarria, J., Richards-Tutor, C., Chinn, V., & Ratleff, P. (2011). Did they get it? The role of fidelity in teaching English learners. *Journal of Adolescent and Adult Literacy, 54*(6), 425–434.

Echevarria, J., Short, D., & Powers, K. (2006). School reform and standards-based education: An instructional model for English language learners. *Journal of Educational Research, 99*(4), 195–210.

Eggington, K., Eggington, W., & Zeichner, K. (2010). Teacher research used to evaluate sheltered instruction in a science classroom setting. *Electronic Journal of Literacy Through Science*, 9.

Friend, J., Most, R., & McCrary, K. (2009). The impact of a professional development program to improve urban middle-level English language learner achievement. *Middle Grades Research Journal, 4*(1), 53–75.

González, M. (2016). Preparing teacher candidates for the instruction of English language learners. *Networks, 18*(2). DOI: 10.4148/2470-6353.1005

Gruver, J., & Bowers, J. (2020). Evolution of inquiry questions in a cyclic professional development program. *Canadian Journal of Action Research, 20*(3), 3–18.

Guarino, A.J., Echevarria, J., Short, D., Schick, J.E., Forbes, S., & Rueda, R. (2001). The Sheltered Instruction Observation Protocol. *Journal of Research in Education, 11*(1), 138–140.

Guzman, R. (2015). *A study of the impact of English language learners: Literacy development through the SIOP Model.* ProQuest Dissertations Publishing, 3701484.

Hayden, R. (2019). *English proficiency in classes using Sheltered Instruction Observation Protocol (SIOP) compared to classes not using SIOP.* Capella University, ProQuest Dissertations Publishing, 22616011.

Hanson-Thomas, H., Langman, J., & Farias, T. (2018). The role of language objectives: Strengthening math and science teachers' language awareness with emergent bilinguals in secondary classrooms. *LACLIL, 11*(2), 193–214. doi: 10.5294/laclil.2018.11.2.2

Himmel, J., Short, D.J., Richards, C., & Echevarria, J. (2009). *Using the SIOP Model to improve middle school science instruction.* Washington, DC: Center for Research on the Educational Achievement and Teaching of English Language Learners. Retrieved from http://www.cal.org/create/publications/briefs/using-the-siop-model-to-improve-middle-school-science-instruction.html

Honigsfeld, A., & Cohan, A. (2008). The power of two: Lesson study and SIOP help teachers instruct ELLs. *Journal of Staff Development, 29*(1), 24–28.

Inceli, O. (2015). The perceptions of English teachers to the SIOP Model and its impact on limited English proficiency. *Journal of Ethnic and Cultural Studies, 2*(1), 15–28.

Ingram, S. (2018). *An analysis of the Sheltered Instruction Observation Protocol Model on academic performance of English language learners.* ProQuest Dissertations Publishing, 0355555247.

Li, J., Steele, J., Slater, R., Bacon, M., & Miller, T. (2016). Teaching practices and language use in two-way dual language immersion programs in a large public school district. *International Multilingual Research Journal, 10*(1). 31–43. DOI: 10.1080/19313152.2016.1118669

Kang, A. (2005). How to promote comprehension and participation in CBI courses: The SIOP Model. *English Teaching,* 12, 159–196.

Kareva, V. & Echevarria, J. (2013). Using the SIOP Model for effective content teaching with second and foreign language learners. *Journal of Education and Training Studies, 1*(2), 239–248.

Kim, S., Song, K., & Coppersmith, S. (2018). Creating an interactive virtual community of linguistically and culturally responsive content teacher-learners to serve English learners. *Contemporary Issues in Technology and Teacher Education, 18*(2), 442–466.

Koura, A. & Zahan, F. (2017). The impact of the Sheltered Instruction Observation Protocol Model on student teachers' teaching skills and self-efficacy. *Journal of Language Teaching and Research, 8*(4), 704–714. DOI: http://dx.doi.org/10.17507/jltr.0804.09

Li, J., Steele, J., Slater, R., Bacon, M., & Miller, T. (2016). Teaching practices and language use in two-way dual language immersion programs in a large public school district. *International Multilingual Research Journal, 10*(1), 31–43. DOI: 10.1080/19313152.2016.1118669

Merritt, E.G., Palacios, N., Banse, H., Rimm-Kaufman, S.E., & Leis, M. (2016). Teaching practices in Grade 5 mathematics classrooms with high-achieving English learner students. *The Journal of Educational Research.* DOI: 10.1080/00220671.2015.1034352

McIntyre, E., Kyle, D., Chen, C., Muñoz, M., & Beldon, S. (2010). Teacher learning and ELL reading achievement in sheltered instruction classrooms: Linking professional development to student development, *Literacy Research and Instruction, 49*(4), 334–351.

Nakagawa, H. (2017). *The Teacher Perception and Receptiveness of Sheltered Instruction Observation Protocol (SIOP) Model within a Japanese University Context.* Northcentral University, ProQuest Dissertations Publishing, 10608145.

O'Neal, D., Ringler, M.C., & Lys, D.B. (2009). Skeptics to partners: University teams with district to improve ELL instruction. *Journal of Staff Development, 30*(4), 52–55.

Owen, S. (2018). *The effect of emphasizing key vocabulary on Student achievement with English learners.* (Doctoral dissertation). Retrieved from https://scholarcommons.sc.edu/etd/5021

Piazza, S., Williams, C., Protacio, M.S., David, V., Tigchelaar, M., & Kuo, H-C. (2020). Improving instruction for English learners: A professional development study using SIOP. *Journal of Teacher Education and Educators, 9*(3), 283–405.

Polat, N., & Cepik, S. (2015). An exploratory factor analysis of the Sheltered Instruction Observation Protocol as an evaluation tool to measure teacher effectiveness. *TESOL Quarterly, 50*(4), 817–843. DOI 10.1002/tesq.248

Portillo, C. (2015). *Teachers' perceptions on the use of Sheltered Instruction Observation Protocol as a districtwide professional development reform.* (Doctoral Dissertation) Available from ProQuest Dissertations and Theses database. (UMI No. 3723058)

Reyes, J., & Gentry, J. (2019). Pre-service administrators' experiences with effective research-based learning strategies for English language learners. In K. Young, C. Brown & S. Harris (Eds.). *Educational Research Review*, 20, 23–38.

Rivera, E. (2019). *The impact of the sheltered instruction observation (SIOP) on the achievement of English language learners* (Order No. 27736339). Available from ProQuest Dissertations & Theses Global: The Humanities and Social Sciences Collection. (2377940533).

Rodriguez Moux, S. (2010). *Teacher's perceptions of sheltered instruction observation protocol for teaching young English language learners: A qualitative case study.* ProQuest Dissertations Publishing, 3398868.

Shi, Y., Zaier, A., & Maina, F. (2019). *Preservice teacher perspectives and practices working with multilingual learners.* Paper presented at the 2019 annual meeting of the American Educational Research Association. DOI: https://doi.org/10.3102/1434337

Short, D., Cloud, N., Morris, P., & Motta, J. (2012). Cross-district collaboration: Curriculum and professional development. *TESOL Journal, 3*(3), 402–424.

Short, D., Echevarria, J., & Richards-Tutor, C. (2011). Research on academic literacy development in sheltered instruction classrooms. *Language Teaching Research, 15*(3), 363–380.

Short, D., Fidelman, C., & Louguit, M. (2012). Developing academic language in English language learners through sheltered instruction. *TESOL Quarterly, 46*(2), 333–360.

Short, D., & Himmel, J. (2013). *Moving research on sheltered instruction into curriculum and professional development practice.* Paper presented at American Educational Research Association (AERA) Annual Meeting, San Francisco, CA, April 2013.

Song, K. (2016, February). Systematic professional development training and its impact on teachers' attitudes toward ELLs: SIOP and guided coaching. *TESOL Journal.* Retrieved from http://onlinelibrary.wiley.com/doi/10.1002/tesj.240/full doi: 10.1002/tesj.240

Song, K. (2016). Applying an SIOP-based instructional framework for professional development in Korea. *TESL-EJ, 20*(1).

Song, S. Y. & Samimy, K. (2015). The beliefs of secondary content teachers of English language learners regarding language learning and teaching. *International Journal of TESOL and Learning, 4*(1), 3–19.

Suweken, G., Waluyo, D., & Okassandiari, N. L. (2017). The improvement of students' conceptual understanding and students' academic language of mathematics through the implementation of SIOP Model. *International Research Journal of Management, IT & Social Sciences, 4*(4), 51–60. DOI: 10.21744/irjmis.v4i4.519

Torres, N. (2006). *Administrative support for English language learners: How the SIOP Model empowers teachers, administrators, and English language learners.* (Doctoral Dissertation) Available from ProQuest Dissertations Publishing. (No. 3231250).

Üzüm, B., & Petrón, M. (2018). Glocal experiences in your own backyard: Teacher candidates developing understanding of equity, diversity, and social justice. In A. F. Selvi and N. Rudolph (Eds.), *Conceptual shifts and contextualized practices in education for glocal interaction, intercultural communication and language education.* Singapore: Springer Nature. https://doi.org/10.1007/978-981-10-6421-0_6

Üzüm, B., Petrón, M., & Berg, H. (2014). Pre-service teachers' first foray into the ESL classroom: Reflective practice in a service learning project. *TESL-EJ, 18*(3), 1–15.

Vidot, J. L. (2011). *The efficacy of sheltered instruction observation protocol (SIOP) in mathematics instruction on English language learners.* (Doctoral dissertation) Available from http://scholarworks.waldenu.edu/dissertations/943/

Watkins, N. M., & Lindahl, K. M. (2010). Targeting content area literacy instruction to meet the needs of adolescent English language learners. *Middle School Journal, 41*(3), 23–32.

Welsh, L., & Newman, K. (2010). Becoming a content-ESL teacher: A dialogic journey of a science teacher and teacher educator. *Theory Into Practice, 49,* 137–144.

Whittier, L. E., & Robinson, M. (2007). Teaching evolution to non-English proficient students by using Lego Robotics. *American Secondary Education, 35*(3), 19–28.

Wong, C.Y., Meadows, B., & Ober, G. (2020). Using the SIOP instruction model for narrative writing: A case study of a teacher's experience of using the model in a high school setting. *TESL Reporter 53*(1–2), 37–58.

Ye He, W.J. & Faircloth, J. (2018). Preparing teachers for English learners: Integrating academic language and community service projects, *The Social Studies, 109*(1), 13–26, DOI: 10.1080/00377996.2017.1403874

Zito-Nash, J. (2017). *Impact of Sheltered Instruction Observation Protocol (SIOP) Strategies on reading achievement of English language learners in the primary grades.* ProQuest Dissertations Publishing, 0355139677.

■ Research Application Of SIOP

Balconi, A., & Spitzman, E. Content area teachers' challenges writing language objectives: A document analysis. *TESOL J.* 2020; 00:e530. https://doi.org/10.1002/tesj.530

Colburn, A., & Echevarria, J. (1999). Meaningful lessons. *The Science Teacher*, 66(2) 36–39.

Coppersmith, S., Slapac, A., & Song, K. (2019). Infusing linguistically and culturally responsive practices for English learners in social studies methods. *Social Studies Education Review, 8*(1) 45–66.

Dumas-Landisi, M. & Honigsfeld, A. (2010). ELL instruction that works for all. *Educator's Voice*, 3, 74–81.

Echevarria, J. (2006). Helping English language learners succeed. *Principal Leadership, 6*(5), 16–21. National Association for Secondary School Principals.

Echevarría, J., & Colburn, A. (2006). Designing lessons: Inquiry approach to science using the SIOP® Model. In A. Fathman & D. Crowther, (Eds.), *Science for English language learners* (pp. 95–108). National Science Teachers Association Press.

Echevarria, J., Frey, N., & Fisher, D. (2015). What it takes for English learners to succeed. *Educational Leadership, 72*(6), 22–26.

Echevarria, J., Powers, K., & Elliott, J. (2004). Promising practices for curbing disproportionate representation of minority students in special education. *Issues in Teacher Education, 13*(1), 19–34.

Echevarria, J., & Short, D. (2010). Programs and practices for effective sheltered content instruction. In California Department of Education (Ed.), *Improving education for English learners: Research-based approaches* (pp. 251–303). Dept. of Education.

Echevarria, J., & Short, D. (2004). Using multiple perspectives in observations of diverse classrooms: The Sheltered Instruction Observation Protocol. In H. Waxman, R. Tharp, & R. Hilberg (Eds.), *Observational Research in U.S. Classrooms* (pp. 21–47). Cambridge Univ. Press.

Echevarria, J., Short, D., & Powers, K. (2008). Making content comprehensible for non-native speakers of English: The SIOP Model. *The International Journal of Learning*, Volume 14, Issue 11, pp. 41–50. Article: Print (Spiral Bound). Article: Electronic (PDF File; 639.531KB).

Echevarria, J., & Vogt, M. (2010). Using the SIOP Model to improve literacy for English learners. *New England Reading Association Journal* (NERAJ), *46*(1) 8–15.

Hansen-Thomas, H. (2008). Sheltered Instruction: Best practices for ELLs in the mainstream, *Kappa Delta Pi Record, 44*(4), 165–169. DOI: 10.1080/00228958.2008.10516517

Lomashvili, L. (2022). How to incorporate language form, function, and structure in the SIOP Model lessons. *International Journal of English Language Teaching, 9*(2), 8–18.

Murillo, R., & Alejandro, H. (2013). Adapting features from the SIOP component: Lesson delivery to English lessons in a Colombian public school. *Profile Issues in Teachers Professional Development, 15*(1), 171–193.

Nora, J., & Echevarria, J. (2016). *No more low expectations for ELLs* (N. Duke & E. Keene, Eds.), *Not This But That* series. Heinemann.

Prabjandee, D. (2016). Sheltered Instruction Observation Protocol (SIOP): Overview, misconceptions, and considerations for implementation. *Journal of Education, 27*(3), 1–17.

Qabaja, Z.M.M., Nafi, J.S., & Abu-Nimah, M.I. (2016). The effect of using the "SQP2RS via WTL" strategy through science context to 10th graders' reading comprehension in English in Palestine. *Journal of Education and Practice, 7*(26), 137–151.

Shanahan, T., & Echevarria, J. (2019). Policies the support improving the literacy levels of English learners. *State Education Standard*. National Association of State Boards of Education.

Short, D. (2017). How to integrate language and content learning effectively for English language learners. EURASIA *Journal of Mathematics Science and Technology Education*, *13*(7b), 4237–4260. DOI: 10.12973/eurasia.2017. 00806a

Short, D. (2000). What principals should know about sheltered instruction for English language learners. *NASSP Bulletin*, *84*(619), 17–27. DOI:10.1177/019263650008461902

Short, D. (2013). Training and sustaining effective teachers of sheltered instruction. *Theory Into Practice*, *52*(2), 118–127.

Short, D., & Echevarria, J. (December 2004/January 2005). Promoting academic literacy for English language learners. *Educational Leadership*, *62*(4) 8–13.

Short, D., & Echevarria, J. (1999). *The sheltered observation protocol: A tool for researcher-teacher collaboration and professional development.* (Educational Practice Report No. 3). Center for Research on Education, Diversity, & Excellence.

Vogt, M.E. (2012). English learners: Developing their literate lives. In R.M. Bean & A.S. Dagen (Eds.), *Best practice of literacy leaders: Keys to school improvement* (pp. 248–260). The Guilford Press.

Vogt, M.E. (In press). Reaching linguistically diverse students through exemplary language, literacy, and content teaching. In S. B. Wepner, D. S. Strickland, & D. Quatroche (Eds.), *The administration and supervision of reading programs,* 6th ed. Teachers College Press.

Vogt, M.E. (2020). Academic Language and literacy development for English learners. In R.M. Bean, & A.S. Dagen (Eds.), *Best practice of literacy leaders: Keys to school improvement* (2nd ed.). The Guilford Press.

Vogt, M., & Echevarria J. (2015). Reaching English learners: Aligning the ELA/ELD framework with SIOP. *The California Reader*, *49*(1), 33.

Glossary

Academic language: Language used in formal contexts for academic subjects and purposes. The aspect of language connected with literacy and academic achievement. This includes technical and general academic terms (*see* Cognitive/Academic Language Proficiency–CALP) and reading, writing, listening, and speaking skills as used in school to acquire new knowledge and accomplish academic tasks.

Assessment: The orderly process of gathering, analyzing, interpreting, and reporting student performance, ideally from multiple sources over a period of time. Assessment data are used to inform instruction and measure student progress.

Basic Interpersonal Communicative Skills (BICS): Face-to-face conversational fluency, including mastery of pronunciation, vocabulary, and grammar. English learners typically acquire conversational language used in everyday activities before they develop more complex, conceptual, academic language proficiency. (*See* Social language.)

Bilingual education: School instruction using two languages, generally the home language of the student and a second language. The amount of time that each language is used depends on the type of bilingual program, its specific objectives, and students' level of language proficiency.

Cognitive/Academic Language Proficiency (CALP): Language proficiency associated with schooling, and the abstract language abilities required for academic work. A more complex, conceptual, linguistic ability that includes analysis, synthesis, and evaluation. (*See* Academic language.)

Content-based language instruction: An instructional approach in which content topics are used as the vehicle for second language learning. A system of instruction in which teachers use a variety of instructional techniques as a way of developing second language, content knowledge, and cognitive and study skills. It is often delivered through thematic units and tied to the subject area instruction that multilingual learners receive. Also known as *content-based ESL* and *content-based ELD*.

Content objectives: Statements that identify what students should know and be able to do in a subject area for a given lesson. They support school district and state content standards and learning outcomes, and they guide teaching and learning in the classroom.

Content standards: Definitions of what students are expected to know and be capable of doing for a given content area; the knowledge and skills that need to be taught in order for students to reach competency; what students are expected to learn and what schools are expected to teach. May be national, state, or district standards.

Co-Teaching: A setting in which professionals, typically an English language development specialist and a general education teacher, collaborate to provide effective instruction for multilingual learners. The process involves using SIOP as a guide for co-planning, co-teaching, co-assessing, and co-reflecting on the lesson.

Culturally responsive teaching: An approach to classroom instruction and communication that respects the different cultural characteristics of all students. The learning environment reflects high expectations for all and builds on students' linguistic, experiential, socio-emotional, cultural, and familial assets. Class discussions are open to cultural viewpoints, student ways of knowing are elicited, collaboration is frequent, pedagogical materials are multicultural, and values are shared and affirmed. The goal is equitable access for all to high quality instruction. Also known as culturally relevant teaching and culturally sustaining pedagogy.

Culture: The customs, lifestyle, traditions, behavior, attitudes, and artifacts of a given people. Culture also encompasses the ways people organize and interpret the world, and the way events are perceived based on established social norms. A system of standards for understanding the world.

Differentiated instruction: In order to create a learning environment that addresses the diversity of abilities and language proficiency levels represented in many classrooms, teachers adjust the pace, amount, level, or kind of instruction to meet the individual needs and abilities of each learner. Teachers may differentiate the way new information is presented, the texts and materials being used, the tasks being required of students, or the grouping of the learners.

Disciplinary literacy: The convergence of specialized, content knowledge and the ability to read, write, listen, speak, and think critically about it. Rigorous state standards suggest that teaching students to read, write, discuss, and think about discipline-specific texts, including primary sources, will help them develop disciplinary literacy skills.

Dual language program: A type of bilingual education where the goal is developing bilingualism and biliteracy. English and a target language are used for instruction. It may follow a 90-10 model (where the earliest grades use the target language 90% of the instructional time and move to 50% by fifth grade) or a 50-50 model (where each language is used 50% of the instructional time in all grades). Sheltered instruction, like SIOP, is needed in classes when non-native speakers are present and learning through a language in which they are not proficient. (Also called *two-way immersion*).

Emergent bilinguals: Refers to students who are in the process of acquiring a new language in addition to their home language. The term reflects the goal of bilingualism so students develop both languages to a proficient level. These students may also be referred to as *multilingual learners, English learners,* or *English language learners* in some regions.

Engagement: When students are fully taking part in a lesson, they are said to be engaged. This is a holistic term that encompasses active listening, reading, writing, responding, and discussing. The level of students' engagement during a lesson may be assessed to a greater or lesser degree. A low SIOP score for engagement would imply frequent chatting, daydreaming, nonattention, and other off-task behaviors.

English language development (ELD): Used in some regions to refer to programs and classes to teach students English as a second (additional) language. May refer to the language teaching specialists and their teaching certifications or endorsements. (*See* ESL.) May refer to some state or district standards. (*See* English language proficiency [ELP] standards.)

English language proficiency (ELP) standards: Definitions of what students are expected to know and be capable of doing in English; the knowledge and skills that need to be taught in order for students to reach competency; what students are expected to learn and what schools are expected to teach. May be national, state, or district standards. Each state is required by the federal government to have ELP standards and related assessments. (*See* English language development [ELD].)

English learners: Children and adults who are learning English as a second or additional language. This term may apply to learners across various levels of proficiency in English. English learners may also be referred to as *English language learners, emergent bilingual students, limited English proficient* (LEP) *students*, and *multilingual learners.*

English-only: Used in some regions, English-only refers to students whose native language is English.

ENL: English as a new language. Used in some regions to refer to programs and classes to teach students English as a new (or second or additional) language.

ESL: English as a second language. Used to refer to programs and classes to teach students English as a second (additional) language. May refer to the language teaching specialists and their teaching certifications or endorsements.

ESOL: English speakers of other languages. Students whose first language is not English and who do not write, speak, and understand the language as well as their classmates. In some regions, this term also refers to the programs and classes for English learners.

Home language: The language, or languages, spoken in the student's home by people who live there. Also referred to as first language (L1), primary language, or native language.

Informal assessment: Appraisal of student performance during lessons; characterized as frequent, ongoing, continuous, and involving simple but important techniques such as verbal checks for understanding, teacher-created assessments, observations, and other nonstandardized procedures. This type of assessment provides teachers with immediate feedback to inform subsequent instruction.

Instructional conversations (IC): An approach to teaching that is an interactive dialogue with an instructional intent. An IC approach encourages thoughtful discussion around a concept or idea with balanced participation between teacher and students.

Integrated ELD: A term used in the California ELA/ELD framework for subject area classes that develop both content knowledge and academic language, with scaffolding to support students. Similar to sheltered instruction.

Inter-rater reliability: Measure of the degree of agreement between two different raters on separate ratings of one assessment indicator using the same scale and criteria.

L1: First language. A widely used abbreviation for the first language learned. Also known as primary, home, or native language.

L2: Second language. A widely used abbreviation for the second (or additional) language learned.

Language minority: In the United States, a student whose native language is not English. The individual student's ability to speak, listen, read, and write in English will vary.

Language objectives: Statements that identify what students should know and be able to do while learning English (or another language) in a given lesson. They support students' language

development, often focusing on vocabulary, functional language, language skills in reading, writing, listening, and speaking, grammatical knowledge, and language learning strategies.

Language proficiency: An individual's competence in using a language for basic communication and for academic purposes. May be categorized as stages of language acquisition. (*See* Levels of language proficiency.)

Learning strategies: Mental processes and plans that people use to help them comprehend, learn, and retain new information. There are several types of learning strategies, such as cognitive, metacognitive, and language-based, and these are consciously adapted and monitored during reading, writing, and learning.

Levels of language proficiency: Students learning language progress through stages. To date, the stages or levels have been labeled differently in a number of states. In seminal work in this area, Krashen and Terrell (1983) described the stages as the following: Preproduction, Early production, Speech emergence, Intermediate fluency, and Advanced fluency. At present, many states have levels similar to those in the WIDA's English language proficiency standards (WIDA, 2020):

Entering (Level 1): Lowest level, essentially no English proficiency. Students are often newcomers and need extensive pictorial and non-linguistic support. They need to learn basic oral language and literacy skills in English.

Emerging (Level 2): Second lowest level. Students use phrases and short sentences and are introduced to general content vocabulary and lesson tasks.

Developing (Level 3): Next level of proficiency. Students can use general and specific language related to the content areas; they can speak and write sentences and paragraphs although with some errors, and they can read with instructional supports.

Expanding (Level 4): Akin to an intermediate level of proficiency. Students use general, academic, and specific language related to content areas. They have improved speaking and writing skills and stronger reading comprehension skills (compared to the Developing level).

Bridging (Level 5): Akin to advanced intermediate or advanced level of proficiency. Students use general academic and technical language of the content areas. They can read and write with linguistic complexity. Students at this level may have exited the ELD program, but their language and academic performance is still monitored.

Reaching (Level 6): At or close to grade-level proficiency. Students' oral and written communication skills are comparable to those of native English speakers at their grade level. Students at this level have exited the ELD program, but their language and academic performance is still monitored.

Limited English proficient (LEP): A term used to refer to a student with restricted understanding or use of written and spoken English; a learner who is still developing competence in using English. The federal government continues to use the term *LEP,* while *multilingual learner, emergent bilingual, English learner,* or *English language learner* are more commonly used in schools.

Long-term English learner: A term used for students who have been enrolled in U.S. schools and designated as English learners for more than five years. Some states or districts may have slightly different definitions and consider progress toward language and academic proficiency as well as time in the program.

Multilingual learners: A term used to refer to individuals who are not yet proficient in English language and literacy skills (reading, writing, speaking, and listening). Multilingual learners may be at any level of English proficiency. These students may also be referred to as *English learners, emergent bilinguals,* or *English language learners* in some regions.

Multi-tiered System of Support (MTSS): MTSS is a process used is to identify at-risk learners early and, with a tiered system of supports, provide effective instruction in general education classrooms first (typically called Tier 1) followed by targeted intervention (Tiers 2 and 3) as needed.

This process is designed to reduce the number of students eligible for and in need of special education services. The focus is on finding ways to change instruction (or student behaviors) so the learner can be successful. MTSS involves data-based problem solving and decision making, then documenting changes in behavior or performance as a result of intervention and assessments. Also called Response to Intervention (RTI) in some districts. (*See* Response to intervention [RTI].)

Native English speaker: An individual whose first language is English. (*See* English-only.)

Native language: An individual's primary, home, or first language (L1).

Newcomer program: Specially designed academic programs for students newly arrived in U.S. schools who are not proficient in English. Newcomers attend these programs for a limited period of time in order to develop academic English, acculturate to U.S. schools, and build subject area knowledge. The programs may be located within an existing school or at a separate site.

Next Generation Science Standards (NGSS): A set of Grades K–12 science standards, adopted fully or to some degree by about 45 states in the United States and the District of Columbia, as of 2018.

Non-native English speaker: Individuals who do not speak English as a first language. May be at any level of proficiency in English.

Nonverbal communication: Paralinguistic messages such as intonation, stress, pauses, and rate of speech, and nonlinguistic messages such as gestures, facial expressions, and body language that can accompany speech or be conveyed without the aid of speech.

Primary language: An individual's home, native, or first language (L1).

Pull-out instruction: Students are "pulled out" from their regular classes for separate classes of ELD instruction, remediation, or acceleration. These are more commonly found in elementary programs.

Realia: Real-life objects and artifacts used to supplement teaching; can provide effective visual scaffolds for multilingual learners.

Reliability: Statistical consistency in measurements and tests, such as the extent to which one assessment will repeatedly produce the same results given the same conditions and student population.

Response to Intervention (RTI): A schoolwide multi-tiered process that is designed for supporting students who are struggling academically. More commonly referred to as MTSS. (*See* Multi-Tiered System of Support [MTSS].)

Rubrics: Statements that describe indicators of performance, which include scoring criteria, on a continuum; may be described as "developmental" (e.g., emergent, beginning, developing, proficient) or "evaluative" (e.g., exceptional, thorough, adequate, inadequate).

Scaffolding: Support for student learning of new information and performance of the tasks. Often provided by the teacher through demonstration, modeling, verbal prompts (e.g., questioning), feedback, graphic organizers, language frames, and more, across successive engagements. These supports are gradually withdrawn, to transfer more autonomy to the learner, leading to independence.

Science of Reading (SOR): The body of published research studies spanning decades that explain how individuals learn to read.

Self-contained ESL class: A class consisting solely of multilingual learners for the purpose of learning English or a subject area. An alternative to pull-out instruction.

Sheltered instruction: A means for making content comprehensible for multilingual learners while they are developing academic English proficiency. The SIOP Model is an empirically validated model of sheltered instruction. Sheltered classrooms may include a mix of native English speakers and multilingual learners or only multilingual learners. SIOP lessons integrate language and content learning and may include culturally responsive instruction as well. (*See* SIOP®.)

SIOP®: The term for an empirically validated model of sheltered instruction designed to make grade-level academic content understandable for multilingual learners while at the same time developing their academic English language proficiency. Formerly spelled out as the Sheltered Instruction Observation Protocol, the acronym SIOP is more commonly used in schools and in the professional literature. SIOP refers to the observation protocol and the lesson planning guide which ensure that teachers are consistently implementing practices known to be effective for multilingual learners. It is often used as an adjective too, as in SIOP teachers, SIOP lessons, and SIOP classrooms.

SLIFE: Students with limited or interrupted formal education. They are typically newly arrived to U.S. schools and have experienced significant gaps in their education. They are assessed as below-grade level in academic skills, and often have weak reading and writing skills in their home language. In some regions these learners are known as SIFE.

Social emotional learning (SEL): The set of skills individuals need to navigate situations and relationships throughout their life. SEL is commonly described by five core competencies: self-awareness, self-management, responsible decision making, relationship skills, and social awareness.

Social language: Basic language proficiency associated with fluency in day-to-day situations, including the classroom. Also referred to as *conversational language*. (*See* Basic Interpersonal Communicative Skills [BICS].)

Sociocultural context: The environment or situation in which people live, work, or go to school that includes social and cultural elements. Student learning in a classroom may be influenced by social and cultural factors from outside the classroom, such as economic status, level of parental education, family structure, and discrimination.

Standards-based assessment: Assessment involving the planning, gathering, analyzing, and reporting of a student's performance according to the English language proficiency and/or content standards.

Translanguaging: Refers to the process by which multilingual students use their full linguistic repertoire in two or more languages strategically to accomplish a task. Translanguaging in a SIOP classroom is a pedagogical practice that encourages students to use and apply the knowledge they have gained through any language medium (e.g., meaning of words in their home language, science knowledge gained in English from a lab experiment) to make meaning and perform instructional activities. As a dynamic, asset-based approach, translanguaging allows students and teachers to use more than one language in the classroom for effective communication.

Unaccompanied minors: This term refers to students who have come to the United States without their parents. A large influx of such students over the years has called attention to the struggles they experienced on their journey to the United States as well as the educational challenges many of them face once they are enrolled in schools.

Validity: A statistical measure of an assessment's match between the information collected and its stated purpose; evidence that inferences from evaluation are trustworthy.

References

Afflerbach, P., Pearson, P. D., & Paris, S. G. (2008). Clarifying differences between reading skills and reading strategies. *The Reading Teacher, 61*(5), 364–373. https://doi.org/10.1598/RT.61.5.1

Aldakhil, A., & Alfadda, H. (2021). The implementation of Sheltered Instructional Observation Protocol (SIOP) Model in Saudi schools: A study of EFL teachers' perspectives. English Language Teaching, 14 (9), 67–79.

Alnusayan, I. S., & Al-Salouli, M.S. (2020). The effectiveness of Sheltered Instruction Observation Protocol (SIOP) Model of developing mathematical achievement in preparatory year female students at Al-Imam Mohammad Ibn Saud Islamic University. *Journal of Educational and Psychological Sciences, 4* (25), 93–113. DOI: https://doi.org/10.26389/AJSRP. E180220

Anderson, L. Q., & Krathwohl, D. R. (Eds.). (2001). *Taxonomy for learning, teaching, and assessing: A revision of Bloom's Taxonomy of Educational Objectives*. Longman.

Anderson, R. C. (1994). Role of the reader's schema in comprehension, learning, and memory. In R. Ruddell, M. Ruddell, & H. Singer (Eds.), *Theoretical models and processes of reading* (4ᵗʰ ed.), International Reading Association (now International Literacy Association), 469–482.

Aronson, E., Blaney, N. T., Stephan, C., Rosenfield, R., & Sikes, J. (1977). Interdependence in the classroom: A field study. *Journal of Educational Psychology, 69*, 121–128.

August, D., & Shanahan T. (Eds.). (2006). *Developing literacy in second-language learners: A report of the National Literacy Panel on Language-Minority Children and Youth*. Erlbaum.

August, D., & Shanahan, T. (2010). Effective English literacy instruction for English learners. In California Department of Education (Ed.), *Improving education for English learners: Research-based approaches*. CDE Press, 209–249.

Bailey, F., & Pransky, K. (2014). *Memory at work in the classroom*. Association for Supervision and Curriculum Development.

Baker, S., Lesaux, N., Jayanthi, M., Dimino, J., Proctor, C.P., Morris, J., Gersten, R., Haymond, K., Kieffer, M.J., Linan-Thompson, S., & Newman-Gonchar, R. (2014). *Teaching academic content and literacy to English learners in elementary and middle school* (NCEE 2014-4012). National Center for Education Evaluation and Regional Assistance (NCEE), Institute of Education Sciences, U.S. Department of Education. http://ies.ed.gov/ncee/wwc/publications_reviews.aspx

Balconi, A., & Spitzman, E. (2021). Content area teachers' challenges writing language objectives: A document analysis. *TESOL Journal, 12*:e530. https://doi.org/10.1002/tesj.530

Bárcena-Toyos, P. (2022). CLIL and SIOP: An effective partnership? *International Multilingual Research Journal.*

Barnes, M. A., Ahmed, Y., Barth, A., & Francis, D.J. (2015). The relation of knowledge-text integration processes and reading comprehension in 7ᵗʰ- to 12ᵗʰ-grade students. *Scientific Studies of Reading, 19*(4), 253–272.

Batt, E. (2010). Cognitive coaching: A critical phase in professional development to implement sheltered instruction. *Teaching and Teacher Education 26,* 997–1005.

Bear, D. R., Invernizzi, M., Templeton, S., & Johnston, F. (2019). *Words their way: Word study for spelling, phonics, and vocabulary instruction* (7ᵗʰ ed.). Pearson.

Beck, I. L., McKeown, M. G., & Kucan, L. (2002). *Bringing words to life: Robust vocabulary instruction*. Guilford Press.

Blachowicz, L. Z., ., & Fisher, P. (2000). Vocabulary instruction. In R. L. Kamil, P. B. Mosenthal, P. D. Pearson, & R. Barr (Eds.), *Handbook of reading research* (Vol. 3), 503–523. Erlbaum.

Boswell, K. (2015). *Write this way: How modeling transforms the writing classroom.* Capstone Classroom.

Brooks, K., & Thurston, L. (2010). English language learner academic engagement and instructional grouping configurations. *American Secondary Education, 39*(1), 45–60.

Brozo, W. (2010). The role of content literacy in an effective RTI program. *The Reading Teacher, 64*(2), 147–150.

Bruner, J. (1983). *Child's talk: Learning to use language.* W. W. Norton.

Calderon, C. T., & Zamora, E. (2014). Factors affecting the implementation of sheltered instruction observation protocols for English language learners. *National Forum of Educational Administration & Supervision Journal, 31*(3), 20–32.

California Department of Education. (2014). *ELA/ELD Framework.* Author. http://www.cde.ca.gov/ci/rl/cf/elaeldfrmwrksbeadopted.asp

Cardenas-Hagen, D. (2020). *Literacy foundations for English learners: A comprehensive guide to evidence-based instruction.* Brookes Publishing.

Carnoy, M., & Garcia, (2017). *Five key trends in U.S. student performance.* Report from the Economic Policy Institute. https://files.epi.org/pdf/113217.pdf

Carr, D., A., Shearer, B. A., & Vogt, M.E. (2019) *Reading specialists and literacy coaches in the real world* (4th ed.). Waveland Press, Inc.

Cazden, C. (2001). *Classroom discourse: The language of teaching and learning.* Heinemann.

Chamot, A.U., & O' Malley, J.M. (1994). *The CALLA handbook: Implementing the Cognitive Academic Language Learning Approach.* Addison Wesley Longman.

Chandler, P. T. (2020). Implementing the SIOP Model to support English language learners. *All Theses And Dissertations.* 315. https://dune.une.edu/theses/315

Chappuis, S., Commodore, C., & Stiggins, R. (2017). *Balanced assessment systems: Leadership, quality, and the role of classroom assessment.* Corwin Press.

Chen, C-T, Kyle, D., & McIntyre, E. (2008). Helping teachers work effectively with English language learners and their families. *The School Community Journal, 18*(1), 7–20.

Cioé-Peña, M. (2021). Raciolinguistics and the education of emergent bilinguals labeled as disabled. *Urban Rev, 53,* 443–469. https://doi-org.csulb.idm.oclc.org/10.1007/s11256-020-00581-z

City, E. (2014). Talking to learn. *Educational Leadership, 72*(3), 10–16.

Cloud, N., Healey, K., Paul, M., Short, D., & Winiarski, P. (2010). Preparing adolescents for the academic listening demands of secondary school classrooms. In N. Ashcraft & A. Tran (Eds.), *Listening: TESOL classroom practice series* (pp. 151–167). TESOL Press.

Cohan, A., Honigsfeld, A., & Dove, M. G. (2019). *Team up, speak up, fire up! Educators, students, and the community working together to support English Learners.* ASCD.

Cook, L., & Friend, M. (1995). Co-teaching: Guidelines for creating effective practices. *Focus on Exceptional Children, 28, 1-16.*

Coppersmith, S., Slapac, A., & Song, K. (2019). Infusing linguistically and culturally responsive practices for English learners in social studies methods. *Social Studies Education Review, 8*(1), 45–66.

Crossley, S., Allen, D., & McNamera, D. (2012). Text simplification and comprehensible input: A case for an intuitive approach. *Language Teaching Research, 16*(1), 89–108. https://doi.org/10.1177/1362168811423456

Cummins, J. (2000). *Language, power and pedagogy.* Multilingual Matters, Ltd.

Cummins, J. (2016). Reflections on Cummins, 1980. The cross-lingual dimensions of language proficiency: Implications for bilingual education and the optimal age issue. *TESOL Quarterly, 50*(4), 940–944.

Custodio, B., & O'Loughlin, J. (2017). *Students with interrupted formal education: Bridging where they are and what they need.* Corwin Press.

Daniel, S., & Pray, L. (2017). Learning to teach English language learners: A study of elementary school teachers' sense-making in an ELL endorsement program. *TESOL Quarterly*, *51*(4), 787–819.

Darling-Hammond, L. (1998). Teacher learning that supports student learning. *Educational Leadership*, *55*(5), 6–11.

Darling-Hammond, L., Hyler, M. E., & Gardner, M. (2017). *Effective teacher professional development.* Learning Policy Institute.

Davin, K. J. (2013). Integration of dynamic assessment and instructional conversations to promote development and improve assessment in the language classroom. *Language Teaching Research, 17*(3), 303–322. https://doi.org/10.1177/1362168813482934

Dean, C. B., Hubbell, E. R., Pilter, H., & Stone, BJ. (2012). *Classroom instruction that works* (2nd ed.). Association for Supervision and Curriculum Development.

Dove, M. G., & Honigsfeld, A. (2017). *Co-teaching for English learners: A guide to collaborative planning, instruction, assessment, and reflection.* Corwin Press.

Dove, M. G., & Honigsfeld, A. (2019). From isolation to collaboration. *Breaking down the wall: Essential shifts for English learners' success.* Corwin Press.

Duke, N. K., & Cartwright, K. (2021). The science of reading progresses: Communicating advances beyond the Simple View of Reading. *Reading Research Quarterly*, *56*(S1), S25–S44.

Duke, N. K., Ward, E., & Pearson, P. D. (2021). The science of reading comprehension instruction, *The Reading Teacher, 74*(6), 663–672.

Dyer, K. (2021). *75 digital tools and apps teachers can use to support formative assessment in the classroom.* NWEA. www.nwea.org/blog/2021/75-digital-tools-apps-teachers-use-to-support-classroom-formative-assessment/

Ebe, A., Soto, M., Freeman, Y., & Freeman, D. (2021, September). Translanguaging in bilingual and ESL classrooms. *TESOL Connections.* http://newsmanager.commpartners.com/tesolc/downloads/features/2021/2021-09_Translanguaging_AEbe%20et%20al.pdf

Ebedy, H. G. M. (2019). Developing reading comprehension skills using Sheltered Instruction Observation Protocol (SIOP) among EFL students. *Journal of Research in Curriculum, Instruction and Educational Technology, 5*(2), 197–220.

Echevarría, J. (1995). Interactive reading instruction: A comparison of proximal and distal effects of instructional conversations. *Exceptional Children, 61*(6), 536–552.

Echevarría, J., (1998). *A model of sheltered instruction for English language learners.* Paper presented at the conference for the Division on Diversity of the Council for Exceptional Children, Washington, DC.

Echevarría, J., & Graves, A. (2015). *Sheltered content instruction: Teaching English learners with diverse abilities* (5th ed.). Allyn & Bacon.

Echevarría, J., Frey, N., & Fisher, D. (2015). What it takes for English learners to succeed. *Educational Leadership*, *72*(6), 22–27.

Echevarría, J., Richards-Tutor, C., & Vogt, M.E. (2015). *Response to intervention (RTI) and English learners: Using the SIOP Model* (2nd ed.). Allyn & Bacon.

Echevarría, J., Richards-Tutor, C., Canges, R., & Francis, D. (2011). Using the SIOP Model to promote the acquisition of language and science concepts with English learners. *Bilingual Research Journal, 34*(3), 334–351.

Echevarría, J., Richards-Tutor, C., Chinn, V., & Ratleff, P. (2011). Did they get it? The role of fidelity in teaching English learners. *Journal of Adolescent and Adult Literacy*, *54*(6), 425–434.

Echevarría, J., & Short, D. (2010). Programs and practices for effective sheltered content instruction. In California Department of Education (Ed.), *Improving education for English learners: Research-based approaches.* CDE Press, 250–321.

Echevarría, J., & Short, D. (2011). *The SIOP Model: A professional development framework for a comprehensive school-wide intervention. CREATE Brief.* Center for Applied Linguistics.

Echevarría, J., Short, D., & Powers, K. (2006). School reform and standards-based education: An instructional model for English language learners. *Journal of Educational Research*, *99*(4), 195–211.

Echevarría, J., Vogt, M.E., & Short, D. (2000). *Making content comprehensible for English language learners: The SIOP Model.* Allyn & Bacon.

Echevarría, J., Short, D., & Vogt, M.E. (2008). *Implementing the SIOP Model through effective professional development and coaching.* Pearson/Allyn & Bacon.

Echevarría, J., Vogt, M.E., & Short, D. (2010). *The SIOP Model for teaching mathematics to English learners.* Pearson/Allyn & Bacon.

Essa, H. (2016). *Teach us your name.* Huda Essa, Publisher.

Fleur, D. S., Bredeweg, B., & van den Bos, W. (2021). Metacognition: Ideas and insights from neuro- and educational sciences. *Science of Learning 6(*13), 1–11. https://doi.org/10.1038/s41539-021-00089-5

Friend, M. (2008). Co-teaching: A simple solution that isn't simple after all. *Journal of Curriculum and Instruction, 2*(2), 9–19.

Friend, J., Most, R., & McCrary, K. (2009). The impact of a professional development program to improve urban middle-level English language learner achievement. *Middle Grades Research Journal, 4*(1), 53–75.

Frøytlog, J. I., & Rasmussen, I. (2020). The distribution and productivity of whole-class dialogues: Exploring the potential of microblogging. *International Journal of Educational Research, 99.* https://doi.org/10.1016/j.ijer.2019.101501

Fuchs, D., Fuchs, L., & Compton, D. (2012). Smart RTI: A next-generation approach to multilevel prevention. *Exceptional Children, 78*(3), 263–279.

Futrell, M., & Gomez, J. (2008). How tracking creates a poverty of learning. *Educational Leadership, 65*(8), 74–78.

Gándara, P., & Rumberger, R. (2008). Immigration, language, and education: How does language policy structure opportunity? *Teachers College Record, 111*(3), 750–782.

García, G. E., & Godina, H. (2017). A window into bilingual reading: The bilingual reading practices of fourth-grade, Mexican-American children who are emergent bilinguals. *Journal of Literacy Research, 49*(2), 273–301 https://doi.org/10.1177/1086296X17703727

Garcia, G. E., Sacco, L., & Guerrero-Arias, B. (2020). Cognate instruction and bilingual students'
improved literacy performance. *The Reading Teacher, 73*(5), 617–625.

García, O., Ibarra Johnson, S., & Seltzer, K. (2017*). The translanguaging classroom: Leveraging student bilingualism for learning.* Caslon Publishing.

Gass, S., Behney, J., & Plonsky, L. (2020). Second language acquisition: An introductory course. (5th ed.). Routledge.

Gay, G. (2018). *Culturally responsive teaching: Theory, research, and practice.* (3rd ed.). Teachers College Press.

Genesee, F., Lindholm-Leary, K., Saunders, W., & Christian, D. (2006). *Educating English language learners: A synthesis of research evidence.* Cambridge University Press.

Geva, E. (2006). Second-language oral proficiency and second-language literacy. In D. August & T. Shanahan (Eds.), *Developing literacy in second-language learners: Report of the National Literacy Panel on Language Minority Children and Youth.* Lawrence Erlbaum Associates.

Gibbons, P. (2015). *Scaffolding language, scaffolding learning* (2nd ed.). Heinemann.

Gillies, R. (2014). Cooperative learning: Developments in research. *International Journal of Educational Psychology, 3*(2), 125–140. doi:10.4471/ijep.2014.08

Goldenberg, C. (2020). Reading wars, reading science, and English learners. *Reading Research Quarterly, 55*(S1), 131–144.

Goldenberg, C. (2021). The science of reading should make room for skepticism (Just not for ignorance). *Education Week.* https://www.edweek.org/teaching-learning/opinion-the-science-of-reading-should-make-room-for-skepticism-just-not-for-ignorance/2021/09

Goldenberg, C., & Coleman, R. (2010). *Promoting academic achievement among English learners: A guide to the research.* Corwin Press.

Goodlad, J. (1984). *A place called school: Prospects for the future.* McGraw-Hill.

González, M. (2016). Preparing teacher candidates for the instruction of English language learners. *Networks, 18*(2). DOI: 10.4148/2470-6353.1005

Gonzalez, N., Moll, L., & Amanti, C. (Eds.). (2005). *Funds of knowledge: Theorizing practices in households, communities, and classrooms*. Routledge.

Gottlieb, M. (2016). *Assessing English language learners: Bridges to educational equity: Connecting academic language proficiency to student achievement*. Corwin Press.

Graff, G. (2003). *Clueless in academe*. Yale University Press.

Graham, S. (2019). Changing how writing is taught. *Review of Research in Education, 43*(1), 277–303.

Greenberg M. J. (2015). *Time to reclassification: How long does it take English learner students in Washington Road Map Districts to develop English proficiency?* (REL 2015-092). U.S. Department of Education, Institute of Education Sciences, National Center for Education Evaluation and Regional Assistance, Regional Educational Laboratory Northwest. http://ies.ed.gov/ncee/edlabs

Gruver, J., & Bowers, J. (2020). Evolution of inquiry questions in a cyclic professional development program. *Canadian Journal of Action Research, 20*(3), 3–18.

Guarino, A. J., Echevarría, J., Short, D., Schick, J. E., Forbes, S., & Rueda, R. (2001). The Sheltered Instruction Observation Protocol. *Journal of Research in Education, 11*(1), 138–140.

Guglielmi, R. (2008). Native language proficiency, English literacy, academic achievement, and occupational attainment in limited-English-proficient students: A latent growth modeling perspective. *Journal of Educational Psychology, 100*(2), 322–342.

Gunderson, L. (2021). The consequences of English learner as a category in teaching, learning, and research. *Journal of Adolescent and Adult Literacy, 64*(4), 431–439

Guzman, R. (2015). *A study of the impact of English language learners: Literacy development through the SIOP Model* (Publication No. 3701484) [Doctoral Dissertation, University of St. Francis]. ProQuest Dissertations Publishing.

Hammond, Z. (2014). *Culturally responsive teaching and the brain: Promoting authentic engagement and rigor among culturally and linguistically diverse students*. Corwin Press.

Haneda, M., & Wells, G. (2012). Some key pedagogic principles for helping ELLs to succeed in school. *Theory into Practice, 51*(4), 297–304.

Hanson-Thomas, H., Langman, J., & Farias, T. (2018). The role of language objectives: Strengthening math and science teachers' language awareness with emergent bilinguals in secondary classrooms. *LACLIL, 11*(2), 193–214. doi: 10.5294/laclil.2018.11.2.

Hayden, R. (2019). *English proficiency in classes using Sheltered Instruction Observation Protocol (SIOP) compared to classes not using SIOP* (Publication No. 22616011) [Doctoral dissertation, Capella University]. ProQuest Dissertations Publishing.

Hattie, J. (2008). *Visible learning: A synthesis of over 800 meta-analyses relating to achievement*. Routledge.

Helman, L., Bear, D., Templeton, S., & Invernizzi, M. (2012). *Words their way with English learners: Word study for phonics, vocabulary, and spelling* (2nd ed.). Pearson.

Hendy, E., & Cuevas, J. (2020). The effects of instructional conversations on English language learners, *Georgia Educational Researcher, 17*(2). https://digitalcommons.georgiasouthern.edu/gerjournal/vol17/iss2/5

Hiebert, E. H., Goodman, A. P., & Cervetti, G. N. (2017). Core vocabulary: Its morphological content and presence in exemplar texts. *Reading Research Quarterly, 50*(2), 1–21.

Himmel, J., Short, D. J., Richards, C., & Echevarría, J. (2009). *Using the SIOP Model to improve middle school science instruction* (CREATE Brief). Center for Research on the Educational Achievement and Teaching of English Language Learners/CAL.

Holder, C., Bell, J., & Toppel, K. (2019, February 15). *Using the SIOP model to support successful co-teaching*. Fresh Ideas for Teaching. https://blog.savvas.com/using-the-siop-model-to-support-successful-co-planning/

Hollins-Alexander, S., & Law, N. (2021). *Collective equity: A movement for creating communities where we all can breathe*. Corwin Press.

Hollins-Alexander, S., & Law, N. (2022). *Collective equity: A movement for creating communities where we all can breathe*. Corwin Press.

Honigsfeld, A., & Cohan, A. (2008). The power of two: Lesson study and SIOP help teachers instruct ELLs. *Journal of Staff Development, 29*(1), 24–28.

Honigsfeld, A., & Dove, M. G. (2019). *Collaborating for English learners: A foundational guide to integrated practices*. Corwin Press.

Hunter, M. (1982). *Mastery teaching: Increasing instructional effectiveness in secondary schools, college, and universities*. TIP Publications.

Ingram, S. (2018). *An analysis of the Sheltered Instruction Observation Protocol Model on academic performance of English language learners* (Publication No. 0355555247) [Doctoral dissertation, Capella University]. ProQuest Dissertations Publishing.

Jensen, E., & McConshie, A. (2020). *Brain-based learning: Teaching the way students really learn*. (3rd ed.). Corwin Press.

Jeong, H., Eggleston, L., & Samaniuk, J. (2021). Culturally and linguistically responsive pedagogy in a digitally mediated classroom: Practices, challenges, and needs. *NYSTESOL Journal, 8*(1), 40–52.

Kaefer, T. (2020). When did you learn it? How background knowledge impacts attention and comprehension in read-aloud activities. *Reading Research Quarterly, S5*(S1), S173-S183.

Kangas, S. E. N. (2018). Breaking one law to uphold another: Service provision for English learners with disabilities. *TESOL Quarterly, 52*(4), 877–910. https://doi-org.csulb.idm.oclc.org/10.1002/tesq.431

Kangas, S. (2021). "Is it language or disability?" An ableist and monolingual filter for English learners with disabilities. *TESOL Quarterly* 55 (3), 673–683.

Kieffer, M. J., & Parker, C. E. (2016). *Patterns of English learner student reclassification in New York City public schools* (REL 2017–200). U.S. Department of Education, Institute of Education Sciences, National Center for Education Evaluation and Regional Assistance, Regional Educational Laboratory, Northeast & Islands. http://ies.ed.gov/ncee/edlabs

Kieffer, M. J., & Thompson, K. D. (2018). Hidden progress of multilingual students on NAEP. *Educational Researcher, 47*(6), 391–398.

Kim, S., Song, K., & Coppersmith, S. (2018). Creating an interactive virtual community of linguistically and culturally responsive content teacher-learners to serve English learners. *Contemporary Issues in Technology and Teacher Education, 18*(2), 442–466.

Klinger, J., & Eppolito, A. (2014). *English language learners: Differentiating between language acquisition and learning disabilities*. Council for Exceptional Children.

Koura, A., & Zahan, F. (2017). The impact of the Sheltered Instruction Observation Protocol Model on student teachers' teaching skills and self-efficacy. *Journal of Language Teaching and Research, 8*(4), 704–714. DOI: http://dx.doi.org/10.17507/jltr.0804.09.

Krashen, S. (1985). *The input hypothesis: Issues and implications*. Longman.

Krashen, S., & Terrell, T. (1983). *The Natural Approach: Language acquisition in the classroom*. Alemany Press.

Langhanns, C., & Müller, H. (2018). Effects of trying 'not to move' instruction on cortical load and concurrent cognitive performance. *Psychological Research 82*, 167–176. https://doi.org/10.1007/s00426-017-0928-9

Lee, H. (2015). *To kill a mockingbird*. Harper Perennial.

Lems, K., Miller, L. D., & Soro, T. M. (2017). *Building literacy with English language learners: Insights from linguistics*. Guilford Publications.

Li, J., Steele, J., Slater, R., Bacon, M., & Miller, T. (2016). Teaching practices and language use in two-way dual language immersion programs in a large public school district. *International Multilingual Research Journal, 10*(1), 31–43. DOI: 10.1080/19313152.2016.1118669

Linares, R. (2018). Meaningful writing opportunities: Write-alouds and dialogue journaling with newcomer and English learner high schoolers. *Journal of Adolescent and Adult Literacy, 62*(5), 521–530. https://doi.org/10.1002/jaal.932

Lipson, M., & Wixson, K. (2013). *Assessment of reading and writing difficulties: An interactive approach* (5th ed.). Longman.

Lomashvili, L. (2022). How to incorporate language form, function, and structure in the SIOP Model lessons. *International Journal of English Language Teaching, 9*(2), 8–18.

Lou, Y. (2013). Within class grouping: Arguments, practices, and research evidence. In *International guide to student achievement* (pp. 180–182). Routledge.

Lyster, R., & Saito, K. (2010). Oral feedback in classroom SLA. *Studies in second language acquisition, 32*, 265–302. doi:10.1017/S0272263109990520

Marshall, J. (2000). Research on response to literature. In R. L. Kamil, P. B. Mosenthal, P. D. Pearson, & R. Barr (Eds.), *Handbook of reading research* (Vol. 3). Lawrence Erlbaum Associates, 381–402.

McIntyre, E., Kyle, D., Chen, C., Muñoz, M., & Beldon, S. (2010). Teacher learning and ELL reading achievement in sheltered instruction classrooms: Linking professional development to student development. *Literacy Research and Instruction, 49*(4), 334–351.

McGrath, K. & Van Bergen, P. (2015). Who, when, why, and to what end? Students at risk of negative student–teacher relationships and their outcomes, *Educational Research Review, 14*, 1–17. https://doi.org/10.1016/j.edurev.2014.12.001.

McLaughlin, M., & Allen, M.B. (2009). *Guided comprehension: A teaching model* (2nd ed.). International Reading Association.

Mellon, P., Hixon, R., & Weber, J. (2019). *With a little help from my friends: Conversation based instruction for culturally responsive and linguistically diverse (CLD) classrooms.* Teachers College Press.

Mellon, P., Straubhaar, R., Balderas, C., Ariail, M., & Portes, P. R. (2018). "They come with Nothing:" How professional development in a culturally responsive pedagogy shapes teacher attitudes towards Latino/English language learners. *Teaching and Teacher Education, 71,* 98–107.

Menken, K., Kleyn, T., & Chae, N. (2012). Spotlight on long-term English language learners: Characteristics and prior schooling experiences of an invisible population. *International Multilingual Research Journal, 6*(2), 121–142. doi 10.1080/19313152.2012.665822

Merritt, E. G., Palacios, N., Banse, H., Rimm-Kaufman, S. E., & Leis, M. (2016). Teaching practices in Grade 5 mathematics classrooms with high-achieving English learner students. *The Journal of Educational Research.* DOI: 10.1080/00220671.2015.1034352

Moll, L. C. (1994). Literacy research in community and classrooms: A sociocultural approach. In R. B. Ruddell, M. R. Ruddell, & H. Singer (Eds.), *Theoretical models and processes of reading* (4th ed., pp. 179–207). International Reading Association (now International Literacy Association).

Moll, L. C., Amanti, C., Neff, D., & Gonzalez, N. (1992). Funds of knowledge for teaching: Using a qualitative approach to connect homes and classrooms. *Theory into Practice, 31*(2), 132–141.

Murillo, R., & Alejandro, H. (2013). Adapting features from the SIOP component: Lesson delivery to English lessons in a Colombian public school. *Profile Issues in Teachers Professional Development, 15*(1),171–193.

Nassaji, H., & Kartchava, E. (Eds.). (2017). *Corrective feedback in second language teaching and learning: Research, theory, applications, implications.* Routledge.

National Academies of Sciences, Engineering, and Medicine (NASEM). (2017). *Promoting the educational success of children and youth learning English: Promising futures.* National Academies Press. https://doi.org/10.17226/24677

National Center for Learning Disabilities. (2020). *Significant disproportionality in special education: Trends among English learners.* Author. https://www.ncld.org/wp-content/uploads/2020/10/2020-NCLD-Disproportionality_-English-Learners_EL_FINAL.pdf

National Council on Teacher Quality. (2015). *2014 Teacher prep review: A review of the nation's teacher preparation programs.* Author. https://www.nctq.org/dmsView/Teacher_Prep_Review_2014_Report

National Institute of Child Health and Human Development (NICHD). (2000). *Report of the National Reading Panel. Teaching children to read: An evidence-based assessment of the scientific research literature on reading and its implications for reading instruction.* (NIH Publication No. 00–4769). U.S. Department of Health and Human Services.

Neuman, S. B., Kaefer, T., & Pinkham, A. (2014). Building background knowledge. *The Reading Teacher, 68*(2), 145–148.

New York City Department of Education. (2022, February). *Chancellor Banks announces increased high school graduation rate for class of 2021 amid pandemic.* [Online article]. https://www.schools.nyc.gov/about-us/news/announcements/contentdetails/2022/02/16/chancellor-banks-announces-increased-high-school-graduation-rate-for-class-of-2021-amid-pandemic

Nieto, S., & Bode, P. (2017). *Affirming diversity: The sociopolitical context of multicultural education* (7th ed). Pearson.

Oakes, J. (1985). *Keeping track: How schools structure inequality.* Yale University Press.

Ogle, D. (1986). K-W-L. A teaching model that develops active reading of expository text. *The Reading Teacher, 39,* 564–570.

Olson, C. B., Land, R., Anselmi, T., & AuBuchon, C. (2011). Teaching secondary English learners to understand, analyze, and write interpretive essays about them. *Journal of Adolescent and Adult Literacy, 54*(4), 246–256.

O'Malley, J. M., & Chamot, A. U. (1990). *Learning strategies in second language acquisition.* Cambridge University Press.

O'Neal, D., Ringler, M. C., & Lys, D. B. (2009). Skeptics to partners: University teams with district to improve ELL instruction. *Journal of Staff Development, 30*(4), 52–55.

Oczkus, L. (2018). *Reciprocal teaching at work: Powerful strategies and lessons for improving reading comprehension* (3rd ed). ASCD.

Palincsar, A. S., & Brown, A. L. (1984). Reciprocal teaching of comprehension-fostering and comprehension-monitoring activities. *Cognition and Instruction, 1*(2), 117–175. https://doi.org/10.1207/s1532690xci0102_1

Pappamihiel, N. E. (2012). Benefits and challenges of co-teaching English learners in one elementary school in transition. *Tapestry, 4*(1), 2.

Paterson, K. (2021). *Using home language as a resource in the classroom: A guide for teachers of English learners.* TESOL International Association.

Pawan, F., Daley, S., Kou, X., & Bonk, C. (2022). *Engaging online language learners: A practical guide.* TESOL International Association.

Pearson, P. D., & Gallagher, M. (1983). The instruction of reading comprehension. *Contemporary Educational Psychology, 8*(3), 317–344.

Peregoy, S. F., & Boyle, O. F. (2017). *Reading, writing, and learning in ESL: A resource book for K-12 teachers* (7th ed.). Pearson.

Piazza, S., Williams, C., Protacio, M. S., David, V., Tigchelaar, M. & Kuo, H-C. (2020). Improving instruction for English learners: A professional development study using SIOP. *Journal of Teacher Education and Educators, 9*(3), 283–405.

Poldrack, R., Clark, J., Pare-Blagoev, E., Shohamy, D., Creso Moyano, J., Myers, C., & Gluck, M. (2001). Interactive memory systems in the human brain. *Nature, 414,* 546–550.

Porath, S. (2014) Talk less, listen more. *The Reading Teacher, 67*(8), 627–635.

Pratt, S. M., Imbody, S. M., Wolf, L. D., & Patterson, A. L. (2017). Co-planning in co-teaching: A practical solution. *Intervention in School and Clinic, 52*(4), 243–249.

Quin, D. (2016). Longitudinal and contextual associations between teacher–student relationships and student engagement: A systematic review. *Review of Educational Research, 82* (2), 345–387.

Rivera, E. (2019). *The impact of the sheltered instruction observation (SIOP) on the achievement of English language learners* (Publication No. 27736339) [Doctoral dissertation, Florida Gulf Coast University]. ProQuest Dissertations & Theses Global: The Humanities and Social Sciences Collection.

Rodriguez, D., Carrasquillo, A., Garcia, E., & Howitt, D. (2020). Factors that challenge English learners and increase their dropout rates: Recommendations from the field. *International Journal of Bilingual Education and Bilingualism,* 1–17. https://doi.org/10.1080/13670050.2020.1722059

Rogers, K. (Spring, 2019). Comprehensible Input FAQs. *Journal of Classics Teaching, 20*(39), 33–36. DOI: https://doi.org/10.1017/S2058631019000059

Rosen, L. D. (2012). *iDisorder.* St. Martin's Press.

Rosenshine, B. (2012, Spring). Principles of instruction: Research-based strategies that all teachers should know. *American Educator,* 12–19, 39.

Rothenberg, C., & Fisher, D. (2007). *Teaching English learners: A differentiated approach.* Pearson/Merrill/Prentice Hall.

Rowe, M. (2003). Wait-time and rewards as instructional variables, their influence on language, logic and fate control: Part one—wait-time. *Journal of Research in Science Teaching,* 40.

Ruddell, M. R. (2007). *Teaching content reading and writing* (5th ed.). John Wiley & Sons.

Rui, N. (2009). Four decades of research on the effects of detracking reform: Where do we stand?—A systematic review of the evidence. *Journal of Evidence-Based Medicine, 2*(3) 164–183.

Rumelhart, D. E. (1980). Schemata: The building blocks of cognition. In R. J. Spiro, et. al (Eds.), *Theoretical issues in reading comprehension* (pp. 33–58). Erlbaum.

Safir, S., & Dugan, J. (2021). *Street data: A next-generation model for equity, pedagogy, and school transformation.* Corwin Press.

Samway, K. Davies, Pease-Alvarez, L., & Alvarez, L. (2020). *Supporting newcomer students: Effective advocacy and Instruction for English learners.* W.W. Norton and TESOL Press.

Saunders, W., & Goldenberg, C. (1999). The effects of instructional conversations and literature logs on limited and fluent English proficient students' story comprehension and thematic understanding. *The Elementary School Journal, 99,* 277–301.

Saunders, W., & Goldenberg, C. (2007). Talking texts: How speech and writing interact in school learning. In R. Horowitz (Ed.), *The effects of an instructional conversation on English language learners' concepts of friendship and story comprehension* (pp. 221–252). Erlbaum.

Saunders,W., & Goldenberg, C. (2010). Research to guide English language development instruction. In California Department of Education (Ed.), *Improving education for English learners: Research-based approaches* (pp. 21–81). CDE Press.

Saunders, W., & Marcelletti, D. (2013). The gap that can't go away: The catch-22 of reclassification in monitoring the progress of English learners. *Educational Evaluation and Policy Analysis, 35*(2), 139–156.

Saunders, W., & O'Brien, G. (2006). Oral language. In F. Genesee, K. Lindholm-Leary, W. Saunders, & D. Christian (Eds.), *Educating English language learners: A synthesis of research evidence* (pp. 14–63). Cambridge University Press.

Schleppegrell, M. (2020). The knowledge base for language teaching: What is the English to be taught as content? *Language Teaching Research, 24*(1). https://doi.org/10.1177/1362168818777519

Schmoker, M. (2006). *Results now.* Association for Supervision and Curriculum Development.

Schmoker, M. (2018). *Focus: Elevating the essentials to radically improve student learning* (2nd ed.). ASCD.

Seidlitz, J., & Perryman, B. (2011). *7 steps to a language-rich interactive classroom.* Canter Press.

Seilstad, B., & Kim, S. (2020). "Colibri" 'hummingbird' as translanguaging metaphor. In Z. Tian, L. Aghai, P. Sayer, & J. L. Schissel (Eds.), *Envisioning TESOL through a translanguaging lens* (pp. 253–273). Springer.

Shanahan, T., Callison, K., Carriere, C., Duke, N. K., Pearson, P. D., Schatschneider, C., & Torgesen, J. (2010). *Improving reading comprehension in kindergarten through 3rd grade: IES Practice Guide,* NCEE 2010-4038. National Center for Education Evaluation and Regional Assistance, Institute of Education Sciences, US Department of Education.

Shearer, B. A., Carr, D. A., & Vogt, M.E. (2019). *Reading specialists and literacy coaches in the real world* (4th ed.). Waveland Press, Inc.

Shearer, B. A., Ruddell, M. R., & Vogt, M.E. (2001). Successful middle school intervention: Negotiated strategies and individual choice. In T. Shanahan & F. V. Rodriguez (Eds.), *National Reading Conference Yearbook, 50.* National Reading Conference (now Literacy Research Association), 558–571.

Shi, Y., Zaier, A., & Maina, F. (2019). *Preservice teacher perspectives and practices working with multilingual learners.* Paper presented at the 2019 annual meeting of the American Educational Research Association. DOI: https://doi.org/10.3102/1434337

Shin, J., Savic, V., & Machida, T. (2021). *The 6 principles for exemplary teaching of English learners: Young learners in a multilingual world.* TESOL International Association.

Short, D. (2013). Training and sustaining effective teachers of sheltered instruction. *Theory Into Practice, 52*(2), 118–127.

Short, D., & Boyson, B. (2012). *Helping newcomer students succeed in secondary schools and beyond.* Center for Applied Linguistics.

Short, D., Cloud, N., Morris, P., & Motta, J. (2012). Cross-district collaboration: Curriculum and professional development. *TESOL Journal, 3*(3), 402–424.

Short, D. J., & Echevarría, J. (2016). *Developing academic language with the SIOP Model.* Pearson.

Short, D. J., Echevarría, J., & Richards-Tutor, C. (2011). Research on academic literacy development in sheltered instruction classrooms. *Language Teaching Research, 15*(3), 363–380.

Short, D., Fidelman, C., & Louguit, M. (2012). Developing academic language in English language learners through sheltered instruction. *TESOL Quarterly, 46*(2), 333–360.

Short, D., & Fitzsimmons, S. (2007). *Double the work: Challenges and solutions to acquiring language and academic literacy for adolescent English language learners.* Report to Carnegie Corporation of New York. Alliance for Excellent Education.

Short, D., & Himmel, J. (2013). *Moving research on sheltered instruction into curriculum and professional development practice.* Paper presented at American Educational Research Association (AERA) Annual Meeting, San Francisco, CA.

Short, D. J., Vogt, M.E., & Echevarria, J. (2011). *The SIOP Model for teaching history-social studies to English learners.* Pearson.

Short, D. J., Vogt, M.E., & Echevarria, J. (2017). *The SIOP Model for administrators* (2nd ed.). Pearson.

Silverman, R., & Hines, S. (2009). The effects of multimedia-enhanced instruction on the vocabulary of English-language learners and non-English-language learners in pre-kindergarten through second grade. *Journal of Educational Psychology, 101*(2), 305–314. https://doi.org/10.1037/a0014217

Snow, C.E., Burns, S., Griffin, P. (Eds.). (1998). *Preventing reading difficulties in young children.* National Academy Press.

Snyder, S., & Staehr Fenner, D. (2021). *Culturally responsive teaching for multilingual learners: Tools for equity.* Corwin Press.

Song, K. (2016a). Applying a SIOP-based instructional framework for professional development in Korea. *TESL-EJ, 20* (1).

Song, K. (2016b). Systematic professional development training and its impact on teachers' attitudes toward ELLs: SIOP and guided coaching. *TESOL Journal.* Retrieved from http://onlinelibrary.wiley.com/doi/10.1002/tesj.240/full doi: 10.1002/tesj.240

Song, S. Y., & Samimy, K. (2015). The beliefs of secondary content teachers of English language learners regarding language learning and teaching. *International Journal of TESOL and Learning, 4* (1), 3–19.

Stahl, S., & Nagy, W. (2006). *Teaching word meanings.* Lawrence Erlbaum Associates.

Stauffer, R. (1969). *Teaching reading as a thinking process.* Harper & Row.

Steele, J. L., Slater, R. O., Zamarro, G., Miller, T., Li, J., Burkhauser, S., & Bacon, M. (2017). Effects of dual-language immersion programs on student achievement: Evidence from lottery data. *American Educational Research Journal, 54*, 282S–306S.

Sugarman, J. (2019). *The unintended consequences for English learners of using the four-year graduation rate for school accountability.* Migration Policy Institute.

Swain, M. (1985). Communicative competence: Some roles of comprehensible input and output in its development. In S. Gass & C. Madden (Eds.), *Input in second language acquisition* (pp. 235–256). Newbury House.

Texas Education Agency. (n.d.). *Content-based language instruction (CBLI): Quick guide.* Author.

TESOL International Association. (2018). *The 6 principles for exemplary teaching of English learners: Grades K-12.* Author.

Tharp, R., & Gallimore, R. (1988). *Rousing minds to life.* Cambridge University Press.

Tobiason, G., Chang, S., Heritage, M., Jones, B., & Herman, J. (2014). *Building blocks, learning goals, and success criteria: Planning instruction and formative assessment for K-8 math standards.* The Regents of the University of California. https://csaa.wested.org/wp-content/uploads/2019/11/BuildingBlocks_Math.pdf

Tobin, K. (1987). The role of wait time in higher cognitive level learning. *Review of Educational Research, 57,* 69–95.

Tomlinson, C., & Imbeau, M. (2010). *Leading and managing a differentiated classroom.* Association of Supervision and Curriculum Development.

Toppel, K., Hyunh, T., & Salva, C. (2021). *DIY PD: A guide to self-directed learning for educators of multilingual learners.* Seidlitz Education, Inc.

Toppel, K. (2022). Cultivating collaboration with multiple teams. In A. Honigsfeld & M.G. Dove (Eds.), *Portraits of collaboration: Educators working together to support multilingual learners* (pp. 88–103). Seidlitz Education.

Torgesen, J. (2012). Catch them before they fall: Identification and assessment to prevent reading failure in young children. *Reading Rockets.* http://www.readingrockets.org/artivel/225/

Tracy, D. H., & Morrow, L. M. (2017). *Lenses on reading: An introduction to theories and models* (3rd Ed.). The Guilford Press.

Turkan, S., de Oliveira, L., Lee, O., & Phelps, G. (2014). Proposing a knowledge base for teaching academic content to English language learners: Disciplinary linguistic knowledge. *Teachers College Record, 116*(1), 1–30.

Umansky, I. M. & Reardon, S. F. (2014). Reclassification patterns among Latino English learner students in bilingual, dual immersion, and English immersion classrooms. *American Educational Research Journal, 51*(5), 879–912.

U.S. Department of Education. (2016). *Non-regulatory guidance: English learners and Title III of the Elementary and Secondary Education Act (ESEA), as amended by the Every Student Succeeds Act (ESSA).* Author. https://www2.ed.gov/policy/elsec/leg/essa/essatitleiiiguidenglishlearners92016.pdf

U.S. Department of Education (2022). *A guide to individualized education program.* Retrieved from https://www2.ed.gov/parents/needs/speced/iepguide/index.html#contents

U.S. Department of Education, Office of English Language Acquisition. (2017). *English learner tool kit* (2nd Rev. ed.). Author. Available at: http://www2.ed.gov/about/offices/list/oela/english-learner-toolkit/index.html

U.S. Department of Education, Office of English Language Acquisition. (2020). High school graduation rates for English learners. *Fact Sheet.* Author. Retrieved from https://ncela.ed.gov/files/fast_facts/20200916-ELGraduationRatesFactSheet-508.pdf

U.S. Department of Education, Office of English Language Acquisition. (2021a). *The biennial report to Congress on the implementation of the Title III State Formula Grant Program, school years 2016-2018.* Author.

U.S. Department of Education, Office of English Language Acquisition. (2021b). English learner absenteeism, suspension and retention. *Fact Sheet.* Retrieved from https://ncela.ed.gov/files/fast_facts/202109-Del4-4ELAbsenteeismSuspensionandRetention-508.pdf

U.S. Department of Education, Office of English Language Acquisition. (2021c). English learners in advanced placement and international baccalaureate courses. *Fact Sheet.* Author. Retrieved from https://ncela.ed.gov/files/fast_facts/20210803-Del4-4EL-AP-IB-FactSheet508.pdf

U.S. Department of Education, Office of English Language Acquisition. (2021d). Migratory children who are English learners. *Fact Sheet.* Author. https://ncela.ed.gov/files/fast_facts/Del4-4MigratoryELs_20210610_508%20(1).pdf

U.S. Department of Education, National Center for Education Statistics. (2021). *Digest of education statistics.* https://nces.ed.gov/programs/digest/2021menu_tables.asp

U.S. Department of Education, OSERS. (2016). Memo to State Directors of Special Education, Preschool/619 State Coordinators. Head Start Directors. https://specialeducationaction.com/a-response-to-intervention-cannot-be-used-to-delay-or-deny-an-evaluation-for-special-education-services/

U.S. Department of Justice, Civil Rights Division, & U.S. Department of Education, Office of Civil Rights. (2015). *Dear colleague letter: English learner students and limited English proficient parents.* Authors. Available at http://www2.ed.gov/about/offices/list/ocr/letters/colleague-el-201501.pdf

Uribe, M., & Nathenson-Mejía, S. (2008). *Literacy essentials for English language learners: Successful transitions.* Teacher's College Press.

Üzüm, B., Petrón, M., & Berg, H. (2014). Pre-service teachers' first foray into the ESL classroom: Reflective practice in a service learning project. *TESL-EJ, 18*(3), 1–15.

Valentino, R. A., & Reardon, S. F. (2015). Effectiveness of four instructional programs designed to serve English learners. Variation by ethnicity and initial English proficiency. *Educational Evaluation and Policy Analysis, 34*(4), 612–637. Available online at http://epa.sagepub.com/content/early/2015/04/01/0162373715573310.abstract

Verhoeven, L., Perfetti, C., & Pugh, K. (2019). Cross-linguistic perspectives on second language Reading. *Journal of Neurolinguistics, 50,* 1-6.

Vidot, J. L. (2011). *The efficacy of sheltered instruction observation protocol (SIOP) in mathematics instruction on English language learners.* (Doctoral dissertation) Available from http://scholarworks.waldenu.edu/dissertations/943/

Virginia Dept. of Education. (2016). *Virginia Mathematics Standards of Learning: Algebra.* Author. https://www.doe.virginia.gov/testing/sol/standards_docs/mathematics/index.shtml#2016

Vogel, S., & Garcia, O. (2017). *Translanguaging. Oxford Research Encyclopedia*, pp. 1–21. DOI: 10.1093/acrefore/9780190264093.013.181

Vogt, M.E. (2020). Academic language and literacy development for English learners (2nd ed.). In S. Swan & R. M Bean (Eds.), *Best practices for literacy leaders: Keys to school Improvement* (pp. 325–343). The Guilford Press.

Vogt, M.E. (2022). Reaching linguistically diverse students through exemplary language, literacy, and content teaching. In S. B. Wepner & D. Quatroch (Eds.), *The administration and supervision of literacy programs* (6th ed.). Teachers College Press.

Vogt, M.E., & Echevarría, J. (2008). *99 ideas and activities for teaching English learners with the SIOP model.* Pearson.

Vogt, M.E., & Echevarríia, J. (2022). *99 ideas and activities for teaching English learners with the SIOP model* (2nd ed.). Pearson Education, Inc.

Vogt, M.E., Echevarría, J., & Washam, M. A. (2015). *99 more ideas and activities for teaching English learners with the SIOP Model.* Pearson.

Vogt, M.E., & Shearer, B.A. (2016). *Reading specialists and literacy coaches in the real world.* (3rd ed.) Waveland Press.

Vygotsky, L. (1978). *Mind and society: The development of higher psychological processes* (M. Cole, V. John-Steiner, S. Scribner, & E. Souberman, Eds. and trans.). Harvard University Press.

Waring, R., & Nation, I. S. P. (2004). Second language reading and incidental vocabulary learning. *Angles on the English Speaking World, 4,* 97–110.

Wasik, B. A., & Hindman, A. H. (2013/2014). Realizing the promise of open-ended questions. *The Reading Teacher 67*(4): 302–311.

Wasik, B., & Iannone-Campbell, C. (2012). Developing vocabulary through purposeful, strategic conversations. *The Reading Teacher, 66*(2), 321–332.

Watkins, N. M., & Lindahl, K. M. (2010). Targeting content area literacy instruction to meet the needs of adolescent English language learners. *Middle School Journal, 41* (3), 23–32.

Webb, N. L. (1997). Determining alignment of expectations and assessment in math and science education. *NISE Brief, 1*(1), National Institute for Science Education, University of Wisconsin, Madison, 1–8.

Webb, S., & Nation, I. S. P. (2017). *How vocabulary is learned.* Oxford University Press.

Welsh, L., & Newman, K. (2010). Becoming a content-ESL teacher: A dialogic journey of a science teacher and teacher educator. *Theory Into Practice, 49,* 137–144.

Whittier, L. E., & Robinson, M. (2007). Teaching evolution to non-English proficient students by using Lego Robotics. *American Secondary Education, 35* (3), 19–28.

WIDA. (2017). *STEM discourse: Strengthening reasoning, strengthening language.* Focus Bulletin, January 2017. https://wida.wisc.edu/sites/default/files/resource/FocusOn-STEM-Discourse.pdf

WIDA. (2020). *WIDA English language development standards framework, 2020 edition: Kindergarten–grade 12.* Board of Regents of the University of Wisconsin System.

Wilkinson, I., Murphy, K.P., & Binici, S. (2015). Dialogue-intensive pedagogies for promoting reading comprehension: what we know, what we need to know. In L. B. Resnick, C. S. C. Asterhan, & S. N. Clarke (Eds.). *Socializing intelligence through academic talk and dialogue* (pp. 37–50). American Educational Research Association.

Wong, C-Y., Meadows, B., & Ober, G. (2021). Using the SIOP Instruction Model for narrative writing: A case study of a teacher's experience of using the model in a high school setting. *TESL Reporter 53*(1-2), 37–58.

Wong, C. Y. C., & Turkan, S. (2022). "No one knows who I am:" What school leaders can learn from ESL teachers' voices. *NYS TESOL Journal*, 9(1), 30–38.

Ye He, W. J. & Faircloth, J. (2018). Preparing teachers for English learners: Integrating academic language and community service projects, *The Social Studies*, 109: 1, 13–26. doi: 10.1080/00377996.2017.1403874

Yoon, B. (Ed.). (2021). *Effective teacher collaboration for English language learners: Cross-curricular insights from K–12 settings.* Routledge.

Young, E. (1996). *Lon po po.* Philomel Books.

Zike, D. (2011). *Dinah Zike's notebook foldables for spirals, binders and composition books.* Dinah-Might Adventures.

Zike, D. (2013). *Foldables and VKVs for phonics, spelling and vocabulary, preK-3.* Dinah-Might Adventures.

Zucker, T., Cabell, S., & Pico, D. (2021). Going nuts for words: Recommendations for teaching young students' academic vocabulary. *The Reading Teacher, 74*(5), 581–594.

Zwiers, J., & Crawford, M. (2011). *Academic conversations: Classroom talk that fosters critical thinking and content understandings.* Stenhouse Publishers.

Zwiers, J., & Hammerla, S. R. (2017). *The K-3 Guide to Academic Conversations: Practices, Scaffolds, and Activities.* Corwin Press.

Zwiers, J., & Soto, I. (2017). *Academic language mastery: Conversational discourse in context.* Corwin Press.

Index